# LUDIC PROOF

*Greek Mathematics and the Alexandrian Aesthetic*

REVIEL NETZ

CAMBRIDGE UNIVERSITY PRESS
Cambridge, New York, Melbourne, Madrid, Cape Town, Singapore, São Paulo, Delhi

Cambridge University Press
The Edinburgh Building, Cambridge CB2 8RU, UK

Published in the United States of America by Cambridge University Press, New York

http://www.cambridge.org
Information on this title: www.cambridge.org/9780521898942

© Reviel Netz 2009

This publication is in copyright. Subject to statutory exception
and to the provisions of relevant collective licensing agreements,
no reproduction of any part may take place without
the written permission of Cambridge University Press.

First published 2009

Printed in the United Kingdom at the University Press, Cambridge

*A catalogue record for this publication is available from the British Library*

Library of Congress Cataloguing in Publication data
Netz, Reviel.
Ludic proof : Greek mathematics and the Alexandrian aesthetic / Reviel Netz.
p. cm.
Includes bibliographical references and index.
ISBN 978-0-521-89894-2 (hardback)
1. Mathematics, Greek.  2. Technical writing.  3. Greek language, Hellenistic (300 B.C.–600 A.D.)
I. Title.
QA22.N28 1008
510.938 – dc22    2008053182

ISBN 978-0-521-89894-2 hardback

Cambridge University Press has no responsibility for the persistence or
accuracy of URLs for external or third-party internet websites referred to
in this publication and does not guarantee that any content on such
websites is, or will remain, accurate or appropriate.

*To Maya, Darya and Tamara*

# LUDIC PROOF

This book represents a new departure in science studies: an analysis of a scientific style of writing, situating it within the context of the contemporary style of literature. Its philosophical significance is that it provides a novel way of making sense of the notion of a scientific style. For the first time, the Hellenistic mathematical corpus – one of the most substantial extant for the period – is placed center-stage in the discussion of Hellenistic culture as a whole. Professor Netz argues that Hellenistic mathematical writings adopt a narrative strategy based on surprise, a compositional form based on a mosaic of apparently unrelated elements, and a carnivalesque profusion of detail. He further investigates how such stylistic preferences derive from, and throw light on, the style of Hellenistic poetry. This important book will be welcomed by all scholars of Hellenistic civilization as well as historians of ancient science and Western mathematics.

REVIEL NETZ is Professor of Classics at Stanford University. He has written many books on mathematics, history, and poetry, including, most recently, *The Transformation of Mathematics in the Early Mediterranean World* (2004) and (with William Noel) *The Archimedes Codex* (2007). *The Shaping of Deduction in Greek Mathematics* (1999) has been variously acclaimed as "a masterpiece" (David Sedley, *Classical Review*), and "The most important work in Science Studies since Leviathan and the Air Pump" (Bruno Latour, *Social Studies of Science*). Together with Nigel Wilson, he is currently editing the Archimedes Palimpsest, and he is also producing a three-volume complete translation of and commentary on the works of Archimedes.

# Contents

| | | |
|---|---|---|
| Preface | | *page* ix |
| | Introduction | 1 |
| 1 | The carnival of calculation | 17 |
| 2 | The telling of mathematics | 66 |
| 3 | Hybrids and mosaics | 115 |
| 4 | The poetic interface | 174 |
| | Conclusions and qualifications | 230 |
| *Bibliography* | | 242 |
| *Index* | | 251 |

# *Preface*

This, my third study on Greek mathematics, serves to complete a project. My first study, *The Shaping of Deduction in Greek Mathematics* (1999) analyzed Greek mathematical writing in its most general form, applicable from the fifth century BC down to the sixth century AD and, in truth, going beyond into Arabic and Latin mathematics, as far as the scientific revolution itself. This form – in a nutshell, the combination of the lettered diagram with a formulaic language – is the constant of Greek mathematics, especially (though not only) in geometry. Against this constant, the historical variations could then be played.[*] The historical variety is formed primarily of the contrast of the Hellenistic period (when Greek mathematics reached its most remarkable achievements) and Late Antiquity (when Greek mathematics came to be re-shaped into the form in which it influenced all of later science). My second study, *The Transformation of Mathematics in the Early Mediterranean* (2004), was largely concerned with the nature of this re-shaping of Greek mathematics in Late Antiquity and the Middle Ages.

This study, finally, is concerned with the nature of Greek mathematics in the Hellenistic period itself. Throughout, my main concern is with the form of writing: taken in a more general, abstract sense, in the first study, and in a more culturally sensitive sense, in the following two.

The three studies were not planned together, but the differences between them have to do not so much with changed opinions as with changed subject matter.

I have changed my views primarily in the following two ways. First, I now believe my reconstruction of the historical background to Greek

---

[*] Some reviewers have made the fair criticism that my evidence, in that book, is largely drawn from the works of the three main Hellenistic geometers, Euclid, Archimedes, and Apollonius (with other authors sampled haphazardly). I regret, in retrospect, that I did not make my survey more obviously representative. Still, even if my documentation of the fact was unfortunately incomplete, it is probably safe to say that the broad features of lettered diagram and formulaic language are indeed a constant of Greek mathematics as well as of its heirs in the pre-modern Mediterranean.

mathematics, as formulated in Netz 1999, did suffer from emphasizing the underlying cultural continuity. The stability of the broad features of Greek mathematical writing should be seen as against the radically changing historical context, and should be understood primarily (I now believe) in the terms of self-regulating conventions discussed in that book (and since, in Netz 2003a). I also would qualify now my picture of Hellenistic mathematics, as presented in Netz 2004. There, I characterized this mathematics as marked by the "aura" of individual treatises – with which I still stand. However, as will be made obvious in the course of this book, I now ground this aura not in the generalized polemical characteristics of Greek culture, but rather in a much more precise interface between the aesthetics of poetry and of mathematics, operative in Alexandrian civilization.

Each of the studies is characterized by a different methodology, because the three different locks called for three different keys. Primarily, this is an effect of zooming in, with sharper detail coming into focus. In the first study, dealing with cross-cultural constants, I took the approach I call "cognitive history." In the second study, dealing with an extended period (covering both Late Antiquity and the Middle Ages), I concentrated on the study of intellectual practices (where I do detect a significant cultural continuity between the various cultures of scriptural religion and the codex). This study, finally, focused as it is on a more clearly defined period, concentrates on the very culturally specific history of style. Taken together, I hope my three studies form a coherent whole. Greek mathematics – always based on the mechanism of the lettered diagram and a formulaic language – reached its most remarkable achievements in the Hellenistic period, where it was characterized by a certain "ludic" style comparable to that of contemporary literature. In Late Antiquity, this style was drastically adjusted to conform to the intellectual practices of deuteronomic texts based on the commentary, giving rise to the form of "Euclidean" science with which we are most familiar.

My theoretical assumption in this book is very modest: people do the things they enjoy doing. In order to find out why Hellenistic mathematicians enjoyed writing their mathematics (and assumed that readers would be found to share their enjoyment), let us look for the kinds of things people enjoyed around them. And since mathematics is primarily a verbal, indeed textual activity, let us look for the kind of verbal art favored in the Hellenistic world. Then let us see whether Greek mathematics conforms to the poetics of this verbal art. This is the underlying logic of the book. Its explicit structure moves in the other direction: the introduction and the first three chapters serve to present the aesthetic characteristics of

Hellenistic mathematics, while the fourth chapter serves (more rapidly) to put this mathematics within its literary context.

The first chapter, "The carnival of calculation," describes the fascination, displayed by many works of Hellenistic mathematics, with creating a rich texture of obscure and seemingly pointless numerical calculation. The treatises occasionally lapse, as it were, so as to wallow in numbers – giving up in this way the purity of abstract geometry.

The second chapter, "The telling of mathematics," follows the narrative technique favored in many Hellenistic mathematical treatises, based on suspense and surprise, on the raising of expectations so as to quash them. I look in particular on the modulation of the authorial voice: how the author is introduced into a seemingly impersonal science.

The third chapter, "Hybrids and mosaics," discusses a compositional feature operative in much of Hellenistic mathematics, at both small and large dimensions. Locally, the treatises often create a texture of variety by producing a mosaic of propositions of different kinds. Globally, there is a fascination with such themes that go beyond the boundaries of geometry, either connecting it to other scientific genres or indeed connecting it to non-scientific genres such as poetry.

This breaking of boundary-genres, in itself, already suggests the interplay of science and poetry in Hellenistic civilization. The fourth chapter, "The literary interface," starts from the role of science in the wider Hellenistic genre-system. I also move on to describe, in a brief, largely derivative manner, the aesthetics of Hellenistic poetry itself.

In my conclusion, I make some tentative suggestions, qualifying the ways in which the broadly descriptive outline of the book can be used to sustain wider historical interpretations.

The book is thematically structured: two chronological questions are briefly addressed where demanded by their thematic context. A final section of chapter 2, building on the notion of the personal voice in mathematics, discusses the later depersonalization of voice in Late Antiquity giving rise to the impersonal image of mathematics we are so familiar with. A discussion of the basic chronological parameters of Hellenistic mathematics is reserved for even later in the book – the conclusion, where such a chronological discussion is demanded by the question of the historical setting giving rise to the style as described.

The focus of the book is description of style – primarily, mathematical style. I intend to write much more on the mathematics than on its literary context, but the reasons for this are simple: the poetics of Hellenistic literature are generally more familiar than those of Hellenistic mathematics while I, myself, know Hellenistic mathematics better than I do Hellenistic literature. Further, there are gaps in our historical evidence so that more can be said at the descriptive level than at the explanatory one. Most important, however, is that my main theme in this work is sustained at the level of style, of poetics or – even more grandly put – of semiotics. The precise historical underpinning of the semiotic practices described here is of less concern for my purposes.

This brings me to the following general observation. A few generations back, scholars of Hellenistic literature identified in it a civilization in decline, one where the poet, detached from his polity, no longer served its communal needs but instead pursued art for art's sake. More recently, scholars have come to focus on the complex cultural realities of Hellenistic civilization and on the complex ways by which Hellenistic poetry spoke for a communal voice. This debate is framed in terms of the historical setting of the poetry. Any attempt, such as mine, to concentrate on the style, and to bracket its historical setting, could therefore be read – erroneously – as an effort to revive the picture of Hellenistic poets as pursuing art for art's sake. But this is not at all my point: my own choice to study Hellenistic style should not be read as a claim that style was what mattered most to the Hellenistic authors. I think they cared most for gods and kings, for cities and their traditions – just as Greek geometers cared most for figures and proportions, for circles and their measurements. Style came only after that. So why do I study the styles, the semiotic practices, after all? Should I not admit, then, that this study is dedicated to a mere ornament, to details of presentation of marginal importance? To the contrary, I argue that my research project addresses the most urgent question of the humanities today: where do cultural artifacts come from? Are they the product of the universally "human," or of specific cultural practices? My research focuses on mathematics, the human cultural pursuit whose universality is most apparent. I try to show how it is indeed fully universal – in its objective achievement – and at the same time how it is fully historical – in the terms of its semiotic practices, which vary sharply according to historical and cultural settings. Seen from this research perspective, it becomes important indeed to look at the semiotic practices typical of the third century BC.

I hope this serves to contextualize this project for my readers, whether they come from science studies or from Hellenistic literature and history. A few more qualifications and clarifications will be made in the conclusion – where once again I address the difficulties involved in trying to account for the semiotic practices in terms of their historical setting. A few preliminary clarifications must be made right now. The title of my book is a useful slogan but it may also mislead if taken literally. I therefore add a glossary, so to speak, to the title.

First, the title mentions an "Alexandrian" aesthetic. The city of Alexandria no doubt played a major role in the cultural history of the period, but I use the word mostly for liking the sound of "Alexandrian aesthetic" better than that of "Hellenistic aesthetic." (For an attempt to quantify the well-known central position of Alexandria in post-classical science, see Netz 1997. In general on the cultural role of Alexandria the best reference remains Fraser 1972.) "Hellenistic" would have been the more precise term, but it too would not be quite precise: the period of most interest to us lies from the mid-third to the mid-second centuries BC, i.e. not the "Hellenistic" period as a whole. The death of Alexander, as well as the ascendance of Augustus, both had little to do, directly, with the history of mathematics.

Second, the term "the aesthetics of X" might be taken to mean "the aesthetics that X has consciously espoused," so that a study of, say, the aesthetics of Hellenistic poetry could be understood to mean an analysis of ars-poetic comments in Hellenistic poems, or a study of ancient treatises in aesthetics such as Philodemus' *On Poems*. This is of course an important field of study, but it is not what I refer to in my title. I use the term "the Hellenistic aesthetic" as an observer concept, to mean "the aesthetics identifiable (by us) in Hellenistic texts," referring to the stylistic properties of those texts, regardless of whether or not such stylistic properties were articulated by the Hellenistic actors themselves.

Third, the "Greek mathematics" in my title sometimes means "Greek geometry" (this terminological looseness is inevitable with the Greek mathematical tradition), and nearly always refers to elite, literate mathematical texts. This does not deny the existence of other, more demotic practices of calculation, measurement and numeracy, which obviously fall outside the scope of this book, as belonging to very different stylistic domains. (For the less-literate traditions, see Cuomo 2001, a study rare for its bringing the literate and the demotic together.)

Fourth, the word "Ludic" in the title typically encodes a certain playful spirit and, in one central case, it encodes the mathematics of a certain game – the Stomachion. But most often in this book "ludic" should be read as no more than an abbreviated reference to "works sharing certain stylistic features" (which, to anticipate, includes in general narrative surprise, mosaic structure and generic experiment, and, in an important set of works, a certain "carnivalesque" atmosphere). I do not suggest that Hellenistic mathematics – or, for that matter, Hellenistic poetry – were not "serious." Even while serious, however, they were definitely sly, subtle, and sophisticated – a combination which the term "ludic" is meant to suggest.

To sum up, then, this book is about the study of a certain sly, subtle, and sophisticated style identifiable by us in elite Greek mathematical (especially geometrical) works of about 250 to 150 BC, as seen in the context of the elite poetry of the same (and somewhat earlier) period.

The book serves at three levels. The first, as already suggested, is descriptive. It offers a new description of Hellenistic mathematics, one focused on a neglected yet major aspect, namely its style of writing. The second is explanatory: by situating mathematics within its wider cultural context, it aims to explain – however tentatively – both its form, as well as its very flourishing at that period. The third is methodological. I am not familiar with extended studies in the history of mathematics – or indeed of science in general – focused on the aesthetics of its writing. This is an obvious lacuna and, I believe, a major one. There are of course references to aesthetics as a phenomenon in science. Since Hutcheson in the eighteenth century – indeed, since Plato himself – it has been something of a commonplace to discuss the "beauty" of certain scientific objects (possessing symmetry, balance, simplicity, etc.). Scientists and mathematicians not infrequently refer to the aesthetic impulse driving their work (see e.g. Chandrasekhar 1987 for a physicist, or Aigner and Ziegler 1998 for a mathematical example). There is a minor research tradition in the philosophy of science, looking for "beauty" as a principle accounting for the scientific choice between theories; McAllister 1996 forms an example. With rare and marginal exceptions, all of this touches on the aesthetics of the scientific object of study and not on the aesthetics of the scientific artifact itself.

The brief argument above – that people do what they enjoy doing – should suffice to point our attention to the importance of such studies. I realize, of course, that more argument is required to make the claim for the need for studies in the historical aesthetics of science. This book, then, makes the argument by providing one such study.

My gratitude extends widely. Audiences at Stanford, Brown, and Groningen helped me think through my argument. Serafina Cuomo, Marco Fantuzzi, Paula Findlen, and Sir Geoffrey Lloyd all read through my entire text and returned with useful comments. Susan Stephens' comments on an early version were especially valuable in helping me rethink my interpretation of the interface of science and poetry in the Hellenistic world. Errors and omissions, I know, remain, and remain mine. The first draft of this book was composed through the year of a fellowship at Stanford's Center for Advanced Studies in Behavioral Sciences. The draft was made into a book at Stanford's Department of Classics, and Cambridge University Press has seen it into publication. I am grateful to have resided in such places that welcome all – including the playful.

# *Introduction*

So this book is going to be about the style of mathematics. Does it mean I am going to ignore the substance of mathematics? To some extent, I do, but then again not: the two dimensions are distinct, yet they are not orthogonal, so that stylistic preferences inform the contents themselves, and vice versa. For an example, I shall now take a central work of Hellenistic mathematics – Archimedes' *Spiral Lines* – and read it twice, first – very quickly – for its contents, and then, at a more leisurely pace, for its presentation of those contents. Besides serving to delineate the two dimensions of style and content, this may also serve as an introduction to our topic: for *Spiral Lines* is a fine example of what makes Hellenistic science so impressive, in both dimensions. For the mathematical contents, I quote the summary in Knorr 1986: 161 (fig. 1):

> The determination of the areas of figures bounded by spirals further illustrates Archimedes' methods of quadrature. The Archimedean plane spiral is traced out by a point moving uniformly along a line as that line rotates uniformly about one of its endpoints. The latter portion of the treatise *On Spiral Lines* is devoted to the proof that the area under the segment of the spiral equals one-third the corresponding circular sector . . . The proofs are managed in full formal detail in accordance with the indirect method of limits. The spirals are bounded above and below by summations of narrow sectors converging to the same limit of one-third the entire enclosing sector, for the sectors follow the progression of square integers. This method remains standard to this very day for the evaluation of definite integrals as the limits of summations.

Since I intend this book to be readable to non-mathematicians, I shall not try to explain here the geometrical structure underlying Knorr's exposition. Suffice for us to note the great elegance of the result obtained – precise numerical statements concerning the values of curvilinear, complex areas. Note the smooth, linear exposition that emerges with Knorr's summary, as if the spiral lines formed a strict mathematical progression leading to a quadrature, based on methods that in turn (in the same linear progression,

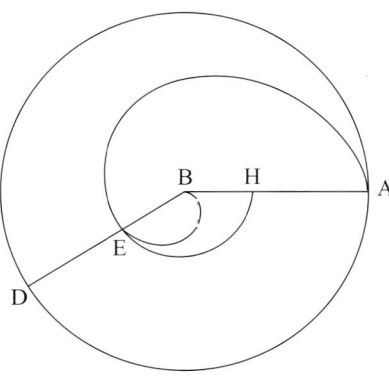

Figure 1

now projected into historical time) serve to inform modern integration. One bounds a problem – the spiral contained between external and internal progressions of sectors – and one then uses the boundaries to solve the problem – the progression is summed up according to a calculation of the summation of a progression of square integers. Such is the smooth, transparent intellectual structure suggested by Knorr's summary.

Let us see, now, how this treatise actually unfolds – so as to appreciate the achievement of Hellenistic mathematics in yet another, complementary way.

We first notice that the treatise is a letter, addressed to one Dositheus – known to us mainly as Archimedes' addressee in several of his works.[1] The social realities underlying the decision made by several ancient authors, to clothe their treatises as letters, are difficult for us to unravel. A lot must have to do with the poetic tradition, from Hesiod onwards, of dedicating the didactic epic to an addressee, as well as the prose genre of the letter-epistle as seen, e.g., in the extant letters of Epicurus.[2] The nature of the ancient mathematical community – a small, scattered group of genteel amateurs – may also be relevant.[3] In this book we shall return time and again to the literary antecedents of Hellenistic mathematics, as well as to its character as refined correspondence conducted inside a small, sophisticated group – but this of course right now is nothing more than a suggestion.

---

[1] See Netz 1998b for some more references and for the curious fact, established on onomastic grounds, that Dositheus was probably Jewish.
[2] I return to discuss this in more detail on pp. 104–5 below.
[3] See Netz 1999, ch. 7 for the discussion concerning the demography of ancient mathematics.

Let us look at the introduction in detail. Archimedes mentions to Dositheus a list of problems he has set out for his correspondents to solve or prove. Indeed, he mentions now explicitly – apparently for the first time – that two of the problems were, in fact, snares: they asked the correspondents to prove a *false* statement. All of this is of course highly suggestive to our picture of the Hellenistic mathematical exchange. But even before that, we should note the texture of writing: for notice the roundabout way Archimedes approaches his topic. First comes the general reminder about the original setting of problems. Then a series of such problems is mentioned, having to do with the sphere. Archimedes points out that those problems are now solved in his treatise (which we know as *Sphere and Cylinder* ii), and reveals the falsity of two of the problems. Following that, Archimedes proceeds to remind Dositheus of a second series of problems, this time having to with conoids. We expect him to tell us that some of those problems were false as well, but instead he sustains the suspense, writing merely that the solutions to those problems were not yet sent. We now expect him to offer those solutions, yet the introduction proceeds differently:[4]

> After those [problems with conoids], the following problems were put forward concerning the spiral – and they are as it were a special kind of problems, having nothing in common with those mentioned above – the proofs concerning which I provide you now in the book.

So not a study of conoids, after all. We now learn all of a sudden – four Teubner pages into the introduction – that this is going to be a study of spirals. And we are explicitly told that these are "special," "having nothing in common" – that is, Archimedes explicitly flaunts the exotic nature of the problems at hand. We begin to note some aspects of the style: suspense and surprise; sharp transitions; expectations raised and quashed; a favoring of the exotic. No more than a hint of that, yet, but let us consider the unfolding of the treatise.

Now that the introduction proper begins, Archimedes moves on to provide us with an explicit definition of the spiral (presented rigorously but discursively as part of the prose of the introduction), and then asserts the main goals of the treatise: to show (i) that the area intercepted by the spiral is one third the enclosing circle; (ii) that a certain line arising from the spiral is equal to the circumference of the enclosing circle; (iii) that the area resulting from allowing the spiral to rotate not once but several times about the starting-point is a certain fraction of the enclosing circle,

---
[4] Heiberg 1913: 13–17.

defined in complex numerical terms; and finally (iv) that the areas bounded between spirals and circles have a certain ratio defined in a complex way. Following that Archimedes recalls a lemma he shall use in the treatise (used by him elsewhere as well, and known today, probably misleadingly, as "Archimedes' Axiom"). At this point the next sentence starts with εἰ κα κατά τινος γράμμας, "if on some line," i.e. without any particle, so that the reader's experience is of having plunged into a new sequence of prose and, indeed, the proofs proper abruptly begin here.

Before we plunge ourselves into those proofs, I have two interrelated comments on the introduction. The first is that the sequence of goals seems to suggest an order for the treatise, going from goal (i), through (ii) and (iii), to (iv). The actual order is (ii) – (i) – (iii) – (iv). The difference is subtle, and yet here is another example of an expectation raised so as to be quashed. The second is that the goals mentioned by Archimedes are put forward in the discursive prose of Greek mathematics of which we shall see many examples in the book – no diagram provided at this point, no unpacking of the meaning of the concepts. The result is a thick, opaque texture of writing, for example, the third goal:

And if the rotated line and the point carried on it are rotated for several rotations and brought back again to that from which they have started out, I say that of the area taken by the spiral in the second rotation: the <area> taken in the third <rotation> shall be twice; the taken in the fourth – three times; the taken in the fifth – four times; and always: the areas taken in the later rotations shall be, by the numbers in sequence, multiples of the <area> taken in the second rotation, while the area taken in the first rotation is a sixth part of the area taken in the second rotation.

This is not the most opaque stated goal – the most opaque one is (iv). In fact I think Archimedes' sequence from (i) to (iv) is ordered in a sequence of mounting opaqueness, gradually creating a texture of prose that is heavy with difficult, exotic descriptions, occasionally rich in numerical terms. One certainly does not gain the impression that Archimedes' plan was to make the text speak out in clear, pedagogic terms.

This is also clear from the sequence of the proofs themselves. For no effort is made to explain their evolving structure. We were told to expect a treatise on measuring several properties of spirals, but we are first provided with theorems of a different kind. The first two propositions appear like physical theorems: for instance, proposition 2 shows that if two points are moved in uniform motions (each, a separate motion) on two separate straight lines, two separate times [so that altogether four lines are traced by

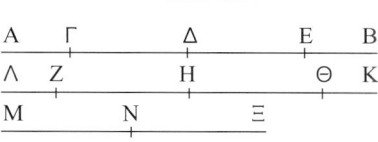

Figure 2

the two points each moving twice] the resulting lines are proportional. (See fig. 2.) Modern readers cannot but be reminded of Aristotle's *Physics*,[5] but for Archimedes' contemporary reader probably what came most to mind – as the scientific field where motions are discussed – was astronomy.[6] All the more surprising, then, that the motions discussed are *along a straight line* – i.e. related, apparently, neither to stars nor to spirals. It should be stressed that Archimedes simply presents us with the theorems, without a word of explanation of how they function in the treatise. So the very beginning does two things: it surprises and intrigues us by pointing in a direction we could not expect (theorems on linear motion!), and it underlines the fact that this treatise is about to involve a certain breaking down of the border between the purely theoretical and the physical. Instead of papering over the physical aspect of the treatise, Archimedes flags it prominently at the very beginning of the treatise. (I shall return to discuss this physical aspect later on.)

Do we move from theorems on linear motion to theorems on circular motion? This would be the logical thing to expect, but no: the treatise moves on to a couple of observations (not even fully proved) lying at the opposite end of the scientific spectrum, so to speak: from the physical theorems of 1–2 we move to observations 3–4 stating that it is possible in general to find lines greater and smaller than other given circles – the stuff of abstract geometrical manipulation. No connection is made to the previous two theorems, no connection is made to the spiral.

---

[5] See e.g. the treatment of the proportions of motion in such passages as *Physics* vii.5.
[6] By the time Archimedes comes to write *Spiral Lines*, Aristotle's Lyceum was certainly of relatively little influence. The texts of course were available (see Barnes 1997), but, for whatever reason, they had few readers (Sedley 1997 suggests that the very linguistic barrier – Attic texts in a *koine*-speaking world – could have deterred readers). On the other hand, it does appear that Archimedes admired Eudoxus above all other past mathematicians, and would probably expect his audience to share his admiration. (Introduction to *SC* i, Heiberg 4.5, 11; introduction to *Method*, Heiberg 430.2, in both places implicitly praising himself for rising to Eudoxus' standard. No other past mathematician is mentioned by Archimedes in such terms.) Eudoxus was, among other things, the author of *On Speeds* (the evidence is in Simplicius, on Arist. *De Cael.* 488.3 ff.) – an astronomical study based on the proportions of motion. I believe this would be the natural context read by Archimedes' audience into the first propositions of *Spiral Lines*.

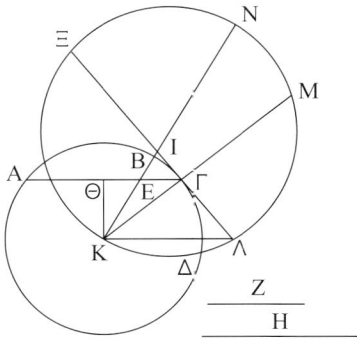

Figure 3

And immediately we switch again: if 1–2 were physical, while 3–4 were rudimentary geometrical observations, now we have a much richer sequence of pure geometry. So pure, that the relation to the spiral becomes even more blurred. Propositions 5–9 solve interesting, difficult problems in the geometry of circles, involving complex, abstruse proportions: for instance (proposition 8):

> Given a circle and, in the circle, a line smaller than the diameter, and another, touching the circle at the end of the <line>[7] in the circle: it is possible to produce a certain line from the center of the circle to the <given> line, so that the <line> taken of it between the circumference of the circle and the given line in the circle has to the <line> taken of the tangent the given ratio – provided the given ratio is smaller than that which the half <line> of <line> given in the circle has to the perpendicular drawn on it from the center of the circle.

(In terms of fig. 3, the claim is that given a line in the circle AΓ and the tangent there ΞΛ, as well as the ratio Z:H, it is possible to find a line KN so that BE:BI::Z:H.) A mind-boggling, beautiful claim – of little obvious relevance to anything that went before in the treatise, or to the spirals themselves.

But this is as nothing compared to what comes next. For now comes a set of two propositions that do not merely fail to connect in any obvious way to the spirals – they do not connect obviously to anything at all. These are very difficult to define. Archimedes' readers would associate them with proportion theory, perhaps, or with arithmetic, but mostly they would consider those proofs to be *sui generis*. They would definitely consider

---

[7] Here and in what follows, text inside pointed brackets is my supplying of words elided in the original, highly economic Greek.

*Introduction* 7

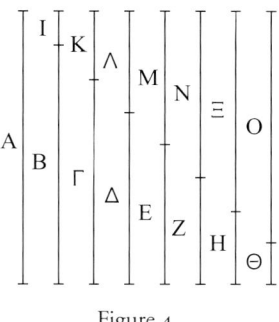

Figure 4

them enormously opaque. I quote the simpler enunciation among them, that of proposition 10:

If lines, however many, be set consecutively, exceeding each other by an equal <difference>, and the excess is equal to the smallest <line>, and other lines be set: equal in multitude to those <lines mentioned above>, while each is <equal> in magnitude to the greatest <line among those mentioned above>, the squares on the <lines> equal to the greatest <i.e. the sum of all such squares>, adding in both: the square on the greatest, and the <rectangle> contained by: the smallest line, and by the <line> equal to all the <lines> exceeding each other by an equal <difference> – shall be three times all the squares on the <lines> exceeding each other by an equal <difference>.

In our terms, in an arithmetical progression $a_1, a_2, a_3, \ldots, a_n$ where the difference between the terms is always equal to the smallest $a_1$, the following equation holds:

$$(n+1)a_n^2 + (a_1 * (a_1 + a_2 + a_3 + \cdots + a_n))$$
$$= 3(a_1^2 + a_2^2 + a_3^2 + \cdots + a_n^2)$$

This now makes sense, to some of us – but this is only because it is put forward in familiar terms, and such that serve to make the parsing of equations a lot easier.[8] The original was neither familiar to its readers nor spelled out in a friendly format. This was a take-it-or-leave-it statement of a difficult, obscure claim. And the proof does not get any easier. The addition of a diagram (fig. 4) certainly helps to parse the claim, but the operations are difficult, involving a morass of calculations whose thread is difficult to follow (I quote at random):

---

[8] It is also helpful to try and check the validity of the equation, so try this: with 1, 2, 3, 4 you have (5∗16)+(1∗10) = 3(1+4+9+16), which is in fact correct!

and since two <rectangles> contained by B, I are equal to two <rectangles> contained by B, Θ... [a long list of similar equalities] and two <rectangles contained> by Δ, Λ are equal to the <rectangle contained> by Θ and the <line> six times Δ – since Λ is three times Δ... [a statement of a set of similar equalities, stated in a complex abstract way] – so all <rectangles taken twice>, adding in the <rectangle> contained by Θ and by the <line> equal to A, B, Γ, Δ, E, Z, H, Θ, shall be equal to the <rectangle> contained by Θ and by the <line> equal to all: A and three times B and five times Γ, and ever again, the following line by the odd multiple at the sequence of odd numbers.

We see that no effort is made to compensate for the obscurity of the enunciation by a proof clearly set out. The difficulty of parsing the statements is carried throughout the argument, serving to signal that this pair of propositions, 10–11, is a special kind of text, marked by its exotic nature.

We also notice that a new kind of genre-boundary is broken. If the first two propositions were surprising in their *physical* nature (having to do with a study of motions along lines), these two propositions 10–11 depend on calculation and in general suggest an arithmetical, rather than a geometrical context. One can say in general that Greek geometry is defined by its opposition to two outside genres. It is abstract rather than concrete, marking it off from the physical sciences, while, inside the theoretical sciences, it is marked by its opposition to arithmetic.[9] Archimedes, in this geometrical treatise, breaks through the genre-boundaries with *both* physics and arithmetic.

And yet this is geometry, indeed the geometry of the spiral. We were almost made to forget this, in the surprising sequence going from physics, through abstract, general geometrical observations, via the geometry of

---

[9] In Aristotle's architecture of the sciences we often see the exact sciences as falling into geometrical and arithmetical, in the first place, and then the applied sciences related to them (e.g. music to arithmetic, optics to geometry: *An. Post.* 75b15–17, 78b37–9). Plato's system of *mathēmata* famously (*Resp.* 525a–531d) includes arithmetic, geometry, astronomy and music, with stereometry uneasily accommodated: since astronomy is explicitly related to stereometry, Plato would presumably have meant his audience to keep in mind the relationship of music to arithmetic, though he merely points out in the conclusion of this passage that the relationship between the sciences is to be worked out (530c9–d4), and he does echo the Pythagorean notion of "sisterhood" of astronomy and music (they are, more precisely, *cousins*) – perhaps derived from Archytas' fr. 1 l.7 (Huffman 2005: ii.1.). It is not clear that anyone in Classical Antiquity other than Aristotle would have explicitly objected to the mixing of scientific disciplines (Late Antiquity is of course already much more self-conscious of such boundaries; it is curious to note that, when Eutocius makes an apology for what he perceives to be a potentially worrisome contamination of geometry by arithmetic – *In Apollonii Conica*, Heiberg 1893: ii.220 ll. 17–25 – he relies explicitly on the notion of the sisterhood of the disciplines!); the same is true, in fact, for literary genres. It may well be that the explicit notion of a scientific discipline – as well as a literary genre – in the age of Aristotle could, paradoxically, facilitate the hybridization of genres characteristic of the third century. But on all of this, more below.

circles and tangents, and finally leading on to a *sui generis* study of arithmo-geometry – none of these being relevant to any of the others. Yet now – almost halfway through the treatise – we are given another jolting surprise. All of a sudden, the text switches to provide us with its proper mathematical introduction! And we now have the explicit definitions of the spiral itself and of several of the geometrical objects associated with it. One is indeed reminded of how we have learned only well into the introduction that this treatise is going to be about spirals, but the surprise here is much more marked, as the very convention of a geometrical introduction is subverted, rather like Pushkin remembering to address his muse only towards the *end* of the first canto of his *Eugene Onegin*. Of course this belated introduction now serves to mark the text and divide it: what comes before is strictly speaking introductory, and the geometry of the spiral itself now unfolds in the following propositions.

And what a mighty piece of work this geometry now is! Having put behind us the introductory material with its ponderous pace, the treatise now proceeds much more rapidly, quickly ascending to the results proved by Archimedes in his introduction. It takes surprisingly little effort, now, to get to goal (ii), where a certain straight line defined by the spiral is found to be equal to a circumference of the circle. Quite a result, too: for after all this is a kind of squaring of the circle. Archimedes obtains this in proposition 18, in a proof that directly depends upon the subtle problems 5–9 having to do with tangents to circles, and indirectly depends upon the first two, physical theorems – which therefore now find, retrospectively, their position in the treatise. And, contrary to the expectation established in the introduction, he does not see proposition 18 as a conclusion for its line of inquiry. Proposition 18 determines an equality between a circumference of a circle and a line produced by a *single* rotation of the spiral. Proposition 19 then shows that the same line produced by the second rotation of the spiral is twice a given circumference, and moves on to generalize to the much more striking (and arithmetized) result, that the rotation of a given number produces a line which is as many times as the given number the circumference of the circle, while the following proposition 20 moves on to show a similar result for a different type of straight line. The single goal (ii) sprouts into an array of results, heavily arithmetical in character.

At this point a new attack on the spiral develops – the most central one, giving rise to the measurement of the area of the spiral. But the reader of Archimedes would be hard pressed to know this.

Archimedes has just proved goal (ii) set, far back, in the introduction, and then went on to add further consequences, not even hinted at in that introduction. At this point, therefore, the reader is thoroughly disoriented: the next proofs can be about some further consequences of goal (ii), or about goal (iii), (i), or anything else. There is no way for us to know that now begins, in effect, the kernel of the book.

The introduction of a further conceptual tool also serves to mystify. In proposition 21 Archimedes starts by introducing the notion of bounding the spiral area between sectors of circles – no suggestion made of how and where this fits into the program of the treatise. And instead of moving on to utilize this bounding, Archimedes moves on in proposition 22 to generalize it to the case where the spiral rotates *twice*, and then generalize further in the same proposition to any number of rotations; in proposition 23 he generalizes it to the case of a partial rotation. Archimedes could easily have followed the argument for a single rotation, and only then generalize it, in this way making the conceptual structure of the argument somewhat less obscure. He has made the deliberate choice not to do so. In fact the reader by now may well think that Archimedes has plunged into a discussion of the relationship between spiral areas and sectors of circles – so extended is the discussion of the bounding of spirals between sectors, and so little outside motivation is given to it.[10]

Then we reach proposition 24 and now – only now! – the treatise as a whole makes sense, in a flash as it were.

The enunciation, all of a sudden, asserts that the spiral area is one-third the enclosing circle (this is said in economic, crystal-clear terms – the first simple, non-mystifying enunciation we have had for a long while). No mention is made in the enunciation of the sectors of circles. The proof starts by asserting that if the area is not one-third, it is either greater or smaller. Assume it is smaller, says Archimedes – and then he recalls the enclosing sectors. And then he notes almost in passing – in fact, he uses the expression "it is obvious that" – that the figure made of enclosing sectors instantiates the result of proposition 10, *a result which only now is provided with its meaning in the treatise*. It then follows immediately that the assumption that the spiral area is smaller than one-third the circle ends up with the enclosing sectors as both greater and smaller than one-third the circle. The analogous result is then quickly shown for the case that the

---

[10] A mathematically sophisticated reader would no doubt identify the potential of such limiting sectors for an application of what, in modern literature is called the "method of exhaustion." But Archimedes does not assert this at any point, and what is even more important, no hint is provided as to how such sectors can be measured and so serve in the application of this method. This will be made clear in retrospect only, as Archimedes would soon reveal the relation of this sequence of sectors to proposition 10.

*Introduction*

area is assumed greater, and the result is now proved. The reader hardly has any time to reflect upon the application of proposition 10, and he has already before him the main result of the treatise.

The shock of surprise is double: as you enter proposition 24, you do not know what to expect; and as you leave, you suddenly realize why proposition 10 was there all along. This moment of double surprise is certainly the rhetorical climax of the treatise, appearing appropriately at its geometrical climax.

And yet the treatise does not end there. Just as with goal (ii) – which sprouted unanticipated consequences – so Archimedes goes on in proposition 25 to generalize the result for further rotations of the spiral. The result (as we can now guess) also involves complex arithmetical relations. Proposition 26 then generalizes to the case of the partial rotation, giving rise to an especially complex proof – of a result not even hinted at in the introduction!

Once again: at this point the reader can hardly remember the (obscurely stated) goals (iii)–(iv), and even if he did remember them, he has no way of knowing which should come first. Nor would he be able to tell whether goal (i) has indeed been exhausted. Thus, as we move into proposition 27, the reader is in the dark. Clearly he does feel that the roll nears its end, and indeed only two propositions remain.

Proposition 27 feels at first to be another elaboration of the previous propositions – we hardly notice that this is goal (iii) stated at the introduction. What is most significant about it is the following: that it is hardly a piece of geometry at all. What it does is to offer a complex arithmetical manipulation of the preceding theorems, in order to show a striking arithmetical relation between the spiral areas resulting from consecutive rotations. No geometrical considerations are introduced, numbers are juggled instead.

Goal (iv) is finally shown in the last proposition of the treatise, number 28. And once again: more than involving any geometrical manipulation, this proposition uses the main results 24–6 and manipulates them by proportion theory and arithmetic, so as to derive a striking numerical relation between areas intercepted between spiral areas. The treatise thus concludes, in the pair of propositions 27–8, in a final surprising note, moving away from the main geometrical exercise of the treatise into the more arithmetical manipulation of quantitative terms.

Having surveyed the treatise in its unfolding, we can now sum up some of its overall aspects.

A feature we saw repeatedly is the surprising role of calculation. The unorthodox propositions 10–11, as well as the concluding pair of propositions 27–8, involve a sequence of difficult calculations that have little directly to do with geometry. Those are not at all marginal to the treatise: the pair of propositions 10–11 occupies a position right at the center of the treatise (immediately prior to the belated definitions), and is highly marked by its unorthodox character; it is also of course key to the main achievement of the treatise. As for the propositions 27–8, these are after all at the very end of the treatise. Indeed, because of their lengthy enunciation, their statement as goals (iii)–(iv) dominates the introduction. The treatise therefore, for all of its geometry, feels like an argument leading on to the complex arithmetical results of 27–8, based on the complex arithmetical results of 10–11.

Generalizing the role of calculation, another – central – feature of the treatise is its breaking of genre-boundaries. We have noticed the breaking of the boundary between geometry and calculation but, as mentioned above, the treatise further breaks the boundary between the geometrical and the physical. This is seen not only in the first pair of propositions involving results in motion but, much more essentially, in the nature of the spiral itself. That is – I recall – the spiral is defined (in the belated definitions) as follows:

If in a plane a straight line is drawn and, while one of its extremities remains fixed, after performing any number of revolutions at a uniform rate, it returns again to the position from which it started, while at the same time a point moves at a uniform rate along the straight line, starting from the fixed extremity, the point will describe a spiral.

The crucial point is that the spiral can be constructed only if the two motions are both kept going, throughout, at the same speed ("at a uniform rate"): any disturbance, a slackening of the pace, would lead to a disturbance in the shape of the line. Thus time enters the definition in an essential way. Compare for instance the way in which a cone, too, may be constructed by rotation: we take a right-angled triangle and rotate it about one of its perpendicular sides (this is in fact the Euclidean definition). This may appear to be a definition involving motion, and yet the motion is quite distinct from any physical realization as we may start by, say, rotating the triangle for one-third a full rotation, then leave it to one side and come back to it later, to rotate it at our leisure, until finally the cone is constructed by the full rotation – the time and pace within which we produce the cone are completely arbitrary, and so in a sense time is not a consideration and so no real motion is involved. But with the spiral, two motions are synchronized, they must be kept simultaneously without stopping. And so the actual times and speed of motion enter the very definition of the object. In this way Archimedes is here felt to study an object not merely of geometry but also of physics.

Finally, the most striking feature of the rhetoric of this treatise is not merely that it straddles the boundary of geometry and calculation – or even that of geometry and physics – but rather that, in general, it creates a mosaic of seemingly unfitting pieces, coming from different domains in unexpected sequence: and which all, of course, finally function together. I have stressed throughout the role of surprise in the rhetoric of the treatise. The surprise is generated by the seemingly ungoverned sequence of seemingly unrelated material. Variety and surprise are closely intertwined in this treatise.

One could think of two possible types of mathematical presentation, each different from that of Archimedes in this treatise. One is the type we automatically associate with mathematics – the linear axiomatic presentation. There, ideally, each result is the most natural one (in some sense) following upon all previous results. Each proposition adds another brick to the structure that ultimately gives rise to a conclusion flowing in a smooth fashion.

Another type of structure is the one most frequently met in contemporary mathematics (especially at the textbook level), and may be called pedagogic. In this case, even if the steps along the way to a conclusion are not all of a single piece, still an effort is made to signpost the general structure of the argument so that the reader may follow why each type of tool is brought in at the place it is required.

What we see is that Archimedes, in this treatise, deliberately eschews both the axiomatic as well as the pedagogic. Of course he could do either. He could have produced an axiomatic treatise by dividing it into books: one on lines, where the sequence of propositions 5–9 would lead on naturally to the sequence of argumentation 12–20, another on areas, where he would simply present the results of 21–30, adding that the main results of "being equal to one third" is proved in a separate lemma (and then providing propositions 10–11 as an appendix to the book on areas). Or he could have produced a pedagogic treatise. This would have been the easiest way: he could do this simply by adding in a more helpful introduction, one that explains why the various components of the treatise are all required.

In short, Archimedes made a deliberate choice to produce a mystifying, obscure, "jumpy" treatise. And it is clear why he should have done so: so as to inspire a reader with the shocking delight of discovering, in proposition 24, how things fit together; so as to have them stumble, with a gasp, into the final, very rich results of propositions 27–8.

Archimedes made a deliberate aesthetic choice, so as to have a deliberate aesthetic effect. The element of free choice in presenting his results in the way he did, suggests the freedom of the dimension of style from that of contents. However, the two are indeed not orthogonal: the very contents seem to display a similar aesthetic as that of their presentation. Let me move on to elaborate on this observation.

### THE AESTHETICS OF SCIENCE: MOTIVATING THE STUDY

We can sum up the above discussion saying that Archimedes' *Spiral Lines* is a remarkable achievement in two ways. It is remarkable in its mathematical content, where a result is found approaching the squaring of the circle, in a manner that anticipates the calculus. It is also remarkable in its aesthetic structure, where variety and surprise are systematically deployed to good effect.

Archimedes' immortality is firmly based on mathematical achievement. The same mathematical content, expressed ponderously and clumsily, would still have earned Archimedes his glory, although as we have suggested already, it would be difficult to present a result as striking as that of *Spiral Lines* without something of its brilliance shining through the style of the writing. And conversely: the same rhetorical structure, expressing poorly thought-out mathematics, would have been quickly forgotten. Of the two dimensions of the treatise – the mathematical and the aesthetic – the mathematical is of course the dominant one.

And yet, as hinted already, one can make a plausible argument that the very mathematical content of *Spiral Lines* is due to the aesthetic temperament revealed in the writing. For after all it is not a dictate that one should study spirals. No one did, in fact, prior to Archimedes.[11] More precisely: I said above that it is difficult to imagine a writing whose mathematical content is that of *Spiral Lines* that does not shine with brilliance. But this is not because the mathematical content is brilliant independently of its aesthetic clothing. It is because the mathematical content, in itself, already

---

[11] Or Archimedes' immediate associates: a famous, obscure reference, Pappus IV. 21 Hultsch 234.2, asserts that Conon proposed (προὐτεῖνε) the theorem concerning the spiral. Knorr 1978 may have been the first modern historian to believe in this report, but I see no reason to doubt Pappus on this point: nothing hangs on it as the cultural setting for the invention of the spiral would in any case be the same. See pp. 126–7 below, however, for the alternative treatment of the spirals reported by Pappus.

suggests a certain aesthetic. I have described above an aesthetic whose key components are variety and surprise. And indeed the spiral itself is marked by its multi-dimensional structure – combining linear and circular motion, straddling the geometrical and the physical; while the key results obtained by Archimedes – a certain line being equal to a circumference of the circle, a certain area being one third that of the circle – are all important because they are so *surprising*, given the expectation of the impossibility of measuring the circle. There is nothing preposterous, then, about suggesting that, in this case at least, the aesthetic temperament drives the mathematical quest. A culture where rich, complex, surprising objects are aesthetically valued, would also value the study of the spiral.

The aesthetic dimension then may even be a force driving the contents of science. But independently of such strong claims, we may certainly make the modest claim – one that is nearly tautologically obvious – that the aesthetic dimension is *part* of a scientific text. It is a text, after all, and therefore has to be shaped in *some* way. As we have seen above, Archimedes had freedom in choosing his mode of presentation, and each choice would have given rise to a somewhat different aesthetic effect. Even if Archimedes' decisions, in making his choice of presentation, were not primarily about aesthetics (I believe they were), they still could not fail to have aesthetic consequences. Thus – among many other things – the scientist must always make decisions that are aesthetically meaningful: he or she is committed to writing texts, a type of object that cannot fail but have – among many other things – an aesthetic dimension.

And there is something further that the scientist then cannot fail but do. He or she does not merely produce a text of a certain aesthetic impact; they produce a text whose aesthetic impact is sensed by a specific readership. One may debate whether or not the mathematical content is timeless. It may be that there is such a thing as "the contents of *Spiral Lines*" that transcends the third century BC – a possible view, however much I would wish to qualify it myself. But in the case of the aesthetic impact of a work, the need for cultural context is even more obvious. Of course we too can appreciate the aesthetic effect of *Spiral Lines*, even though we do not live in the third century BC, but this is not the point. The point is that the work was written with a third-century BC audience in mind and so, when Archimedes was calculating the impact the work would have on its readership, he had to consider the sensibilities of a third-century audience. What else could he have done? Who else could he have in mind as readers? The aesthetic impact, after all – perhaps unlike the mathematical content – cannot exist *apart* from an audience.

One may of course argue that there is something timeless about aesthetics (just as there is something timeless about the mathematical). Human aesthetic reactions are likely to be dictated not just by culturally specific attitudes, but also by universal properties of the mind. The recognition of narrative surprise, or the ability to pick up the variety of different discourses, are both perhaps specimens of innate human capacity related to the universal linguistic capacity itself. It may be that our appreciation of the beauty of texts is therefore always rooted, in some way, in such universals. And yet such universals cannot in themselves dictate the precise choice of aesthetics dominating a given text, for after all a basic fact of aesthetic value judgment is its historical and cultural variety. Beauty may be timeless, but different beautiful things are preferred in different times and places. When we look for Archimedes' choices in the presentation of his works – that is, for his aesthetic preferences – we must then study the aesthetic preferences that were available to him in his culture and that he could assume among his readers. He did not have to satisfy his readers' appetite; but he had to be aware of it, and we shall only understand his choices if we are aware of it ourselves. To understand the aesthetics of *Spiral Lines*, then, we need to understand the aesthetics of the third century BC.

This task will bring us, I shall argue, to the poetry of Alexandria. Now this, in itself, is not a foregone conclusion of what was said above. When I say that a scientific text must be written with a view to the aesthetics of its era, I do not necessarily mean that its aesthetic structure must copy that of contemporary poetry. Not at all: one may well have cultures where the dominant aesthetics of science and of poetry diverge, so that science, among other things, marks itself by being non-poetical while poetry, among other things, marks itself by being non-scientific. It is a specific historical claim I shall make, throughout this book, that this was not the case in the Hellenistic world. A distinctive feature of its science and poetry is that they did not mark themselves from each other but, to the contrary, strived for an aesthetic that breaks such generic boundaries.

Such then is the program of the book: I shall first try to describe a certain aesthetic operative in Greek mathematical texts, and then show how it is tied to a wider aesthetics, seen also in Alexandrian poetry. We begin with a carnival.

CHAPTER I

# *The carnival of calculation**

## I.I THE *STOMACHION*: MOTIVATING THE DISCUSSION

My moment of revelation – indeed, the starting point for writing this book – was while trying to make sense of Archimedes' *Stomachion*. This treatise, surviving on a single parchment leaf containing the introduction, a preliminary proof, and one stump of a proof – all mutilated and difficult to read – has gained little scholarship since its first publication by Heiberg in 1915.[1] I would have never paid it much attention myself – it did not appear to be a "serious" work – but it is after all a page out of the Archimedes Palimpsest, and just looking at the parchment one could not resist the temptation to work on it. The page looked to be in such a bad shape, surely Heiberg did not manage to read it satisfactorily!

My reading did not add many words to those read by Heiberg. But I was probably the first person in many years to have read, slowly and attentively, the introduction to the *Stomachion*. I quote a tentative translation:

As the so-called Stomachion has a variegated *theoria* of the transposition of the figures from which it is set up, I deemed it necessary: first, to set out in my investigation of the magnitude of the whole figure each of the <figures> to which it is divided, by which <number> it is measured; and further also, which are <the> angles, taken by combinations and added together; <all of the above> said for the sake of finding out the fitting-together of the arising figures, whether the resulting sides in the figures are on a line or whether they are slightly short of that <but so as to be> unnoticed by sight. For such considerations as these are

---

* I beg permission to use the word "carnival" even though I do not intend it in precisely the meaning made canonic by Bakhtin's great study. Bakhtin's notion of "carnival" is firmly rooted in a specific historical experience of France in the sixteenth century and so should not be easily applicable to Alexandria of the third century BC. The way in which I wish to use the terms will become clear through this chapter, and I return in the conclusion to discuss its precise relation to Bakhtin.

[1] A further source for the treatise, an Arabic version of (apparently) one of its results was published in Suter 1899: a faulty edition, never revisited since. A better translation of the Arabic is in Minonzio 2000.

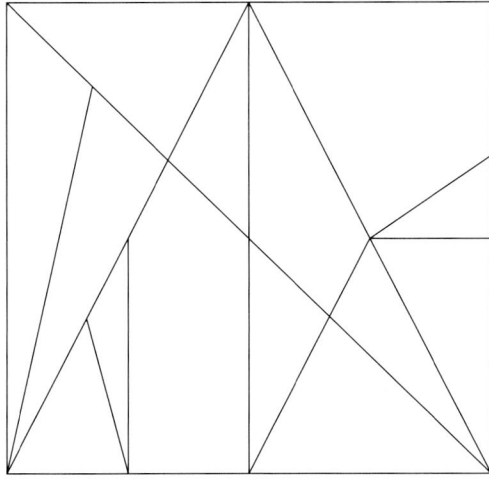

Figure 5

intellectually challenging;[2] nor, if it is a little short of <being on a line> while being unnoticed by vision, the <figures> composed are not for that reason to be rejected.

So then, there is not a small multitude of figures made of them, because of its being possible to rotate them (?)[3] into another place of an equal and equiangular figure, transposed to hold another position; and again also with two figures, taken together, being equal and similar to a single figure, and two figures taken together being equal and similar to two figures taken together – <then>, out of the transposition, many figures are put together.

We knew all along, from the Arabic fragment (as well as from some late testimonies) that Archimedes' term "Stomachion" was a reference to a tangram game of the shape of fig. 5. But what was the mathematical point of the exercise? I assumed – as a generation of scholars was trained to assume – that Greek mathematics, certainly in its canonical form seen in the works of Euclid, Apollonius, and Archimedes, systematically foregrounded geometrical considerations. This would lead one to look for a geometrical study having to do with the tangram shapes of the Stomachion – which indeed must have formed part of the structure of Archimedes' treatise. The proof and a fragment of a proof we have following the introduction do indeed deal with the angles and sides in a Stomachion-type figure,

---

[2] An anachronistic rendering of *philotechna*, "<worthy of> the love of the art."
[3] The translation of a single, crucial word is difficult, as the word is both difficult to read and, likely, corrupt.

though the example of *Spiral Lines* above (and we shall see many more such examples in the next chapter) may lead us to suspect that the treatise had a surprising mosaic structure, so that following a few propositions dealing with, say, the angles of the figures, came several other propositions of a totally different kind, and so on. If anything, as in a Shakespearean play, Archimedes' tendency was to postpone the entrance of the main figures. Not much can be learned then from these fragments of preliminary proofs.

And indeed Archimedes' words, when attended to, are quite clear. The treatise did not foreground geometry. It foregrounded a certain number. Here in fact was the most important new reading: "there is not a small *multitude* of figures..." The word "multitude" was not read by Heiberg who consequently did not quite see what Archimedes was saying about those figures. But what he was saying was that there were *many* of them. How come? This Archimedes explained in the second paragraph of the introduction: figures might be internally exchanged and in this way new figures are created. The meaning is clear once it is considered that the task of the Stomachion game was probably, in the standard case, to form a *square*. Once a single solution ("figure") is found, another can be obtained by exchanging some of the segments in the square with others, congruent with them (or by internally rotating a group of segments).

It appears then that Archimedes pointed out in his introduction that the square of the Stomachion game can be formed in many ways, which can be found by considering the internal rotations and congruences of the segments, in turn dependent upon area and angle properties of the figure. One can immediately see how the treatise could have displayed the "variegated *theoria*" promised by Archimedes in the first words of the introduction, in a rich mosaic leading via surprising routes to a conclusion. The nature of the conclusion is also clear: it would have to be a number stating how many such solutions exist. So this must have been a treatise in geometrical combinatorics.

Combinatorics! Before 2002, I would never even have considered this interpretation – putting this treatise so far outside the mainstream of geometrical study that we have always associated with Hellenistic mathematics. But I was fortunate to attend Fabio Acerbi's talk at Delphi in that year, where Hipparchus' combinatoric study was finally recovered for the history of Greek mathematics. The evidence, once again, is slim, yet – in retrospect – clear. In a couple of passages, Plutarch reports a calculation by Hipparchus (the great mathematician and astronomer of the second century bc), determining the number of conjunctions Stoic logic allows with ten assertibles, without negation (103,049) or with it (310,954).[4] Assuming that Greek mathematicians did not care for such calculations, one tended to ignore this passage, seeing in it, perhaps, some obscure joke. Probably Hipparchus did mean this to be, among other things, funny, but it is now clear that his mathematics was very seriously done. Two recent mathematical publications have shown that the numbers carry precise combinatoric meaning – these are not mere abracadabra numbers and so must represent a correct, precise solution to a combinatoric number.[5] Subsequent to this mathematical analysis, the philosophical and mathematical context for Hipparchus' work has been worked out in detail by Acerbi.[6] The existence of sophisticated Greek combinatorics is therefore no longer in question. And the role of calculation is surprising, as there is no short-cut that allows one to get the numbers out of a single, simple formula. The numbers can be found only by an iterated sequence of complicated calculations.

So much for one difficulty with my interpretation of the Stomachion: it could be a piece of combinatorics. But was it? Is there an interesting story to tell about the geometrical combinatorics of the Stomachion square? For this I asked my colleague at Stanford Persi Diaconis, a noted combinatorist, to help me solve what I assumed to be a simple question: how many ways are there to put together the square? (I was rather embarrassed that I could not find the answer myself.) It took Diaconis a couple of months and collaborative work with three colleagues to come up with the number of solutions – 17,152 – independently found at the same time by Bill Cutler (who relied on a computer analysis of the same problem). The calculation is inherently complicated: once again, there is no single formula providing us with the number, but instead a set of varied considerations concerning various parts of the figure, each contributing in complex ways to the final result.

We find that there were at least two ancient treatises in combinatorics, both leading via complex calculations to a big, unwieldy number.

Not quite what one associates, perhaps, with Greek mathematics. Yet once you begin looking for them, they are everywhere: treatises leading up, via a complex, thick structure of calculation, to unwieldy numbers. This is what I refer to as the *carnival of calculation*. In this chapter I show

---

[4] See Plutarch, *On the Contradictions of the Stoics* 1047C–E and *Convival Talks* VIII 9 732F. The manuscripts of the *Table Talk* carry the figure 101,049, this is corrected from the parallel passage in the text of *On the Contradictions of the Stoics*. The second figure is given in Plutarch's manuscript as 310952, this was emended by Habsieger *et al.* 1998.
[5] Stanley 1997, followed by Habsieger *et al.* 1998.  [6] Published in Acerbi 2003.

its existence and try to find its main themes, which I identify as follows: (1) attempting to capture the unbounded, (2) opaque cognitive texture of calculation, (3) non-utilitarian calculation and (4) a fascination with size. The evidence for the existence of the phenomenon will be presented as we follow the four themes, in sequence, in the following sections 1.2–1.5. Section 1.6 is a brief summary of the carnival.

## 1.2 ATTEMPTING TO CAPTURE THE UNBOUNDED

Archimedes' treatise *On the Measurement of the Circle* certainly falls well into the mainstream of Greek mathematics, having as its subject matter the circumference of the circle – a subject as geometrical as can be imagined. It may rank second to Euclid's *Elements* alone, as the most influential Greek mathematical work through the ages.[7] Knorr has argued in very great detail that the shape in which we have the work may be very far from that in which Archimedes left it,[8] but the argument rests on no more than certain assumptions of what ought to have been Archimedes' writing methods. Whether or not these assumptions were right ultimately would have to be decided on the basis of the extant corpus so that, at most, Knorr could have argued that Archimedes' *Measurement of the Circle* was unlike other Archimedean works – which I am not sure it is. In what follows I discuss this question briefly but leave it moot as, in this case, relatively little hangs on the question of authenticity: even if the main proposition of the treatise is not by Archimedes himself – which I doubt – it is still, most likely, Hellenistic in origin.

In considering the subject matter of the work, there is nothing specifically "carnivalesque" about this work attempting to capture the unbounded: this after all is a solid mathematical goal that can be quite sober in character. Before us is the circle, and our task is to measure it, i.e. to find a rectilinear figure equal to it. As the catchphrase has it, then, our goal is to square the circle.

[7] A large part of Clagett 1984 deals with the Medieval Latin reception of this work; it is also – alongside *Sphere and Cylinder* – the only work by Archimedes to have been widely known in the Arab-speaking world (see Lorch 1989).
[8] This forms the bulk of Knorr 1989 – pp. 375–816, a major monograph on its own right, bulky, full of insight and an enormously rich resource for the tradition of the measurement of the circle through antiquity and the Middle Ages. Its textual argument as regards the non-Archimedean provenance of the extant treatise is of course possible enough – as such skepticism always is – but ultimately is based on very little evidence. See Appendix to this chapter, pp. 63–65.

The treatise, brief as it is, displays the mosaic structure we are familiar with. It begins – there is no extant introduction – with a strictly geometrical proposition, showing that the circle is equal to a right-angled triangle one of whose sides is equal to the perimeter of the circle, the other – to its radius. This is a strong result, rather simply obtained, and at first sight it appears to constitute already a squaring of the circle – though a moment's reflection (not made explicit in the treatise as we have it) reveals that we are not quite there as, after all, we still need to measure the perimeter of the circle.

The next proposition states, falsely, that the circle has to the square on its diameter the ratio of 11 to 14. (Of course, such a statement can be made only as an approximation – of which there is no hint.) Besides being false, the proposition is also dependent not only on the first proposition, but also (obviously) upon some kind of measurement of the circumference of the circle in terms of the radius, or what in modern times is often referred to as an estimate of π. This is not offered or even hinted at inside proposition 2 itself. An estimate of π is indeed offered in proposition 3 – to which I shall immediately turn. Now, it is logically possible to have a deductively sound treatise without adhering to the principle that results required by proposition $n$ are all proved in propositions $n-1$ or less. In fact any permutation of propositional order within a deductively sound treatise still remains deductively sound: deductive soundness depends not on the sequence of presentation (at heart, a stylistic concern), but on the absence of circular paths of demonstration. The *Measurement of the Circle* as it stands is therefore deductively sound. Still, it is remarkably outside the norm of Greek mathematical writing which – as a very strong rule – does not allow such permutations of propositions. This, coupled with the falseness of proposition 2, makes most modern readers believe proposition 2 is a late interpolation. It is indeed a very brief statement, that could be made as some kind of scholion providing the readers with something to "take home" from the *Measurement of the Circle*. Or else it could be a hoax on Archimedes' part, along the line of the false results reported in the introduction to *Spiral Lines* . . . I myself believe the stronger likelihood is that of a late interpolation, so I shall not try to enlist proposition 2 into my survey of the ludic in Hellenistic mathematics.

I now turn to proposition 3, which forms the bulk of the treatise. Indeed, if proposition 2 is stripped away, the treatise that remains is an exercise in opposites: a relatively brief, elegant result in pure geometry (proposition 1); followed by a very substantial piece of calculation (proposition 3). At this point I would say that – unlike Knorr (who imagined the treatise to form some kind of degenerate version of an original, lengthier work) – I see no reason to doubt the authenticity of the emerging structure. This is the Hellenistic mosaic texture with which we are already familiar, brought to its logical perfection of a pair of opposites, each performing an opposite kind of *tour de force*: maximal geometrical elegance followed by the maximal carnival of calculation.

Proposition 3 asserts that the circumference of the circle stands to its diameter in a ratio which is three times and – more than a seventh, but less than ten to seventy-one. What follows is a complex set of calculations based on geometrical considerations.

Here then is a case of a calculation by Archimedes attempting to capture the unbounded. What I claim is that this attempt ends up with something less than a solution: to some extent it does capture the unbounded, but, no less, it signals the unboundedness of that object on which the attempt was made. Instead of showing how a problem may be simplified and solved, the act of calculation serves to underline how difficult, how inherently complex, the problem is.

One should make the following comparison. The Greek mathematical interest in providing boundaries, in setting precise terms, even numerical terms, has a significant pedigree. One can identify a philosophical tradition starting from the Pythagoreans such as Philolaus, and maturing into Platonic doctrine, where the model of music is taken as a prime example of how science can throw light on a piece of reality by showing the strict terms bounding it. Philolaus' philosophy has the basic pair of opposites of the limiter and the unlimited, with the presence of the "limiter" as providing reality with its structure and value.[9] Such, in broad outline, seems to be Plato's position in dialogues such as the *Republic* and the *Philebus* and, surprisingly perhaps, Aristotle too may have shared this worldview. Already Philolaus mentions "harmony" as a central principle of this doctrine, and it is clear that music is the model informing Plato's and Aristotle's thinking, as well, on the subject.[10] Now there the application of numerical terms is indeed quite striking. What mathematical musical theorists have found was that, essentially, the system of musical harmonies can be brought down

---

[9] Huffman 1993: 37–53.
[10] For Plato, see the discussion in Burnyeat 2000, esp. 47–53, focusing on the *Republic*, as well as Huffman 2001, focusing on the *Philebus*. (Of course, one should also mention the role of music in the contruction of the world-soul in the *Timaeus*.) For Aristotle, see in particular Sorabji 1972.

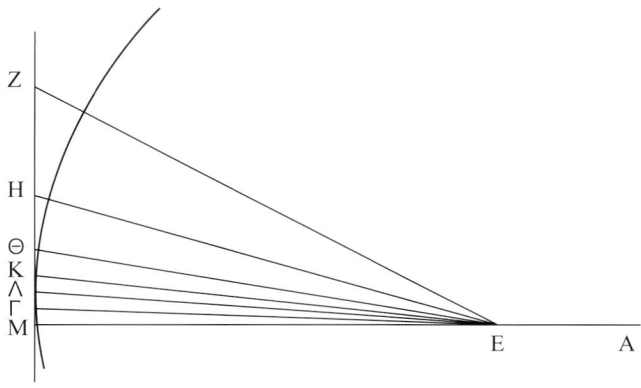

Figure 6

to some very few numerical ratios – essentially, all one needs are the three ratios:

1:2 (standing for the octave)
2:3 (standing for the fifth)
3:4 (standing for the fourth)[11]

where all other musical relations can then be seen as functions of these basic concords.

This then is a case where an otherwise difficult, irregular piece of reality – musical experience with its variety of alternative tunings – is captured by numerical calculation that serves to show how, essentially, the system is all regular.[12] This would be an attempt to capture the unbounded ending up with it changing its character – the unbounded of pre-theoretical musical experience ends up being bounded by musical theory. It is all simple, after all! Such, I argue, is not the case with Archimedes' measurement of the circle. No simple ratios here, no sense of an accomplishment.

We begin by looking at straight lines bounding the circle from the outside, first with an angle such as ZEΓ being one third a right angle (ΓZ is a tangent, ΓE – a radius).

---

[11] What is meant by these ratios is essentially that, say, two similar pieces of string with the ratios of their length 1:2 will produce sounds an octave apart, etc.; though the Greeks would have a variety of other examples, and of physical theories, accounting for this relation.

[12] Pre-theoretical musical experience would have felt complex enough for the Greeks – with (i) the bewildering variety of keys that, of course, prior to theory could not be seen as variations on a single model, and with (ii) the rich structures available to perception, especially given that the system incorporated quarter-tones. See the introduction to Barker 1989 for an overview of the problems involved.

*Attempting to capture the unbounded*    25

I move now to supply an explanation omitted by Archimedes.[13] The construction makes the triangle ΓEZ one-half of an equilateral triangle (remember that in an equilateral triangle all three angles are equal to two-thirds of a right angle). ZE is twice ZΓ, and the square on ZE is four times that on ZΓ, so, by Pythagoras' theorem, the square on ΓE is three times that on ZΓ. This will make the ratio of ΓE to ZΓ to be what we would call the square root of three, itself an irrational number. In other words, this value can be bounded but not stated. Archimedes mentions none of the above and does not even mention that the ratio cannot be measured precisely, instead proceeding directly to state – without an explanation – that the ratio of ΓE to ΓZ is that of 265 to 153 (while that of ZE to ZΓ is 306 to 153 – also stated without an explanation, but obviously meaning the same as 2:1). I shall return to discuss the apparent falsehood below.

Now the following geometrical consideration holds (this time made explicit by Archimedes). Bisect the angle ZEΓ by EH, and you have the geometrical consequence

ZE:EΓ::ZH:HΓ, also (ZE+EΓ):ZΓ::EΓ:ΓH

This would allow us to state, based on the above, that 571:153::EΓ:ΓH,
   but Archimedes asserts that 571:153<ΓE:ΓH.

In other words, Archimedes suddenly owns up – no account being given – to the approximative nature of the original ratio 265:153.

At which point, once again without an explanation (the underlying geometrical principle is Pythagoras' theorem) Archimedes states that EH has to HΓ, in square, the ratio of 349,450 to 23,409. (The preceding inequality is once again treated, misleadingly, as an equality.) From which, it is claimed, it follows that EH has to HΓ the ratio of 591 and an eighth to 153. (This taking of the square root is once again an unacknowledged approximation.)

Now Archimedes bisects the angle ΓEH and asserts that "because of the same <arguments>" (a fantastic expression, given that Archimedes has so far revealed only part of the reasoning underlying the calculations)

EΓ:ΓΘ>(1162 and an eighth):153.

And he proceeds to provide the numbers resulting for the following two bisections ending up in the ratio of EΓ to ΛΓ (the angle ΓEΛ now being a forty-eighth of a right angle). This turns out to be greater than

(4,673 and a half):153.

---

[13] I use the name "Archimedes" instead of the cumbersome phrase "the author of the proposition." I do indeed believe this text is by Archimedes but, even if it isn't, it is an intelligent piece of mathematical work: the implication of the name "Archimedes" is not misleading.

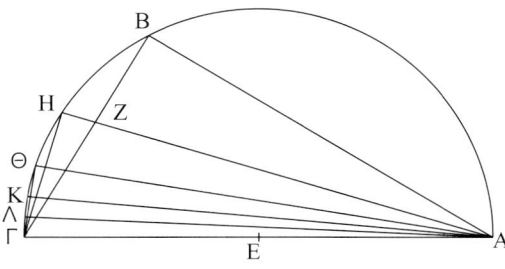

Figure 7

At this point Archimedes explains in detail how this can be used as an expression of the ratio of the perimeter of the 96-gon to the radius of the circle. This ratio is then 14,688:(4673 and a half) which, Archimedes shows, once again in clear detail, is less than 3 and a seventh, which provides Archimedes with the upper boundary on the ratio of the perimeter of the circle.

Then Archimedes moves on to the lower boundary, where he starts in this case with the half-equilateral triangle ABΓ inscribed within a circle (fig. 7). Based on a similar estimate of the square root of three, Archimedes now begins by stating that

AB:BΓ<1351:780.

He then bisects angle A by AH and produces in detail the geometrical proportion:

(BA, AΓ taken together):BΓ::AH:HΓ

which then allows him to make a series of bisections, simplifying the ratios along the way, to arrive at AΓ:ΓΛ<(2017 and a quarter):66. He then explains how this can be used for calculating the ratio of the inscribed 96-gon to the diameter of the circle, which is found to be greater than three and the ratio ten to seventy one.

There are several features I wish to stress here.

First, we notice the thick structure of nearly incomprehensible calculation, to which I shall return below as an independent stylistic feature. The main outcome here is to stress the difficulty of the operation.

Second, we notice the systematic ambiguity between equalities and inequalities. While Archimedes' end result is a mere statement of upper and lower boundaries, he keeps making statements concerning precise ratios, statements that strictly speaking are false. It is absurd to suggest that Archimedes was unaware of the difference between equality and inequality (the relation between the two is very carefully handled in the actual calculation, even if the presentation very often ignores the distinction). It is also clear that Archimedes had the language to express the difference between a ratio being the same as another, and a ratio being greater than another. It is also obvious that the nature of upper and lower bounding is what the treatise is about: surely Archimedes could not think the clear statement of a boundary as such – and not as an equality – was a trivial detail. Since Archimedes knew about the difference, knew how to express it and cared about it, and yet so often expressed it in such a misleading way, my conclusion is that he made a choice to mystify his readers at this point. But even without any such assumptions concerning the author's intentions, it is clear that the *outcome* of the proposition is indeed to leave the reader confused as to the precise structure of equalities and inequalities underlying Archimedes' calculation.

This is not merely a stylistic, but also a mathematical point. In order to calculate with inequalities, one needs to follow precise rules of algebra: from A>B and B>C, A>C may be deduced, but from A>B and B<C, nothing can. Archimedes never makes the slightest effort to clarify this algebraic structure underlying his calculations, although, once again, his actual calculations are all impeccable and so done with a clear understanding of the nature of the inequalities involved; and although mathematical Greek had a vocabulary of dealing with such structures.[14] The reader is deliberately left in the dark.

Third, we notice the essentially open-ended nature of the exercise. Archimedes clearly intended his readers to see that the operations of bounding the circle could be extended *ad infinitum*, with the same type of calculations being extended. There is no inherent reason to stop with the 96-gon.

Fourth, we notice that Archimedes' final result is explicitly weaker than it needs to be. On both boundaries, Archimedes obtains a rather complex ratio which he then simplifies, at the price of getting a less precise ratio. The ratio of the circumference to the diameter was bounded by Archimedes into a range smaller than the (3 and a seventh) – (3 and ten to seventy one) range he ultimately uses. The range chosen was clearly preferred for its relatively simple and elegant form (few words, and "seven" elegantly appearing on both sides), and the loss in precision was quite minimal (about a myriadth – though this will not be apparent from Archimedes' numbers themselves). And yet, the outcome is to suggest once again how arbitrary

---

[14] This would be the πολὺ μαλλόν connector (or just πολλῷ), "by much," used in the context (i) A>B, (ii) B>C, (iii) πολλῷ A>C. While this is used in Archimedes' writings, and even, in two places (Heiberg 240.10, 242.17) in the *Measurement of the Circle* itself, most of Archimedes' calculations of inequalities in this treatise are not marked by the connector.

the choice of the boundaries stated is: not only is the result arbitrarily obtained for the 96-gons, it is then also arbitrarily simplified.

Fifth and most elementary, we notice the nature of the result in terms of boundaries rather than a precise number. This of course is in the nature of the problem – but it is a striking result in a quest for exactitude. Of course Archimedes could not have found a precise value for π. But he did make the choice of writing a treatise in which an estimate is made for the ratio of a circumference to the diameter, that is he made the choice of writing a treatise whose outcome is stated in terms of boundaries. Not here the simple ratios of musical theory.

To sum up (slightly revising the order): the *Measurement of the Circle* (1) foregrounds the difficulty of calculating the ratio of the circumference to the diameter, it ends up by (5) finding mere boundaries, (2) through a process where the interplay of equalities and inequalities is completely obscured, (3) stressing the arbitrariness of ending the process at any particular point and of (4) setting out its outcome in any particular way. This is my ground for making the following suggestion: that while Archimedes does indeed make an attempt to capture the unbounded – the ratio of the circumference to the diameter – he ends up with an ambiguous result, on the one hand a triumph of bounding a complex structure, on the other hand a display of the complexity and recalcitrance of a structure which is only imperfectly bounded.

One part of this is the very choice of a problem whose nature is asymptotic. To offer a solution is – with such a problem – to reach not an end but a step along a way, whose lack of clear termination is suggested by the solution itself. Any solution based on upper and lower boundaries has a similar character. Aristarchus' treatise on the *Sizes and Distances of the Sun and the Moon* – to which I now turn – reveals the same principle. As the title suggests, Aristarchus is indeed attempting to capture the unbounded, in fact he is trying, literally, to reach for the stars. While doing so, he is also going to uncover a universe of staggering dimensions: the results of the mathematical calculation end up, in a way, delimiting the universe, but also end up expanding it relative to established notions. The sun for instance is found to be much greater than the earth – to be precise, or, more precisely, to be *imprecise*, the sun is found (in proposition 16 of the treatise) to have to the earth a ratio greater than that which 6,859 has to 27, but less than that which 79,507 has to 216 (!). Aristarchus, just like Archimedes in the *Measurement of the Circle*, ends up with an asymptotic result, merely bounding the sizes and the distances instead of offering precise values.

Aristarchus' mathematical operation is based on trigonometric calculations starting from simple astronomical observations. Aristarchus emphasizes the tentative nature of the calculation by choosing values for the simple observations that are just obviously too pat. He gives the angle Moon-Sun-Earth at the exact moment of dichotomy of the moon as 1/30 a right angle – while the correct value is far lower, about nine minutes. More troubling (since this is much easier to measure) is the very false value provided for the seen angle of the moon, 1/45 a right angle (the true value is one-fourth that; anyone who can measure anything in the sky should be able to see the difference).[15] And then he proceeds very similarly to Archimedes: offering calculations whose details are not explicated, giving rise to inequalities. At heart, the asymptotic nature of the treatise is directly comparable to that of Archimedes: both are effectively producing trigonometric calculations and can do no better than approximate trigonometric functions. Aristarchus has achieved a stupendous piece of calculation, bounding the cosmos – along the way suggesting the tentative and approximative nature of the exercise. And indeed, a century later, Hipparchus would attempt the same calculation again – based on a different geometrical approach – this time coming up with different and (naturally) bigger numbers – according to Ptolemy's later re-calculation, the sun's distance is 1,210 radii of the earth, its volume 170 times that of the earth.[16] This of course is typical of Greek polemical intellectual life, where claims are made so as to be challenged; but the very nature of approximation is to invite future correction. We shall see below the same pattern of claim and corrections with another case of astronomical calculation, this time of the earth itself. And we should notice that Archimedes' achievement of the calculation of ratio of the circumference of the circle to its diameter was indeed corrected by later authors, foremost by Apollonius himself. This is reported to us, tantalizingly, by Eutocius, towards the end of his commentary to Archimedes' *Measurement of the Circle* (Heiberg 258.15–260.1) – tantalizingly, because Eutocius merely notes the existence of other numbers by Apollonius and by Philo of Gadara, without providing us with the actual numbers. But then again, we would hardly need Eutocius' report to guess that such numbers existed: the obvious asymptotic nature of his calculation, together with Archimedes' authority as well as the grandeur

---

[15] The value for the diameter of the moon would be obviously false; the value for the angle at bisection would be obviously unattainable. Van Helden's comments are worth quoting at some length (1985: 7): "[D]etermining the exact moment of dichotomy and then measuring the angular separation of the two luminaries accurately is a hopeless task. Even a small error in the time of dichotomy leads to a significant error in <MES [the angle Moon-Earth-Sun], itself difficult to measure accurately . . . a small error in <MES will produce a proportionally much larger error in the all-important <MSE . . ."

[16] Those are the numbers provided by Ptolemy, which may reflect Ptolemy's own calculations. Other ancient authors mention bigger numbers for Hipparchus, for instance Theon of Smyrna (Hiller 197.9–11) makes the sun 1,880 times the earth. For the main piece of evidence, see Ptolemy v.14–16.

of the theme (measuring the circle!) formed an invitation for polemic that future authors could not ignore.

Trigonometric functions are not the only route leading to the approximative. Some other problems by their nature allow merely an asymptotic solution. Consider for instance Eratosthenes, setting out to capture prime numbers – an attempt to capture the unbounded if ever there was one. (Euclid's *Elements* IX.20 – apparently designed as a culmination of Euclid's theory of numbers[17] – ends up by showing that prime numbers are more than any given magnitude.) According to a report in Nicomachus' *Arithmetic* (1.13), Eratosthenes has written a simple algorithm for determining prime numbers, which he has colorfully labeled the *Sieve*: take a list of all odd numbers and, starting from 3, add marks by going three steps at a time (from 3 to 9, to 15, to 21 . . .), then starting from 5, add marks by going five steps at a time, etc . . . Clearly, every time you reach an unmarked odd number in this way, you have identified a prime number. And at the same time – the operation underlines its own open-endedness. The sieve has infinitely many holes at its bottom: one can get nearer and nearer to defining the set of prime numbers, and yet one is also infinitely distant from completing this task.

This is the capturing of the unbounded as an exercise in impossibility. A famous study by Archimedes is dedicated precisely to a central poetic trope of the impossible – trying to count grains of sand.[18] In the *Sand-Reckoner*, Archimedes' goal is a measurement of the number of grains of sand it would take to fill the cosmos. Which brings us to a double unbounded, as the goal is both below and above measure. The grains of sand are too small to measure, chaotic in their minuscule structure. They are also imagined to fill up the immeasurable dimensions of the cosmos. This brings to mind Aristarchus – who is indeed mentioned by Archimedes, not directly for *The*

---

[17] Euclid's arithmetical books have a complex narrative structure, in that they are designed with two culminating points: the ending itself, IX.36, producing an algorithm for finding a perfect number (one equal to the sum of all its factors, e.g. $6 = 1+2+3$), and then IX. 20 which, as Mueller puts it, "stands in isolation" – i.e. does not serve further deductive purposes – while, to quote Mueller again, "There is a dramatic change after IX.20" (Mueller 1981: 103). The isolation of IX.20, the shift immediately following it and its obvious striking achievement, all serve to mark it as a culmination point. The interesting fact is that the two culmination points – IX.20 and IX.36 – speak to very different aesthetic sensibilities. The main fact of IX.20 is a certain lack of closure. The main fact of IX.36 is a certain closure, literally: the Greek word for "perfect," *teleion*, may equally be translated as "brought to its complete end," "made complete," indeed – if only the Greeks were inclined to speak in such words – "closured." That IX.36 is chosen to serve as the major culmination, may speak to Euclid's own aesthetic, or perhaps metaphysical preferences.

[18] For the literary trope, see e.g. Nisbet and Hubbard 1970: 321; we shall of course return below to discuss this interface of the mathematical with the poetic. For tropes of the uncountable in general, see Mccartney 1960.

*Sizes and Distances of the Sun and the Moon* but for his other famous (and now lost) treatise, where a heliocentric model of the universe was offered. Such a model involves a much bigger universe, so as to avoid any parallax even with the much-extended motions of the terrestrial observer, and my guess is that Aristarchus produced this model precisely for the sake of such extravagant size.

Such speculation aside, extravagant calculation is clearly what Archimedes' treatise is about. First, he presents a special counting tool that allows the representation of extremely big numbers. This is based on a principle of iteration: myriad myriads are taken as the unit of the "second numbers," myriad myriad those – as the unit of the third numbers, etc., and then myriad myriads of the myriad-myriad numbers are taken as the unit of the first numbers of the "second period," the unit of the second period being myriad-myriads of the myriad-myriads numbers of the second period, etc., until one hits myriad myriads of the myriad-myriad numbers of the myriad-myriads period, which is a very big number indeed if you pause to think of it. I have pointed out in a previous article (Netz 2003) that the interpretation often offered in the literature, as if this is some kind of attempt by Archimedes to present a version of our decimal system, is clearly off-mark: Archimedes' system is deliberately cumbersome in its notation (even though it does allow calculation of multiplication by the addition of the exponents), aiming at preserving the texture of natural language – which is precisely the opposite of the decimal system. At the same time, and most importantly for our immediate purposes, the system is explicitly *bounded*. Unlike our decimal numbers, Archimedes' numbers in the *Sand-Reckoner* are distinguished by their having an end-point. The reader then sees Archimedes reaching for the goal of numbering the largest possible numbers – achieving much and yet also, obviously, failing, as he ends up pathetically distant from infinity, with merely the myriad myriads of the myriad-myriad numbers of the myriad-myriad period as the biggest number . . .

But this is just one aspect of the asymptotic nature of Archimedes' treatise. Of course one other aspect we predict already: trying to offer an estimate for the size of the cosmos under Aristarchus' assumptions, Archimedes would have to present a boundary estimate based on a complicated, not fully articulated trigonometric calculation. But there's even more. The system developed by Archimedes could in principle allow precise calculation – for instance imagine that there are two numbers:

A – Three of the third numbers of the second period and one of the second numbers of the first period;

B – Two of the third numbers of the second period and two of the second numbers of the first period.

Then A+B is:

five of the third numbers of the second period and three of the second numbers of the first period.

But clearly this calculation would quickly get out of hand if more complex relations are involved. Imagine summations where one needs to cross thresholds of "numbers" and "periods!" Bear in mind that the "numerator" would quickly become more complicated that two or three, reaching expressions such as "thirty two myriads, two thousand five hundred and seventy three of the one hundred and twenty first numbers . . ." Most important, bear in mind that each number may have a rich structure containing a host of constituents from different periods and numbers (the preceding example would be just a single constituent). In fact, it is natural to expect that a precise value for a number would involve *all* the periods and numbers, starting from the highest required by the calculation, going all the way down to the ordinary numbers smaller than a myriad myriads: indeed, each number-and-period combination may host as many as 100,000,000 integers.

In other words, Archimedes' numerical system is not at all useful for precise calculations, and it is useful *only* for providing boundaries (where one may always cut all the terms except for the biggest). This is precisely what Archimedes produces in the *Sand-Reckoner*. Of course, as we expect him to do, he goes through a thick, difficult calculation, where inequalities are continually traded for each other. And he ends up by showing that the number obtained – the number of grains of sand it would take to fill the earth – is less than a thousand of the seventh numbers. This is in fact a gloriously compact formulation (and one is reminded of the prominence of the number seven in the *Measurement of the Circle* itself), but it is also a misleadingly compact formulation: as any sophisticated reader would have to notice, Archimedes could have obtained this value only by reducing his problem to that of *bounding* the number of grains. If asked actually to *number* those grains, he would do no better than Pindar did. The treatise attempts to capture the unbounded, and fails to do so – failing better and better – three times:

- The numerical system aims at numbers as big as possible, only to end up with an absurdly big and yet finite number.
- The astronomical calculation provides an absurdly big, heliocentric universe – and can only provide an asymptotic, bounding measure of it.

- The actual calculation of the grains of sand succeeds by reducing the problem (appearing to be that of providing a number) to a mere boundary problem.

In all cases, Archimedes' approach not merely ends up with an asymptotic result but also underlines the impossibility of going beyond it.

Archimedes has tried to count the grains of sand; Hipparchus, a century later, went on to count the stars. Thus both poetic tropes of futile counting were literally attempted by Hellenistic mathematicians.[19] Hipparchus' catalogue is lost, and so, much less can be said of it. We do have an extant catalogue of fixed stars as books VII–VIII of Ptolemy's *Almagest*, and there are many indications – in particular, the comments made by Hipparchus on Aratus' astronomical poem (of which more at pp. 168–71 below) – that the catalogue by Ptolemy is modeled on Hipparchus'. We cannot tell what the exact form of Hipparchus' original work was, but there are comments – e.g. by Pliny, II.95 – according to which Hipparchus aimed to produce a checklist against which any new appearances in the sky could be compared. This then suggests the aim of a *complete* star catalogue so that, in simple words, Hipparchus counted the stars (and probably *measured* them too – the concept of applying degrees of brightness to stars may have originated with him).[20] It is a pity we do not have his actual number, but as the star catalogue of Ptolemy contains over a thousand stars and that of Hipparchus could not have been much smaller, we get the order of magnitude (a number often repeated by modern scholars is that of 850 Hipparchean stars).[21] This is finite, and yet remarkable enough – especially given that one would have to go through those stars one by one, providing each with some numerical coordinates (measured, perhaps, in complex fractions of angles) as well as a degree of brightness; this work must have presented its readers with a dazzling array of numbers, much as does Ptolemy's catalogue.

The stars, whatever the poets make of them, present a relatively simple problem of counting. Yet sometimes the numbers of a mathematical problem can be so big as to defy solution. Consider, for this purpose, Archimedes' *Cattle Problem*:

---

[19] For the trope of counting stars see McCartney 1960: 83–4 (curiously, the earliest extant poetic source is in this case Callimachus, *Hymn to Delos* 175–6).

[20] Thus, for instance, in the passage quoted, Pliny mentions not only the possibility of new stars appearing but also that of stars growing or diminishing – to investigate this, one would need to have some kind of measurement of the "magnitude" of the star at the time of the making of the catalogue, i.e. the notion of degree of brightness.

[21] This is based on extrapolation, but there are strong statistical arguments why the number must be in about this range. See the discussion in Grasshoff 1990: 34–42.

Measure for me, friend, the multitude of Helios' cattle,
Possessing diligence – if you partake of wisdom:
How many did once graze the planes of Sicily,
The Island Thrinacian? Divided in four herds,
In color varied . . .
. . . The white bulls
Were of the black a half and then a third
And then the whole of yellows, friend, do know this . . .

So begins the treatise. It survives on a path separate from the main tradition of the works by Archimedes, but ancient testimonies make us believe it is indeed by Archimedes. And yet: a poem! (We shall of course return below to discuss this formal aspect.) It sets out a list of conditions, seven equations and two geometrical requirements that the various segments of Helios' herd must have satisfied. All taken together give rise to a problem whose simplest solution involves a number which, in our writing, takes 206,545 digits.[22] It is certain that no one in antiquity ever solved the problem, but what could have been Archimedes' point? This is not at all clear – but the sense of setting out the task of capturing the impossible is palpable (one, indeed, reaches to capture Helios' cattle at one's own risk).

Asymptotic calculation is then merely one side of capturing the unbounded. The very size and complexity of numbers may sometimes contribute to such a sense. Remember once again the comparison with musical theory. There, the totality of musical experience is captured by such simple numerical relations as 1:2, 2:3, and 3:4. Now, any calculation that comes up with a number that is big and complicated – even if this number is precisely calculated – gives rise to a sense that the object number somehow has not been "captured." The end result of a calculation that ends up with a complex number is not to show that the object numbered is well behaved but rather to show – in a precise way – how badly behaved it is. Consider now Hipparchus' own combinatoric calculation, coming up with 103,049 (for the simpler problem) or 310,954 (for the more complex one). This is in the context of an attempt to debunk Chrysippus, who apparently asserted airily that those numbers are "more than a million." Hipparchus substitutes a precise calculation for Chrysippus' boundary (which is truly unsatisfactory, being a *lower* boundary). He captures a seemingly unbounded, what appears to be a "more than a million" (i.e. huge) number. Yet he does this by irreducibly complex calculations

---

[22] See Amthor 1880, where the transmission of the problem is discussed as well.

that end up with an irreducibly complex number, one that does not appear to have any special meaning, any special structure to it. Hipparchus ends up finding that the number of solutions is indeed huge and unwieldy – just in a different way from that imagined by Chrysippus.

Or a number may be much smaller, but still decidedly "unwieldy" or, so to speak, "unmusical." We learn from Ptolemy's *Almagest* (1.12), for instance, about a discussion by Eratosthenes of the obliquity of the ecliptic. This was often represented in the Greek case as the ratio between, on the one hand, the angular distance between the points of the two solstices and, on the other hand, the circumference of the sky as a whole. Ptolemy himself, who divides the sky into 360 degrees (as we also do, ultimately following Babylonian practice) derives a value between $47\frac{2}{3}$ and $47\frac{3}{4}$ degrees. Eratosthenes, so Ptolemy tells us, provided the ratio 11:83 (which was then followed by Hipparchus himself). This is an extraordinary value to state, as anyone who has ever tried to divide a circle into eighty-three equal parts would have to agree. There are efforts in modern literature to try to account for such numbers in terms of a putative method of calculation that naturally gives rise to them, or in terms of the geographical and astronomical data underlying the number.[23] I do not deny the value of such discussions but I wish to note that they ignore one point: that Eratosthenes could have been satisfied with such numbers – instead of returning to his abacus to find another, more accessible way of stating his ratio (especially seeing that the number must have been understood, anyway, as an approximation).[24] Of course we know nothing about the original context of Eratosthenes' text, but we surely see here another example of a Hellenistic calculation ending up with strange, unwieldy numbers. That those are among the most central numbers defining the skies makes this even more curious. Was some joke intended with Plato's world-soul as its butt?[25]

The above is speculation. As usual, we should turn to Archimedes to see the full variety of the unwieldy in action. Now I return to the *Stomachion* – a

---

[23] See e.g. Fowler 1999: 50–1, Taisbak 1984, Jones 2002.
[24] A very close approximation involving some very "neat" numbers is 2/15 minus 1/1200 (which suggests that 2/15 itself is tolerably good). One wonders if, in the observational context of pre-Hipparchan astronomy, the quarter of a degree separating 2/15 and 11/83 would have mattered so much.
[25] In Plato's *Timaeus*, a famous strange cosmological-metaphysical passage, 35b–36b, involves the construction of the world-soul as a kind of musical correlate to the heavenly scheme, where the main terms are "the same" and "the other," in some sense corresponding to the diurnal and annual rotation, so that their ratios would correspond to the ecliptic; Plato implies that all the numbers involved are reduced to powers of 2 and 3, on the model of mathematical musical theory. Eratosthenes' actual ratio involves two considerably bigger, not at all "pretty" prime numbers.

work, indeed, where the actual structure of calculation is no longer extant. But it is a safe bet that Archimedes made a correct calculation of the number of combinations: his extant works are short on errors. If so (assuming he would opt for the most expansive definition of what counts as a combination), the treatise would have ended with the reply "17,152" – a number striking for its precision as well as for its meaninglessness. This would have been another attempt to capture the unbounded, hobbled by its unwieldy, in a sense unbounded outcome. But there would be more than this: the continuation of the treatise must have dealt with another, qualitatively different problem, for which I quote again from the introduction to the treatise:

... <all of the above> said for the sake of finding out the fitting-together of the arising figures, whether the resulting sides in the figures are on a line or whether they are slightly short of that <but so as to be> unnoticed by sight. For such considerations as these are intellectually challenging; nor, if it is a little short of <being on a line> while being unnoticed by vision, the <figures> composed are not for that reason to be rejected.

It appears quite clear that, having studied the problem of the solutions assuming perfect alignment, Archimedes added on some further study of the problem arising where less than perfect solutions are allowed, namely ones where the line segments align at angles that are slightly, invisibly "off" straight lines.

The first kind of study, with its "17,152" conclusion, would offer the unbounded of the unwieldy; the second kind of study – whose solution we cannot really guess – would offer the unbounded of the asymptotic. For there is no single "correct" way of defining what counts as a *slightly* non-linear angle. Having produced one answer, definite and yet unwieldy, Archimedes then went on to point out that in practice, the number of allowed solutions is even bigger, even more unwieldy – and in fact, so he would imply, can only be approximated. This then may be the formula: in many Hellenistic mathematical works we see calculations that give rise to values that are big and unwieldy, or else are only asymptotically found. Such calculations end up not with the satisfaction of having simplified a complex domain, but almost the opposite of that: a sense of reveling in a domain's complexity. A similar sense of reveling in complexity is seen not only in the result itself, but also in the process of calculation leading to it – to which we now turn.

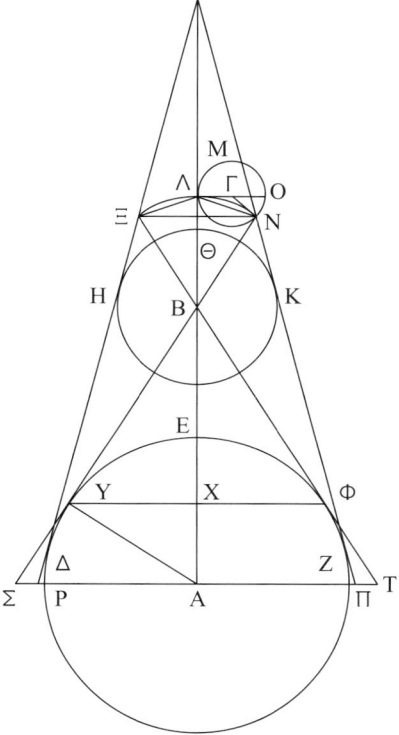

Figure 8

## 1.3 OPAQUE COGNITIVE TEXTURE OF CALCULATION

I start with a relatively simple example, one where calculation is relatively transparent. This is from Aristarchus' *Sizes and Distances of the Sun and the Moon*, proposition 13 (fig. 8):

(1) But NΓ has to ΛΓ a ratio greater than that which 89 has to 45, (2) that is, the <square> on NΓ has to the <square> on ΛΓ a greater ratio than 7921 to 2025; (3) therefore: the <square> on ΞN, too, has to the square on NΓ a greater ratio than 7921 to 2025, (4) and ΞN has to ΛO a greater ratio than 7921 to 4050. (5) And 7921 has to 4050 a greater ratio than 88 to 45; (6) therefore NΞ has to ΛO a greater ratio than 88 to 45.

I wish to draw our attention to the cognitive divide between several types of argument in this passage.

First, there is the direct trading of equivalences, in the verbal scheme "A stands in the relation P to B, B to C, therefore A to C" (with P a transitive relation). This is a purely verbal move that can be easily parsed without any special training (all that is called for is familiarity with the terms involved). This is the trivial move from (4) and (5) taken together to (6). (Notice incidentally the transition from referring to ΞN in (4), to referring to NΞ in (6) – that this can be done in the course of such an equivalence statement is a mark of the degree to which the operation is mediated by referring to the concrete diagram, rather than to the symbolic layer alone.)

The concrete diagram underlies the second type of argument. First, there is the assumption that a diameter is twice a radius, where the status of ΛΓ as a radius and of ΛΟ as a diameter is unproblematically encoded into the diagram. Geometrical reasoning aided by the diagram is the most direct tool available to the mind – certainly the Greek mind – in such a context, so that within the transition from (3) to (4) this adaptation is implicitly made.

Further, there is a more complex combination of geometry and proportion-theory involved in the same move. By the construction, the triangles ΞΛΝ, ΝΓΝ are similar, so that one has *inter alia* the proportion

$$\Xi\Lambda : \Lambda N :: \Lambda N : \Lambda \Gamma$$

which is asserted in the transition from (2) to (3). Further, from the same similarity of triangles the trained Greek mathematical reader automatically deduces (the two expressions are nearly notational variations for him):

$$\Xi\Lambda^2 : \Lambda N^2 :: \Xi\Lambda : \Lambda \Gamma$$

(please excuse the anachronistic, algebraic presentation).

This, together with the implicit transition from radius to diameter, underlies the most interesting part of the passage above, namely the move from (3) to (4).

The geometrical type of argument actually displays variety. Of the arguments considered above, one is geometrical and purely visual, another is geometrical but also involved proportion-theoretical considerations. I have no doubt a Greek reader would parse the transition from (2) to (3) without any effort at all, while the transition from (3) to (4) would require no more than a moment's reflection. Most important, the Greek reader, just by reflecting upon the transition from (3) to (4), would be able to affirm it to his satisfaction: this is the general rule for geometrical arguments as such.

Such is no longer the case with the remainder of the passage and the final type of arguments it displays. I refer to the transitions from (1) to (2), as well as that stated in (5). The transition from (1) to (2) is relatively easy, and one can see how a person with good training in calculation could work this out. But notice that this calls for being worked out. The reader cannot simply reflect upon the equality

$(89:25)^2 = 7,921:2,025$

to perceive its validity, but instead must need to break it down into its constituents (how much is 89 times 89? It is, e.g., 80 times 80 plus 9 times 9 plus twice 9 times 80 . . .), referring to some concrete medium for calculation (a calculator or a pen and paper in our case, most likely the abacus in the Greek case). To verify the equation, one must detach oneself momentarily from the text, though most likely one simply takes the statement on faith, reflecting that it is in principle easy to verify.

This is no longer true when considering the last and most difficult type of argument made in this passage: the statement made in the course of (5), that

$7,921:4,050 > 88:45$.

The verification of such a statement is inherently difficult (it involves a multiple set of divisions), but more than this: there is no clear way to know that the statement is not merely a *correct* inequality statement, but also a *useful* approximation statement. For the implication is that by the transition from 7,921:4,050 to 88:45, some precision is lost, but that this is compensated for by the greater simplicity of 88:45. The implicit trade-off is little precision lost for much simplicity gained. But do we really know that this is a good approximation, the best possible? Perhaps there is a ratio with terms smaller than 88 and 45, that is even nearer the original ratio of 7921 to 4050? We are not provided any handle on this question and so, while the *validity* of the statement at (5) may in principle be checked by detaching ourselves, once again, from the proposition, its *value* as an approximation is not even subject to serious thought. No hint is made at the mechanism producing the approximation, so that no arguments can be raised for or against it. This is truly a take-it-or-leave-it statement.

We see therefore a fundamental divide: while the geometrical component of Aristarchus' reasoning is meant to be parsed as the reader goes along, and so to be confirmed by the reader's knowledge of geometry and of proportion-theory (always bringing into play the concrete diagram), the arithmetical component is reduced to a series of take-it-or-leave-it statements that the reader just takes for granted. This duality is characteristic of all of Greek mathematical texts. In a more geometrical context the resulting text displays rigorous logical standards, admirably open to the reader's inspection. It was on this end of Greek mathematical writing that I concentrated in my book, *The Shaping of Deduction in Greek Mathematics* (1999), and of course I still stand behind my characterization there of the cognitive experience of reading Greek geometrical proof. But one should also notice that when the text begins to have a considerable arithmetical component – as in Aristarchus' treatise on the *Sizes and Distances of the Sun and the Moon* – the nature of the reading experience begins to shift. In the geometrical case, the reading experience is of a continuous stream of statements whose validity is parsed and confirmed by the mind through the application of certain known equivalences, of the diagram, and of the verbal texture: to read is to understand and agree. In the more arithmetical case, disbelief has to be occasionally suspended. The effort of understanding gives way to the effort of merely remembering – even, merely perusing – the complex numerical values involved. The reader is no longer a *judge*, but is instead a *spectator*. And with the puncturing of the seamless sequence of parsed deductions, the reading experience is no longer continuous, but is much more discrete, each statement standing on its own. Thus, as the text loses its overarching deductive structure, and as it is no longer under the reader's intellectual control, its overall texture becomes more opaque and difficult. This is the thick texture of calculation.

In the case seen above from Aristarchus – relatively mild as it was – the sense of opacity was related to the sheer size and complexity of the numbers involved (after all, calculating the squares of 12 and 8, say, would not pose the same cognitive hurdle as calculating those of 89 and 25). But the same effect may be obtained with rather simple numerical values.

We have noticed above Archimedes' numerical coda to *Spiral Lines*, where the last two propositions develop in detail the numerical ratios inside the sequence of outward-extending spirals. This in fact may have been an Archimedean technique: to conclude a mostly geometrical work with an arithmetical coda. Instead of returning once again to *Spiral Lines*, then, let us consider another example: the second book on *Planes in Equlibrium*. Here Archimedes finds the center of gravity of a parabolic segment. The first eight propositions, clearly geometrical in character, develop the geometrical proportions required for this purpose. The final, tenth proposition, is a heavily arithmetical exercise where the various segments involved are added together and calculated. Most interestingly, this calculation is based on the mostly arithmetical result of proposition 9. Here we move into a territory much more opaque than Aristarchus' (quoting first the enunciation):

If four lines are proportional in a continuous proportion, and that ratio which the smallest has to the excess, by which the greatest exceeds the smallest – let some <line> be taken, having this <ratio> to three fifths of the excess of the greatest of the proportional <lines> of the third <line>; while that ratio which the <line> equal to twice the greatest of the proportional <lines> and four times the second and six times the third and three times the fourth to the <line> equal to five times the greatest and ten times the second and ten times the third and five times the fourth – let some <line> be taken, having this <ratio> to the excess, by which the greatest <line> exceeds the third – then the taken <lines>, taken together, shall be two fifths of the greatest.

One may well appreciate Dijksterhuis' judgment (1987: 356): "The two propositions 9 and 10, as they stand, are about the most indigestible thing in all Greek mathematics." Dijksterhuis then proceeds to a beautiful exposition that does help to reduce the opacity of these two propositions, but which also relies heavily on modern equations. No doubt the reader expects me now to translate the expression above into such equations as, quite simply, without this modern tool the very statement of relations involving numbers poses a serious cognitive difficulty. As purely verbal expressions, complex relational terms such as "five times" or "ten times" do not provide the mind with useful mnemonic handles. In the Greek context, in particular, such terms also necessitate a move away from the concrete diagram (where one can represent a line, but not "five times a line"). And yet I resist the translation into an equation: the entire point is that no such translation was available to the Greek reader. In other words, we see once again the divide between inspectable, geometrical relations, and opaque, numerical relations. The Greek focus on making geometrical relations inspectable gives rise to the centrality of the diagram as the main cognitive tool mediating the text, and so serves to mark further non-visual relations as inherently opaque. Reading an enunciation such as that of *Planes in Equilibrium* 9, the reader must once again suspend disbelief or in this case, more precisely, suspend ignorance. To put it crudely, I have no doubt that the Greek reader – just like you – simply did not understand what proposition 9 was saying. And yet he went along, relying on Archimedes to have made sense, however opaque that sense might appear.

The very cognitive constraints on mental calculation (as opposed to the mental parsing of geometrical argument) are part of the cognitive divide separating the numerical and the geometrical in Greek writings. But another part has to do with deliberate choice on the part of the ancient authors. As we have seen already several times, the real intellectual challenge with calculation involves approximation, that is, the effective use of inequalities. There are intellectual traditions where the problems of numerical approximation are made explicit and the logic of inequalities is clarified, especially in Eastern traditions from China to the Muslim world leading into an important strand of modern Western mathematics.[26] One can find the topic more carefully discussed in some later Greek works: Eutocius' commentary to Archimedes' *Measurement of the Circle*, for instance, does go in much greater detail into the actual calculations, while Ptolemy, in particular, makes a real effort to be explicit about the significance of his approximations.[27] Yet the rule in Hellenistic mathematics is, first, to present approximations without comment and, second, to deal cursorily if at all with the logic of inequalities.

A witness for the ancient practice of take-it-or-leave-it approximations is the modern cottage industry of trying to account for such ancient calculations. Fowler (1999, section 2.4), goes through some of the most celebrated examples (I mention three, which we have already seen): what was Eratosthenes' 83:11 an approximation of, and why? How did Aristarchus get to 7,921:4,050>88:45 and, even more remarkable (in the same proposition), 71,755,875:61,735,500>43:37? How did Archimedes approximate the square root of 3 with 265:153? Fowler suggests that anthyphairetic calculations could give rise to those numbers, and there are other accounts elsewhere in the literature.[28] Clearly those modern interpretations address a serious question, as the ancients must have come up with those numbers *somehow*. But my point right now is that, no less important than how those numbers were found, is how those numbers were presented. Eratosthenes may have perhaps said more about his methods of calculation – we do not know (I suspect, based on the comparative evidence, that he did not). But we can see that Aristarchus and Archimedes remained silent – making the deliberate choice to mystify their audiences.

A similar decision, even more difficult to account for, is the Greek treatment of inequalities. Here the situation is especially curious, since the elliptic treatment of inequalities is not limited to the numerical case. In general, the arguments in Greek geometry and proportion theory are almost without exception rooted in a relatively small toolbox of

---

[26] See Chemla 1994. The numerical extraction of roots is a field rich in possibilities for the problems of approximation, and it served as one of the main areas of work for both Chinese and Arabic medieval mathematicians, giving rise along the way to our own decimal fractions.

[27] Ptolemy's elementary development of trigonometry (*Almagest* 1.10) is explicit and sophisticated about the nature of the approximations used – even if in the practical application of his calculations his treatment of approximations will often be quite opaque. (A notorious debate: how come Ptolemy's numbers end up being so round? See Grasshoff 1990: 156–73.)

[28] Fowler 1999: 53–5, with further references there. See also e.g. Heath 1921: II. 324–5.

well-known results, corresponding – and this is the crucial observation – to *a subset of Euclid's Elements* (see Netz 1999 chapter 5, section 4, and especially Saito 1997). The one major exception to that is proportional inequalities. For instance, Greek authors will often make assertions of the form "line AB has to line CD a ratio greater than line EF to line GH; therefore, alternately, line AB has to line EF a ratio greater than line CD to line GH." Such assertions extend results proved by Euclid for the equalities of ratios (in this case, *Elements* v.16), into their corresponding inequalities. It may be that our version of Euclid's *Elements* is in some sense defective and that at least some ancients operated with a more systematic elementary work for proportion theory. A common tradition of modern scholarship involves the micro-analysis of the text of the *Elements*, detecting layers of edition and thus recovering lost, earlier stages of Greek mathematics.[29] Indeed, it is inherently likely that Greek mathematicians active prior to the third century operated on the basis of a toolbox at least slightly different from that enshrined in Euclid's *Elements*. But this is beside the issue: the point is precisely that later Greek mathematicians have been content with the extant, incomplete book v.[30] On the other hand, it is inconceivable that Greek mathematicians assumed, falsely, that all the results for strict proportions are *ipso facto* true of proportion inequalities as well. The net result is that with inequalities – quite unlike any other field of Greek geometry and proportion theory – Greek mathematicians operated on the basis of an intuitive sense of validity. This logical lacuna is no more than a minor blemish within the context of Greek geometry (usually the results for strict proportion do apply to inequalities as well, and Greek mathematicians of course stick to only such results that can indeed be intuitively seen to hold). But for numerical theory this is much more serious: the deliberate choice not to map the logic of inequalities would block the very possibility of a theory of approximation. We see then that as Greek mathematics moves from the geometrical to the numerical it loses its anchoring in the cognitive support of Greek mathematics – the diagram – as well as in its logical support – the toolbox of results in Euclid's *Elements*.

The very experience of reading numerical statements, then, would be different from that of reading geometrical statements. One lowers one's cognitive and logical expectations, surrendering oneself instead to a

---

[29] For book v see e.g. Gardies 1991 and, even closer to our main concern – the absence of the systematic treatment of proportion inequalities in the extant book v – Knorr 1978, Acerbi 2003a.

[30] And content they were: a passage in Pappus' *Collection* (vii. 45–53), providing such results as *specific* lemmata for a specific work by Apollonius, shows that Pappus was both aware of the absence of such results from the *Elements* – and was at the same time happy to operate without them elsewhere.

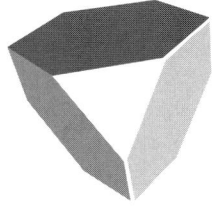

Figure 9

declamation of a text that often failed, almost, to make simple sense. One should quite seriously consider the experience of numerical text as incantation. Let us consider for instance a report in Pappus of a (lost) work by Archimedes, studying the possibilities of constructing semi-regular solids. These generalize the five Platonic solids to polyhedra where the faces are all regular polygons, all meeting in identical solid angles – but where more than a single type of regular polygons is allowed. In fig. 9 the simplest such object is visualized, contained by four equilateral triangles and four regular hexagons. The report by Pappus does not provide us with a sense of Archimedes' method of finding (correctly) that there are precisely thirteen such (non-trivial) solids, but it likely reflects some results obtained by Archimedes himself. I quote therefore the statement on the first types of solids, starting from the one mentioned above. To properly appreciate the sense of numerical incantation, bear in mind that Greek words such as "triangle" and "hexagon" carry, to the Greeks, apparent numerical markers (think, e.g., of a "threeangle" and a "sixangle"):

Now, since the first of the 13 irregular solids is contained by 4 triangles and 4 hexagons, it has 12 solid angles, and 18 sides; for the angles of the four triangles are 12, as also the sides are 12, while the angles of the hexagons are 24, as also the sides are 24; so as the number of all comes to be 36, the number of solid angles is necessarily a third part of the aforementioned number, since also each of its solid angles is contained by three plane angles, and the numbers of sides is half the number, that is of 36, so that there shall be 18 sides.

Of the 14-hedra, the first is contained by 8 triangles and 6 squares, so that it has 12 solid angles (for each angle of it is contained by four plane angles) and 24 sides. And since the second of the 14-hedra is contained by 6 squares and 8 hexagons it shall have 24 angles (for each of its angles is contained by 3 plane angles) and 36 sides. And since the third of the 14-hedra is contained by 8 triangles and 6 octagons, it shall have 24 solid angles and 36 sides . . .

And so on the text continues, evolving into a litany of numerals. We cannot know how much more discursive the text was originally (it may be that Archimedes was more explicit in detailing all the calculations or – more likely – it may be that Pappus inserts explications where the original had uninterrupted calculations). The overall texture of the text is clear: a sequence of numerical values that in fact make sense (the principle underlying the calculation is in this case clear and intellectually satisfying, and the numbers are generally at the level open to mental calculation). And yet, even while making sense, they also begin to add up to something else, beyond logical structure: they begin to form an incantation.

Number words are not referential – unlike the usual terms of Greek geometry, which refer to a diagram. There is no mental picture associated with "24 solid angles and 36 sides." And so, in the absence of a mental picture, the overriding experience in reading this text is that of verbal texture. This may be defined as the repetition of ever-rising numbers in close sequence. This is the same verbal texture seen many times already – in the more numerical results of *Spiral Lines*, in the third proposition of the *Measurement of the Circle*, in Aristarchus' calculation, indeed whenever the numerical intrudes into Greek geometry. In the experience of the reader, logic recedes, and the sheer sound of number words takes over.

The most fundamental point is that those numbers do not supply the reader with any cognitive advantage. This is in strict opposition to the pattern in many other mathematical traditions, where the use of numerical values is in fact utilitarian and cognitively meaningful. I proceed now to make this comparison.

### 1.4 NON-UTILITARIAN CALCULATION

The use of numerical values is by no means a special feature of Greek carnivalesque proofs. To the contrary: whenever we look at any mathematical tradition aside from the Greek, what we find are mostly numerical values, starting from our very earliest texts, such as the Moscow Mathematical Papyrus – a nineteenth-century BC text from Egypt. Here, for example, is problem number 42 (most problems have the same nature):

Method of calculating b'ku of a cobbler:
If it is said to you "b'ku of a cobbler:" if he cuts
it is 10 per day; if he finishes it is 5 per day.
If he cuts and finishes how many will it be per day?
Then you calculate the parts of this 10 together with this 5.
Then the sum results as 3. Then you divide 10 by this.
Then 3 3 times result.
Behold, it is 3 3 per day.

As Immhasuen explains in 2003, this problem deals with a cobbler's *per diem* sandal production.

Much later in time – the third century AD – but from a very different tradition, is a text from the *Nine Chapters*, the central Chinese mathematical classic. Here is the 18th problem of the sixth book (once again, most other problems in the *Nine Chapters* are of the same nature):

Suppose that 5 persons share 5 coins in such a way that what the two superior persons obtain is equal to what the three inferior persons obtain. One asks how much each obtains.

Reply:

The first (*Jia*) obtains 1 coin 2/6 coin
The second (*Yi*) 1 coin 1/6 coin
The third (*Bing*) obtains 1 coin
The fourth (*Ding*) obtains 5/6 coin
The fifth (*Wu*) obtains 4/6 coin.[31]

The problem (if not the solution to it) is self-explanatory (see Chemla 2003 for more on the motivation and solution to the problem).

Perhaps at about the same time as the *Nine Chapters* were composed in China, Diophantus produced his own remarkable work in arithmetical theory. Here is the main part of the relatively simple proposition 1.10 (for ease of presentation here, I ignore Diophantus' special symbolism and print as if his text was written in natural Greek):

To two given numbers: to add to the smaller of them, and to take away from the greater, and to make the resulting <number> have a given ratio to the remainder.

Let it be set forth to add to 20, and to take away from 100 the same number, and to make the greater four-times the smaller.

Let the <number> which is added and taken away from each number <sc. of the two given numbers> be set down, <namely> number, one. And if it is added to twenty, results: number 1, units 20. And if it is taken away from 100, results: units 100 lacking number 1. And it shall be required that the greater be 4-times the smaller. Therefore four-times the smaller is equal to the greater; but four-times the smaller results: units 400 lacking number 4; these equal number 1 units 20.

Let the subtraction be added <as> common, and let similar <terms> be taken away from similar <terms>. Remaining: numbers, 5, equal units 380. (10) And the number results: units, 76.

---

[31] One can equally go back to the earliest extant Chinese mathematical text (in fragmentary state), the Suàn Shù Shū from the second century BC, e.g.: "There are 3 *zhū* and 5/9 *zhū* of gold. Now it is desired to pay out 6/7 *zhū* of it. Question: how much is the remaining gold?" (S28,29, from Cullen 2004: 44).

Finally, several centuries later but now firmly within the mainstream of the Greek mathematical tradition, one may turn to the oldest extant full manuscript of Euclid, the Bodleian Ms. D'Orville, produced at Constantinople in the year AD 888. Here, at the recto of leaf 31, one finds the famous diagram to Pythagoras' theorem (Euclid's *Elements* 1.47). The argument preceding the figure is developed in the abstract geometrical format we are accustomed to from mainstream Greek geometry, of course without any mention being made of any specific numerical values. Then, onto the diagram, someone has inscribed tiny glosses. The glosses are: the numeral 3 next to one of the sides of the squares, 4 next to another and 5 next to the side of the square on the hypotenuse; 9 inside one of the squares, 16 inside another and 25 inside the square on the hypotenuse. Once again: this has no correlate in the text itself and is an extraneous addition to the manuscript tradition of Euclid. It is, as it were, the standard cultural practice we see from across global mathematical traditions – impinging upon the special world of Greek geometry. This may have been done later than AD 888 but probably reflects a widespread and earlier practice: one notes this type of numerical approach applied systematically in the works of Hero (first century AD), with expressions such as (*Metr.* 1.6, 14.18–20): "Let ABG be an obtuse angled triangle having 13 units, BG 11 units and AG 20 units." (We can see the context, not at all distant from Pythagoras' theorem: an extension of the study of right-angled triangles to general triangles).[32]

We can easily sum up the standard practice across many cultures: it is to represent mathematical problems in terms of simple, accessible numerical values.

By referring in the title to this subsection to "non-utilitarian calculation" I do not mean that a utilitarian calculation is one which allows you to direct the labor of cobblers, or to divide up money, or to do your practical arithmetical and geometrical calculations. What I have in mind in particular is that the use of calculation can often be utilitarian in a cognitive sense: the numerals serve a mnemonic and pedagogic function and so enhance, rather than stymie, the mathematical parsing.

This is very clear with the simple algebraic relations that most mathematical traditions focus upon. While our modern algebraic notation is certainly a useful tool in the explication of such relations, even today the learning of such relations is enhanced by the study of simple examples. It

---

[32] The mostly Heronian *Codex Constantinopolitanus* has – which is natural – numerals inserted, systematically, next to the measured objects in the diagram. (See Bruins 1964, vol. 1 *passim*.) De Young 2005 looks more closely at some details of the transmission of Euclid's diagrams in Arabic manuscripts, with one of the major issues being the insertion of such numerical values.

is clear that the author of the Moscow Papyrus problems was not really interested in a particular cobbler who indeed produced exactly three and a third sandals each day. It was rather the case that the solution of such a production problem is very difficult in the abstract, indeed quickly would degenerate, absent any concrete values, into the kind of morass we have seen – for example – in Archimedes' *Planes in Equilibrium* II.9. The same is of course clear with Diophantus: he is trying to deal with problems more general than just those numerical problems studied, and the particular choice of numerical values is meant as a kind of arithmetical equivalent to the role of the concrete diagram in Greek geometry: it supplies the mind with a concrete example it can follow and digest. The effort to make Diophantine arguments accessible to the mind in a more general form would give rise, indeed, to modern symbolism as we know it. Yet, without such algebraical symbols, the best available tools of representation are the numerals themselves.

In some cases we can see pedagogic logic at work. A central interpretation of Chinese mathematical texts considers them in the context of the Chinese examination system.[33] The various routes to achievement in the Chinese Imperial world mostly went through an Imperial examination; a few of these (not the most valuable ones) went through a mathematical examination. The *Nine Chapters* formed, in effect, the problem set for this examination, providing teachers and students with hands-on experience of solving problems that are variations on a theme. You solve in practice one division problem, having to do with coins; in the actual examination you will solve another, say with horses. The world of simple numerical problems is pedagogically useful not only in that the simple numbers provide one with a handle on the question, but also because they allow simple variations (the same numerals referring to other objects, or the numerals slightly tweaked), so that one may have a set of problems to solve and, by doing so, build up the student's skill and confidence.

The examples from the manuscript tradition of Euclid (or from Hero) are especially instructive. At first it is more difficult to see the direct pedagogic contribution the numerals make: after all the argument proceeds in the main text as it did before, without any numerals and, in the kind of geometrical argument used by Euclid, such numerals cannot really figure usefully. And yet it is clear that the numbers are helpful (and come up regularly in the modern pedagogic context): they are a way of fleshing out what is even *meant* by saying that two squares equal a third one. What

[33] Siu and Volkov 1999.

we see is that quantitative relations are more directly present to the mind when they are presented by numerals – as long of course as the numerals themselves are easy to parse. Simple numbers are the best format for the representation of quantity.

Nothing of this is visible in the main tradition of Greek geometry. The only tool used to concretize the problems is the non-numerical, qualitative diagram. Of course, some of the quantitative relations stated inside Greek geometry refer to numbers: it is after all the precise achievement of Archimedes to show that the sphere, say, is two-thirds the cylinder enclosing it, while the parabolic segment is four-thirds the triangle it encloses. But such results are obtained with very little explicit reference to numbers, the simple values obtained at the end arising out of more basic equalities. Indeed, the relations obtained are expressed not in terms of numbers, but in terms of ratios, emphasizing the more abstract and less numerical character of the discovery. (Where the ratios involved are as simple as 3:2, or 4:3, as in the cases above, one is indeed reminded of mathematical musical theory: the sphere as well as the parabolic segment were truly captured by Archimedes, in that they were delimited by a truly simple structure.)

We thus find a systematic, remarkable pattern. There are many cases where Greek mathematics deals with the straightforward presentation of results that are meant to be directly grasped – results such as the elementary results of Euclid, or the simpler results obtained by Archimedes, as well as any geometrical argument where the emphasis is on the accessibility of the demonstrative structure. This type of presentation is universally aided, across all non-Greek cultures, by the use of simple numbers. Yet in the Greek case numbers are effectively excluded from this type of presentation. On the other hand, whenever numbers assume center stage in Greek mathematics, this is precisely where straightforward presentation fails – as seen in the preceding sections. The function of the application of numbers is precisely to thicken the structure of an opaque presentation. The net result is to isolate and mark the Greek use of numerals: not only are numerals in mainstream Greek mathematics applied in the context of opaque presentation, this is in fact the *only* context in which they are applied.

An example of the radically non-utilitarian nature of Greek numerical texts is called for – and one can hardly do better than Apollonius' numerical study of the hexameter line.

This survives in a curious, doubly fragmentary state. The original treatise is no longer extant, but it formed the basis for a lengthy and detailed commentary by Pappus, constituting the entirety of the second book of

Pappus' *Collection*. This, in turn, is extant only in part (the whole of book I, as well as the beginning of book II of the *Collection*, were lost at an early stage from the codex upon which our knowledge of Pappus rests, Vat. Gr. 218). It seems that the commentary is extant from proposition 14 onwards, where the original treatise by Apollonius contained twenty-six propositions followed by a sequence of calculations.

Pappus must have thought highly of this treatise. Among the extant books of the *Collection*, the only one to have the formal structure of a commentary on a single treatise is book II. Of course, Pappus is also the author of a commentary on Euclid's *Elements* X, extant only in Arabic, and it is likely that he produced even more commentaries. But it is still striking that he considered this work by Apollonius to be worthy of commentary. In fact, the need for commentary may have been precisely a consequence of Apollonius' non-utilitarian numerical practices. Since we do have such a detailed commentary, we may reconstruct those practices in detail. Thus, for instance, we may quote the commentary to proposition 17, where Pappus in turn quotes the enunciation by Apollonius (Pappus II. 7.6–11):

Let there be a multitude of numbers, that on which are the A's, of which <numbers> each is smaller than hundred while being measured by ten, and let there be another multitude of numbers, that on which are the B's, of which each is smaller than thousand while being measured by hundreds, and it is required to state the solid number <produced> by the A's, B's, without multiplying them.

Pappus' commentary then goes on to offer a concrete example with specific numerical values. All of this is continuous with what we have seen so far: mainstream Greek demonstrative practice based on the diagram alone; pedagogic explications of the same practice then introduce simple numerical relations. But there is more to the non-utilitarian character of numerals in mainstream Greek mathematics in this case.

I first explain the basic theoretical tools of Apollonius' treatise. The first is the notion of the "base" where, e.g., the "base" of 70 is 7, of 300 is 3 etc. The second is the notion of "double myriad," "triple myriad," etc.: a double myriad is a myriad-myriads, a triple myriad is a myriad-myriad-myriads, etc.

Pappus' commentary first puts forward the case where there are four A's, whose bases are 1, 2, 3, 4 (the A's are 10, 20, 30, 40), and four B's, whose bases are 2, 3, 4, 5 (the B's are 200, 300, 400, 500). He then multiplies all eight bases to obtain 2,880.

Then he moves back to the language of Apollonius himself in his proof. Apollonius constructs Z as the number of A's and twice the number of

B's, which he then has shown to be relevant to the solution as follows: "the solid number <produced> of all the <numbers> on which are the A's, B's, is as many myriads, of the same name [ = i.e of the same power of ten] as the number Z, as there units in E." Pappus in his commentary unpacks this to mean that, since Z in the case produced by Pappus himself is 12, the number resulting is a triple myriad (we can see that a myriad is the equivalent of ten taken four times), and the value as a whole, Pappus finally shows, is 2880 triple myriads.

The few explicit quotations Pappus makes of Apollonius suffice to determine the original nature of the Apollonian proposition: it was an abstract, quasi-geometrical proof, accompanied by a diagram showing line segments on which lay the letters A and B (several times each) as well as E and Z (once each). The argument was all couched in general terms, no specific values being mentioned – going as far as treating even the number of A's and B's (tacitly determined by the diagram) as if it were indeterminate. That is: the diagram would have had (I suspect) exactly four lines next to each of which was written the letter A; and the text would still speak of "as many as there are A's." All of this would be standard Greek demonstrative practice. Notice also how opaque the resulting text would be. No doubt Apollonius himself did not provide concrete numerical examples, or otherwise Pappus' commentary would have been truly otiose: for indeed Pappus hardly does anything besides providing those numerical values. And note, even in my brief example above, how important those numerical values are for clarifying the text! Once again, we see the value of simple numbers as expository aids, the numbers in this case being very simple indeed – no more than those going from 1 to 5.

We may also begin to perceive the purpose of the treatise. It has to do with the calculation of the multiplication of numbers, each of which is an integer multiple (the integer no greater than 9) of a power of ten: numbers of the form $k*10^n$, where $1 \leq k \leq 9$. This is of very little practical value: in practice, multiplications become truly complex where the multiplicands are each a sum of different powers of ten. Not to mention the fact that multiplications, after all, are not a major practical obstacle for calculation: the real difficulty usually begins with division.

But Apollonius' study has one immediate application. The major type of numerals used in the Greek literary context are known as "alphabetic numerals," where the twenty-four characters of the Greek alphabet (to which are added three *ad-hoc* symbols) are associated with the twenty-seven values one obtains with $k*10^n$, where $1 \leq k \leq 9$ as well as $0 \leq n \leq 2$, that is the values 1, 2, 3, . . . , 9, 10, 20, 30, . . . , 90, 100, 200, 300, . . . , 900. Apollonius' system is thus a method for the multiplication of letters of the Greek alphabet considered as numerals. This is precisely how Apollonius himself applied his system. We learn from Pappus' commentary that, following the sequence of twenty-six or so abstract, quasi-geometrical propositions, Apollonius produced a sample calculation. (The book, that is, could have had twenty-seven propositions – did Apollonius *intend* such numerical puns?) The letters taken for multiplication were not accidental, but instead were those of a hexameter line (Pappus, II 21.1):

Ἀρτέμιδος κλεῖτε κράτος ἔξοχον ἐννέα κοῦραι

(Nine maidens, praise Artemis' excellent power).

Conceived as alphabetical numerals, these are:

1, 100, 300, 5, 40, 10, 4, 200, 20, 30, 5, 10, 300, 5, 20, 100, 1, 300, 300, 60, 200, 5, 70, 60, 50, 5, 50, 50, 5, 1, 20, 60, 400, 100, 1, 10.

Incidentally, it does not appear to me that Apollonius selected his hexameter line for its high numerical value. I did not attempt an explicit calculation with random Greek hexameter lines, but it would be apparent that some high-value letters such as Φ (500), and especially the frequent letter ω (800) are nowhere present in this line. One can also easily have lines with more tokens of Σ (200), a very common letter indeed.[34] The choice of the line is however extraordinarily apt, as the treatise is precisely about reducing calculations to nine bases – the numerals from 1 to 9. Those, and those alone, suffice "to praise the power of Artemis," quite excellent and outstanding in this case: the line comes out to produce, in multiplication, what we write as 196,036,848,000,000,000. I shall of course return to discuss the wit of this line (unknown otherwise – was it invented by Apollonius?), later on in this book.

But first: how explicit was Apollonius in his own calculation? It is difficult to say with certainty, but it is interesting to note that Pappus' commentary, besides following the detail of this particular calculation, goes on to add another one produced by Pappus himself, this time of the (pseudo?)-Orphic line:[35]

Μῆνιν ἄειδε θεὰ Δημήτερος ἀγλαοκάρπου

(Sing, Goddess, the wrath of Demeter the bearer of beautiful fruit), which comes out merely as 21,849,440,256,000,000.

---

[34] Packard 1974, a study of sound patterns in Homer, lists many lines with repeated letters, some of which happen to be of high numerical value. A line that gets repeated, formulaically, four times (*Iliad* 3.127, 3.131, 3.251, 8.71), may well be the highest in Homer: Τρώων θ' ἱπποδάμων καὶ Ἀχαιῶν χαλκοχιτώνων, with six omega's and three chi's . . . (I thank Jack Mitchell for the reference).

[35] Aside from Pappus, this is attested only once, at Pseudo-Justinus Martyr, *Cohortatio ad Gentiles*, Morel 17C2 (a second-century AD work) where the line is ascribed to Orpheus. I have no idea why Pappus should choose this perverse line instead of the obvious *Iliad* 1.1 itself.

My guess would be that Pappus was driven to add this extra calculation since, in this case, the original text already possessed an explicit calculation for the case of the nine maidens (so that it left less room for commentary).[36] One should gain a sense of what the calculation feels like. This is from the multiplication of the bases:

For one <multiplied> by 1 produces 1, by 3 produces 3, by 5 produces 15, by 4 produces 60, by one produces 60, by 4 produces 240, by 7 produces 1,440, by 2 produces 2,880, by 2 produces 5,760 [I skip many steps] . . . by 3 produces 907 myriads and 2,000 units, by 7 produces 6,350 myriads and 4,000 units [I skip many steps again] . . . by 2 produces 7,001 triple myriads and 3,160 double myriads, by 7 produces 4 quadruple myriads and 9,009 triple myriads and 2,220 double myriads, by 4 produces 19 quadruple myriads and 6,036 triple myriads and 8480 double myriads.

The last expression is Apollonius' rather elegant way of expressing the number above, 196,036,848,000,000,000. The opaque structure of the calculation is by now familiar to us, as is the outcome of a sense of a futile attempt to capture the unbounded. Even though the result is quite elegant, in its way, what is most striking for the reader is how big and unwieldy a number is obtained from a single, simple-looking hexameter line (what would happen with the entirety of the Homeric epic, one would have to wonder!). This is most of all reminiscent of the familiar example of the chessboard with a single grain on its first square, two grains on its second, four on its third etc. – ending with the incredibly many, $2^{63}$ grains on the last square (which, funnily enough, happens to be of a similar order of magnitude to the number obtained by Apollonius).

I argue that Apollonius' treatise had the following structure. (i) First came a prolonged set of abstract propositions solving, in quasi-geometrical terms, the problems of multiplying powers of ten. Here the reader was asked to exert his mental powers considerably, as the diagram is of relatively little use in parsing the abstract structures of calculation. Yet, in principle, the propositions could be followed as a pure deductive exercise. (ii) This was followed by an explicit, *tour-de-force* of a calculation, where the reader was left gasping at the ever-rising numerical values produced by the actual calculation, hardly expected, in reality, to check the validity of the calculation.

[36] Hultsch, in his edition, doubts the authenticity of both sets of explicit calculation. This has no clear motivation and is part and parcel of Hultsch's ultra-critical textual practice, throughout his edition of Pappus.

The duality at play is remarkable. The use of simple numerical examples would have been of great expository value in the *first* section – as is witnessed by Pappus' commentary which is based entirely on such numerical examples. But there it was altogether avoided. Numbers however came to their own in the second, non-deductive parts of the treatise, where their function was not to instruct but instead to dazzle and overwhelm. This, then, in a nutshell, forms the non-utilitarian character of numerical examples within mainstream Greek mathematics. While in all other pre-modern cultures, numerical examples are constitutive to the pedagogic process of parsing the mathematical argument, in Greek mathematics numbers are denied playing any argumentative role. Instead, numbers are brought in – surprisingly often – where the text moves beyond the pedagogic and the expository, towards a carnivalesque show of dazzling, incomprehensible calculation.

We begin to develop a sense for why the term "carnivalesque" may be appropriate. To support this argument, I wish to return to the notion of an attempt to capture the unbounded, concentrating now on what appears to be the role of *size* as such.

### 1.5 A FASCINATION WITH SIZE

Cleomedes – a second-century AD author of a handbook of astronomy – tells us of two Hellenistic approaches to a single problem. The first is by Eratosthenes, from the mid-third century BC, while the second is by Posidonius, from the early first century BC: the two constitute the time-limits of our study. Throughout this period, we find, people were interested in the size of the earth (for both approaches, see Cleomedes 1.7).

The chronologically later method, by Posidonius, is based on Canobus, a very bright, southerly star. Of course, from any given point on the earth, some stars are never visible (which is why the southern skies are different from the northern skies): a consideration familiar to Greek astronomers starting from the very first authors we possess, such as Autolycus, of the fourth century BC. Now Canobus is said, according to Posidonius, to become visible precisely at the moment one passes Rhodes on the way south. Upon reaching Alexandria, it is said to be at the maximal elevation of exactly one quarter a zodiacal sign. Furthermore, Rhodes is taken to be directly north of Alexandria so that one has now acquired an argument for taking the distance of Rhodes from Alexandria to be one forty-eighths the circumference of the earth. The distance between Rhodes and Alexandria is taken to be 5,000 stades and the earth's circumference is now measured at 240,000 stades. One notes immediately the way this argument is strewn with the hypothetical – the obviously pat assumptions that Rhodes and Alexandria are *exactly* 5,000 stades apart, Canobus is *exactly* one-fourth a zodiacal sign above the horizon. (The assumption that Rhodes and Alexandria lie effectively on the same meridian was perhaps too culturally entrenched to be much in doubt.) Cleomedes in his report repeatedly stresses the hypothetical nature of those assumptions, though of course this could be Cleomedes' own contribution. At any rate, while scholars have tried to find here a hypothetical-deductive method favored by Posidonius,[37] it is clear to us by now that this hypothetical calculation is in line with the Hellenistic way of attempting to capture the unbounded, while signaling the limits of that attempt. But what an attempt! Prior to Columbus, Posidonius sets out to circumnavigate the earth.

Not the first to do so, either. Eratosthenes' method was no less striking. He compares Alexandria not to Rhodes, but to Syene, a site at the extreme south of the Ptolemaic empire. He takes his measurements based on an object even brighter than Canobus, namely, the sun. Syene is assumed to lie under the ecliptic so that, in the midsummer noon – besides being very hot – it also casts no shadow. Take at the same time Alexandria and measure the angle of the shadow cast at midday. This angle is now taken to be the same as the angular distance of Alexandria and Syene. (The geometry is straightforward, so long as we take the distance of the sun from the earth to be effectively infinite: either another pat hypothesis, or an implicit reference to Aristarchus.) The angle is measured to be one-fiftieth of a full circle (since the observation of shadows allows for precise measurement, this may well be the safest part of the calculation), while Syene is assumed to be – once again! – precisely 5,000 stades, precisely south from Alexandria – and Eratosthenes' world is circumnavigated at 250,000 stades.

One notes the centrality of Alexandria to both calculations, and the way in which the geography chosen by each author is a reflection of that author's political position. Eratosthenes, the Alexandrian librarian, chooses a calculation that juxtaposes the center and the limit of the Ptolemaic kingdom;

---

[37] So Kidd 1988: 728, in his discussion of this passage from Cleomedes (fragment 202): "he was not trying to be a scientist, but as a philosopher demonstrating another method . . . [i]t was not apparently the calculations which interested him as much as the theory." This is based on the judgment passed earlier (p. 727): "Posidonius seems to have been content, not to attempt to establish exact data for himself, but simply to accept figures which he knew to be inexact . . . and observational measurement which he knew to be inaccurate . . ." – this I endorse, adding the qualification that this seems to be quite typical of geographical and astronomical measurement, based on geometry, in the Hellenistic period. Such practice does *not* mark Posidonius off from, say, Eratosthenes.

Posidonius, the philosopher active at Rhodes, chooses a calculation that juxtaposes Rhodes with the great center of Mediterranean life – to which Rhodes still referred, even as late as the first century – that of Alexandria. With both, the limits of one's political horizon could be used – by reference to the stars – as a launching pad for a daring flight of imagination, right around the globe. Going beyond the Alexandrian world, one could say something about the earth as a whole.

Of course this is not an isolated moment in Hellenistic cultural life. This is a civilization of expansion, whose very moment of inception is marked by an urge to reach out for the totality of the earth. Even prior to Eratosthenes or Posidonius trying to measure the earth based on the observations at Alexandria, one had to set up Alexandrias across the known world – and to build power that reached as far as such exotic places as Syene. This moment of Alexandrian conquest also coincided, as is well known, with Pytheas' travels into the Atlantic, reaching into a northern extreme untouched by Alexander himself.[38] Alexander and Pytheas, as well as Eratosthenes and Posidonius, all tried to capture the earth. We have considered already the meaning of this effort as an attempt to capture the unbounded. Here I want to emphasize the gigantic aspect of this effort. This at least is surely clear: Eratosthenes and Posidonius cared about *size*.

Size is an appropriate theme with which to sum up the evidence considered in this chapter. It is evident in a series of cosmic measurements – not only those of the earth just seen here, but also those of the cosmos offered by Aristarchus at least once, in the *Sizes and Distances of the Sun and the Moon* (and perhaps once again in the treatise where the Heliocentric thesis was put forth), as well as by Archimedes in the *Sand-Reckoner*.[39] And beyond the cosmic lies the divine and the mythical: the fantastically huge number representing the fancifully described cattle of Helios (in Archimedes' *Cattle Problem*), the extraordinarily large number arising from trying to mathematize "the excellent power of Artemis." One is tempted to bring into this context the problem of finding two mean proportionals between two given

---

[38] On Pytheas see, e.g. – critically – Strabo 11.4.1. Little is known of substance of Pytheas' travels, except that they definitely took him into the Northern Atlantic. For a recent survey of the evidence, see Magnani 2002. The reception of Pytheas – from antiquity down to the present day – is fascinated with the problems of authenticity: what did Pytheas actually do? More relevant to us is what cultural role he was trying to assume. Magnani's speculative summary ends up with the image of Pytheas (pp. 241–2) as engaged primarily in the autoptic confirmation of Eudoxean mathematical geography. In other words, what Pytheas represents is the desire to make the theoretical, universal reach of mathematics concrete.

[39] See more on mostly the later, Renaissance history of such cosmic measurements in Henderson 1991. Likely, Hipparchus himself was once again a key contributor to this domain, though in this case as in so many others his achievement is only indirectly reported (Swerdlow 1969).

lines that is being reinterpreted by Eratosthenes, in a fragment preserved by Eutocius (as well as in his *Platonicus*) as a problem of "doubling the cube" – the form in which it is still familiar to us today. Let us quote Eratosthenes, then, addressing the king:

Eratosthenes to king Ptolemy, greetings.
They say that one of the old tragic authors introduced Minos, building a tomb to Glaucos, and, hearing that it ought to be a hundred cubits long in each direction, saying:
*You have mentioned a small precinct of the tomb royal;*
*Let it be double, and, not losing this beauty,*
*Quickly double each side of the tomb.*

*This seems to have been mistaken; for, the sides doubled, the plane becomes four times, while the solid becomes eight times. And this was investigated by the geometers, too: in which way one could double the given solid, the solid keeping the same shape; and they called this problem "duplication of a cube": for, assuming a cube, they investigated how to double it.*

One notices not only the mythical dimensions inserted by Eratosthenes, but a more basic point still: a sober geometrical exercise in finding proportional lines is presented, by Eratosthenes, as a problem of *making something bigger* – indeed making something bigger precisely in the context, well understood by a Ptolemaic audience, of royal architectural grandeur. This reinterpretation of the problem of two mean proportionals as one of "doubling the cube" has become so successful that we have now come to think of it as the natural *mathematical* representation – but we must be aware of its specific Alexandrian origins.

The *Sand-Reckoner* – with its measuring out of the universe by grains of sand – reminds us that these two are interconnected: the fantastically big and the fantastically small. In a precise way, it is their combination that creates the sense of size. Measured in "earth circumferences," for instance, the earth comes out as having the size of 1, not at all a remarkable result ... For us to be impressed by Eratosthenes' and Posidonius' numbers, measure has to be provided in *stades*. And so we should also follow the measurements of the fantastically small as an exercise in fantastically big numbers. The obvious example is in the attempt to provide a precise calculation of the ratio of the circumference of the circle to its diameter, in Archimedes' *Measurement of Circle*. But is the focus on the extremely small not at the very heart of Hellenistic mathematics? For even at its most sober, geometrical moments, its achievements are those of precise curvilinear measurements based on the method of exhaustion, whose essence is the consideration of differences fantastically small – *smaller than any given size*. Of course there is an internal intellectual reason why such studies bring up the notion of the extremely small. Precise measurement of irrationals must, as a matter of logic, involve the potential infinitesimal. But at the same time, we may also begin to identify a cultural resonance that this notion might have had in antiquity, going beyond any significance purely internal to mathematics. After all, no one has forced the Greek mathematicians to attempt to measure curvilinear objects *with precision*. Before them, no one did. They did so, because this measurement meant something to them. Among other things, I suggest, it meant the juxtaposition of the extremes of big and small.

Still, the main theme we have followed in this chapter is that of *big* numerical size. We may review the main numbers we have seen above:

| | |
|---|---|
| c. 1,000 | Number of fixed stars (Hipparchus). |
| 17,152 | Number of Stomachion combinations (Archimedes). |
| 103,049/310,954 | Number of Stoic sentences (Hipparchus). |
| 240,000 stades | Size of earth (Posidonius). |
| 250,000 stades | Size of earth (Eratosthenes). |
| 14,688:(4,673 and a half)/(2,017 and a quarter):66 | Boundaries on ratio of circumference to diameter (Archimedes). |
| 6,859:27/79,507:216 | Boundaries on ratio of sun to earth (Aristarchus). |
| 196,036,848,000,000,000 | Multiplying a hexameter line (Apollonius). |
| Thousand "seven" numbers ($= 10^{68}$) | Grains of sand to fill the cosmos (Archimedes). |
| A 206,545 digits number | The cattle of Helios (Archimedes). |
| Approaching infinity | The "sieve" for finding primes (Eratosthenes). |
| Approaching infinity | Heliocentric model for the size of the cosmos (Aristarchus). |

Such are some of the fantastically large numbers to have greeted the readers of Hellenistic mathematics. Of these, only four are extant, including Aristarchus' heliocentric measurement and three works by Archimedes: *Measurement of the Circle*, *Sand-Reckoner*, and *Cattle Problem*. This chapter has dealt mostly with lost works. Clearly, aside from the fame of Archimedes – which made Byzantine readers interested in preserving anything they had under his name – such works did not survive at all beyond Late Antiquity. Manuscript selection favored works of a more geometrical character – and we shall return in the next chapter to consider why this was the case.

And yet, in its original Hellenistic setting, we find that fantastically rich numbers were among the staples of mathematical writing, contributing to a sense of dazzlement, of the carnivalesque. I move on now to a summary unpacking this notion of the carnival of calculation.

## 1.6 THE CARNIVAL OF CALCULATION

There is nothing metaphorical about Bakhtin's notion of "carnival." In his well-known masterpiece, *Rabelais and his World*, Bakhtin returned time and again to the actual practices of the late medieval celebration of carnival, where entrenched social positions were momentarily inverted and the taboo areas of sex and excrement openly celebrated. The relationship between such events and Rabelais' prose was understood not in a formal sense (with, say, some structural properties of Rabelais' writing shown to be an inversion of established norms), but at the level of contents, so that Bakhtin's main task was to document the role of social inversion, and the celebration of sex and excrement, within Rabelais' fictional world.

None of this then applies to my case, and I am almost deterred from using the term "carnival" – as, indeed, this in recent parlance has become so closely associated with Bakhtin (true, in a rather loose manner, so that in point of fact my usage, if not true to Bakhtin, is still in line with current practice in literary theory). Of course one could imagine a true, social, Bakhtinian grounding of my material, and this would not be completely without merit. I hinted as much when considering the urge of expansion at the inception of Alexandrian civilization – and would it not be appropriate to bring the Ptolemaic *pompē* as context for the fascination with size described in this chapter? One may well quote at this point the summary by Green:[40]

> The procession, held in the city stadium, showed [. . .] ultramontane extravagance. Nike (Victory) figures with gold wings, satyrs with gilt leaves of ivy on their torches, 120 boys carrying saffron on gold platters, gold-crowned Dionysiac revelers, a Delphic tripod eighteen feet high, a four-wheeled cart twenty-one feet long by twelve feet wide, a gold mixing bowl that held 150 gallons, a wineskin stitched together from leopard pelts, with a 30,000-gallon capacity (dribbling out its contents along the route), a giant float with fountains gushing milk and wine, the biggest elephants, the tallest actors, six hundred ivory tusks . . . Perhaps to our way of thinking the most outré item was a gaudily painted gold phallus, almost two hundred feet long – how did it negotiate corners? . . .

In this culture numbers such as 196,036,848,000,000,000 are not out of place. Green himself, in commenting on the cultural impact of this context, suggests that "No wonder an intellectual like Callimachus said

---

[40] Green 1990: 160, summing up a few details from Callixenus of Rhodes' *Great Procession of Ptolemy Philadelphus*.

big books were a big evil: elegant miniaturism was one of the few permissible outlets against this relentless and all-pervasive ostentation" – which belongs in the outdated tradition of assuming Hellenistic intellectuals had to be dissidents[41] (why should they? No regime was holding them back in Alexandria; to the contrary, they have mostly *chosen* to settle there and to relate, at least, to court life there). No: what we see is that, in Hellenistic culture, *size matters*. This is the age of building up the Pharos as well as the Colossus, two wonders of the world – and also, in all likelihood, the age of compiling such lists of wonders; the one that came down to us is definitely based on the principle of size.[42] Indeed, reflecting the new sensibilities of the age, the very word "colossus" changes its meaning, from "archaizing statue" to "huge monument":[43] almost as if, when earlier Greeks looked at big statues, they saw primarily a *style* whereas, from now on, they primarily saw a *size*. Closer at home to mathematics, this is also the very age of competitive shipbuilding, giving rise to gigantic shipbuilding – one memorable case involving a special mechanism for pulling a ship whose inventor, reportedly, explained by the principle of δώς μοι ποῦ στῶ καὶ κινῶ τὰν γᾶν[44] – a piece of the Archimedean legend which we can now interpret as yet another striking contrast between the small (the single man's position) and the huge (the earth). The miniaturism of some Hellenistic works is best seen as that of the sand-grain: a small unit with which to attempt an extravagant task.

Still, there are many features of what I call the carnival of calculation that do not translate well into such broad cultural terms. What do we make of the self-defeating nature of the attempt to capture the unbounded, or of the opaque, non-utilitarian use of numerical values? Those seem to have an internal mathematical meaning for which there is no obvious correlate

---

[41] Furthermore, this is in truth inspired by a very old-fashioned reading of Callimachus' *Telchines*, as if Callimachus was arguing that one should write, to borrow Green's phrase, in a "miniaturist" manner. Cameron 1995 is largely dedicated to debunking this reading, see esp. ch. 12.

[42] See Clayton and Price 1988, Hoepfner 2003 (concentrating on the Colossus at Rhodes but with further useful notes). The earliest mention is in an epigram by Antipater (of Sidon, apparently, so also Argentieri 2003), *Anth. Pal.* 9.58, i.e. mid-second century BC; a plausible argument is that the list would most likely have been compiled between the dedication of the last wonder (the Pharos, at about 280 BC) and the earliest destruction, that of the Colossus by the earthquake at Rhodes (226 BC), i.e. the list itself goes back to the mid-third century BC. (This list, however, is unlikely to go back to Callimachus himself, as suggested by some authors. The *Suda* entry on Callimachus does mention a "survey of wonders of the world arranged by place," but the title as well as everything else we know of Callimachus' practices suggests a comprehensive survey of a great many paradoxa, rather than a celebration of a few selected monuments.)

[43] Benveniste 1932. Kosmetatou and Papalexandrou 2003 argue that this semantic shift can be seen in process in Posidippus 68.

[44] For the story of this Syracusan ship, the Syracusia (later Alexandris) likely to contain an element of truth but of cultural interest even if it does not, see Spada 2002.

in the world of the *pompē*. My use of the carnival, then, is more abstract, and I beg the reader's indulgence in using the Bakhtinian term with a more structural, formal meaning in mind.

The essence of the phenomena described here is a certain contrast. On the one hand is standard, pure geometrical reasoning – where no numerical values are used, and where the argument is inspected throughout for its compelling logic. On the other hand are passages of calculation, where numerical values are everywhere, serving little geometrical function, producing a textual experience where logical reading must give way to a more passive assent, indeed to a reading where the text becomes a pattern of sound more than of meaning.

As I argued in my *The Shaping of Deduction in Greek Mathematics* (1999), valid, inspectable reasoning is the defining feature of a Greek geometrical text. Let us not forget after all that the culture that produced all the works mentioned above, was also the culture of Archimedes' great proofs. Apollonius was not only the author of a study calculating a hexameter line; he was also the author of the *Conics*. And throughout we have not mentioned Euclid, whose writing, with very rare, marginal exceptions,[45] shows none of the features discussed in this chapter. Greek mathematics, not least the Greek mathematics of the third century BC, was fundamentally about the deductive unfolding of geometrical truths.

All of which does not invalidate any of what we have seen above in this chapter, but rather serves to frame it. The numerical, opaque texts found in third-century Greek mathematics functioned against the expectations created by canonical, geometrical writing. They create a kind of alternative space – a holiday from reasoning. It is this alternative, "holiday" aspect that motivates my notion of the "Carnival of calculation."

The alternative space of writing is a matter not only of the experience of reasoning, but also of its goal. It is in this context that I wish to interpret the phenomenon of the attempt to capture the unbounded. Here the two opposites poles – mainstream geometrical rigor and its inversion by opaque calculation – intertwine dialectically. The goals of completion

---

[45] I have in mind especially the more calculatory character of book XIII, as well as a certain intended opacity and thick structure characteristic of book X – both, incidentally, among the less pedagogic works and possibly the more original works of the *Elements*. I shall return to discuss the character of Euclid again in this book, but one notices immediately that, in general, his works may owe more to earlier fourth-century models, and may also be much earlier than those by Archimedes, Apollonius, and their followers. (This is not as certain as once assumed: the usual dating of Euclid to the later fourth century is now doubted by the scholars in the field, though one is hard pressed to find anyone committing himself in print to denying this ancient convention of dating . . . Perhaps the earliest such expression of doubt is in Schneider 1979: 104, n. 105). I return to this in the conclusion to the book.

and precision are derived from the geometrical character of the proofs; they are then undercut by the reality of limited, provisional numerical approach. Built into the claims of complete control – the size of the sun! the circumference of the circle! – is the ironic doubt of a never-ending, asymptotic calculation.

And here finally one may also bring in the more obviously cultural aspect of those texts, their very fascination with size. For one consequence of such a fascination is that concrete size – the actual size of physical things – becomes important. Into the abstract world of geometrical reasoning, then, the world of calculation brings in a fascination with materiality in its literally overpowering form: the entire mass of the cosmos may suddenly be flung upon the reader of geometry.

Against the central promise of Greek geometrical works – made explicit already by Plato – of masterful reason, of complete control, and of the purity of abstraction – Hellenistic treatises of calculation set up a mathematical universe where reason is suspended, control is loosened – its very possibility ironically challenged – the concrete looming large. None of this is ever done so as to cut away from mainstream Greek geometrical traditions. The texts remain logically rigorous, precision is obtained within the limits possible, the arguments can usually be followed in abstraction from their material referents. Still, against the backdrop of pure geometrical proofs, the opposition would be starkly evident to the ancient reader.

The essence of the "Carnival of calculation," then, is that within many mathematical works produced in the Hellenistic world, authors extended the standard format of geometrical reasoning to encompass passages that are nearly the precise inversion of this standard. The standard format is marked by austerity and control and its inversion involves a loosening and contamination. This is what underlies my metaphorical extension of Bakhtin's terminology.

The main result, for us, is the practice of extending a genre so as to encompass its opposite. This approach to genre – and to compositional structure – will be of great interest to us later in the book. Most immediately I shall now move on to consider Hellenistic mathematics from this compositional perspective, concentrating on narrative structure. We have concentrated in this chapter on a large, often neglected, species of Hellenistic mathematics yet, still, no more than a single species. In what follows our discussion becomes much wider in scope: many of the same structural forces seen in this chapter will be seen, in a different form, in mainstream geometry itself.

APPENDIX. MEASUREMENT OF CIRCLE, KNORR, AND OUR
KNOWLEDGE OF ANCIENT TEXTS: A BRIEF NOTE

*Knorr's discussion of Measurement of Circle* is launched at (1989) p. 375 by mentioning four observations: that proposition 2 is false, and falsely placed as it relies on proposition 3 (the view that this brief proposition should be seen, for this reason, as a late interpolation, is in my view sound); that Hero (*Metrica* 1.37) refers to a result on the measurement of sectors which is absent from the extant text (this is an interesting, but not a compelling argument – since the result on the sectors follows as a very obvious corollary from the extant text, it would be completely possible for an ancient author to say that the *authority* for the sector result is Archimedes' *Measurement of Circle* – which was, perhaps, the most famous piece of mathematics in antiquity – even without there being an explicit statement of the sector theorem in the Archimedean work; though one of course cannot rule out there having been such a brief, now lost corollary, in the original work); that the text uses *tomeus*, in proposition 1, where it should use *tmēma* (this is obviously a weak argument in the extreme for making a text non-Archimedean.); most fundamentally, that – as already pointed out by Heiberg – the text is "so negligent as to betray the hand of an excerptor, rather than of Archimedes." On this – and on this alone, really – the argument stands (Dijksterhuis, who is also quoted by Knorr to support his skepticism in n. 3, p. 396, mentioned, as well, the koine dialect [Dijksterhuis 1987: 222]). I believe – based on personal communication from Henry Mendell – that Knorr was better aware of the extent to which the apparent Doric dialect of many other extant treatises was shaped by the editor Heiberg (on this, see Netz forthcoming) and for this reason preferred not to rely on this further, weak argument). But where does this negligence lie? Partly in the very presence of proposition 2; but more importantly for our purposes, in those features of proposition 3 which make – as we saw – for a rough reading experience. However, there is no positive argument for revising our text for proposition 3. Knorr enjoys the game of comparing ancient alternative versions of proposition 1 – of which one can find a few in the commentators (Knorr 1989, chapter 2): but there are no alternative, pre-Arabic sources for proposition 3, and even the Arabic sources are not essentially different from the extant Greek text. (Knorr 1989, chapter 4, e.g. p. 482: "variations among DC [the extant text] and the several medieval versions of prop. 3 are slight".) And finally, no one can doubt the sheer intelligence of the extant proposition 3. So, who knows? Perhaps our text for proposition 3 is indeed deeply flawed (but this is an argument one can apply anywhere else in the manuscript tradition). Or, better from a methodological point of view, we should try and understand the kind of writing where the "negligence" to which Heiberg refers could make sense from the hand of the author. Which is what I try to achieve in my discussion.

The issue is deep and of deep significance to my project of analyzing the style of Greek mathematical writing. How to account for the *style*, given such indirect evidence? Indeed, laypersons are always stunned to discover how mediated our textual tradition is (what? The manuscripts are closer in time to us than they are to antiquity?), and among the historians of science – many of whom were not trained as classicists – such skepticism lingers. Would the texts of classical mathematics not be drastically recast through the process of transmission? Classicists tend to be less skeptical today: "source analysis" lost its fascination as we came to recognize the greater agency of authors – as well as the much more limited agency of scribes. The growing study of book culture, starting from Reynolds and Wilson 1974, has made us much more aware of the reality of a transmission based on commissioned copying. Of course, not all that is extant is genuine: while overwhelmingly an act of mere copying, transmission is indeed prone to corruption. Some authors become foci for forgery (for a good introduction to the subject, from a field not unrelated to our authors, see Thesleff 1961, 1965). In the Greek-speaking world, however, the only mathematical author for whom this is at all likely is Euclid; it is only in the Arabic-speaking world that Archimedes became a pseudepigraphic focus (for which see Sesiano 1991). Even so, pseudepigraphy is not the same as radical recasting: the pseudepigraphic work then becomes subject to the same conservative forces of authentic transmission. The real issue is whether or not mathematical texts became "unprotected" in the sense promoted by Zetzel 1993: those marginal works whose "authenticity" did not matter, such as the cookbook, the legal compendium, or the magical collection (as opposed to texts used inside school curriculum, where textual variation is much less common). As Nagy 1996 points out, the same would hold for performance texts as well and we may indeed view the cookbook, the legal compendium, or the magical collection precisely as aides in performance. Were Greek mathematical texts like cookbooks or like school curricula texts? Some were more, some were less. Accomplished pieces of argumentation, attached to well-known authorial figures (Archimedes?), copied for the school (Euclid?), or for the private collection of prized writings from the past (again, Archimedes?) – such works would not be likely candidates for drastic recasting. Other works may have been considered more as repositories of past results that merit less protection (Hero? Perhaps Apollonius'

*Conics* – a mere "elementary" work, whose author was not quite as famous as Archimedes, and which did not become part of a school curriculum in any sense). For the Heronian text, see Hoyrup 1997, for Apollonius' *Conics* see Decorps-Foulquier 2000; for the overall character of nature of editorial intervention and a critique of Knorr's more expansive position see Cameron 1990.

Yet a final word on this subject. Knorr has done much to reopen the question of the authenticity of the extant Greek texts. In particular, Knorr 1996 is an interesting introduction to the possibility that some portions of the Arabic transmission of Euclid's *Elements* could be superior to the Greek transmission. (See Djebbar *et al.* 2001 for discussion of this thesis). This argument – calling into question the validity of the Greek text of the best-attested Greek mathematical authors – may have an unfortunate misleading effect: in point of fact, the discrepancies between the Greek and the Arabic, while not trivial, are not at all dramatic (at the range of less than 1 percent of the transmitted text). The rather small discrepancy between the Greek and the Arabic tends, if anything, further to support our overall faith in the textual transmission of Greek mathematical texts – which, of course, should always be qualified by the usual awareness of the possibility of local corruption.

CHAPTER 2

# *The telling of mathematics*

## 2.1 THE *SPHERE AND CYLINDER*: MOTIVATING THE DISCUSSION

The *Stomachion* lies at the edges of our knowledge of ancient mathematics, hardly figuring in any of the modern histories of mathematics. This may represent a more modern bias (the game it studies was called in antiquity "the box of Archimedes,"[1] which suggests that Archimedes' treatment of it became widely known), but even so, no one would suggest this represents the core of Archimedes' fame. For this we have to turn to the *Sphere and Cylinder*. After all, there is the famous report by Cicero, according to which Archimedes chose those two figures for his tombstone – defining them as his crowning achievement.[2] And one can easily see why. With all we have seen in the previous chapter concerning the fascination shown by Greek mathematicians towards the complex and the unwieldy, nothing could beat sheer elegance. And what elegance in this result! The cylinder (defined as having its height equal the diameter of its base) is one-and-a-half times the sphere it encloses. Exactly so – in other words, the two objects are like the harmonic notes of the fifth. And is not the sphere as elusive as the circle, with the added complexity of the third dimension? To compare the sphere with the simpler cylinder is to measure it, in a sense, and this result obtained by Archimedes is the closest that Greek mathematicians – or any other since – have ever come to squaring the circle. It is therefore quite appropriately the crowning achievement not only of Archimedes' work but of Greek mathematics as a whole.

---

[1] *Grammatici Latini* VI. 100–1 (Asmonius), 271–2 (Caesius Bassus).
[2] *Tusc.* V.23. Even if Cicero is making up his story (so that he never set eyes on this tomb), he is in all likelihood doing so on the basis of written reports stating how the tomb *would* have looked or, at the very least, tacitly endorsing a view prevalent at Cicero's time that this was how the tomb *should* have looked. For a full treatment of this Ciceronian episode, see Jaeger 2008.

# The Sphere and Cylinder

We should therefore follow the telling of it. For the sense of cunning surprise is quite palpably there – not in the unwieldiness and complexity of the result itself, but in the route leading there.[3]

We turn to read the book now known as "the first book of Archimedes' *Sphere and Cylinder*" (a misleading modern appellation: two works by Archimedes were put together, in later time, to constitute "Archimedes on *Sphere and Cylinder*" in two books; each was originally an autonomous work).[4] This has for its starting point a discursive introduction (addressed to Dositheus, a colleague), where the goal of the treatise is set out explicitly. Archimedes proudly says he has discovered fundamental results about the sphere, as mentioned above: that its volume is two-thirds the cylinder enclosing it, and also that its surface is equal to four times the great circle. I shall return in this chapter to discuss in detail the role of the introduction – a characteristic of the Hellenistic mathematical genre – in the telling of mathematics. Right now I want to stress two features. First, the introduction is highly personal: it has an element of personal autobiography (reminding Dositheus – as Archimedes was to do time and again – of the loss of Archimedes' friend, Conon), and it stresses Archimedes' personal pride in his new achievement (which, he is keen to assert, compares with those of the great Eudoxus). Such an introduction is very far from any conception of an austere, impersonal mathematics.

Second, we see already another fundamental function of an introduction, namely, it creates expectations. Let us see then what happens to those expectations.

Having stated the results, Archimedes moves on to offer a set of axioms or postulates, very subtle and none at all closely related to the sphere. For instance, he defines in detail the concept of concavity and presents an axiomatic foundation for the comparison of concave lines. Such discussions have nothing to do with the three dimensional nor indeed, in any obvious way, with the sphere (on which all lines are similarly concave). Closer at

---

[3] The following discussion expands my previous treatment of narrative structure in Greek mathematics, Netz 2005.
[4] This claim is questioned by Sidoli 2005: 148, in a review of Netz 2004: this questioning must represent a misunderstanding as the point I make is quite straightforward. When I say the two works are autonomous, I point out the simple fact that they were separately released by Archimedes, and not in the accidental sense that he had two pieces of papyrus in which to send two installments of the same single work, but in the sense that they were understood by him to constitute two separate projects. Of course, the claims of the so-called second book could only be seen to be valid by a reader acquainted with the proofs of the first. Even so, Archimedes made sure to recall explicitly, introducing the second book, those results of the first that are used in the second, so as to make a separate reading feasible (a separate reading does not mean, of course, being conceptually independent). For all of this, see Archimedes' introduction to the second book (Heiberg I.168.3–170.2).

home to the three dimensional, Archimedes defines, for instance, the "solid rhombus." This is the outcome of two equilateral cones stuck to each other at their bases so that their axes are collinear – a nice object, but what has it got to do with the sphere?

Archimedes tells us nothing. A quick, first result – more part of the introduction than part of the main deductive sequence[5] – deals with polygons; then another, seemingly unrelated problem deals with general geometrical proportion theory. Only then does Archimedes move on to the first main substantial sequence of problems (propositions 3–6), which allows him to construct polygons and circles in defined proportion. Once again, I stress: the introduction did nothing to prepare us for such results, nor does Archimedes suggest anywhere how they are supposed to contribute to the measuring of the sphere. And he does not even stick to such results. In the mosaic structure we are familiar with already, Archimedes lurches in all directions: following this first set of results come propositions 7–12, now theorems dealing with the surfaces of *pyramids* – at least the immediate subject matter of three dimensional measurements, but what have pyramids to do with spheres? No answer to this is forthcoming from Archimedes. Instead, propositions 13–20 move on to the surfaces of *cones* (and of various figures composed of segments of cones). Still no word of the sphere although, with cones, we at least move into something resembling the *cylinder*. We edge closer – and then suddenly are flung far away: the following two propositions 21–2 move out to totally new territory. Instead of having anything to do with three-dimensional figures, they return to the polygons of propositions 3–6 and for them state very complex and specialized results, having to do with proportions of lines drawn through the polygons. Those lines do not seem to have any relevance to anything – certainly not to spheres (fig. 10). These two results simply have no obvious parallels or connections with anything else in the corpus of Greek mathematics. Why on earth would Archimedes wish to draw such figures, to prove such results? How does all the above tie together?

Archimedes does not answer this question directly. Instead, in proposition 23, we are asked to make a thought experiment. We rotate the circle, polygon and lines from fig. 10, and obtain in this way a sphere in which is enclosed a figure composed of segments of cones (fig. 11). It now becomes obvious that the results concerning polygons, and those concerning cones, can be put together and (with the aid of the specific claims made about proportion, as well as about pyramids), can immediately give rise to the

---

[5] On this structure of gradual transition from introduction to main text, see pp. 100–4 below.

*The* Sphere and Cylinder 69

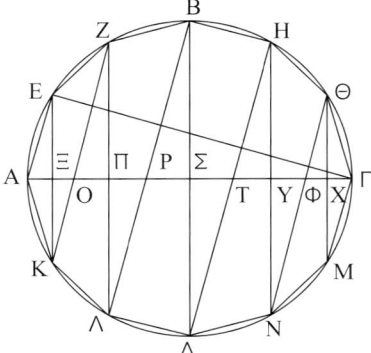

Figure 10

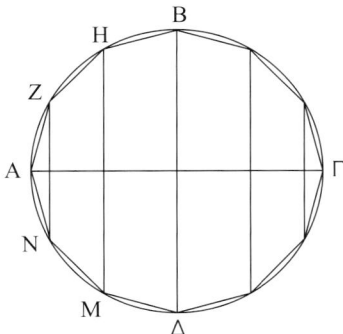

Figure 11

proportions determining the surface and volume of a sphere. The seemingly irrelevant and long preparation – just about half the book – is suddenly found to be directly relevant so that, indeed, the main line of reasoning can now proceed fairly quickly to obtain Archimedes' main results in propositions 33–4. (The book moves on to a further set of results concerning segments of sphere, derived in propositions 35–44; in context, these appear as a kind of appendix, moving from the elegance of the main results into a more opaque and unwieldy set of results. For my purposes right now, I prefer to concentrate on the central structure of the book, leading to the climax of propositions 33–4.)

It is not my intention to celebrate the genius of Archimedes. That Archimedes was a genius of narrative is of course what I subjectively feel.

In more objective terms, however, what I am concerned with is just stating the narrative structure that appears to emerge here. Perhaps the simplest way to state this is by noting that Archimedes had alternative ways of presenting his argument. The most obvious one – and the one with potentially the greatest harm for his apparent narrative goals – would have been to *start* with the thought-experiment of proposition 23. This after all has a very general character, not so much a proposition as an observation, almost a definition. It could easily belong in an introduction. And it is also clear that, in such a case, the sense of a brilliant master-stroke would have been completely eroded. We notice incidentally a fundamental fact: the mathematical kernel of an argument – whatever we take *this* to be – only very weakly underdetermines the form it may take. The mathematician makes decisions for the form, decisions that are mathematically undetermined (in a traditional, narrow sense of mathematics) and therefore have to be dominated by narrative functions.

In this case the results of the narrative choices made by Archimedes can be spelled out as follows. First, the narrative structure is difficult to follow, in the sense we are familiar with from the previous chapter. Above all, it is dazzlingly surprising, which must have been the key point for Archimedes: the reader would all the more appreciate Archimedes' genius as he would pick up, for himself, all the threads leading into and away from proposition 23.

My main claim in this chapter is that narrative structures of complexity and surprise are everywhere in Hellenistic mathematics. These are works that cannot be construed as marginal in any sense: we still consider them among the most important achievements of Hellenistic mathematics. I will show this narrative structure at its two levels – first at the local level of the individual proposition, in section 2.2, and then at the more global level of a treatise taken as a whole (as we have just noted for *Sphere and Cylinder* I), in section 2.3.

I will also show in this chapter how the narrative is introduced by an authorial voice: how Hellenistic mathematicians personalize their works via the characteristic tool of the introduction. Of course the main structure of argumentation keeps to a certain ideal of abstract impersonality, sustaining in this way the claim of perfect, objective validity. Once again, one can identify in Hellenistic mathematics a certain dialectic, where the genre characterized by its impersonality acquires within itself a place for the personal voice. This modulation of the personal and the impersonal is the subject of section 2.4.

Ending this chapter is section 2.5: "Coda – triumph of the impersonal." I consider the ludic narrative style of Hellenistic mathematics in its wider

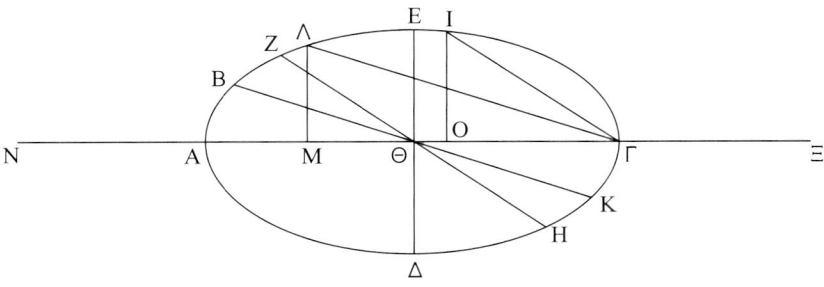

Figure 12

context of stylistic options. This coda is also an intermezzo, positioned as it is halfway through the book. This section is dedicated to the question of the aftermath – whatever happened to the ludic in the later reception of Greek mathematics? This follows on naturally from the discussion of the personal voice as, indeed, the perception of mathematics as impersonal seems to be the main force moving later mathematics away from its Hellenistic forms.

## 2.2 THE TELLING OF THE PROOF

I begin with a work reputed for its tough-minded seriousness: Apollonius' *Conics*. For my first example, I will do my best to follow in detail the key piece of argumentation in an advanced part of book VII, i.e. a very advanced piece of mathematics indeed. Apollonius proves a series of inequalities resulting with lines constructed on conic sections. The text is extant only in Arabic translation, but it is clear that (with the exception of possible interpolated glosses) the translation is very close to the original. I provide a translation of parts of VII.41 adapted from Toomer's edition (in a language somewhat closer to Greek geometrical style than Toomer's). I provide numerals for the steps in the argument. The enunciation, which I do not translate, asserts a number of *minimum* results, among them the one whose proof we shall follow – that the sides of a rectangle constructed on the major axis[6] of the ellipse are smaller than the sides of the same type of rectangle constructed on any other diameter. I skip the construction, as well, which is implicit in fig. 12.

---

[6] It is sufficient for our purposes here to say that the rectangle involved is produced by the two sides of the diameter and the *latus rectum* of the ellipse. It will take too long to explain here what a *latus rectum* is, for which the reader should turn to Apollonius' *Conics* I.13. For our purposes this might be taken as a mystery line associated, according to precise rules, with each given diameter of the ellipse.

ΑΓ is the major axis, ΔΕ the minor, and the points Ν, Ξ are found by ΓΝ:ΑΝ::ΑΞ:ΞΓ::(ΑΓ:*latus rectum*).

(1) And as the square on ΑΓ to the square on the line equal to: the diameter ΑΓ together with the *latus rectum* of the figure constructed on it, so the square on ΝΓ to the square on ΝΞ,[7] (2) and as the rectangle <contained by> ΝΓ,ΑΞ to the square on ΝΞ, (3) since the rectangle <contained by> ΝΓ,ΑΞ is equal to the square on ΝΓ. (4) And as the square on ΑΓ to the square on ΕΔ, so ΝΓ to ΓΞ, (5) since it was proven in proposition 15 of Book I that as the square on ΑΓ to the square on ΔΕ so ΑΓ to its *latus rectum*.[8] (6) And as ΝΓ to ΓΞ, so the rectangle <contained by> ΝΓ, ΓΞ to the square on ΓΞ, (7) while as the square on ΔΕ to the square on the line equal to: the line ΔΕ together with the *latus rectum* of the figure constructed on it, so the square on ΓΞ to the square on ΝΞ, (8) also because of what was proven in proposition 15 of Book I. (9) Therefore as the square on ΑΓ to the square on the line equal to: the diameter ΔΕ together with the *latus rectum* of the figure constructed on it, so the rectangle <contained by> ΝΓ, ΓΞ to the square on ΓΞ, (10) and it was shown that as the rectangle <contained by> ΝΓ,ΑΞ to the square on ΓΞ, so the square on ΑΓ to the square on the line equal to the line ΑΓ together with the *latus rectum* of the figure constructed on it, (11) therefore the ratio of ΑΓ to: ΑΓ together with the *latus rectum* is greater than the ratio of ΑΓ to: ΔΕ together with the *latus rectum*.

From Step 11 it follows that ΑΓ together with its *latus rectum* is smaller than ΔΕ together with its *latus rectum*, which is already part of the required proof. I therefore stop at this point, as we can already see here how Apollonius obtains his essential results.

The basic structure of the argument is the quick obtaining of Step 2 (based on 1, 3), followed by the somewhat more involved obtaining of Step 9 (based on Steps 4–8). Step 2 is recalled as Step 10 and then 9 and 10 together yield 11.

For the reader, life is not as easy as that. While the Greek particles would have made the navigation of the text almost as transparent as my numerals and logical chart make it, still the major derivations involve considerable mental labor.

Consider first the easier case, of Step 2. This is, in modern notation, $ΑΓ^2:(ΑΓ+latus)^2::(ΝΓ×ΑΞ):ΝΞ^2$.

---

[7] The Arabic has here throughout the expression, less natural in Greek, "the ratio of . . . to . . . is as the ratio of . . . to . . . ". I translate as if the original Greek had "as . . . to . . . , so . . . to . . . ", and return to the Arabic (more natural in Greek with an inequality) in Step 11. Of course I may be wrong in this "emendation" of the Arabic text; nothing hangs on it.

[8] Step 5 is likely to be a gloss added by some Arabic reader, since explicit cross-references are natural in scholia.

This is derived from Step 1 – that $A\Gamma^2:(A\Gamma+latus)^2::N\Gamma^2:N\Xi^2$ – together with the rather obvious observation, made as an afterthought in Step 3, that $N\Gamma^2$ equals $N\Gamma \times A\Xi$ ($N\Gamma$ and $A\Xi$ are constructed by exactly the same ratio and it is therefore indeed quite evident that they are equal). However, how do we get at Step 1? Toomer (n. 199) hints at a likely route: by construction, $\Gamma N:AN::A\Gamma:latus$, and so by the proportion theory operation of "adding," $\Gamma N:(\Gamma N+AN)::A\Gamma:(A\Gamma+latus)$, which we may promptly square (and change order for easier parsing) as $A\Gamma^2:(A\Gamma+latus)^2::\Gamma N^2:(\Gamma N+AN)^2$, at which point a few substitutions may be made based on the geometrical equalities obtaining. For instance, we are already familiar with the equality $\Gamma N=A\Xi$. So instead of $\Gamma N^2$ we may write down $N\Gamma \times A\Xi$. Further, instead of $\Gamma N+AN$ we may write down $\Gamma N+\Gamma\Xi$ or (as can be immediately seen in the diagram) $N\Xi$. Now we can write $A\Gamma^2:(A\Gamma+latus)^2::(N\Gamma \times A\Xi):N\Xi^2$, the desired Step 2. The complexity of the implicit reasoning is notable, especially because it combines abstract proportion theory manipulations together with geometrical, indeed diagram observations.

Step 9 is derived via another complex route. From Step 4 we have

(4) $A\Gamma^2:E\Delta^2::N\Gamma:\Gamma\Xi$

(which is simply a general observation about ellipses), while from Step 6 we have

(6) $N\Gamma:\Gamma\Xi::(N\Gamma*\Gamma\Xi):\Gamma\Xi^2$

(this is of course an automatic expansion of any ratio into a valid proportion). An implicit result is

(6*) $A\Gamma^2:E\Delta^2::(N\Gamma \times \Gamma\Xi):\Gamma\Xi^2$,

but note that (6*) is not asserted explicitly by Apollonius. Further, Step 7 asserts

(7) $\Delta E^2:(\Delta E+latus)^2::\Gamma\Xi^2:N\Xi^2$.

This is not however a direct application of a well-known observation, but a more complex derivation. Step 8 is correct in making the dependence of Step 7 on 1.15 quite vague, as 1.15 proves a very different result. There it is shown (implicitly!) that minor and major axes such as our $A\Gamma$, $\Delta E$, with their two *latera recta*, form a continuous proportion as follows:

(i) $\Delta E:(its\ latus)::(A\Gamma's\ latus):A\Gamma$.

Toomer suggests effectively as follows. First, we know by construction that

(ii) $A\Gamma's\ latus:A\Gamma::AN:\Gamma N$.

So that (i) above becomes

(ii) $\Delta E:(its\ latus)::AN:\Gamma N$.

Further, a proportion theory manipulation transforms (ii) into

(iv) $\Delta E:(\Delta E+its\ latus)::AN:(AN+\Gamma N)$

And AN, AN+ΓN respectively are easily transformed by the diagram into ΓΞ, NΞ respectively:

ΔE:(ΔE+its *latus*)::ΓΞ:NΞ.

At which point one may square each of the terms to obtain Step 7, finally! Once again, note the combination of diagrammatic and proportion theory grounds involved in the implicit argument.

Let us now return to recall Step 7 together with the (implicit) Step 6*:

(6*) AΓ²:EΔ²::(NΓ*ΓΞ):ΓΞ²

(7) ΔE²:(ΔE+*latus*)²::ΓΞ²:NΞ².

Here a proportion theory manipulation ("by the equality") allows us to remove middle terms and obtain a new proportion:

AΓ²:(ΔE+*latus*)²::(NΓ×ΓΞ): NΞ².

This indeed is the desired Step 9.

To sum up, Step 9 is based on the combination of three claims – Steps 4, 6, and 7. Its obtaining is implicit in two ways. First, the three steps taken together do not yield the result, unless one considers a possible implicit result of 4 and 6 taken together, namely 6*. Second, Step 7 is based on a complex, implicit argument.

With both parts of the argument – reaching Step 2, and reaching Step 9 – we see a similar structure. The text confronts the reader with a difficult, yet soluble puzzle. At first the statements seem to arrive from out of the blue. A more careful reading, based on a close acquaintance with the Greek mathematical toolbox and close attention to the diagram, suggests how the statements are in fact valid. The filling-in of the interim arguments is indeed difficult, but not at all impossible. It should be stressed that the cognitive experience involved here is not "opaque" in the sense mentioned above for calculations. There is nothing useful for the clever reader to do, faced with a long list of calculations – short of the numbing operation of trying to re-do the calculations. Yet here the clever reader is invited to look up the solution to the puzzle: how to obtain the results? A challenge that gives rise to considerable pleasure in its pursuit and achievement.

Now, it would not have been at all difficult for Apollonius to spell out explicitly all those interim steps. This would have made the text transparent, pedagogically useful, and deadly slow. There are of course texts in Greek mathematics that are exactly that, in particular the earlier propositions of Euclid's *Elements*. But especially in the more advanced parts of Greek mathematics – clearly intended for the true aficionado of geometry – such passages as Apollonius' VII.41 are frequently found.⁹ Here then is one kind of experience an advanced Greek geometrical proof is meant to elicit: that of the puzzle intended for the erudite reader. This need not take only the form of sending the reader to look for hidden arguments. For instance, Diocles offers a solution to a problem first set by Archimedes, of dividing a sphere by a plane so that its two parts stand to each other at a given ratio. The solution to the problem is merely sketched, in the Greek mode of analysis (where the problem is assumed as solved, and consequences of this assumption are followed until an understanding emerges of how the problem is to be solved). Providing an actual solution to the problem is left as an exercise to the reader.[10] The sense is obvious: that providing the explicit solution would be otiose. The reader can do so himself! This is the sense animating many advanced Greek geometrical writings: much of the work is left for the reader, so as to keep his mind exercised rather than numbed.

A somewhat different experience may be represented by one of the more famous results in Greek mathematics – the first proposition of Archimedes' *Method*. I follow the outline of the argument (see fig. 13). First, a parabolic segment ABΓ has its base AΓ bisected at Δ. The tangent at Γ is ΓZ; the diameter ΔB is extended to E, with AZ parallel to it. An arbitrary line MNOΞ is then drawn, also parallel to ΔB. Furthermore, a balance is

---

[9] To quantify such passages is very difficult, especially since a precise definition is impossible – when does a normal application of the toolbox become complex enough to be considered as a "puzzle?" Eutocius' commentaries often concern themselves with the solution of such puzzles (with the remarkable exceptions of the historical excursi in the commentary to *SC* ii), with which however he is far from exhaustive. (The commentary on book i, other than the discussion of the axioms, concerns itself nearly entirely with such puzzles: about thirty puzzles in a relatively simple work.) An even better measure is in Heiberg's numbered footnotes which all deal either with textual issues or with the solution of puzzles (straightforward references to the toolbox are made through parenthetical references to the *Elements* or other works). I count 514 numbered footnotes by Heiberg whose function is to solve such puzzles. Heiberg's numbering of the corpus has 199 propositions, if I am not mistaken, that is about three puzzles per proposition on average, but here it must be admitted that the counting is still very impressionistic. Heiberg's footnotes span the spectrum from the trivial to the truly perplexing. It would be a very valuable exercise to go systematically through the entire corpus of Archimedes and Apollonius and to analyze all those arguments that go beyond a mere evocation of toolbox results. I checked *Spiral Lines* for that, and I find there some forty-odd footnotes by Heiberg that solve a genuine puzzle: more than one per proposition on average. This is at the "advanced" end of the spectrum. My very non-quantitative impression is that all advanced mathematical works contain a number of more difficult propositions, each with a handful of true puzzles. More in this qualitative vein, below.
[10] The text survives in two forms: as prop. 8 in Diocles' *On Burning Mirrors* (in Arabic translation) and as a fragment preserved in Eutocius' commentary to Archimedes' second book on *Sphere and Cylinder*. The second fragment does include a synthesis, but this may well be supplied by Eutocius himself, especially because in the Arabic version the synthesis is explicitly avoided (Rashed 2000: 125.16).

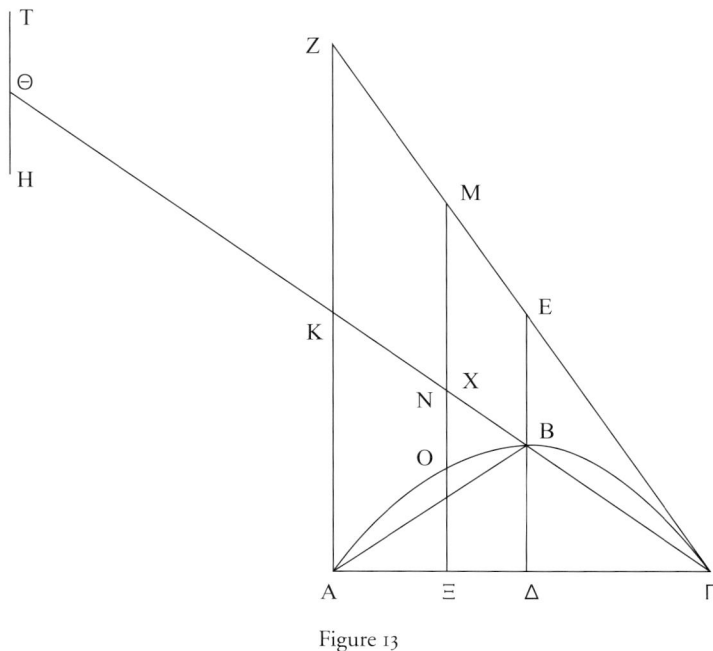

Figure 13

imagined (a strange move in geometry!) located at the line ΓB, extended until KΘ= KΓ.

Archimedes notes a number of results obtainable from the theory of conic sections: EB is equal to BΔ (with the ensuing equalities, based on similarities of triangles, MN = NΞ, ZK = KA). A more complex result, stated without proof but indeed provable from the theory of conic sections, is

ΓA:AΞ::MΞ:ΞO

which Archimedes manipulates in a rather straightforward way to obtain

ΘK:KN::MΞ:ΞO.

I now proceed to quote the following, main part of the argument:

(1) And since the point N is a center of the weight of the line MΞ, (2) since MN is equal to NΞ), (a) therefore if we set TH equal to ΞO, and Θ its < = TH's> center of the weight,[11] (4) so that TΘ is equal to ΘH, (5) TΘH shall balance MΞ – <MΞ> remaining in the same place, (6) through the fact that ΘN is cut reciprocally to the weights TH, MΞ, (7) and as ΘK to KN, so MΞ to HT. (8) So that K is a center

---

[11] This is not part of the argument, but a piece of the construction, delayed intentionally until this part of the argument where it can be more effectively read.

of the weight of the weight <composed> of both <MΞ and TH>. (9) And also similarly: however many <lines> shall be drawn in the triangle ZAΓ parallel to EΔ, they shall balance – remaining in the same place – the <lines> taken by them, of the segment, transposed to Θ, so that K is center of the weight of the <weight composed> of both. (10) And since the triangle ΓZA has been composed of the <lines> in the triangle ΓZA, (11) while the segment ABΓ has been composed of the <lines> in the segment taken similarly to ΞO, (12) therefore the triangle ZAΓ, remaining in the same place, shall balance the segment of the section, positioned around Θ as center of the weight, at the point K, (13) so that K shall be center of the weight of the <weight> composed of both <triangle and segment>.

At this point the main result is already obtained. Archimedes merely needs to point out that a triangle's center of the weight (as he himself has shown in his book on *Balancing Planes*) is at a point Ξ where KΞ is a third of KΓ, while KΓ = KΘ by the construction, so that the distances of the two weights, triangle and segment, from their center of the weight are at a 1:3 ratio, so that so must be their weights (by another result shown by Archimedes in the same *Balancing Planes*), so that the parabolic segment is measured as one-third the triangle AZΓ or (by a simple geometrical manipulation) a third as much again as the triangle ABΓ.

Notice that the argument has much less the aspect of an explicit puzzle than Apollonius'. Indeed Archimedes is occasionally remarkably explicit: pointing out the obvious consequence of the construction Step a in Step 4; going in great detail from one statement of a balance to its equivalent representations (from Step 5 to Steps 7 and 8, and then again from Step 12 to Step 13). The surface experience could therefore be that of reading a fully explicit, almost pedagogic text. And yet the text is anything but transparent. It is marked by two major moments of a radical thought-experiment. First, at the construction Step a, a copy of the line cut at the parabolic segment is positioned elsewhere in the diagram, and the geometrical result is then restated as a result concerning a balance. This suddenly recasts the previous geometrical derivation, endowing it with a new, quasi-physical meaning – a delightful moment where, with a gasp, we realize the point of the previous exercise (this is directly comparable to the role of proposition 23 in Archimedes' first book on *Sphere and Cylinder* as seen in the preceding section). Second, and more significant, Steps 10–11 invite us to reconsider the triangle and the parabolic segments as composed of the arbitrary parallel lines drawn through them, so that the center of the weight of both figures together then becomes the same as the center of the weight of each couple of lines.

This second thought-experiment is very well known in the history of mathematics, as Archimedes here seems to be suggesting some kind of integration. The interesting aspect for us is the breathtaking ease with which this suggestion is broached. Archimedes does not really imply that there is some kind of major thought-experiment involved and, for the naïve reader, this appears like a standard demonstrative move where a self-evident truth is asserted. The effect in this case is quite different from that of Step a mentioned above. There, the reader was invited to share the delight in discovering, retrospectively, a beautiful correlation. Here, a further effect is involved, intended for some very discerning readers only. For here Archimedes has laid a kind of trap. Is the argument at all valid? That is, are we allowed to transform a result for arbitrary lines into a result concerning the objects through which the lines are drawn? Are we allowed to conceive of a figure as if it were many lines glued together? Indeed Archimedes suggests at the introduction to the *Method* that the results proved through the special method introduced in the treatise are in some sense not quite valid. However he does not explain in the introduction what the special method is, and where its invalidity lies (I shall return to discuss this in greater detail below). Steps 10–11 may well be understood to constitute the *Method*'s Achilles heel. But if so, how carefully Archimedes avoided exposing it! The naïve reader would not notice any difficulty; the very sophisticated one will realize the difficulty but will also be at a loss to state Archimedes' true position. As against the puzzle of Apollonius' vii.41 – a tough but doable problem, a challenging exercise for the sophisticated geometrical reader – this moment in the *Method* is a trap for the naïve and an insoluble riddle for the expert.

We have seen three types of experience elicited by the telling of the proof: the challenging puzzle, meant for the erudite (Apollonius' vii.41); the gasp of delight at a clever combination, retrospectively grasped (Archimedes' *Method* 1, Step a); the trap or the riddle (the same, Steps 10–11). These are but examples, of course. How representative are they? I will not try to study this question in a quantitative way. But the following should be noted.

First, the bulk of the transmission of Greek mathematics in the West concentrated on Euclid's *Elements*, i.e. the Greek work least marked for its use of the challenging puzzle (while some of its books, such as book x, are indeed difficult, this is not because they set the readers explicit puzzles, but rather because of the complex, non-intuitive character of their results). This is obvious for a tradition made by compilers with little geometry and produced for the benefit of readers with little geometry. There is no fun in a puzzle you cannot solve. As for the more advanced works of Greek geometry, many of them survive in Arabic only (such as

Apollonius' *Conics*, books v–vii – from which our example was taken – or Diocles' *On Burning Mirrors*, where we have seen an analysis with the synthesis left as an exercise). The major body of advanced Greek geometry transmitted in the West is that of the works of Archimedes, and it is striking to see how often the text is interpolated by readers who wished, precisely, to solve Archimedean puzzles. (Because their solutions are often clumsy, we have reason to believe those are indeed interpolations rather than Archimedes' own words.) The detection of such interpolations – of course always conjectural – was the main editorial task faced by Heiberg in his edition of Archimedes.[12] And finally, it should be noted that the sense of frustration with the puzzling was not limited to medieval geometrical mediocrities. Heath, for instance, commenting on Archimedes' *Method*, sounds a familiar complaint, somewhat different from that of medieval readers but essentially related to it:[13]

Nothing is more characteristic of the classical works of the great geometers of Greece, or more tantalizing, than the absence of any indication of the steps by which they worked their way to the discovery of their great theorems. As they have come down to us, these theorems are finished masterpieces which leave no traces of any rough-hewn stage, no hint of the method by which they were evolved.

Heath's notion – that Archimedes' *Method* was, in his words, "a sort of lifting of the veil" – is of course nonsense.[14] If the veil was lifted, how come we have spent the last century arguing over what's underneath? No, the *Method* is another, more subtle veil. But this is not my point here. What I want to stress is that the modern frustration with the Greek synthetic presentation of results is precisely what I have described so far in this section: a frustration with a certain puzzling appearance, where the author attempts no pedagogic intervention explaining the significance of the flow of the text, instead demanding that the reader work out for himself the line of thought.

The challenging puzzle, meant for the erudite, is standard in the more advanced parts of Greek geometry. As for the trap or the riddle, this is perhaps rare, as indeed only some very special combinations will allow for it. It seems, however, to have been at the very least an Archimedean stylistic principle. We are reminded of course of the false claims sent out by Archimedes as challenges for the mathematical community, so as to trap his competitors (see my discussion of *Spiral Lines*, p. 3 above). But more can be

---

[12] I discuss this editorial practice in detail in Netz forthcoming.  [13] Heath 1921: 6.
[14] Heath repeats a *topos*: the persistent early modern myth of a hidden, ancient *ars inveniendi* (see e.g. Bos 2001: 93–4). The myth must have been false but it is nevertheless revealing: Greek mathematics was perceived to *hide a secret*.

said: whenever Archimedes introduces a fundamentally original principle of reasoning, this is presented in a riddling combination of the explicit and the obscure. Consider his work on *Balancing Planes*, where a very subtle and precise axiomatic model is constructed for the calculation of conditions under which equal and unequal planes will balance. Following that, Archimedes reaches the crucial result (already seen in our example from the *Method*), that planes balance at distances reciprocal to (what we call) their areas. This is the argument towards which the axiomatic model is built, and from which all else flows. And yet here the application of the axioms is left obscure so that a modern controversy rages as to the precise assumptions Archimedes used in this argument (some arguing, indeed, that Archimedes was here guilty of circular reasoning).[15] Less familiar but very similar is a case from the first book on *Sphere and Cylinder*, where Archimedes develops a very sophisticated axiomatic model for the comparison of lines and planes concave in the same direction – the notion of concave is defined in great detail and precise conditions are set out for when lines and planes can be said to be greater or smaller than each other, depending on their relations of concavity. Then the treatise unfolds and Archimedes simply asserts of this line that it is greater than that, of this plane that it is greater than that, never invoking explicitly the rules set out in the axiomatic model. Of course this is in part the usual challenging puzzle, leaving the reader to complete such details on his own. But since no examples are ever provided for how the axiomatic model is applied in practice, the puzzle verges on the riddle: the reader, tantalizingly, is offered a principle of geometrical reasoning, and is then left without indication of how this is to work, so that the principle is admired, implicitly used, but never truly clarified.

In other words, we see a continuity reaching from the puzzle meant to be solved, to the riddle meant to tantalize. Most significant, indeed, is that the three aspects seen above form a unity. In the telling of the advanced Greek geometrical proof, we see an interest in an experience of reading marked by subtlety, surprise, and authorial playfulness. Let us now move on to see more of this, at the level of the treatise taken as a whole.

## 2.3 THE TELLING OF THE TREATISE

We have already seen in detail the logical flow of two treatises by Archimedes – on *Spiral Lines*, and the first book on *Sphere and Cylinder* – where a principle of retrospective surprise seems to have motivated the narrative structure.

[15] See Suppes 1976, Dijksterhuis 1987: 289–304 (with more references there), Mach 1912: 14 ff.

In *Spiral Lines* (discussed in the introduction) the main result concerning the area intercepted by a spiral line being one third its enclosing circle, is introduced unexpectedly as proposition 24 (very late in the book). And it is only in passing that the reader realizes, while reading this proposition, that it relies essentially on proposition 10, which otherwise appears to be totally unmotivated. This is the fundamental retrospective surprise of *Spiral Lines*, and it is neatly reproduced by the first book on *Sphere and Cylinder*. In *Spiral Lines*, the bizarre, unmotivated sequence is the arithmetico-geometrical proportion results 10–11; in *Sphere and Cylinder* I, this is the complex, *ad hoc* geometrical proportion results concerning circles and polygons, 21–2. Both come to be understood belatedly – so that this moment of belated recognition forms the narrative key to the work.

Clearly this was a specifically Archimedean narrative technique. We have seen a very similar technique employed in *Planes in Equilibrium*, book II (see pp. 40–1 above), where the penultimate proposition 9, a complex arithmetico-geometrical result, appears without any motivation, becoming meaningful only through the reading of the following and final proposition 10. Much more extreme is the case of propositions 1–2 in *Conoids and Spheroids*. There, too, Archimedes presents complex, opaque results in abstract proportion theory, e.g. the (simpler) enunciation of 1:

If however many magnitudes, in multitude, have the same ratio, two by two, with other magnitudes (equal <to them> by multitude), as those similarly ordered, and the first magnitudes are said to other magnitudes in however many ratios – whether all or some of them – and the latter magnitudes are in the same ratios to other magnitudes, respectively, <then> all the first magnitudes to all the <magnitudes> they stand in ratio to, have a ratio that all the latter magnitudes have to all the <magnitudes> they stand in ratio to.

This follows immediately upon the introduction where the geometrical definition of conoids and spheroids is developed in great detail, so that the reader should expect a geometrical treatise. Instead, the treatise proper starts with those very involved results in proportion theory, which become applied – once again as in *Spiral Lines*, applied mostly implicitly – only from proposition 21 onwards. (It often takes an Archimedean treatise some twenty propositions "to warm up".)

While very characteristic of Archimedes, this narrative structure based on the play of expectations and surprises has parallels elsewhere. Even Euclid's *Elements* contains at least one book conforming to such a pattern. Significantly, this is the one book where Euclid's *Elements* ceases being a repository of elementary results, to offer a fully fledged advanced geometrical treatise.

Book XIII is marked by the absence of any introduction.[16] What is it about to prove? The first set of six propositions are all about lines cut in extreme and mean proportions (i.e. so that the whole line is to the greater segment as the greater segment is to the smaller), so one may expect a specialized study in the application of proportion theory to geometry. Then a new direction is taken, and the next six propositions are about geometrical relations holding with regular polygons inscribed in a circle. Since it is found in proposition 8 that lines drawn inside a regular pentagon give rise rather naturally to a line cut in extreme and mean proportion, the reader may then expect to see the preceding propositions 1–6 as introductory to the finding of extreme and mean proportions as central geometrical properties of regular polygons. Not so: the treatise finally moves on in proposition 13 to construct a pyramid and inscribe it in a sphere, comparing its side to the radius of the sphere. The remainder of the book then proceeds to do the same with the remaining five regular solids, with the treatise finally rounded up by a comparison of all five sides and a proof that there are exactly five such solids. In other words, we find out only at the end that the book forms a study of the regular solids, and that the results on extreme and mean proportions are there for the sake of some results on regular polygons – which in turn are there for the sake of regular solids. (This is in fact a close parallel for the way in which the results concerning regular polygons in Archimedes' first book on *Sphere and Cylinder* are retrospectively understood as lemmata for results concerning solids.) That this is not quite at the level of awe-inspiring surprise inspired by Archimedes' narrative structures is perhaps merely a mark of Archimedes' genius. The tantalizing, surprising structure is evident in this book by Euclid just as it is in Archimedes. Of course book XIII is exceptional in the context of the *Elements*: but not so in the wider context of Greek mathematics.

Let us turn for instance to Diocles' book *On Burning Mirrors*, not that it is easy to make out the structure of the book. Indeed it is difficult to determine even where it ends. The authorship is heavily mediated, our source being an Arabic text whose structure, as it stands, is peculiar indeed. About a third of the book is, as suggested by its (late?) title, a study of burning mirrors. Then follows a study of the problem of cutting a sphere by a plane so that its two segments have a given ratio to each other. Following that comes a study of the problem of finding two mean proportionals between two given lines. Either Diocles has written a kind

---

[16] The same is true only of books VIII, IX; but it appears that books VII–IX were intended to be read as a single sequence.

of anthology, or three separate treatises by him were put together either in antiquity itself or in late antiquity.[17] I propose now that we look at the first part of the book, the one dealing with burning mirrors properly, and consider how it was supposed to make sense, independently, as a piece of narrative. This then is the text of Toomer (1976: 35–71).[18]

The overall project of this part of Diocles' *On Burning Mirrors* is to show that, with a mirror in the shape of a paraboloid, rays of light are reflected to coincide in a point, resulting in a burning mirror. We can immediately imagine how Archimedes would have structured such a treatise: first, a sequence of results on optics and the reflection of rays of light, starting from first principles; then a study of conic sections, apparently unrelated to the subject at hand; and finally a grand synthesis where the conic sections are found to be no less crucial to the construction of a burning mirror than is optics itself. In other words, we would have a narrative transition moving, in a flash, from obscurity to clarity. Diocles may have intentionally avoided this structure. After all, the following section of *On Burning Mirrors* – the one dedicated to the problem of cutting a sphere – contains the most scathing criticism extant, directed at Archimedes.[19] It may well be that Diocles took pains *not* to write as the old master did.

Instead, his treatise manages to achieve satisfying results without ever attaining more than local narrative clarity. In this treatise, sense is always refracted.

This involves a remarkable narrative practice. The treatise begins with a rich introduction, with historical, astronomical, and practical prolegomena to the problem of setting a burning mirror (the astronomical considerations are brought in for good geometrical reason, on which see below). Diocles makes it quite clear (if not quite convincing) that he is the first to offer a valid theoretical solution to the problem, showing that the mirror is constructed with a paraboloid. So much for the Archimedean surprise. It is appears as if everything is on the table.

Following this long introduction – five Arabic Toomer pages out of the treatise's nineteen – the text then says (Toomer 1976: 44): "Let there be a

---

[17] The last option is mentioned by Toomer 1976 as coming from J. Sesiano, and it is the likeliest explanation.

[18] I follow Toomer in taking so-called proposition 6 to be spurious (narrative considerations of the kind to be discussed later on are relevant here, too: while the five preceding propositions lack authorial explanation, as I describe below, the goal of proposition 6 is explicitly explained in the text).

[19] The same problem was proposed by Archimedes, its solution by him apparently lost in antiquity, so that here was a case of Archimedes promising to solve a problem and failing to deliver on his promise; see Netz 2004 for the general history of the problem, and especially pp. 39–54 for Diocles' treatment of it.

parabola KBM, with axis AZ, and let half the parameter of the squares on the ordinates be line BH . . ."

Here is Diocles' decisive choice. The main point is the following. A Greek mathematical proposition is typically introduced by a general enunciation, where the theorem to be proved, or problem to be solved, is asserted in its most general form ("in every triangle . . . "). Then comes a specific construction in the diagram, where once again the goal of the proof is asserted explicitly, though this time in the particular terms ("I say that the line AB is . . ."). Only then comes the proof proper. This is the typical structure of a Greek mathematical proposition (typically, but not universally applied – see Netz 1998a). Its narrative consequence is obvious: the reader has a clear sense of the goal of the demonstrative discourse, so that he is able to position the steps of the argument in relation to this goal. The author may then be more explicit – in which case the parsing of the argument, in terms of the contribution it makes towards the goal, becomes obvious – or less explicit, where such parsing becomes more challenging and potentially interesting from a narrative point of view.

Diocles, in a move rare in Greek mathematics, in this treatise avoids *both* general enunciation as well as particular setting out. The propositions simply move from construction to proof. Only at the end of each proof are consequences drawn, not quite in general geometrical terms but in optical and then practical terms having to do with the construction of the burning mirror. Thus, following a rather complex proof – through which, I repeat, the reader has no idea what the proof is about! – the text reaches the following passage which I quote extensively (slightly expanding Toomer's translation in pp. 46–8; see fig. 14):

So the angle T, remainder, is equal to the angle PΘ, remainder. So when line SΘ meets line AΘ it is reflected to point D, forming equal angles, PQ and T, between itself and the tangent AΘ. [End of proof, though the reader has no reason to suspect this.[20]] "Hence it has been shown that if one draws from any point on KBM a line tangent to the section, and draws the line connecting the point of tangency with point D, e.g. line ΘD, and draws line SΘ parallel to AZ, then in that case line SΘ is reflected to point D, i.e. the line passing through point Θ is reflected at equal angles from the tangent to the section. And all parallel lines from

---

[20] For whatever its worth, the diagram – the marker of closure in early mathematical manuscripts, as it is invariably situated at the end of the text to which it refers – is here positioned not following this end of the proof, but later on, following the discussion of the optical and practical consequences (Toomer 1976: 120; we have here a positioning of the diagram in the form of a blank space, while the diagrams themselves are missing from this manuscript, a state of affairs not uncommon with medieval manuscripts. At some stage of the transmission, the scribe responsible for putting in diagrams happened to be on holiday).

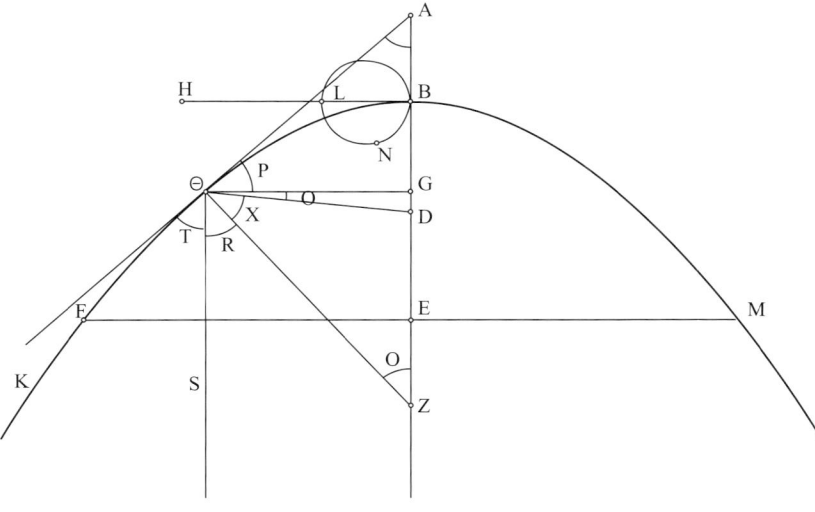

Figure 14

all points on KBM have the same property, so, since they make equal angles with the tangent, they go to point D. [Here ends the general geometrical exposition of the import of the proof – a tantalizing exposition as I shall return to explain below.] Hence, if AZ is kept stationary, and KBM revolved (about it) until it returns to its original position, and a concave surface of brass is constructed on the surface described by KBM, and placed facing the sun, so that the sun's rays meet the concave surface, they will be reflected to point D, since they are parallel to each other.[21]

The text now moves on to offer various variations on the construction of the paraboloid, with resulting consequences for the reflecting rays. I concentrate just on the simplest case discussed right now. The most crucial feature of the construction is that point D – about which angles T, PΘ are equal – is independent of the choice of point Θ. This is what makes all parallel lines such as ΘS reflect towards the same, single point D. However, since the definition of point D is never described in general terms, the reader is to pick up this vital information for himself. Otherwise it could well be that each point Θ defines its own point D with no singularity emerging and no burning. Diocles made the choice to delay his general exposition and

---

[21] Diocles effectively assumes – as did Eratosthenes in his calculation of the size of the earth – an infinitely distant sun. The astronomical discussions in the introduction contribute to make this assumption more plausible. (There, Diocles describes his assumption as treating every point on the surface of the earth as if it were its center.)

to keep to the terms of the particular diagram, for which he pays a heavy price in terms of clarity of exposition. What he gains however is a seamless transition from mathematical proof to mechanical construction. Because the object is always at the particular level of a diagrammatically labeled parabola, he can directly operate on this diagrammatic object as if it were a piece of metal. This is true not only in terms of the discursive transition from the geometrical study to the mechanical consequence. More than this: I would argue that the obscure geometrical demonstration (of whose goal the reader is kept throughout in the dark), turning into a set of mechanical directions, enacts on the page the wonder of machine-making that Diocles aims to simulate. After all there likely never was any Dioclean burning mirror made in brass in the real world – certainly there is none for the reader of this text. The only experience of the burning mirror available to Diocles' readers is that of reading about it. And so let us imagine the experience Diocles is trying to evoke: that of tinkering and toying with a piece of brass, turning and smoothing it until, lo and behold, the sacrificial flesh burns.[22] Diocles cannot tinker and toy with brass, he has only words to tinker with – and this is precisely what he does, then, proceeding with the material diagram, turning and smoothing it, so to speak, in his geometrical reasoning until, lo and behold, it gives rise to a burning mirror.[23]

The next set of proofs[24] shows how a burning mirror is constructed with a spherical surface, at first considering an entire surface and then a sector of a sphere whose angle is one-third a sphere (which for practical terms, Diocles shows, is all one requires). These discussions follow the same structure: a particular geometrical argument, introduced without any general enunciation or particular setting out, seamlessly changes to a mechanical construction.

[22] A passage immediately preceding the mathematical proposition mentions sacrificial flesh as the object to be burned. Toomer doubts its authenticity, especially since it mentions glass – not so common in Diocles' time – and glass-burning as opposed to mirror-burning. To my mind, the very centrality of burned sacrifice in this passage suggests a pagan, and so an early origin – but this is admittedly a weak argument.
[23] We are reminded, then, of the very role of surprise – indeed, wonder – in ancient mechanics. Diocles' mirrors are not at all far off from Ctesibius' and Philo's pneumatic machines (one may, barely, consult Prager 1974 to get a sense of the range of objects produced or contemplated by this third-century author: a submerged, burning torch (chapter 55), whistling water-devices (chapter 60): the operation relies throughout on contrast and surprise). Tybjerg 2003 points to a connection, in the later and possibly more sophisticated author Hero, between mechanical surprise and philosophical wonder. Without wishing to play down this context, I wish to stress the context of Hellenistic mechanics not with Aristotelian epistemology but with Hellenistic poetics, where "wonder" and "surprise" gain a different meaning.
[24] Toomer provides the text with proposition numbers but, as he himself makes clear, those are modern divisions of the text. It is of course crucial to Diocles' discursive goal that the separate proofs are not signposted in any clear way.

The spherical surface is inferior to that of a paraboloid, in that the singularity of reflection is located on a line, not at a point. Still, the structure of the treatise so far was that of presenting us with two methods of constructing a burning mirror. Whereupon Diocles makes the following statement – for the first time, a general statement of a geometrical task (Toomer 1976: 62):

How do we shape the curvature of the burning mirror when we want the point at which the burning occurs to be at a given distance from the center of the surface of the mirror? We draw with a ruler on a given board a line equal to the distance we want: that is the line AB... [and the text now continues in this particular, mechanical detail, without returning to explain what the particular goal is].

Having seen Diocles' game of hide-and-seek above, I cannot believe this general statement of the task is *accidentally* ambiguous. At this stage the reader would not know whether Diocles is looking for the construction of a paraboloid or of a spherical surface. The reference to a "point where the burning occurs" suggests the paraboloid; the reference to the "center of the surface of the mirror" suggests the spherical surface (the notion of the center of a parabolic segment – by which Diocles means the vertex – is not at all entrenched for Diocles' audience). Now it is true that the problem is only meaningful for the case of the paraboloid, but this is a sophisticated geometrical observation, not present at the surface of Diocles' writing. The reader, once again, even when provided with a generally stated task, is left to find out the sense of the argument only from its consequences that end up with the construction of a certain curve – but which? Having constructed it, Diocles then moves on to another geometrical argument, this time without any general enunciation, which, we may realize (if we are very keen geometrical readers) ends up proving that the curve constructed just now happens to be a parabola. Whereupon the treatise abruptly ends.

The overall structure of the treatise is, we now see, not illogical. A study showing the advantages of the paraboloid for the construction of a burning mirror begins by showing how the paraboloid achieves this goal, followed by an implicit comparison to the spherical surface, and then by a solution of the problem of constructing the desired paraboloid under given conditions. All of this makes structural sense, only that this is the *hidden* structure of the treatise. Its surface structure is of a series of plunges into unannounced proofs out of which emerge, miraculously, burning mirrors, surfaces, and parabolas.

To repeat the contrast between the styles of Archimedes and of Diocles: whereas Archimedes typically reaches, in his treatises, a moment of clarity, following which the propositions make continuous, coherent sense, Diocles begins with a sense of coherence, making the introduction very explicit concerning the goals of the treatise. Following that, however, he fashions each proposition as a hide-and-seek game where overall sense is difficult to discern.

Perhaps we should not draw too many conclusions from the narrative structure of the extant Diocles, mediated as it is by Arabic translation (though the treatise is made tantalizingly opaque through marked structural properties, not through some accidental omissions: it is not as if some faulty transmission has introduced noise to an otherwise clear signal). And yet this principle – of a clear introduction followed by a more opaque sequence of propositions – is not at all rare. We may consider for instance the third book of Apollonius' *Conics*. Apollonius' introductory words (in the general introduction to the book as a whole, i.e. right at the beginning of book I) are brief but explicit:

The third book contains many theorems that stretch belief – useful both for the solution of solid loci as well as for the <finding of> limits of possibility <on problems>, of which most – and the most beautiful – are new; more than that, as we conceived them we understood that the three- and four-line locus was not solved by Euclid, but merely a certain part of it – and that, too, only in uncertain terms.[25]

The thrust of book III is therefore clear. It contains new, surprising results on conic sections, whose outcome is to facilitate the solution of solid problems, and in particular leading to a better solution of the problem of three- and four-line locus, i.e. the rather complex problem where three or four lines are given, and where we are looking for points in space from which lines are drawn to the three or four given lines, by given rules, e.g. so that they are perpendicular to the given lines, so that we construct three or four new lines; for which further conditions are required, e.g. – in the four-line case – that the rectangle contained by two of the lines shall be equal to the rectangle contained by the remaining two.

At this point I am somewhat at a loss as to how best to describe briefly the contents of *Conics* III. It appears that nothing short of full quotation of the sequence of enunciations will give a sense of the book. The results are indeed surprising. Time and again Apollonius shows how lines drawn from conic sections, and figures constructed upon them, happen to be

---

[25] My feeble attempt at preserving an original pun (crucial for Apollonius' put-down of Euclid): that only a τυχόν part was solved, and that, too, not εὐτυχῶς. The text goes on with a brief polemic which is irrelevant for our immediate purposes.

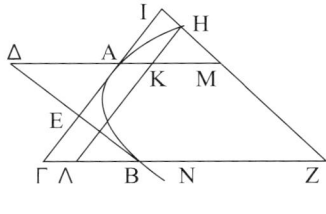

Figure 15

equal or proportional to each other, all for no apparent good reason. Thus for instance III.2 (fig. 15): we take a point, say H, on any conic section (or a circle, for that matter), we draw any two tangents, say AEΓ, BEΔ, where AΔ, BΓ are diameters to the sections; we then have HΛ, IZ drawn through H parallel to the tangents, and extend ΔA to M. Lo and behold: the resulting triangle AIM is equal to the resulting quadrilateral ΓΛHI. Why? The brief demonstration throws the reader back to III.1, and this is typical of the treatise where the magician keeps sending the reader back to the previous acts. Of course the rabbit is a pigeon: after all, we have already seen that the pigeon is inside the hat... The bulk of the treatise is dedicated to such constructions on a particular type of conic section, one that is of great significance for Apollonius (he may have been the first to construct it). This is the very strange, discontinuous object known as "opposite sections," composed of what we may see as two conjugate hyperbolas. (I shall return to discuss the very strangeness of the object, in the following chapter.) Thus for instance III.19 (fig. 16): the two diameters of the sections are AΓ, BΔ; AZ, ZΔ are tangents, and HΘIKΛ, MNΞOΛ are parallel to the tangents. Lo and behold: as AZ to ZΔ, so the rectangle contained by HΛ, ΛI to that contained by MΛ, ΛΞ. Or once again a very general, and striking result, III.37 (fig. 17): on any conic section or circle, we draw two tangents such as AΓ, ΓB and further draw an arbitrary line ΓΔEZ. Lo and behold: as ΓZ to ΓΔ, so ZE to EΔ. Such surprises keep rolling on, with the reader left in complete darkness as to the direction the treatise may take next, as the sequence is largely that of trying out new combinations of lines drawn and new equalities and proportions considered. Finally the last proposition 56 is reached, whose enunciation I now quote, directly from the Green Lion translation – I cannot bring myself to translate this sentence myself (Taliaferro *et al.* 1997: 265):

If two straight lines touching one of the opposite sections meet, and parallels to the tangents are drawn through the points of contact, and straight lines cutting the parallels are drawn from the points of contact to the same point of the other

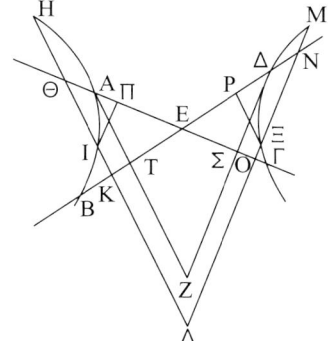

Figure 16

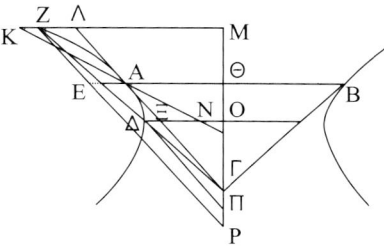

Figure 17

section, then the rectangle contained by the straight lines cut off will have to the square on the straight line joining the points of contact the ratio compounded of the ratio which, of the straight line joining the point of meeting and the midpoint, that part between the midpoint and the other section has in square to that part between the same section and the point of meeting, and of the ratio which the rectangle contained by the tangents has to the fourth part of the square on the straight line joining the points of contact.

The Green Lion edition proceeds to note in the Translator's Appendix (p. 267) that "The three line locus property of conics is easily deduced for the ellipse, hyperbola, parabola and circle from III.54; and for the opposite sections from III.55 and 56." This is an example of the curious way in which modern mathematicians use adverbs such as "easily." Of course Apollonius did not intend his readers to have anything *easy*. If anything, he easily could have inserted a final problem, where the three-line locus problem was stated and solved. This would have produced a more Archimedean-like treatise where the end, at least, would have retrospectively clarified the preceding structure. Apollonius' goal is the opposite: to lead the readers, tantalizingly, through a labyrinth where every turn is surprising, marvelous, and apparently arbitrary, finally reaching not far from the grand prize – the one stated at the introduction – but then ending, without even mentioning that the prize is in sight. All of which answers well the nature of the treatise. It is a study of the counter-intuitive, the surprising. A narrative sequence where surprise is paramount and where the text is left, throughout, at the edge of the intelligible, is called for. Similar structures inform other books in Apollonius' *Conics*: to some extent book II, and in particular book VII (from which comes the puzzle we have seen in the previous subsection, now understood to be part of a wider puzzling strategy). Other books seem to be more systematic and explanatory in character, in particular book V and, in another way, books I, IV, and VI. I shall return to consider such contrasts in the final section of this chapter.

The examples seen in this section all focus on the role of surprise and challenge as narrative strategies underlying a major strand of Hellenistic mathematical writing. Let us return to consider the variety seen here. Euclid's *Elements* XIII possesses a simple structure of gradual assent to a goal via a sequence of narrative surprises. Archimedes' treatises often display a sequence of narrative surprises that has the further, extremely elegant combination of retrospective understanding. Diocles may serve as a more extreme example of a hide-and-seek game where the reader's experience is that of constant transition from obscurity to clarity and back, always at the mercy of the author. Apollonius, finally, is an example of the medley, where the jumble of striking results serves to numb the reader and force an experience of struggling against an opaque, though remarkable, sequence.

In all of the examples considered, the introductory, meta-mathematical presence or absence always serves to determine the narrative progress. Surprises may be created, for instance, by explicitly raising expectations which later on may be qualified and frustrated. The absence of an introduction, on the other hand, forces the reader to make the narrative sequence for himself. Thus the absence of an introduction from *Elements* XIII, as well as its presence in the treatises considered above by Archimedes, Diocles, and Apollonius, all contribute to the narrative possibilities of these works. In general, the mathematical introduction appears to be one of the key narrative inventions of Hellenistic mathematics. Let us now turn to consider it in somewhat greater detail.

## 2.4 INTRODUCING THE AUTHOR

Hypsicles did not fare well with posterity. Few know his name today – although his major extant treatise is a fine piece both as mathematics and as scientific prose. But at an early stage his work was hijacked by the manuscript tradition. Hypsicles' main book was conscripted to serve as "book XIV" of Euclid's *Elements* so that, from an original author, he was turned into an appendix. Especially galling, given the major contrast between Hypsicles' work and that of Euclid: the author of the *Elements* is the most self-effacing of Greek mathematicians, of whom nothing, in truth, is known (more on this below), while Hypsicles tried hard to distinguish himself, as a person, on the space of the page. And yet there is also justice in turning Hypsicles into "book XIV:" his work did refer, intimately, to previous mathematical works, Euclid's book XIII preeminent among them. This interplay of the personal and the intertextual is typical. The rise of the personal voice, in Hellenistic Greek mathematics, is associated with the rise of intertextuality as a feature in mathematical writing.

So let us consider Hypsicles' work in detail. Writing some time in the second century BC, he is a relatively late author in terms of our study. As mentioned above, he is known mainly for book XIV of the *Elements*.[26] The subject matter, as mentioned above, is Euclidean, namely Euclid's book XIII: that is, Hypsicles studies relations between regular solids within the special conditions developed in book XIII. As we have seen already, Euclid inscribes all five regular solids inside a sphere of a given diameter. In this way, the different solids become metrically comparable: one can ask what are the ratios of volume, say, between a dodecahedron and an eicosahedron, when both are inscribed inside the same sphere. The exercise is artificial, in a way: nothing in the construction of the regular solids *demands* the presence of a given sphere. It is as if Euclid has invented a parlor game, "fit solids inside spheres," in which Hypsicles tries his own hand.

Crucially, he was not the first to try. As we move to read the introduction to this book, we see that it reveals the deep role of tradition for Hypsicles. It is worth quoting in detail:

---

[26] His other, minor extant work, the *Anaphoricus*, is not as rich in personal detail, but its narrative structure is worth noticing: starting out in pure arithmetic, the work suddenly plunges into the realities of astronomical observation to bring about a surprising combination of the pure and the applied. (The *Anaphoricus* has a good edition with mathematical commentary: de Falco and Krause with Neugebauer 1966.)

Dear Protarchus: When Basilides of Tyre came to Alexandria and met my father, he spent most of his stay with him, because of their common interest in mathematics. And once, when looking into the tract written by Apollonius about the comparison of the dodecahedron and icosahedron inscribed the same sphere... it seemed to them that Apollonius did not prove those things correctly; accordingly, as I understood from my father, they proceeded to amend and rewrite it. Later, I came across another book published by Apollonius, containing a demonstration of the matter in question... Now the book published by Apollonius is accessible to all; for it has a large circulation in a form which seems to have been the result of later careful elaboration. And I... decided to dedicate to you a treatise in the form of a commentary, because of your proficiency in mathematics... and your intimacy with my father... but it is time to have done with the introduction and to begin my treatise itself.

It is clear that Hypsicles writes with specific people, and books, in mind: his father, Basilides, as well as Apollonius and Protarchus form the axis which interests Hypsicles. It is people and books he mentions in the introduction, and not solids and theorems. No mention is made of what may have been wrong with Apollonius' proofs, according to Basilides and Hypsicles' father; instead, Hypsicles notes the shape of *editions*, such as the later edition of Apollonius he has come across. The work is a "commentary" – not in the literal sense, that it is meant to accompany Apollonius' work, but clearly in that it is dependent upon other works, and is throughout written within a second-order awareness. A typical phrasing of Hypsicles is the very ending of this introduction: "but it is time to have done with the introduction and to begin my treatise itself." In other words, the text becomes explicitly self-reflective. We see that, for Hypsicles, "introduction" and "treatise" are terms of a technical genre, consciously employed.

Let us describe the mathematical contents of the treatise, as this is relevant for understanding the role of the introduction. The field is indeed among the most pleasing in Greek geometry, with many remarkable relationships. If we take regular figures and solids, and inscribe them inside circles and spheres, the properties of the circle give us not only many equal sides, but also many equal angles (the angles in the circle, subtending the equal lines). These can then lead to triangles' congruity or similarity, with resulting equalities and proportions (see Taisbak 1982, chapter 1, which shows how such results inform Euclid's *Elements* XIII and, as a consequence, *Elements* X). The major result is Euclid's *Elements* XIII.10: "If an equilateral pentagon is inscribed in a circle, the square on the side of the pentagon is equal to the squares on the side of the hexagon and on that of the decagon inscribed in the same circle." Such an equality is completely unexpected, and one therefore is led to ask whether similar equalities may not be found with three-dimensional objects; it is perhaps for this reason that the "parlor game" of fitting the regular solids inside the same sphere was developed. In this game, all we are ever interested in is, effectively, a single sphere with all the regular solids inscribed in it; and a single circle, with (potentially) all the regular polygons inscribed in it. It is a feature of this research tradition that reference is made to objects such as "the side of the pentagon," "the side of the dodecahedron," without specifying which pentagon or dodecahedron is intended: the only possible reference is the side of a regular solid of this kind, inscribed in the single given circle or sphere. That is: the intertextual axis is crucial for the very definition of objects. This should be stressed: by working within the instantly recognizable field of literary reference, Hypsicles is also capable of establishing the references of objects which otherwise would be ambiguous, such as "the side of the pentagon."

Throughout the treatise, Hypsicles at least makes the effort to appear to be giving credit to his predecessors (though of course we cannot say how much of what he presents as his own research is indeed original). Two main results are mentioned in this way:

1  Aristaeus proved that the same circle circumscribes both the pentagon of the dodecahedron and the triangle of the icosahedron inscribed in the same sphere. (Aristaeus may have been a contemporary of Euclid, and he is mentioned in the context of the pre-Apollonian theory of conic sections.) With this result, the two aspects of the "game" – solids inside a given sphere, and polygons inside a given circle – become directly related, for the dodecahedron and the icosahedron. This connection is clinched by the following result:

2  Apollonius has shown, in the second edition of his work – which Hypsicles judged to be sound – that the dodecahedron and the icosahedron are to each other as their surfaces (the deep reason for that is that the two surfaces are equidistant from the center of the sphere, so that if both are decomposed, in the Archimedean manner, into pyramids with their vertex at the center, all the pyramids have equal heights, so that their combined volumes are proportional to their "bases" – the surfaces of the solids).

Let us first of all note the mathematical line of thought. Starting from Apollonius' result, we are immediately led to think that, by comparing the surfaces of the dodecahedron and the icosahedron, we will be able to compare those two solids themselves, while Aristaeus' earlier result provides us with an idea for making such a comparison between the surfaces. If the components of the surface – pentagons for dodecahedron, triangles for icosahedron – are circumscribed by the same circle, then all we need to do, in fact, is to compare the pentagon and the triangle inside the same circle, correcting for the different numbers of pentagons and triangles, in the dodecahedron and the icosahedron. This Hypsicles achieves in this treatise.

However he does not achieve this by a simple sequence of theorems. Although the ending of the introduction implies that, having discharged the obligation to introduce the treatise, Hypsicles will now move on to a pure sequence of results, in fact the second-order voice of the last sentence of the introduction continues to inform the following sequence. Hypsicles continually provides the reader with signposts as to the position of the argument. Each argument is presented in the fully fledged impersonal format of Greek deduction (with a general enunciation and a clear setting out of the goal, i.e. unlike Diocles' presentation in *On Burning Mirrors*). And yet, following or introducing most such arguments, a brief passage is inserted of a more discursive nature. Following the first proposition, Hypsicles notes that "It is obvious, from the theorem in the thirteenth book [i.e. of Euclid's *Elements*] that..." introducing a new result (without proof) – notice once again the combination of more discursive prose with the intertextual. And then follows a long passage where the results by Aristaeus and Apollonius are quoted in order (with clear bibliographic references), and then Hypsicles proceeds as follows:

But we too should prove that... [where follows the enunciation of Aristaeus' result], proving as a preliminary that... [where follows another enunciation and proof, and then] With this proved, it is to be proved that [the enunciation of Aristaeus' proof restated, followed by a proof].

We notice several features of the narrative setting. First, Hypsicles deploys little surprise: he announces very clearly which result he is (locally) going to prove, and he even explains in advance that a certain result is introduced as a lemma for that purpose. He also comes clean about a crucial fact: that the result to be proved is a different route to a conclusion previously obtained elsewhere. To some extent, all of this serves to make Hypsicles' text more transparent, less dazzling than some of the texts we have read so far. But this clearly is not Hypsicles' main goal in his explicit use of the second-order voice. His goal is to achieve, simultaneously, his insertion into a tradition of intertextuality – and yet to assert his independence within it. The second order was necessary, so that Hypsicles could alert his audience simultaneously to Aristaeus' work, as well as to Hypsicles' originality.

96    *The telling of mathematics*

Following this remarkable sequence of second-order interventions, Hypsicles briefly reverts to the impersonal mode: Hypsicles' own proof of Aristaeus' result is followed by another result on pentagons, this time presented without any motivation. This is followed by a minor narrative move in the Archimedean fashion: Hypsicles reveals, at the end of this proof, that the consideration of the pentagon actually has surprising consequences for the dodecahedron. He then proceeds, in a minimally second-order intervention: "with this being clear, it is to be proved..." (followed by a fine result concerning solids).

This statement is followed by a proof, whose end gives rise to a very surprising twist: "And it is possible to prove in another way that" [the same result above re-stated] "proving as a preliminary that..." [introducing a new result, this time without explicit enunciation so that it is strongly marked as a mere lemma].

This is very reminiscent of Hypsicles' treatment of Aristaeus' result: he states it, re-proves it himself, with the aid of a lemma, all explicitly signposted. In this case – although of course this might be misleading on Hypsicles' part – it appears as if the result is by Hypsicles himself, so that the text acquires a decidedly second-order nature, with the emphasis put not so much on the contents of results as on how they are obtained. At any rate this twice-repeated doubling – of Aristaeus' result and then of Hypsicles' result, in each case with a further doubling by a lemma – endows the treatise with an intricate, explicitly marked texture. It is not at all a mere sequence of one proof followed by another: instead, it turns and winds its way, repeatedly led by the explicit voice of Hypsicles himself.

Following this turn, Hypsicles several times makes minimal second-order interventions such as: "It is to be proved that...", etc., accumulating a few results whose motivation is not made explicitly clear, until he reaches his final paragraph:

So, with all of these made understood, it is clear that: if a dodecahedron as well as an eicosahedron are inscribed inside the same sphere, the dodecahedron shall have to the eicosahedron a ratio (with a line, whatsoever, divided by an extreme and mean ratio[27]), as, the <line> which is, in square, the whole <line> and the greater segment, to the <line> which is, in square, the whole line and the smaller segment,[28] for since... [followed by a brief argument, without letters, where the various results of the treatise are recalled and brought together to achieve the conclusion].

---

[27] I.e. divided so that the whole is to the greater segment as the greater segment to the smaller one ("the golden section").

[28] Say the whole line is (a+b), the greater segment is a and the smaller is b. Then the ratio is that of $\sqrt{(2a+b)} : \sqrt{(a+2b)}$.

This is a mild Archimedean effect, once again: at the very end, the various results obtained by Hypsicles are brought together to obtain a very counter-intuitive conclusion. But notice how explicit Hypsicles is about this (which is very much unlike Archimedes' understated surprises). He makes sure to remind us that this is obtained "with all of these made understood," that is effectively telling us that he is about to bring together the various conclusions obtained so far. Most important, the nature of the final paragraph is distinct from that of the preceding arguments: it contains no reference to a diagram, merely recalling general statements in their general form. No labeling letters are quoted. Thus the passage, while involved with geometrical reasoning, is also felt to be on a line with the more discursive, second-order passages that pepper Hypsicles' treatise and, with its final position, it leads to an overall sense of closure. The treatise started out in discursive prose, returned to the discursive time and again, and it ends on the same discursive note. And since Hypsicles has started out with such a strong authorial voice, underlining what was personally at stake for him, the return to discursive prose is felt as a triumphant, personal statement. In general: throughout the treatise, the role of the discursive prose was to underline Hypsicles' position in the tradition, so as to introduce the reader to such a tradition and, simultaneously, to mark Hypsicles' own originality. The end result is to localize the text twice: as a product of a literary tradition, and as a product of the author's ingenuity.

In the previous chapter, we noted the tension presented by the various carnivalesque calculations of Hellenistic mathematics: into the austere form of Greek geometrical deduction there erupts an opaque and chaotically textured discourse. A comparable (albeit distinct) tension is seen in such treatises as those of Hypsicles: into the impersonal form of Greek geometrical deduction there erupts a highly personal, culturally bound authorial voice.

Let us consider, as a comparison, the "I say that" of the Greek mathematical proof – where, following the setting out of the particular terms of the proposition, the author states the particular goal as true ("Let . . . and let . . . and let . . . *I say that* line AB is equal to line CD. For since . . ."). We usually think of this formula as a token gesture whose first-person singular is completely eroded by its very formulaic nature. (Indeed, inside Greek Hellenistic technical prose, at least an equally acceptable way of expressing an actual authorial voice would probably be that of the first-person *plural* – the form often used in Hellenistic mathematical introductions). I have argued (in Netz 1999, chapter 6), that the expression serves a highly specialized logical function: it does not merely state the demonstrandum (in which case an impersonal "it is to be proved that . . ." would be appropriate), nor does it already assert the demonstrandum as obtained (in which case a bare statement of the demonstrandum, without any qualifications, would be enough). Instead, it makes the tentative claim that, with the particular terms set out, the demonstrandum is thereby warranted, as the following proof will show. The "I say that" should be seen therefore as an invitation to a demonstration. This special logical role calls for a special formula, to which the "I say that" is indeed appropriate. And indeed, no "I" is felt by the readers of such a formula – nor is any intended.

Thus a text such as Hypsicles' stands in very marked opposition to a Greek mathematical proof, taken in isolation. The intrusion of the personal is very marked indeed. But how marked is it compared to the standard of Greek Hellenistic mathematical writing, considering not only individual proofs but also the introductions to the treatises? This is a much more difficult question, as the nature of the introduction varies. It is very rare to have no introductory material at all; otherwise, introductions vary from the absolutely minimal, impersonal introductory material typical of Euclid's *Elements*, to the highly personal and pervasive introductory material we saw with Hypsicles. A useful division would be into three levels of the personal:

The most impersonal, as suggested above, is that of Euclid's *Elements*, where book 1 famously starts with such phrases as "A point is that which has no part," etc. Even there, however, bear in mind that modern editions are misleading in making such passages even more technical and dispassionate than they are in reality. This is because such passages were neither labeled nor numbered in their original form. Modern (and rarely, ancient) editors have supplied titles such as "Definitions," and then numbered each statement so that "A point is that which has no part" becomes "Euclid's *Elements* book 1, Definition 1." But in their original form, such introductions functioned as discursive passages without titles or internal divisions, to be read as, e.g.: "A point is that which has no part, and a line is breathless length, and points are limits of a line; a straight line is – whichever <line> lies evenly with the points upon it; while a plane is <that> which has breadth and length alone, and lines are limits of a plane . . . " Euclid starts out with such a piece of Greek prose (which reads rather like a sequence of philosophical aphorisms), following which he plunges directly into the sequence of geometrical demonstrations, within which no more shall we see any of the discursive. This then is the most impersonal form of the Greek mathematical introduction.

At the other extreme stand works such as Hypsicles', where the introductory material is highly personalized, putting forward a figure of the author and making claims both for his intertextual position and for his originality. Such material is then sustained throughout the treatise. Hypsicles is by no means the only author of this kind, nor is his example the one to foreground the personal most radically (more on the truly radical examples below). But he is definitely among the more personal authors. His manner of writing closely resembles that already seen above, with Diocles' *On Burning Mirrors* (where, once again, a long second-order introduction continues to inform the rest of the treatise). Or consider the brief report by Eutocius, in his summary of Nicomedes' solution to the problem of finding two mean proportionals: "from the book the man appears to have prided himself immensely, while making great fun of the solutions of Eratosthenes, as impractical and at the same time devoid of geometrical skill" – which is suggestive of a treatise similar in polemical and personal character to that of Hypsicles. Another brief treatise by Diocles, on another problem, that of the cutting of the sphere (preserved as the second part of *On Burning Mirrors*) had a similar character. While small perhaps as a sample, these three authors – Diocles, Hypsicles, and Nicomedes – are also the *only* authors of the second century BC of whose style of writing anything can be said.

Third, most common in Greek Hellenistic writing is a role of the introduction intermediate between, let us say, Euclid and Hypsicles. In this common form, the introduction (as in Hypsicles) serves to set the intertextual and personal coordinates for the work, sustaining a marked authorial voice. This authorial voice also spills over, to a certain extent, into the later passages of the treatise. However, it usually does not become as dominant later on as it does in Hypsicles' treatise, so that there is, on the whole, a division between a highly personal introduction and a usually impersonal sequence of proofs.

This final form is not only the most common one: it is also the one seen in most works of both Archimedes and Apollonius. Apollonius' extant introduction to book I of the *Conics* is striking in its markedly localized nature (slightly correcting the Green Lion translation):

Apollonius to Eudemus, greetings. If you are restored in body, and other things go with you to your mind, well and good; and we too fare pretty well. At the time I was with you in Pergamon, I observed you were quite eager to be kept informed of the work I was doing in conics. And so I have sent you this first book revised, and we shall dispatch the others when we are satisfied with them. For I don't believe you have forgotten hearing from me how I worked out the plan for these conics at the request of Naucratis, the geometer, at the time he was with us studying in Alexandria, and how on arranging them in eight books we immediately communicated them in great haste because of his near departure, not revising them but putting down whatever came to us with the intention of a final going over. And so finding now the occasion of correcting them, one book after another, we send them out. And since it happened that some others among those frequenting us got acquainted with the first and second book before the revision, don't be surprised if you come upon them in a different form.

This marks Apollonius the author in several ways: as the acquaintance, in specified locations, of Eudemus and Naucratis (and, dismissively, of some "others"); as the author of a work with a specified bibliographic history; as a proud author, too, who wishes to make sure his works are known in their most final form. The introduction goes on to become somewhat less personal, somewhat more technical. Apollonius goes through the books and explains their goals (we have seen this above for book III), often however being critical of his predecessors, which once again serves to locate him within the tradition. This highly personalized introduction then changes into a more impersonal one, though one which is still characterized by discursive prose. Apollonius introduces certain definitions, comparable to those of Euclid (always bearing in mind that those definitions were certainly not numbered, and likely not titled in the original: i.e. they formed a more discursive passage). Then starts the sequence of proofs. But it is important to notice that the text is further punctuated by the second order. Another sequence of definitions is introduced following proposition 16, implicitly signaling a narrative transition in the treatise: following the setting up of the basic properties of conic sections, the text switches to more specialized studies of the intersections of conic sections with lines, and of certain basic equalities and proportions. Following a long sequence of such results, the text then moves into a long discursive passage following proposition 51, where a central result is summed up in general, non-diagrammatic terms (this is reminiscent of Hypsicles' conclusion of his treatise). This indeed forms another implicit transition, this time to a sequence of problems where the conic sections are constructed, echoing the basic theorems at the beginning of the treatise. A minimal second-order intervention right at the end of the final proposition 60 ("let these sections be called 'conjugate'") reverts right back to the mode of definitory discursive prose, framing the entire book. This then is an understated but clear example of the model of a text where the authorial voice is strongly introduced at the very beginning and is then allowed to appear, in a more subdued form, throughout the treatise.

Archimedes' treatises typically have a somewhat stronger authorial presence, where the purely introductory and the strictly impersonal are more difficult to tell apart. We may see this, once again, at the first book on

*Sphere and Cylinder*. We have already considered this treatise as a canonical example of Archimedean narrative style and, no less, it forms a canonical example of the Archimedean authorial presence. As mentioned above, at first Archimedes establishes the position of the work in a dedicatory letter to Dositheus. The letter is somewhat impersonal, with the exception of a reference to Conon, Archimedes' dead colleague: "They should have come out while Conon was still alive. For we suppose that he was probably the one most able to understand them and to pass the appropriate judgment."

The effect however is complicated: by bringing up the warmth of Archimedes' relationship towards Conon, Archimedes further marks the cooler tone adopted towards Dositheus himself. (I mention this as, perhaps, the distance established between Archimedes and his dedicatee may prepare the ground for that ironic distance which Archimedes cultivates throughout.) The letter of introduction then turns into a series of mathematical assumptions required by Archimedes (Heiberg, misleadingly, arranges those as numbered "definitions" and "postulates," but the original text has the assumptions in discursive form, inseparable from the preceding dedicatory prose). Following the assumptions, Archimedes notes that "Assuming these it is manifest that if a polygon is inscribed inside a circle, the perimeter of the inscribed polygon is smaller than the circumference of the circle." This claim is followed by no more than a brief sentence of explanation, so that the text still reads as normal discursive prose. The next piece of text (titled by Heiberg "proposition 1") makes the analogous claim – that the circle is smaller than the polygon circumscribed around it – but this time the claim is followed by a more fully fledged proof, with diagram and letters referring to it. Still, the proof is very syncopated, as the letters of the diagram are not explicitly introduced in a setting out. Only the following proposition – a problem in geometrical proportion theory (titled by Heiberg "proposition 2") – is presented in the full format of a proof. All in all, we see a very gradual transition from the normal Greek prose of the dedicatory letter, through the more formal prose of the mathematical assumptions, then through the minimal argument of the claim on inscribed polygons, then through the syncopated proof of the claim on circumscribed polygons, and finally the complete proof of the problem in proposition 2. The text is still marked by an opposition between normal, first-person prose and mathematical, impersonal prose, but the gradual progress from the first to the second means also that there is no moment where the subjective presence of the author all of a sudden disappears: there is the ghost of the author remaining even where the text is in the format of proof with lettered diagram.

The work presents an entire series of such sliding progressions, usually in the opposite direction: from the purely first-order language of geometrical proof towards a more second-order, authorial utterance. A sequence of proofs from propositions 3 to 6, dealing with variations on a similar theme, gradually gets abbreviated until finally the author simply remarks at the end of proposition 6 "and similarly also in the case of the sector;" similarly, a sequence of proofs from propositions 7 to 12 leads to a remarkably long passage where, without any diagrams, the author asserts the consequences of the preceding propositions. (This is very similar to the sequence following proposition 51 in Apollonius' *Conics* I.) Archimedes keeps punctuating the text with such authorial interventions: thus, following proposition 16 comes a brief interlude where elementary results are recalled. (This may or may not – depending on how we choose to emend the text – end up with a meta-mathematical note where Archimedes points out that those results were obtained by previous authors, or by Euclid, implicitly setting himself apart as obtaining even stronger results: this is already suggestive of Hypsicles' authorial use of intertextuality.[29]) Later on, in the grand thought-experiment of proposition 23 (where the sphere with a figure inscribed in it is reconceived as the result of a circle rotating with a polygon inscribed in it), Archimedes does not make any explicit second-order comments, but he does use a new form of presentation, *without* any general statements, serving to mark the proposition as possessing a special authorial "voice" – a special voice which is then repeated in a number of propositions punctuating the remainder of the treatise.

I would like to remind the readers at this point of how a Greek mathematical text is often imagined: as a bipartite text where the first part is an impersonal, numbered list of "axioms" and "definitions," and the second part is an impersonal, numbered list of "proofs." In this image no place is allowed for modulation of style within the two parts, and no place is left, in either, to the author.[30] This image is based on a false reading of Euclid's

---

[29] The text now read from Archimedes' Palimpsest (29r col.1 ll. 3–5) is ταῦτα δὲ πρότερον πάντα ὑπὸ Εὐκλείδου ἀπεδείχθη, which is perhaps to be preferred to Codex A's reading (printed by Heiberg), ταῦτα δὲ πάντα ὑπὸ τῶν πρότερον ἀπεδείχθη.

[30] This is of course no more than a caricature – fitting best, perhaps, what *I* came to believe as an undergraduate! It is an artifact of popular cultural conceptions and I cannot resist quoting *Nature Magazine*, commenting in 2005 upon a recent Mykonos conference on mathematics and narrative (http://www.nature.com/news/2005/050801/full/436622a.html): "The venue was apt, given that ancient Greece was where the gulf between mathematics and story-telling first opened up. 'Plato approved of mathematics, but despised poetry,' says Rebecca Goldstein, a philosopher and novelist based in Hartford, Connecticut, who has used mathematicians as characters in several novels. Other participants blamed Euclid for introducing the impersonal, logical style that has characterized much mathematical writing ever since."

*Elements* 1, but while imprecise, it does fit that book better than it does any other extant Greek work. This image is also a totally false depiction of a work such as Archimedes' *Sphere and Cylinder*. Archimedes seems to strive to blur the border dividing his own personal voice from that of impersonal geometry; he carefully introduces modulations of authorial voice into the structure of the treatise.

The same type of modulation may be seen in nearly all of Archimedes' treatises. I briefly mention two examples. First, *Planes in Equilibrium*: the work starts *in medias res* (in this untypical case, there is no letter of dedication). The text first of all asserts a number of claims that are "requested" (what we would technically call "postulated") by the author. As usual, Heiberg, misleadingly, numbers these as so-called "postulates," but the original text, once again as usual, had the structure of continuous, discursive prose. This prose then does not move directly into a sequence of proofs based on the lettered diagram. Just as with the result on the inscribed polygon in *Sphere and Cylinder*, so here: Archimedes moves on to say that "with those things assumed" certain results follow. In this case, Archimedes runs through a sequence of two micro-propositions, both times making an assertion and completing it with a very brief argument (modern editions misleadingly refer to those two claims as "propositions 1 and 2"). The following claim (misleadingly labeled by modern editors "proposition 3") has a somewhat fuller argument, aided by a lettered diagram. Still, this argument is very brief and it leads on to another very brief claim of the converse, which is said to be "clear" based on the argument of proposition 3, no extra argument added. It is only starting at "proposition 4" that the text assumes the full contours of proofs based on the lettered diagram. This then is, once again, a gradual progression from the meta-mathematical to the geometrical, though this time much less personal in character. My second example, the *Method*, is among the most personal works in the Archimedean corpus. Archimedes dedicates the work to Eratosthenes, a much more important figure than Dositheus, and correspondingly the stakes at the introduction are higher: Archimedes makes claims for the value not only of the results obtained, but for the method of obtaining them, a method which is implicitly presented as his own personal invention. This immediately shifts the focus of the reading from the impersonal, geometrical result, to the personal route leading to the discovery of that result. As usual, the prose letter moves on to a sequence of mathematical assumptions. But there is something special taking place: Archimedes notes in advance which result he is going to prove as the first proposition, and why – this result on the parabolic segment was the first to be obtained by the *Method*. In other words, as the reader parses the text of *Method* proposition 1, he simultaneously gets a piece of geometry *and* of Archimedean biography. It is appropriate therefore that Archimedes does not let the proposition stand alone, but appends to it a quick authorial comment: the result is indeed obtained by the new method, but something is lacking so that another proof is called for (which Archimedes has of course obtained separately, as he tells us). Following that, Archimedes moves on to another result, this time on spheres, and once again he appends a quick comment: having found this result via the method, the thought occurred to him that another result on spheres might be correct, a thought verified in the first book on *Sphere and Cylinder* itself. The sequence of text from the introduction through the first two propositions established the text as a kind of retrospective exhibition set up by Archimedes, where he hangs on the wall his past results together with brief autobiographical comments. It is typical of Archimedes' authorial style – based on the principle of gradation – that, following this more personal beginning, the treatise later on settles into an impersonal sequence of proofs without comments. However, the so-called "proposition 11" is a non-diagrammatic text where Archimedes offers a brief argument based on previous results (compare once again the passage following proposition 51 in Apollonius' *Conics* 1). I note also that we have lost a major moment of transition in the treatise: while the first so-called propositions "1–13" are all based on a certain application of mechanics, this is no longer true from proposition 14 onwards. We have lost the ending of "proposition 13," so we cannot tell if Archimedes originally had some kind of modulation of voice so as to underline this transition; I would be surprised if he did not, but of course nothing can be based on such conjectures.

Leaving the speculative aside, then, we see an important result: Archimedes' mathematical writings were skillfully modulated between the personal and the impersonal.

Throughout this section we have seen the close interrelation between the authorial voice, and the introductory form. By employing the form of an introduction addressed to a reader, the author presents us immediately with two persons – the addressee as well as the author, evidenced even in the formula "X to Y, greetings." (It is the author, indeed, who comes first.) This relation has often been noted in recent scholarship of both the didactic epic as well as the epistle. Konstan sums up the situation well for the didactic form: "It appears that four personae . . . inhabit the space of didactic poetry: the poet-teacher; the authority, standing behind the teacher, who guarantees the value of the precepts; the personal addressee;

and the wider audience that peers over the shoulder of the addressee."[31] So Stirewalt for the epistle, or what he calls the "letter-essay:" "The letter-setting behind the letter-essay is triangular, I-thou-they."[32] Stirewalt points out certain functions for the epistolary form in scientific teaching, in particular, a derivative function. Thus, the author often explicitly maintains that the letter functions as some kind of explanation of another, more difficult work (as is most obvious in the case of Epicurus).[33] This is only rarely the case with Greek mathematical introductions whose function, I argue, is precisely to construct the triangular space of I-thou-they, not so much for the sake of the "thou" as for the sake of the "I." Whence the Hellenistic mathematical letter of introduction? In it, I argue, the Hellenistic mathematical authors capitalize on the reality of geographical dispersion – that makes communication written by necessity – so as to adopt the literary technique of the epistle in such a way as to construct the personal identity of the author.

Before concluding this section, I wish to make two comments. First, note that the recent examples are typical to Archimedes – but I have not yet introduced the text where the authorial presence is most marked. This is his *Sand-Reckoner* – that carnival of calculation where Archimedes counts the grains of sand to fill the cosmos. In this treatise, background and foreground are inverted. Whereas the norm for a Greek mathematical text is that of a text made mostly of impersonal mathematical results and proofs, punctuated (as argued in this section) by the introduction of a personal voice, the *Sand-Reckoner* is ruled throughout by Archimedes speaking in his own voice, occasionally breaking his speech so as to give room for a mathematical proof. It is perhaps typical that this work is fully localized – when Archimedes, at the beginning of the treatise, refers to those

---

[31] Konstan 1994: 12; one should consult Schiesaro *et al.* 1994 as a whole, for a survey of the role of the addressee in didactic epic.

[32] Stirewalt 1991: 169. The difference between Konstan and Stirewalt, between didactic epic and letter-essay, is that in the former, but not in the latter, the Muses are built in into the genre so that, even in their absence, some kind of authority external to the author is expected – largely based on the Hesiodic model. In other words, one result of writing one's teaching in prose is to signal the author's epistemic autonomy.

[33] Stirewalt 1991: 163–6 calls this function "supplementary or substitutive." It is evident, in a sense, in the dedication to Apollonius' *Conics* (which does mention a previous edition) as well as in, say, Archimedes' writings, which mention a previous sending-out of a statement that is only now proved. This, however, blends into the much wider category of "bibliographic specification" – within the introduction, the author explains the bibliographic relation of his work to previous treatises, by himself or by others. This function is not truly "supplementary or substitutive;" the autonomy of the dedicated work is emphasized, instead (one no longer needs any access to Apollonius' previous edition of the *Conics* – which is in fact lost – and one of course has no more interest in Archimedes' previous promises once they are fulfilled).

who believe the amount of sand to exceed number, and claims that they are wrong, he explains that he means "not only that sand which is around Syracuse and the rest of Sicily . . ." – a mathematically gratuitous statement whose only purpose is to position the treatise in Syracuse (which, of course, is highly relevant in the context of a treatise dedicated to the monarch of that city . . . ). I can think of only one other extant Greek mathematical work similar in character, namely Eratosthenes' treatise on duplicating the cube, preserved inside Eutocius' catalogue of solutions to the problem of finding two mean proportionals (in his commentary to Archimedes' second book on *Sphere and Cylinder*). There, as we have seen above (p. 57) Eratosthenes starts with a mythical story on a royal tomb that needed to be doubled. He then moves on to a quasi-historical survey of the geometrical problem, he offers some heavily commented proofs and then rounds up his small treatise with a poem celebrating his achievement. Once again, then: the personal framing is foregrounded, the mathematical contents are backgrounded. These two treatises – the *Sand-Reckoner* as well as Eratosthenes' treatise on duplicating the cube – are both much more personal in character even than works such as Hypsicles' or Diocles' mentioned above. Why is that? These two works are indeed "supplementary," to borrow Stirewalt's term: Archimedes refers explicitly to a previous work, "To (Against?) Zeuxippus" (Heiberg II.216.18–19); Eratosthenes' treatise is an *ekphrasis* of a dedication and stands as a supplement to it. Here, mathematical treatises come closest to resembling the established literary format of the prose epistle. More than this: these two works are also unique in the extant corpus in the nature of their dedicatee. Archimedes dedicates the *Sand-Reckoner* to King Gelon; Eratosthenes dedicates his small treatise to King Ptolemy. We have already seen above the difference that a dedicatee can make: the difference between dedicating a work to, say, Dositheus or to Eratosthenes. The act of dedication defines the nature of the prose: the stronger the personal presence of the dedicatee, the stronger the personal presence of the author has to be. Of course, there is the question of the dedicatee's interests. (Not a professional mathematician, the king would wish to hear more of the author himself.) And yet, the correlation between the nature of the dedicatee and the nature of the prose is striking: once again, it reminds us that the introduction is not detached from the rest of the treatise. The first words that establish the author and his correspondents establish a climate for the treatise as a whole.

My second comment has to do with an emerging chronological pattern. Let us put aside the *Sand-Reckoner* as well as Eratosthenes' small treatise (which we should do, as explained above – those are indeed exceptional works). We find then that, roughly speaking, the later we go in time, the more personal treatises become. Euclid's *Elements* – probably from the very edge of the Hellenistic period – is hardly personal at all (and the same is true, significantly, for the works of Autolycus, produced before the foundation of Alexandria, as well as for the surviving treatise of Aristarchus from the beginning of the third century). Subtle modulations of the personal and the impersonal are typical of the works of Archimedes and his somewhat younger contemporary, Apollonius. In the following generation, that of Hypsicles and Diocles, a more overtly personal style becomes standard. Of course, our sample is corrupt, and it is likely that the actual development of the Hellenistic mathematical introduction was more complicated. But let us assume for a moment that the impression we have is indeed broadly correct and that, over time, treatises did become more personal. This may be taken in two ways. One possible interpretation would be that the characteristics of the Hellenistic style as discussed here evolve and became more marked over time. Another possible interpretation – which I find more likely – is that we see here an example of a widespread phenomenon, what may be called *the inflation of style*. The general structure is very familiar: what was at first striking and original becomes banal and automated so that a new, even more radical departure is required merely in order to capture the original sense of surprise. Thus a style, during its period of growth, tends to become more pronounced – until it is finally discarded. I suspect that a similar phenomenon took place in Greek mathematical writing from the early third century to the late second century BC: the style, based on the modulation of the personal and the impersonal, as well as on playful surprises, grew gradually more pronounced while seeking throughout the same effect of delightful shock.

We bring into consideration, finally, the chronological development. Whatever our view of the growth of the Hellenistic mathematical style during the Alexandrian period itself, we need to account somehow for the later development of mathematical style. This, indeed, is necessary for the very reconstruction of the Hellenistic style itself.

## 2.5 CODA: TRIUMPH OF THE IMPERSONAL

Of course, not all Greek mathematical writing in the Hellenistic world shared the features discussed so far in this book. Some works were more personal, some were less; some were more ludic, some were less. To argue that ludic proof was important in Hellenistic mathematics is to make a statement about relative quantitative and qualitative importance, not about the absolute impossibility of non-ludic writing.

Let us try to position the ludic in the space of stylistic options. To offer a rough classification, we may find three types of Greek mathematical treatises, which I will call here (i) ludic, (ii) survey, (iii) pedagogic.

The ludic is a treatise of the ideal type discussed above: a work based on obtaining results in surprising, intricate ways, where the author brings out his own voice in rich, modulated ways, and where the textual surface is often made deliberately opaque by, say, long passages of calculation. The fundamental narrative structure usually leads to some striking results towards the end of the treatise, and the ludic structure is predicated upon the readers' expectations regarding the route leading to the conclusion – expectations that are deliberately sustained so as to be subverted later. (Such works also exhibit the compositional principle of *variatio*, and may deal with complex, hybrid objects, for which see the following chapter.) In different ways, this description fits well all of Archimedes' extant works, as well as a number of works by other authors (which are often known only by testimony, or else survive through indirect and corrupt routes of transmission – for which see more below). In particular, this description seems to fit well all the minor extant works from the Hellenistic era: from Aristarchus' *Sizes and Distances of the Sun and the Moon* through Eratosthenes' mini-treatise on the *Duplication of the Cube*, all the way down to Diocles' *On Burning Mirrors* and Hypsicles' "Book xiv." It also fits well a few of the books in Apollonius' *Conics*, in particular the more difficult books iii and vii. *Elements* xiii is the only book by Euclid to fit this description at all well.

The survey is a work where a certain field is exhaustively treated. Here a narrative structure is more difficult to make out and very often there may be a rather weak internal deductive ordering, as well. It is less clear that such works are even intended for continuous reading. A typical early example of such a treatise is Euclid's *Elements* x, where a survey is made of some properties of irrationals. Euclid's *Data* offers another very clear case of a survey, where various elementary propositions are collected. All share the same theme: a geometrical object becomes given once another one is; the internal structuring of the book is otherwise fairly weak (and it is also fair to say that it makes for rather boring reading, however mathematically intriguing Taisbak 2003 has made it!). Several other works, many of them known through Pappus' book vii (the "Domain of analysis") or, occasionally, through Arabic translation, must have had a similar character. Thus, for instance, Apollonius' *Cutting off of a Ratio* – which Pappus knew

## Coda: triumph of the impersonal

in the format of two books with 181 propositions (!)[34] – is all dedicated to various cases arising from a single problem in geometrical proportion theory. Exhaustive treatment is the main goal in such a work, and any interesting narrative structure is therefore ruled out. The author has given up on making significant selections, except those having to do with order – but, with little internal deductive structure, the question of order recedes in significance as well. Besides the works mentioned above, it should be noted that some of the books in the *Conics* itself verge on the "survey," especially the more simple books IV and VI.

Finally, some Hellenistic mathematical works had a more pedagogical character: here the narrative structure is paramount, however it is no longer based on surprise but, to the contrary, it is based on gradual, aided discovery on the part of the reader. Opacity is avoided as far as possible, and the authorial presence is muted throughout. Perhaps the only work truly to fit such a description is (large parts of) Euclid's *Elements* itself – which I am not sure we should consider a Hellenistic work (more below) – but there are traces of the pedagogic elsewhere: in some other elementary works, such as Theodosius' *Spherics*; or, to a certain extent, in book I of Apollonius' *Conics*.

One may further note the following. In stylistic terms, the ludic and the pedagogic are at opposite poles, the survey occupying a mid-position: for the survey treatise creates a kind of opaque texture, with a reading experience not unlike that of some ludic treatises. Indeed, going through the 181 permutations of a single geometrical problem – as Apollonius does in the *Cutting off of a Ratio* – is to engage in a combinatoric game not completely unlike those discussed in the preceding chapter. As it were, the exhaustive survey borders on the carnival of calculation. (At the same time, of course, in its attempt to provide a complete picture of a certain mathematical field, the survey also verges on the pedagogic.) The three genres form a certain continuum.

What was the quantitative and qualitative division between those works in the Hellenistic world? Of course we know too little to say much at the level of individual *treatises*, but there is one crucial quantitative observation to make at the level of *authors*. This is that there is only one Hellenistic author in whose writings the ludic appears to have been marginal – Euclid himself. With the exception of the somewhat ludic *Elements* XIII, Euclid's works seem to have the character of either survey or pedagogy. Otherwise all known authors seem to have significantly engaged in some forms of the

---

[34] Pappus II 640.23–4.

ludic. Even Apollonius – who may appear to be a relatively staid author – wrote, after all, the treatise calculating the value of hexameter lines... Besides, the *Conics* itself often displays narrative structures of surprise, modulation of authorial voice, and deliberate opacity. Apollonius certainly has written several works whose character was that of a survey, and there is a trace of the pedagogic in the first book of the *Conics*, but otherwise his books fit well the characteristics described so far in this book. Other authors, from the early Aristarchus to the late Hypsicles, all seem to have produced, mostly, treatises whose character fits well the analyses offered so far here.

To sharpen this, I venture the following speculation. It is true that we know nothing of substance on Euclid's chronology.[35] Still, there is no solid reason to jettison the traditional dating, making Euclid active right at the very beginning of the Hellenistic era, say just at the turn of the fourth century BC. If this is indeed assumed then we reach the striking conclusion: *all* Hellenistic authors active later than about 300 BC had an interest in the writing of ludic treatises; none appears to have had much interest in the pedagogic form (as opposed to the form of survey).

Furthermore, the qualitative significance of the above is obvious: the author whom we can most firmly associate with the ludic form was Archimedes, clearly the towering figure of Hellenistic mathematics.

What is the legacy of such genres? It is difficult to speak in terms of historical continuity. Even through the second century BC our evidence peters out. Hypsicles, active in the middle of the century, may be the last Hellenistic mathematical author of whom we have direct evidence. Hipparchus, the author of at least one remarkable ludic text – his treatise in combinatorics – was active at about the same time, but, for this author, all we have extant is a commentary to Aratus. In itself an interesting example of the breaking of genre in Hellenistic writing (more below), this is already one step removed from the core of mathematical writing. Later than that, even less is known. I mentioned Posidonius, active at the end of the century, in the context of the carnival of calculation – he did measure the size of the earth! – but nothing is extant. And from then on, less is known, probably because less was accomplished. The crisis of direct Roman military intervention, from the third Macedonian War down to the Mithridatic wars, probably formed a physical and moral catastrophe; tradition was broken.[36] At least, little is known to have been written on mathematical themes until the period of the Empire, by authors such as

---

[35] See ch. 1 n.45 above.  [36] See Glucker 1978: 373–80.

Geminus, or Hero of Alexandria – already active in the first century AD. With these authors, a new explicitness emerges: the voice of the author is heard so clearly as to exclude significant modulation, and he speaks with an obvious pedagogic tone. Though, once again we do not really know enough of this entire period of Greek culture. The picture becomes clear only as we move to Late Antiquity, with its own, very different, arrangement of mathematical styles.

The fundamental feature of this later reception of Hellenistic mathematics is a sharp decline in interest in the ludic, correlated with a new emphasis on the pedagogic (the survey preserved to the extent that it is pedagogical). Archimedes forms, of course, a special case. He was the only ancient *famous* mathematician, and his fame did not subside through the generations. The result was that there was a distinct effort made to preserve his works for sheer bibliographical interest, so as to display "the works of Archimedes" in one's library. This can be shown as follows. We typically possess Greek mathematical treatises in the form of codices with various works by various authors, all dedicated to a related theme.[37] Archimedes stands out in that his works survived mostly through three lines of transmission that came down as Heiberg's Codices A, B, and C – where *all* represent medieval attempts (and probably, before that, late ancient attempts) to put together a volume of "collected works of Archimedes." Briefly, then, Archimedes was not preserved for an interest in his mathematics but for an interest in his name. Who were preserved for their mathematics? Nearly all the treatises described so far in this book have survived through an indirect route. Eratosthenes' treatise on duplicating the cube survived only because Eutocius chose to include it in his catalogue of solutions of the same problem (the "catalogue" format turning this originally ludic treatise into a component inside a *survey*), which got attached to a certain Archimedean

---

[37] I have surveyed a sample of Greek, Latin, and Arabic manuscripts in the exact sciences from Paris (those whose holding numbers are multiples of five), as well as all the Greek scientific manuscripts from the Vatican and the Laurentian at Florence. Putting aside the manuscripts that contain a *single* treatise, I find 76 manuscripts arranged by theme, and 19 manuscripts arranged by author. Of the last, three are Archimedes manuscripts, seven are either non-mathematical (e.g. Vat. Gr. 209 – an Aristotle manuscript included in this survey because of a small astrological appendix) or non-classical (e.g. Par. Lat. 7190 – a collection of works by Jordan of Namur), and five are late, sixteenth to seventeenth-century compilations that apparently do not represent an ancient principle of arrangement (one by Diophantus, one by Cleomedes, and three by Hero, all Par. Gr.). In the entire survey, there are only four relatively early manuscripts arranged by an author other than Archimedes: Vat. Gr. 176 (Ptolemy, XIV C.), Laur 28.2 (Euclid, XIV C.), Laur. 28.3 (Euclid, XI C.), Laur 28.10 (Euclid, XV C). One's impression is that those manuscripts, again, did not represent a biobibliographic interest in preserving an ancient *author* as such, but rather perceived in the ancient author – whether Ptolemy or Euclid – an appropriate exponent of an entire *field*.

line of transmission. Hypsicles' book survived because its subject matter was closely related to that of Euclid's *Elements* book XIII so that the decision was made to attach it there as a kind of appendix (once again, turning this highly personal work into a mere pawn inside a larger system). Somewhat comparable is the case of Aristarchus, whose *Sizes and Distances of the Sun and the Moon* got conscripted to form part of an astronomical survey (known as "the small astronomy," to distinguish it from Ptolemy).[38] Several other works have survived only in Arabic (which may perhaps suggest that they were rare already in Late Antiquity): For instance Diocles' *On Burning Mirrors*, or the more complex books of Apollonius' *Conics*. Nothing else survives. All that we know of, say, Eratosthenes' measurement of the size of the earth, or of Hipparchus' work in combinatorics, or even of Apollonius' counting of a hexameter line, is based on indirect testimony. No one in Late Antiquity was interested in ludic treatises.

The mathematical library of Late Antiquity owed little to the Hellenistic achievement itself. The basic works were Euclid, for geometry, Nicomachus,[39] for arithmetic, Ptolemy, for astronomy. The first was written in what I would see as a pre-Alexandrian period; the latter two were written in the second century AD. All three share a marked pedagogic character (nearly perfect in Euclid's case, nearly sublime in Ptolemy's, pedestrian in Nicomachus' – but such differences of quality are irrelevant for our purpose here). The works allow for little surprise, either because they obtain well-known results in direct routes (as in the case of Euclid) or because they are extremely explicit about their own structures (as in Nicomachus and Ptolemy). Among advanced works, it is possible that Apollonius' *Conics* was known: for instance, Galen seems to have been aware of its existence.[40] But even there, the set of works that did survive through the Greek line of transmission is that of books I–IV, i.e. a set dominated by the relatively pedagogical *Conics* I.

I have described (in Netz 2004) the process whereby deuteronomic writings and in particular the commentary came to dominate Late Ancient writing, with consequences for the very contents of mathematics. I shall

---

[38] This collection is referred to – and perhaps in some sense created – by Pappus, who dedicates book VI to a survey of astronomical works. All aside from Aristarchus are pedagogical in character (by Euclid, Theodosius, and Menelaus; the first pre-Hellenistic, the second perhaps, and the third certainly post-Hellenistic). The book was clearly collected in this connection – as is made by clear from Pappus' remarks as well (Pappus II 558.21–560.10) – because its subject matter was also touched upon by Ptolemy.

[39] The historical significance of Nicomachus is often forgotten; see Cuomo 2001: 181 ff.

[40] See Toomer 1985. Note that otherwise Galen – who sets great stock by his knowledge of mathematics – seems to be aware mostly of Euclid.

not repeat the argument of that book, but shall rather sum up briefly what, for our purposes, is its main moral. This is that, in the world of commentary, the pedagogical reigns supreme. The aim is not so much to obtain this or that particular result, but to position the result within a larger system, explicitly accounting for the purpose of each link in the chain. Obviously, this is in direct contradiction to the subtle narrative structures we have noted in this chapter. To mention just one brief example: we have seen above how Archimedes modulates his text, say by gradually abbreviating the mathematical argument so as to move towards a more second-order, authorial voice. One place where this happens is in the sequence of propositions 3–6 in the first book on *Sphere and Cylinder*. The main proof of proposition 6 ends on a very brief note where an argument is only hinted at, merely stating: "through this, then, the circumscribed will be smaller than <them> taken together." What can the commentator Eutocius do? Of course he expands this argument in his commentary, explaining how the derivation actually works in its mathematical detail: "For since the circumscribed has to the inscribed a smaller ratio than..." and so on for three steps of reasoning. Archimedes' entire point was to make direct contact with the reader, to suggest that a certain territory has already been mastered. Eutocius annuls this moment of authorial communication, so that Archimedes' authorial intervention, muffled by the commentator's intervention, turns into another mundane piece of geometrical reasoning. Obviously what I say here is not meant as criticism of Eutocius: he fulfills his duty as he perceives it which is, fundamentally, to endow the text of Archimedes, uniformly, with the same explicitness he finds in Euclid's *Elements*. In a pedagogic context of reading, even Archimedes – the only non-pedagogic author Late Antiquity chose to preserve – is pedagogized.

The irony is that the explicit text of Eutocius – where the author Eutocius so often speaks for himself – depersonalizes not only Archimedes but also Eutocius himself. Since Eutocius' task is so predictable, Eutocius' authorial decisions become invisible. He becomes merely the ghost of Euclid's *Elements* speaking through the works of Archimedes. More than this: the same system of commentary is applied widely in Late Antiquity, to Apollonius by Eutocius himself, to Ptolemy by Pappus, and Theon, probably also (though this is no longer extant) to Diophantus by Hypatia, and of course to Euclid himself by Proclus, Pappus and others. The similar treatment ends up homogenizing the authors of the past: from Euclid to Archimedes, everyone comes to be perceived as filling up different parts of the order of mathematics.

In short, later generations have selected to preserve pedagogic works, have added pedagogic works to the mathematical corpus, and have produced a body of commentary that tends to depersonalize each individual work and that, in aggregate, depersonalizes the corpus as a whole. Mathematics, the impersonal discipline *par excellence*, came to its own in the sixth century AD, to shape from then on our very image of the field and to blind us to the Hellenistic phenomenon of ludic proof.

CHAPTER 3

# *Hybrids and mosaics*

Euclid's *Elements* stand out, among Hellenistic mathematical works, in their pedagogic intent. Yet their very end – book XIII – already suggests the ludic, and at the very end is a theorem, attached as a kind of appendix, that would have been worthy of Archimedes. The theorem is often considered to have been discovered early (though its form may be due to Euclid himself, or even to some later reader of him). However this may be, it may serve as an example of an important compositional phenomenon: the mosaic proof. Here then is the proof that there are exactly five regular solids (adapted from Heath's translation):

(1) For a solid angle cannot be constructed with two triangles (or, in general, <two> planes). [This is based on a definition in book XI and in principle represents a fundamental three-dimensional intuition.] (2) With three triangles the angle of the pyramid is constructed, with four the angle of the octahedron, and with five the angle of the icosahedron [this moves into the mode of exhaustive survey]; (3) but a solid angle cannot be formed by six equilateral and equiangular triangles placed together at one point, (4) for, the angle of the equilateral triangle being two-thirds of a right angle, (5) the six will be equal to four right angles: (6) which is impossible, (7) for any solid angle is contained by angles less than four right angles. [Step 7 is a result proved at *Elements* XI.21. For the fantastic argumentative structure of Steps 3–7, see in more detail below.] (8) So, for the same reasons, a solid angle cannot be constructed by more than six plane angles.[1] (9) By three squares the angle of the cube is contained, (10) but by four it is impossible for a solid angle to be contained, (11) for they will again be four right angles. (12) By three equilateral and equiangular pentagons the angle of the dodecahedron is contained, (13) but by four such it is impossible for any solid angle to be formed, (14) for, the angle of the equilateral pentagon being a right angle and a

---

[1] A sloppy statement: the meaning is that a solid angle cannot be formed by more than six plane angles *under the conditions of a regular solid*. With this proviso attached, Step 8 is a valid *a fortiori* conclusion from Step 7. It is however otiose, as stronger claims will be made in the following (is it an interpolation?).

fifth,[2] (15) the four angles will be greater than four right angles: (16) which is impossible. (17) Neither again will a solid angle be contained by other polygonal figures,[3] (18) by reason of the same absurdity.

This delightful proposition – which as it were keeps tearing up and building toy polyhedra in our mind's eye – also keeps tearing up and building connections between diverse domains of proof. The thread running through the proof is that of exhaustive survey: a field of possibilities is divided up and surveyed until it is exhausted, whereupon certainty is attained. Within this thread runs a basic set of three-dimensional intuitions: that a solid angle is contained by at least three plane angles, whose sums are less than four right angles (whose meeting-up makes not a solid angle, but a plane). Note that this intuition is compelling, but not as obvious as some plane geometry intuitions are. It takes a positive effort of imagination to convince ourselves of the validity of this assumption, and so it is felt to be actively present in the course of the proof, rather than forming some kind of neutral background. Further, one repeatedly requires results in plane geometry: the size of the angles for equiangular polygons. We take it for granted in the course of this proof that the triangle's is two-thirds a right angle, the square's – a right angle, and the pentagon's – a right angle and a fifth (the hexagon's right-and-a-third is left implicit). The result for the pentagon is assigned to a following lemma, that for the square is too obvious to call for any argument, that for the triangle is left as a quick and very straightforward exercise for the reader. In all cases, plane geometry is called to the fore. Finally, the proof repeatedly invokes the very different field of calculation, of a more complex type than we would have in the same context. Euclid counts his angles in the units of right angles, so that the calculation of fractions is required: two-thirds make four when multiplied by six, one and a fifth goes over four when multiplied by four, and (implicitly) one and a third – for the hexagon – makes four already when multiplied by three. Consider again Steps 3–7: "(3) but a solid angle cannot be formed by six equilateral and equiangular triangles placed together at one point, (4) for, the angle of the equilateral triangle being two-thirds of a right angle, (5) the six will be equal to four right angles: (6) which is impossible, (7) for any solid angle is contained by angles less than four right angles."

---

[2] The text provides a further lemma proving this result, which is strictly speaking redundant: all that is required is that the angle of the pentagon is greater than the angle of the square, and it appears that Euclid takes for granted (in the concluding Steps 17–18) that the more-sided polygon has the greater angle.

[3] Once again, the proviso "under the conditions of a regular solid" is tacitly assumed.

The claim of Step 3 is proved by the rapid combination of three independent lines of thought (presented in ascending order of complexity): plane geometry in Step 4, calculation in Step 5, three-dimensional intuition in Step 7.

In a sense we are already familiar with the compositional principle present here, in two of its forms. In the first chapter we have seen how Hellenistic mathematicians juxtapose the geometrical and the arithmetic, to create the striking structures of the carnival of calculation. In the second chapter we have seen how they juxtapose the personal and the impersonal to obtain striking structures of narration. The fundamental principle is that of mosaic composition: the juxtaposition of apparently unrelated threads that, put together, delight with the surprise of a fruitful combination, or startle with the shock of incongruity. In this chapter we follow this principle more generally. We see how, so often, Hellenistic mathematics is couched in the form of the mosaic, while its objects, in turn, are made to be hybrids combining disparate principles.

Section 3.1 is dedicated to the mosaic composition as such, enriching our examples beyond that taken above from Euclid. Section 3.2 looks more closely at the phenomenon of genre-breaking: combining results from more than one field of science. Section 3.3 proceeds to discuss the phenomenon of hybrid objects, which leads on to a vignette presented in section 3.4: the phenomenon of Hellenistic scientific naming. Objects are often metaphorically labeled, so that their very names enshrine the principle of the breaking of boundaries. This role of metaphor within science reminds us finally of the central breaking of genre characteristic of Hellenistic science: the breaking of the boundary between science and literature. This is the subject of section 3.5, which prepares the way for the next and final chapter where Hellenistic literature is brought in.

## 3.1 COMPOSITIONAL VARIATION

We have seen in the final proof of Euclid's *Elements* XIII a combination of plane and solid geometry together with (very elementary) calculation. Any combination of geometry with arithmetic is bound to be striking, but an even more striking combination is that of geometry with the more abstract calculation of proportions; a combination which is so central to Greek mathematics that, habituated, we may fail to be startled by it. I take for example Apollonius' *Conics* 1.23 – one of a series of propositions of "topological," i.e. strictly spatial import. We are given an ellipse ΑΓΒΔ,

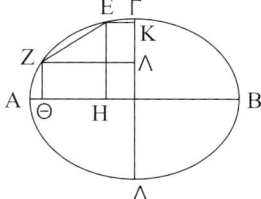

Figure 18

with AB, ΓΔ diameters; we are also given the line EZ, said to be "positioned between the diameters" (i.e. it does not cut them inside the ellipse). We need to show that the line EZ, produced, cuts the two diameters *outside* the ellipse (fig. 18). The argument runs as follows. First, we drop the ordinate lines from the points E, Z (the definition of "ordinate" is complex but for our purposes here we may take the ordinate lines to be perpendicular to the diameters): EK, ZΛ, EH, ZΘ. A central result in the theory of conic sections, already obtained by Apollonius at this stage, is in the purely abstract and quantitative terms of proportions:

Sq.(EH):sq.(ZΘ)::rect.(BH,HA):rect.(BΘ,ΘA)
Sq.(ZΛ):sq.(EK)::rect.(ΔΛ,ΛΓ):rect.(EK,KΓ).

What I mean when I say "purely abstract and quantitative" is that, for the sake of this proportion, it is completely immaterial how we position the segments and, indeed, no actual rectangles are envisaged. This is a mere statement of quantitative relations formed by segments whose spatial position is conceptually elided.

Apollonius asserts those proportions (of course in non-symbolic, natural Greek) and then continues: "And the <rectangle contained> by BHA is greater than the <rectangle contained> by BΘA; for H is closer to the bisection <point>." I explain: this indirectly recalls a result from Euclid's *Elements*, according to which, in a line such as PRST (R being the bisection point of PT) rect.(PS,ST)+sq.(RS) = sq.(PR) (fig. 19).[4] But for this to work, the abstract proportions have to be re-imagined in their concrete form, the eye noting on the space of the diagram (fig. 18) the arrangement of B, H, Θ and A. Another combination, then, of the spatial and the abstract.

---

[4] This is a geometrical way of stating $(a+b)(a-b) = a^2-b^2$, whence it follows that the smaller sq.(RS) is – the closer the division of the two segments is to the bisection point – the closer the rectangle contained by the two segments gets to the square on half the line, i.e. the greater it becomes. All of this in itself forms a complex combination of geometrical and quantitative thinking.

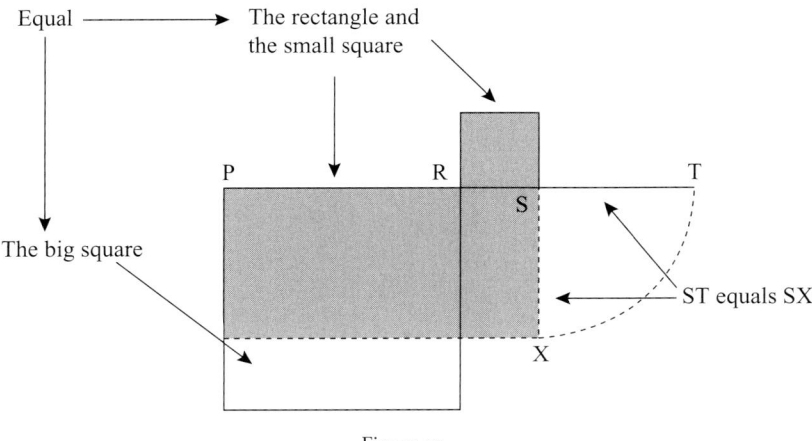

Figure 19

The main transition of the proof, however, translates this spatially obtained information into the quantitative terms presented above. Since we have the proportion sq.(EH):sq.(ZΘ)::rect.(BH,HA):rect.(BΘ,ΘA), and we are provided with an inequality between the rectangles, we may immediately derive – in a purely abstract manner, without reference to the spatial position of the objects involved – the inequality asserted next by Apollonius: "Therefore the <square> on HE, too, is greater than the <square> on ZΘ" (and analogously for the other pair), and this continues in the same purely abstract manipulation of terms: "Therefore HE, too, is greater than ZΘ" (and analogously for the other pair), and here, suddenly, Apollonius reverts to the spatial: "and HE is parallel to ZΘ . . . therefore EZ, produced, will meet the diameter AB outside the section" (and analogously for the other pair). This claim is so tightly based on spatial intuition that, in fact – as is typical for such topological assertions in Greek mathematics – it does not have any direct deductive basis.[5]

---

[5] Apollonius' argument seems to involve the assertion that, if two parallel lines intercepted between two straight lines are unequal, the two intercepting lines are not parallel. With the parallel postulate assumed – as is justified in this context – we may derive this in several ways, but the argument would be complex and non-trivial. One has the impression that Apollonius expects us to perceive the persuasiveness of the argument directly, on the force of the visual intuition: as the straight lines representing the distance get smaller, they will ultimately vanish and the two lines will meet. (A strong intuition to demand, coming from the author of a treatise where asymptotes play such a role; but then again the asymptotes to the hyperbole are much more complex than the straight lines of the situation at hand.)

This proposition is especially typical of Apollonius.[6] But this type of argument is ubiquitous in Hellenistic Greek mathematics: lines keep changing their meaning, once as objects in space, then again as terms in abstract proportions. The translation of results from one domain to another is the trick that allows the authors to obtain strong, surprising results: what is easy to obtain in the abstract domain is surprising in the spatial domain, and vice versa. This duality then plays an important deductive role, and is therefore not just aesthetically motivated. Furthermore, it is so ubiquitous that we may be too habituated to notice its charm of playful combination. But however habituated we may be, let us not forget the very basic sense of delightful surprise we have upon reading a Hellenistic mathematical proof: in the most standard case, this delightful surprise is obtained by this combination of the abstract and the concrete.

So far I have discussed cases (from Euclid and from Apollonius) where the different mathematical strands are so closely woven together as to be almost imperceptible, giving rise to a subtle sense of complexity and variety. Another type of structure is where the different strands are clearly set apart in the telling of the proof, so that the mosaic structure becomes more obvious, even blunt. Consider Archimedes' *Method* 14. In this great proposition (the closest any extant Greek proof comes to the modern calculus), Archimedes has a cylinder enclosed in a prism, with an oblique plane cutting through both prism and cylinder cutting off, from the cylinder, a strange figure bounded by an ellipse, a semi-circle and a cylindrical surface (fig. 20). This figure Archimedes is, amazingly, going to measure. We concentrate on the "base" common to prism and cylinder, as in fig. 21 (the oblique plane is drawn from the diameter HE to the side above ΓΔ). An arbitrary perpendicular to EH is drawn as MN, cutting the base of the cylinder HZEΘ at Σ and a parabolic segment HZE at Λ. The proof, following that, is divided into three discrete parts:

First, Archimedes makes the geometrical assertion – stunning in itself – that the line NΣ is the mean proportional between the lines NΛ, NM. This is saying, in a way, that a circle is the mean between a parabola and

---

[6] A large body of literature has formed in the last quarter of the twentieth century, regarding the question of so-called geometrical algebra: with Zeuthen (1886) identifying, within Greek geometry, one specialized branch where the appearance of a qualitative geometry serves to clothe the contents of a quantitative algebra? Fried and Unguru (2001) – who sum up much of the discussion – argue for a thoroughly qualitative, geometrical Greek mathematics and indeed there is no doubt that Greek mathematical thinking never loses its anchoring in the concrete diagram and its spatial objects. What I suggest here is the following: that in Apollonius' *Conics*, in particular (the major site for this modern debate) the combination of the abstract and the concrete, the geometrical and the "algebraical," is real – and should be seen against the wider cultural interest in the hybridization of genres.

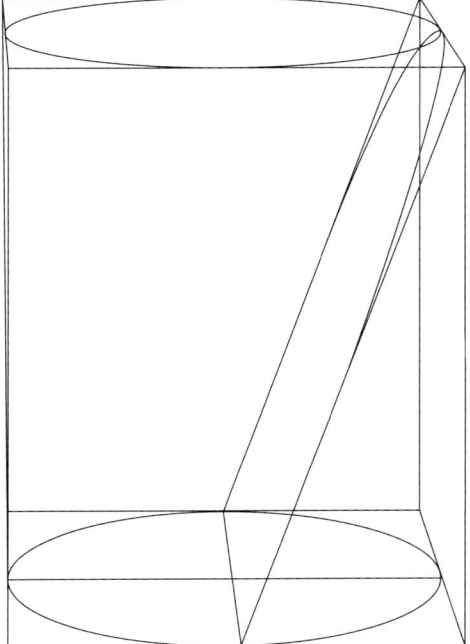

Figure 20

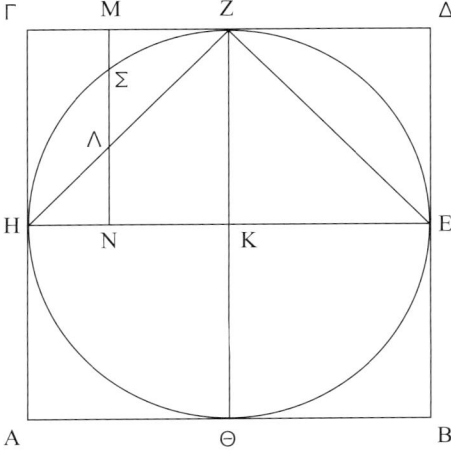

Figure 21

a straight line . . . such a completely unexpected result (based ultimately on the abstract proportion properties of the parabola) is sprung upon the reader as a kind of "exercise," a challenging puzzle of the kind we are familiar with from the previous chapter. Archimedes further draws the more straightforward conclusion from this mean proportional property, namely that, once we consider the triangles cut off by the oblique plane, one on top of MN (the prism triangle) and another on top of ΣN (the cylinder triangle) we have the proportion:

Prism triangle:cylinder triangle::line MN:line NΛ.

This concludes the first part of the proof (Steps 1–14 in Netz *et al.* 2001–2).

Second, Archimedes plunges into a fantastically complex argument where general and very abstract results in proportion theory are applied to this concrete geometrical proportion. The abstract results allow the composition of a set of proportions involving single objects, into a proportion involving the summation of those single objects. In this case the single objects are the various triangles and lines of the preceding proportion, taken for each arbitrary line such as MN drawn through the base; their composition yields a proportion where:

Figure cut from prism:figure cut from cylinder::rectangle:parabolic segment.

Here a different, meta-exercise is set for the reader to puzzle out: how is the result on composition of proportions (proved elsewhere, as *Conoids and Spheroids* 1, but only for the case of finitely many objects) to apply in the case of infinitely many objects? This meta-exercise left for the reader is of course typical to the *Method*, as seen in the preceding chapter. The application of proportion theory to the summation of proportions takes up Steps 14–29 in Netz *et al.* 2001–2.

The following coda to the proof – Steps 30–7 – develops in surprising detail a very simple argument, now of a very different character. Step 29 has established the proportion of the prism and cylinder figures with the rectangle and the parabolic segment. Now, as we recall in Step 30, Archimedes has shown (in the *Quadrature of the Parabola*) that the rectangle is half as much again as the parabolic segment. This in itself could suffice as a measurement of the cylindrical figure, but Archimedes adds on a series of very simple arithmetical manipulations whereby the result is restated to say that the cylindrical figure is one-sixth the entire prism surrounding it.

The three parts each have a very different character, then: advanced geometry (in itself combining the spatial and the abstract) in the first part; completely abstract proportion theory, of a very advanced character, in the second part; and a coda with mere arithmetical calculations. We are now familiar with all those strands, and we may appreciate the craftsmanship with which Archimedes sets them out side by side, in this case quite bluntly, as if to savour the jarring effect of surprising juxtaposition.

If my description of Hellenistic mathematics as a field of variety may be surprising, this is mainly due to an image – based on a somewhat superficial reading of Euclid's *Elements* – according to which the Greek mathematical style is based on mindless, exact repetition. This should be dispelled once and for all. Perhaps the place where this image is most stubborn is our picture of the Q.E.D. – the mindless, mechanical ending to a Greek mathematical proof, asserting, at the very end, the general enunciation preceded by the word "therefore" and appending the three words "which was to be proved" (or in the case of problems, "which was to be done").

The Q.E.D. is in point of fact idiosyncratic to Euclid, and variedly used by him. As pointed out by Acerbi (2004), the systematic application of the Q.E.D. is a late phenomenon in Euclidean manuscripts – that is, yet another example of late pedagogic interests overriding original varied textures of writing. Euclid himself used the formula most of the time, but not always (why he chose to apply it in the precise places he did is not clear to me). Outside of Euclid's *Elements*, the Q.E.D. formula, I believe, was never met in antiquity. It is not present, say, even in Euclid's *Data*. It does occur occasionally, in our manuscripts, for isolated propositions. For instance, at the very end of Archimedes *Planes in Equilibrium* II.8, the manuscripts have a formulaic abbreviation, οι – standing for the beginning and end of the formula ὅπερ ἔδει δεῖξαι, or Q.E.D. The very abbreviation suggests that this is a scribal intervention. One finds more fully spelled out phrases occasionally (e.g. the end of Archimedes' second book on *Sphere and Cylinder*, proposition 2), but the rule is that it is rare to find the formula applied – outside of Euclid's *Elements* – more than once or twice in a given work. One's impression then is that such occurrences may represent a reader well versed in Euclid's *Elements* who went beyond the text to introduce the formula. On the whole, late sophisticated readers such as Eutocius seem to have grasped that this is a formula specific to Euclid's *Elements*, so that in his own proofs Eutocius is careful *not* to introduce the formula. In short, instead of being a mark of mindless repetition, the Q.E.D. is an example of the personal specificity of Greek mathematical style (in that Euclid alone uses it), as well as being an example of the varied structure in the writing of a single author (in that Euclid – the most pedagogic of authors – does not apply it systematically). That it came to appear as mechanical as it does, is a fine representation of the triumph of the impersonal through the Middle Ages.

Less formulaic than the Q.E.D. phrase itself is the overall structure within which it is embedded: an ending where the author reverts to the original enunciation and repeats it now as a proven fact introduced by the particle "therefore." This is a significant stylistic device (turning the mathematical proposition, technically speaking, into a "ring composition").[7] And it is indeed nearly universal in Euclid's *Elements*. Once again, however, the picture gets more complicated when we look elsewhere. Typically, propositions do not end with a return to the general terms introduced in the enunciation. Instead, the ending of propositions keeps to the particular terms referring to the diagram, introduced at the setting-out and at the definition of the goal. The simplest and most direct way to structure this would be to have the ending of the proposition revert to the precise terms introduced by the definition of the goal. Thus the proposition would start with a general enunciation, followed by a particular setting out and a definition of the goal asserting that such and such a relation holds inside the diagram; the ending of the proof then concluding with the very same relation. It is typical of Hellenistic mathematical treatises that they vary their approach to this moment of conclusion. Thus for instance the first four explicit proofs in Archimedes' *Planes in Equilibrium* I (printed by Heiberg as propositions 3–6 – see my discussion at p. 103 above). The first three of these end with the definition of the goal directly obtained, though occasionally with some minimal variation:

*PE* 1.3 def. of goal: " . . . AΓ is smaller than ΓB."
*PE* 1.3 end of proof: " . . . AΓ is smaller than ΓB."

*PE* 1.4 def. of goal: " . . . Γ is center <of the weight> of the magnitude composed of both magnitudes."
*PE* 1.4 end of proof: " . . . Γ is center of the weight of the magnitude composed of A, B."

*PE* 1.5 def. of goal: " . . . the point Γ is center of the weight of the magnitude composed of all magnitudes."
*PE* 1.5 end of proof: ". . . the point which is also center of the weight of the middle <magnitude>, shall be center of the weight of the magnitude composed of all <magnitudes>, too."

---

[7] The *locus classicus* for this stylistic device is van Otterlo 1944. It is typically associated with oral performance and to my knowledge the prevalence of ring composition in Euclid's *Elements* has not yet been considered by literary scholars studying Greek ring composition more generally.

The sequence is obvious: from a precise repetition at the first proposition, towards growing variation. Now, the last proposition in the sequence I chose here – *PE* 1.6 – is also the first proposition in the treatise to display a truly intricate demonstrative structure. Here is the pair in this case:

*PE* 1.6 def. of goal: "... Γ is center of the weight of the magnitude composed of both A, B."
*PE* 1.6 end of proof: "... they shall balance at Γ."

Here Archimedes deliberately varies the mathematical terms, introducing a mathematically equivalent expression: instead of a point being the center of the weight of certain magnitudes, it is stated that certain magnitudes balance at it. The equivalence, indeed, is not altogether tautological, especially as the very terms of "center of the weight" and "balance" were introduced in this treatise (perhaps, in a sense, invented by Archimedes). Thus we see another example of the mathematical puzzle thrown at the reader (indeed, of a very mild variety). However "enigmatic" this end is designed to be (and this particular proposition is perhaps enigmatic as a whole), we may concentrate right now on the compositional principle: variety in the sense of discrepancy between definition of goal and end of proof; this discrepancy itself becoming a tool for variation in that it gradually *grows*. All of which reminds us of a simple fact: the very well-structured nature of a Greek mathematical proof provides us with a system upon which variation can be built. It might appear to be a boring, repetitive feature: proofs must end, predictably, with their goals obtained. But the very fact that each treatise must go through the same ritual several dozens of times allows an element of variety, by going through this ritual somewhat differently each time.

The very need to have a result proved might seem to be a boring task: after all, there is only a finite way of obtaining conclusions. And yet a finite number is quite sufficient for variation. Here I treat a subject – the "alternative proof" – where textual questions are paramount. Not infrequently, a Greek mathematical proposition may be followed by the expression "in another way," following which is the same result, proved again through another route. How to account for that? One possible line of explanation is textual: for instance, let us suppose that the text circulated in two forms, once with proof A, again with proof B; faced with this varied tradition, some later scribe chose to incorporate both proofs.[8] Or another way of accounting for the phenomenon: a mathematically trained reader

---
[8] Vitrac believes this is the rule in Euclid's *Elements*; see Vitrac 2004 for a very full discussion.

finds a proof wanting in some way and so, even though he copies it, he appends to it another proof which he finds better. (This is likely to be the case, e.g., at Archimedes' first book on *Sphere and Cylinder*, proposition 7: here a somewhat complex proof is followed by a simpler one, modeled on another proof in the treatise – more below.) But at least occasionally it appears that the alternative proof is introduced by the author himself, signaling an interest in varied structure for its own sake: even though the proof has already been obtained, another one is offered so as to create a richer reading experience (as we saw, explicitly, in Hypiscles' treatise, p. 96 above). I believe this is the best way to account for such cases as, say, Archimedes' alternative proof to proposition 8 in the *Second Book on Sphere and Cylinder*. The alternative proof is so complicated and so marked in its radical departures from established Greek style, I just cannot imagine a later reader introducing it. So could it be introduced by Archimedes himself as an explicit *alternative*? It makes sense for Archimedes to introduce it at such a point, as the treatise draws to an end and the gradual introduction of strange, marked forms of proof seems to be a stylistic feature of this treatise (see my comments at Netz 2004, esp. 226–7). At any rate, it certainly was not alien to Archimedes' thinking to produce more than a single proof of the same result – he was after all the mathematician who proved *three times* the basic measurement of the parabola (twice, along separate mathematical routes, in the *Quadrature of the Parabola*, for which see more in the following section, and then again in *Method* 1). And if the parabola, then why not the spiral? A set of propositions in Pappus' *Collection* (IV.21–5) reviews some central properties of the spiral obtained via a route separate from that of the Archimedean treatise, and yet Pappus takes no credit for himself and refers to no other mathematician besides Archimedes as the author of the approach (save for asserting, as noted in Intro. n. 11 above, that Conon *proposed* this research). The main line of attack is different from that of the extant *Spiral Lines* – but it is no less inspired. Whereas, in *Spiral Lines*, the sectors of the circle bounding the spiral are directly summed up via a quasi-arithmetic summation of the series of squares, the route taken in Pappus' account is more directly geometrical: each spiralic sector is associated with a cutting of a cone, while the associated circular sector is associated with a cutting of the cylinder; the outcome is to show that the spiral area is to the circle enclosing it as a cone is to a cylinder enclosing it. This beautiful, paradoxical rendering of two-dimensional figures in three-dimensional terms – in itself breaking a boundary of Greek geometry – may well have sprung from the mind of Archimedes. Knorr – who was the first modern historian to take this passage seriously – has taken this as an example of an early, heuristic treatment by Archimedes, discarded precisely because of the uneasy way in which this discussion breaks assumptions concerning geometrical dimensionality.[9] But if this were discarded papers by Archimedes, they did only fractionally worse than those that have come down to us: this was a treatise by Archimedes surviving right into the fourth century AD. A slightly different set of scribal accidents could have left that treatise as the "authoritative" treatment of spiral lines by Archimedes (would we wonder then, had we come to read about the "other" *Spiral Lines*, whether this was an early effort rejected for its uneasy mixing of geometry and arithmetic?). Quite possibly, Archimedes published two – or more, perhaps? – treatises on *Spiral Lines* of which only one survived into the main transmission of his works. (But, of course, an alternative account is possible: that this treatise was a reaction to Archimedes' *Spiral Lines* by some later ancient geometer, whose identity was unknown to Pappus. Although, even so, if this geometer was Hellenistic – which would be in itself likely – this would then serve as an example of the *cultural* accumulation of alternatives in Hellenistic geometry.)

The essence of the juxtaposition of two different proofs is the assertion of equivalence: two separate methods yield an equivalent result. Now, this principle of equivalence is at the heart of the major achievement of Hellenistic astronomy. Here our information is extremely meager: we are told by Ptolemy that a certain technique (ubiquitous in Ptolemy, but hardly attested before him) was due to Apollonius of Perga.[10] We know nothing further about the context of Apollonius' statement of the technique. And yet, this is well worth our attention. For the Ptolemaic passage seems to suggest that Apollonius, already, has shown the equivalence of two radically separate treatments of planetary phenomena. One can either describe them as the result of *eccentrics* – i.e. a uniform motion along a circular circumference, where however the angular velocity is constant relative not to the geometrical center of the circle, but relative to some other point within it. Or one can describe them as the result of *epicycles* – i.e. the uniform motion of a circle whose center, in turn, uniformly rotates, in a circular fashion, about another center. Both methods can describe very well the observed planetary phenomena. And one can obtain this *either way*,

---

[9] Knorr 1978, incorporated into Knorr 1986: 162–3.
[10] In what follows I rely on an expansive reading of Ptolemy XII.1, as if the reference by Ptolemy to a discovery by Apollonius refers to both astronomical models. There is a school of thought that tends to discredit all reports of early Greek mathematical astronomy, represented by Bowen and Goldstein (for this particular problem see Bowen 2001: 821–2.) Obviously, I differ – and see no difficulty in assuming Apollonius to be perfectly capable of producing what, it appears, Ptolemy says he did.

that is: for each arrangement of eccentric motion there is an arrangement of epicyclic motion, which derives exactly the same observed phenomena, and vice versa. This is all we know about Apollonius' discovery. Now, it used to be thought that this argument by equivalence belied an instrumentalist tendency: the ancients, so it was once thought, considered astronomy as a mere mathematical tool for the description of observations, not as a realistic enterprise setting out to discover underlying cosmological systems.[11] To the extent that finality is ever possible on such questions, I would say that Lloyd has refuted this old picture: everything we know about ancient astronomy suggests that its practitioners were interested in cosmology and were understood by their audience to be offering cosmological models.[12] This underlines the radical nature of Apollonius' mathematical discovery of epicycles and eccentrics: even while offering a set of cosmological models which is very effective in describing the sky, Apollonius was undercutting his very own model by the juxtaposition of two, mutually exhaustive but equivalent methods. It is indeed a pity that no more is known about the context of Apollonius' astronomy. Still, it certainly should serve as a prime example of the juxtaposition of equivalent, alternative methods in Greek mathematics.

Apollonius' astronomy must be seen as the most radical case of the juxtaposition of analogous yet different solutions. (More of this would be seen, however, in works of a more meta-mathematical character, such as Archimedes' *Quadrature of Parabola* and the *Method* – of which more in the next section.) But a very common technique is the use of different modes of proof in propositions set *in sequence*. We have seen something of this already in the previous chapter: in modulating the authorial voice, a frequently used technique is the gradual abbreviation, so that propositions going again and again through similar demonstrative routes become more and more abbreviated and as a consequence second order. More than this happens, occasionally: so, for instance, the very example quoted above from the first book on *Sphere and Cylinder*. Both propositions, 7 and 8, measure the surface of a pyramid, somewhat differently constructed in each case. In proposition 7 (the main proof), Archimedes is satisfied with a direct measurement of the surface of the pyramid itself. In proposition 8 a different demonstrative strategy is applied: an *ad hoc* triangle is constructed, equal to the surface of the pyramid, and this triangle (rather than the pyramid itself) is then being measured. (As we recall, a later scribe then chose to imitate this demonstrative strategy of proposition 8, appending

---

[11] This interpretation is due to Duhem 1908.   [12] Lloyd 1978.

an alternative proof to 7.) The difference is minimal, but it does help to create a more varied texture: in this pyramid Archimedes is setting up, each face is slightly different.

### 3.2 THE HYBRID TREATISE

In a way we are very familiar already with this particular narrative structure: a Hellenistic mathematical treatise whose contents unfold "jerkily," by rapid switches from this field to the other. A major example not considered as yet is the *Quadrature of the Parabola* – one of the more striking narrative structures created by Archimedes. As usual, a personal introduction (dedicated to Dositheus) mentions Conon and concentrates mostly on a single meta-mathematical question: the admissibility of (so-called) Archimedes' Axiom. Following that the treatise moves on to a series of results in pure conic theory, leading on to a rather sophisticated result (in proposition 5), which is also used in the first proposition of the *Method*. Immediately thereafter the text switches into another of the Archimedean thought-experiments: a geometrical configuration is re-imagined as the setting for the balance. The assumption that, in the particular setting, the balance is at equilibrium, leads – Archimedes shows – to a certain conclusion: a given ratio obtains between the geometrical objects. Needless to say, the objects at hand have nothing to do with conic sections, so that proposition 6 marks a clean break from the preceding five propositions. The sequence of propositions 6–13 goes on to extend such geometrical results to ever-complex geometrical configurations. Those configurations all involve structures arising from triangles to which smaller triangles are affixed in some quantitatively defined form – of no immediately apparent function. And at this point a new departure is made – which is almost to be predicted. (The Archimedean unit of discourse is about 6 propositions long, and following such a unit the text typically makes some abrupt switch.)

Here arrives an Archimedean moment of synthesis: proposition 14 now has a parabolic segment imagined on the balance, and divided in such a form so as to suggest how it may be reconceived as the limit for a sequence of triangles arranged in a quantitatively defined form. Propositions 14–18 then form a sequence of tightly interrelated propositions – nearly a single, multipartite proposition – where a complex argument shows how, from the thought-experiment of the parabolic segment extended on the balance, its measurement as four-thirds the enclosed triangle follows.

The treatise could have ended here, a typical, though rather brief, Archimedean work: hit in one direction (conic sections), hit in another (triangles on the balance), combine it all (parabola on the balance), and get to the striking result. But wait: the treatise makes yet another fresh start. Propositions 19 to 22 all add in more results on conic sections and the inscribed configurations of triangles. Proposition 23 makes an entirely independent move – as we saw several times already in Archimedes – this time of a nearly arithmetic character: we obtain the sum of a certain geometrical progression. Proposition 24 now returns to the configuration of triangles inscribed inside a parabolic segment, considering it now as a geometrical progression whose summation, once again, yields the measurement of the parabola as four-thirds the inscribed triangle. Here the treatise ends.

This then is a double complex structure: a typical Archimedean structure yields the result in eighteen propositions of three chapters; another one telescopes the same structure into another set of thesis-antithesis-synthesis, where however antithesis and synthesis, in this case, take only a single proposition each (23 and 24). Each of the narrative structures is in itself familiar. What is most striking for us is the overarching structure of the two narratives in sequence. We see here the principle of the alternative proof, now extended to an entire treatise. Here is a hybrid treatise, obtaining the same result twice via different routes. Each of the routes is based on hybrids, on cross-fertilization: abstract conic theory and a concrete theory of the balance, in the first route; abstract conic theory and an even more abstract summation of geometrical progressions, in the second route. But in this sense the hybrids do cross-fertilize and in this way form some kind of organic unity. The relationship within each of the segments – propositions 1–18 and propositions 19–24 – is that of a single mathematical thought. Putting the two segments side by side is a much more radical departure, creating a textured treatise whose two parts are to be read alongside, or against, each other. Is the presence of a more "classical" geometrical proof designed to undercut the first, "mechanical" proof? Or are the two meant to cast light on one another (e.g. in that the mechanical line of thought might explain, in some sense, how one obtains the geometrical one? This is certainly the experience of reading the second following the first). The treatise as a whole throws this kind of meta-mathematical puzzle at the reader and, in a sense, ironically undercuts the very notion of a definitive proof: it highlights, after all, the multiplicity of mathematical routes.

Most significant, however, the treatise highlights a gap: that between the purely geometrical, and the mechanical. By allowing the two treatments to be considered side by side, Archimedes further emphasizes how strange the thought-experiment is, with the parabolic segment laid upon the balance. A single line of argument, all based on the parabolic segment treated as possessing weight, would have favored a sustained suspension of disbelief. The reader would accept that, by the rules established in this treatise, parabolic segments *are* weighted magnitudes. But the double treatment casts doubt on the very suspension of disbelief granted earlier by the reader, suggesting that after all there is something wrong about the application of mechanics to geometry. But if so, why apply it in the first place, when a non-mechanical route is open as well?

This is of course the duality underlying the *Method* itself. This text has a complex mosaic structure. The first division is between propositions 1–11 and the following, 12–17 (? – the final part of the treatise is not extant). The first section, 1–11, is a medley of results, all known to the readers from elsewhere. The second section, 12–17, is dedicated to two interrelated, original results on the measurement of solid cuts of cylinders. The first section, as noted in the preceding chapter, is heavily mediated by the authorial voice; the second section appears to be more restrained in this respect (though this is not certain, as the treatise is preserved in fragmentary form: see p. 104 above). The results in the first section are all based on a combination of mechanics and indivisibles, calling for a double suspension of disbelief. (By *indivisibles* I mean the treatment of a solid as composed of infinitely many planes, or of a plane as composed of infinitely many lines.) The second section presents a much more complex pattern. Each of the two results is proved more than once. The first result (the only one extant in our text) is in fact proved *three* times. First (propositions 12–13) a fantastically complex proof is developed based on both mechanics and indivisibles. A totally unrelated proof is developed in proposition 14, this time based on indivisibles alone (see pp. 120–3 above). Finally, a classical treatment (closely allied to that of proposition 14) is offered in proposition 15. The tripartite arrangement throws the reader into complete confusion: is proposition 14 on the "correct" or the "wrong" side? Is the use of indivisibles alone (but not of mechanics) in itself totally acceptable? But if so, why proposition 15? And if it is not acceptable – why add it on to propositions 12–13? Once again, the end result of having a multipartite text, is to present the reader with an enigma. The goal of the *Method* is not to answer our question, what Archimedes' methodological views were; it is to open this question wide.

Less sophisticated – mathematically – but no less striking in its incongruous juxtaposition is Eratosthenes' treatise on the duplication of the cube. The overall structure is very rich, with the author turning from the literary to the mathematical and back, a context I shall describe in greater detail below. Here I concentrate on a duality within the mathematics itself. Having produced the literary background, Eratosthenes first describes in detail (Heiberg III 90.30–92.24) a purely geometrical construction whereby two mean proportionals are found. Immediately afterwards, he proceeds to set out the mechanical conditions that an instrument is to satisfy (Heiberg III 92.25–94.7): the materials best used and the thinness recommended. This then is all rounded up by quoting a brief recapitulation of the purely geometrical proof (one Eratosthenes has set up in an inscription: Heiberg III 94.15–96.2). In making the transition from the mathematical to the mechanical Eratosthenes is explicit concerning the break (Heiberg III 92.25–7):

So these are proved for geometrical surfaces. But so as we may also take the two means by a machine, a box is fixed etc. . . .

How we are supposed to bridge the gap – whether geometrical proofs automatically apply to mechanical objects, or are perhaps only approximated by them – is a philosophical question Eratosthenes does not touch upon. What I wish to stress is that, in this complex, multipartite text, Eratosthenes emphasizes the multiplicity of approaches taken. He does not smooth over the transition from pure geometry to the mechanical: to the contrary, he foregrounds it.

Is it possible then to suggest that Diocles' so-called *On Burning Mirrors* was originally intended as a surprising, incongruous juxtaposition? The text, as we have seen, is made of three separate lines of argument, one finding some properties of paraboloid mirrors, another solving Archimedes' problem of cutting a sphere, a third finally solving the problem of finding two mean proportionals. It is very likely that the text as we have it is the product of inept, late compilation. Yet it may also be the product of an authorial decision to obtain a jarring, multipartite structure. At least, one should note the complex structures within the separate treatments. We have already observed the complex, surprising way in which Diocles' treatment of the paraboloid mirrors themselves involves both the mechanical and the geometrical – the same duality already seen above several times. The fine detail of Diocles' own treatment is that he begins with the mechanical and then gradually builds up a geometrical treatment until the reader realizes, in surprised retrospect, how the geometrical coincides with the mechanical.

In his treatment of the problem of finding two mean proportionals, Diocles constructs an even more complex multipartite structure. The problem is first raised and solved (proposition 10) purely as a problem in duplicating a cube. The more general problem is solved in proposition 11 based on conic sections; then again it is treated in propositions 12–13 based on applying a specially designed ruler to lines in circles, once each time a ratio is required. This treatment is then generalized in propositions 14–16 into a more economical mechanical method, one which does not require the repeated application of the ruler: instead, a curve solving the problem is mechanically constructed once and for all, and can be used to find the two mean proportionals in whichever ratio they might be required. The overall structure, then, is homologous to that of the treatment of paraboloid mirrors, in that the geometrical is gradually subsumed under the mechanical (thus the transition from a conic-sections based solution to one based on a mechanical curve), though in this case Diocles can exploit a further duality, namely the two ways of conceptualizing the problem (as the duplication of the cube, and as the finding of two mean proportionals). In short, I do not know if Diocles has intended the three parts of his treatise to make a complex diverse structure; but it is clear that complex diverse structures are what he valued most in his compositions. Once again, we also see the centrality of the duality of the geometrical and the mechanical. Alongside the duality of the geometrical and the arithmetic (of which we have seen so much in the first chapter), here is a striking, jarring duality, one which is *conceptually* problematic. A reader of Plato and Aristotle might have wanted Greek mathematicians to avoid such dualities but, instead, we find that they embrace them as providing opportunities for the striking juxtaposition.

So far we have looked mainly into pure geometrical problems – those of the measurement of the parabola, say, or the duplication of the cube. But already Diocles' *On Burning Mirrors* reminds us that the very setting of a mathematical subject matter might involve the same combination of the concrete and the abstract. These are the sciences referred to by Aristotle as "mixed," such as mechanics itself, astronomy, harmonics, or optics. Such sciences deal with physical objects, concentrating on certain mathematically defined features, but in cognizance of further, non-mathematical properties of the objects involved. For instance, optics is not merely a study of straight lines; it is also a study of rays of vision. How is this to be developed in practice? There is no simple answer to that (and it is not too clear what was Aristotle's or indeed Plato's position).[13] One can imagine a purely abstract treatment, where say the rays of vision are postulated once and for all to correspond to straight lines, the following discussion being effectively geometrical; or one can have a richer structure, where the reader is constantly reminded of the physicality of the objects studied. The more abstract route is the one usually taken in the *Optics* ascribed in our manuscripts to Euclid. A striking moment is proposition 36: having shown in the preceding proposition how a circle, viewed obliquely, appears non-circular, the author of the *Optics* moves on to assert in this proposition that wheels, viewed obliquely, do not appear circular! Such moments would tend to foreground the "mixed" nature of a field such as optics, and the sequence from the geometrical proposition 35 to the visual proposition 36 certainly leads to an effect of jarring juxtaposition comparable to those we have seen in the preceding examples. But it should be said that the provenance of this proposition 36 is uncertain and, aside from it, the *Optics* appears as a very smooth reading, avoiding any such jarring juxtapositions. In general the same is true of the *Catoptrics* – the study of mirrors – also ascribed in our manuscript tradition to Euclid (but often considered to be of a later Hellenistic provenance).[14] Yet the very nature of this study seems to defy classification. In pure optics, one talks of properties of sight, which in turn are essentially properties of configurations of straight lines: the underlying geometrical structure is foregrounded, its physical implementation merely noted. But the subject matter of the study of mirrors is not the lines of sight in themselves, but another object, very hard to characterize: the image in the mirror. What to make of proposition 21 of the *Catoptrics*, that "In convex mirrors, the image is smaller than the visible <object>?" The proof immediately transforms the statement into a configuration of lines, one of them curved – for the convex mirror – and all the rest straight. The proof is geometrical, and yet the result is about an eerily physical object, not even the actual object of vision but its derivative, distorted mirror-image – as if in direct parody of Plato's strictures on mathematics. Or what about propositions such as 24 and 25: "In concave

---

[13] Plato's puzzling position in the curriculum passage of the *Republic* – apparently, as if astronomy and harmonics are to be conducted in complete abstraction from their physical implementation – is of course very well known and not very well understood (see e.g. Gregory 2000 and references there). Aristotle's position appears to be more nuanced, but it is difficult to tell what Aristotle intended scientists to do in practice: see e.g. Cleary 1995: 424–38. It is especially unfortunate to us that Hellenistic philosophy of science did not return to focus on such problems (or, if it did, that this is not reflected by our extant sources).

[14] See Knorr 1985.

mirrors, if the eye is positioned at the center, it alone is visible," "In concave mirrors, if the eye is positioned at the circumference or outside the circumference, it is not visible." Such paradoxical statements question the very identity of their underlying subject matter. No physical instantiation of the experiment is possible: you are not going to see a mirror all full of eyes, and you are not going to see an invisible mirror. The geometrical assumptions are so strong that the claim is literally true only for a limiting, impossible case. And yet the statement is not meaningful for purely geometrical objects: to have meaning at all, it must have physical, seeing eyes to instantiate it. The hybrid object required by the study of catoptrics – perfectly turned geometrical mirrors, point-sized eyes – is neither geometrical nor physical. It is a vanishing ghost world: the eye in the circumference of the mirror.

The same may be true for many of the apparently physical objects of Greek mathematics. Above all, what are those planes and solids weighed on the balance and immersed in the water, inside the works of Archimedes? *Balancing Planes* is all about planes, even about lines possessing weight (which, as the reader gradually works out, means *length* for lines, *area* for planes). What is this supposed to mean? A geometrical figure does not possess weight, while a physical magnitude is never a plane or a line . . . Or the *Floating Bodies*: none of these, true, are lines or planes (Archimedes' axiomatics do not encompass the hydrostatic treatment of figures not possessing volume), but the entire treatise leads to the study of complex configurations of bodies immersed in water, whose shape is precisely that of segments of conoids of revolution. Now this is a most extraordinary configuration to be met in nature. Nature – or, for that matter, art – simply do not spend their time rotating conic sections.[15] But this already brings us to the subject of the hybrid object, to which I turn in the next section.

The main observation I wish to make here, still on the subject of the hybrid treatise, is its prevalence in Archimedes' writings. We have noted just now the *Planes in Equilibrium* and the *Floating Bodies*, treatises dedicated to hybrid fields. The *Method* and the *Quadrature of the Parabola*, as mentioned above, were all about the dual, hybrid treatment of a single set of

[15] Landels' (1978: 191) suggestion – that such conoids of revolution might be considered as approximations of hulls of ships – is an interesting suggestion, but notice that nothing in Archimedes' treatment allows any results to be transferred into objects approximating conoids of revolution; everything is predicated on the object being *precisely* of this geometrical description: it is critical to Archimedes' discussion that even small geometrical differences may give rise to hydrostatic results that are qualitatively distinct. (To be fair, Landels himself mentions the possibility merely so as to discard it.)

problems. I have not even mentioned the *Sand-Reckoner* in this section – the clearest example of a hybrid treatise ranging across arithmetic, astronomy, and geometry (not to mention literature, on which more below: another literary-mathematical hybrid, to be mentioned below in more detail, is the *Cattle Problem*). While not hybrids in the strict sense, we have noted time and again the variegated, multipartite structure of several treatises, in particular both books on *Sphere and Cylinder* as well as *Spiral Lines*. Note also, in the same vein, the border-crossing between the arithmetical and the geometrical, in *Conoids and Spheroids*. Finally, I go back once again to the introduction to the *Stomachion*. Little is known of the way that treatise would have unfolded, but Archimedes did leave us with a clear hint concerning his overall stylistic – as well as scientific – preferences. Here is how the treatise begins:

As the so-called Stomachion has a variegated *theoria* of the transposition of the figures from which it is set up, I deemed it necessary . . . [to study its aspects].

At one level Archimedes is telling us merely that because the theory of the Stomachion is many-sided, it calls for several independent lines of study, but at another level – coming right at the starting point of the treatise – this can also be read as a credo, stating why Archimedes studies the Stomachion in the first place. He does so *because* the *theoria* it presents is variegated, many-sided. *Poikile* is the Greek word, which can be translated literally as "many-spangled" though possessing of a wide metaphorical meaning. Richness of texture seems to have been an overarching principle governing Archimedean style. And indeed, we find this richness of texture, this "poikilic" nature, in *all* of Archimedes' works. This word – *poikile* – occurs once in the extant geometrical works, preserved – barely – on a single moldy page towards the end of the Palimpsest (I return below, on p. 146, to another, non-geometrical appearance). We are lucky that it is so saved: I suggest it should serve as the key for the understanding of Archimedes' writing.[16]

## 3.3 THE HYBRID OBJECT

We have already looked at the *Balancing Planes*, not only in the preceding section but also in the preceding chapter. There, I mentioned Archimedes' treatise as an example of the enigmatic treatise. Just what is meant by

---

[16] It is worth recalling at this point that Kroll – the author of the classical case for the centrality of the mixing of genres in Hellenistic poetry – makes the mixing of genres one of two keys to the literature of Alexandria, the other being the principle of *poikilia* (1924: 203, n. 2).

## The hybrid object

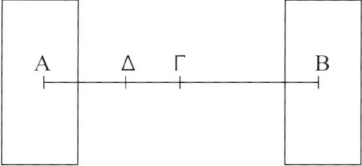

Figure 22

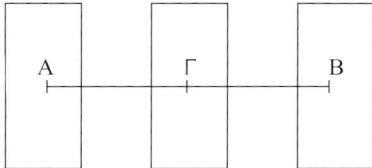

Figure 23

geometrical objects possessing weight, indeed possessing that mysterious "center of the weight?" The last notion might have a clear physical meaning (the point, suspended from which the body remains balanced), but just what is the *geometrical* meaning of the term?

Pursuing this question leads to further senses in which objects can become *hybrids*. It is not only that objects can straddle ontological domains: they may also straddle space. Consider the object constructed at the so-called proposition 4 of *Balancing Planes* (fig. 22):

If two magnitudes do not have the same center of the weight, then center of the weight of *the magnitude composed of both magnitudes* shall be . . . [following is a geometrical method of finding that point]

The diagram – which may well be authorial – represents the two objects not merely as distinct, but as *separate*. In other words, we are allowed to have a single, non-contiguous object. After all, that object has a single center! The impression of the diagram becomes a mathematical necessity in the following proposition, where three magnitudes with equal weight are arranged so that their centers of the weight are positioned on a straight line (fig. 23). To show that the point Γ is center of the weight of all three taken together, Archimedes first shows the point is center of the weight of the magnitude composed of A, B, i.e. of the two magnitudes separated by the magnitude Γ. This technique in fact becomes standard in what follows: to study centers of weight of "normal" objects such as the triangle, for instance, *ad hoc*, "bizarre" objects have to be set up, such as the object composed

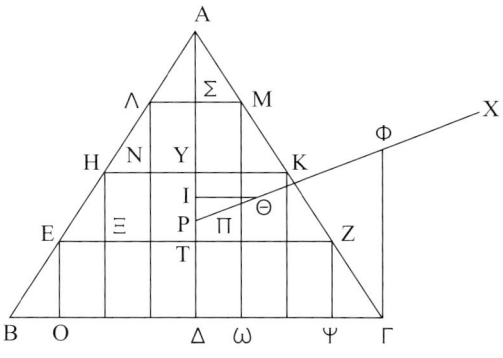

Figure 24

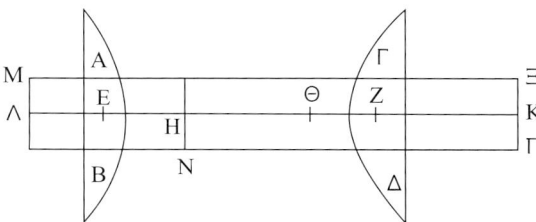

Figure 25

of all triangles along the edges of the triangle ABΓ, such as BOE, EΞH, etc. (Heiberg's proposition 13, see fig. 24). Or in the second book, as the parabolic segment is introduced, it is immediately presented by having two separate parabolic segments with a single center of weight (fig. 25) . . . But in fact the object composed of all edge-triangles in the triangle ABΓ above is hardly unique in Archimedes' writings: the rectification of curvilinear objects often involves some summed-object involving a set of micro-objects positioned along the edge of a large object, a kind of colony of barnacles along the spines of various leviathans. Here the spiral, e.g. *Spiral Lines* 21, fig. 26: all those small sectors of circles. Here the conoid, e.g. *Conoids and Spheroids* 19, fig. 27: all those small rectangles (standing for an even more fantastic object: the figure is three dimensional so that each of the rectangles represents the ring of a hollowed-out cylinder). The reader of Archimedes is used to such objects that stretch the very notion of objecthood. Nor are they specifically Archimedean. Once again, here is the author of solid

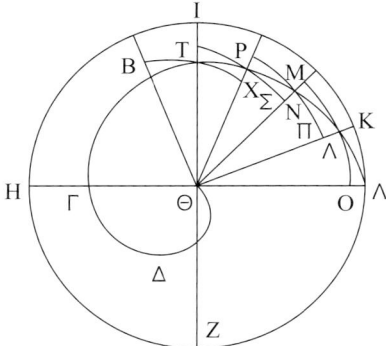

Figure 26

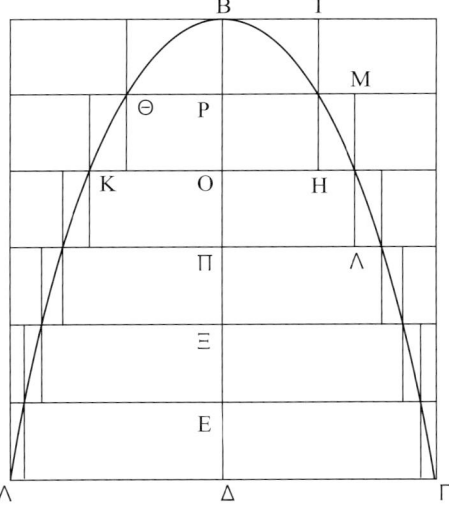

Figure 27

reputation, Apollonius. Perhaps the main contribution Apollonius makes to the elementary study of conic sections is the consideration of the cone itself in new, composite terms. The cone, for Apollonius, is the outcome not of a rotating triangle (Euclid's definition), but that of a line passing through a fixed point, rotating along the circumference of a circle. The outcome of that rotation is the production not of a *single* cone, but of *two*, with the original fixed point serving as their one point of contact

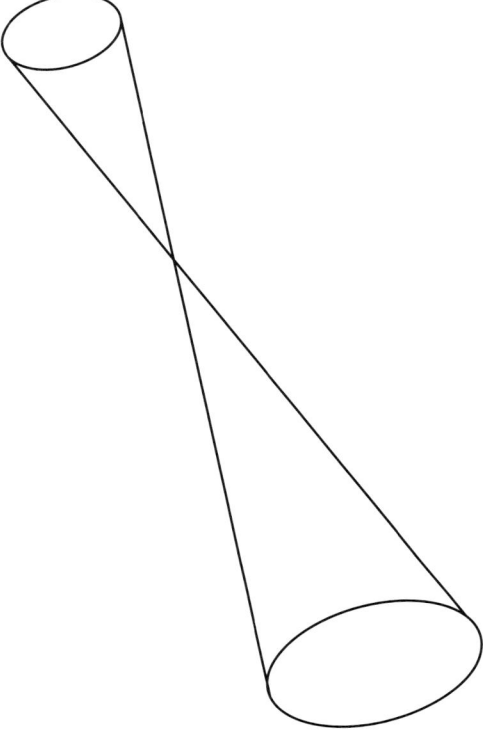

Figure 28

(fig. 28). The consequence of this new definition of a cone is that each hyperbola has another hyperbola correlated with it: the plane producing a hyperbola in the bottom half of the cone must also pass through the top half and produce there, naturally, another hyperbola. Acrobatic enough as an act of imagination – yet Apollonius goes further than that: he insists on considering the pair of hyperbolas thus curved out of the cone as a *single* object (after all, the two were the product of a single conic cut – and what is the definition of a conic section if not the product of a conic *cut*?). Those are baptized as "Opposite sections" (*Conics* I. 14) and, later on in the treatise, Apollonius will systematically prove results for this special kind of conic section.[17] In sum, we find non-contiguous objects

[17] "Apollonius understands curves in a strictly geometrical framework, so that the singular-plural nature of the opposite sections makes them an object of particular fascination, but also the source of a certain uneasiness" (Fried and Unguru 2001: 119).

everywhere – the edge-objects produced by the rectification of curvilinear figures; opposite sections; discontinuous magnitudes with a single center of weight.

Throughout, there is a *choice* involved in considering such sets as single objects. Archimedes could have avoided talking about the center of the weight of the two objects taken together, for instance, stating instead that the two balance at a given point. Apollonius did not need to introduce a special object for the "opposite sections:" he could instead have shown that each hyperbola has another conjoined with it. The edge-objects of rectification could be discussed in purely quantitative terms, as the summation of so many distinct areas or solids, rather than being lumped together as a single composite object. In short, we see a deliberate choice to mark the paradox of non-contiguous identity. Ultimately, this may be the same fascination we have seen above inside the narrative structure itself. At both the level of narrative and at the level of objects narrated, Hellenistic mathematics is interested in what may be termed *non-organic unities* – objects whose principle of individuation involves an internal incongruity. As it were, this is a culture which favors Goodman's grue and bleen over green and blue.

Especially important in this respect is the entire class of objects whose principle of individuation – in the sense of their very mathematical content – involves some kind of internal incongruity. The opposite sections, after all, are indeed the outcome of a single, coherent geometrical act. But what about objects which are the product of *distinct* geometrical acts? Consider for instance the so-called *Quadratrix*, invented perhaps by a certain Hippias.[18] We have a square where the two lines AB, BΓ obviously coincide at the point B (fig. 29). Now think again of the two lines: BΓ should remain in your mind as a side of the square, but re-conceive line AB as the radius of a circle with center at A. The two lines have now become geometrically distinct. More than this: they shall now produce distinct geometrical acts, a bizarre geometrical feat of acrobatics. Line BΓ, the side of the square, should move downwards until it coincides with the bottom line AΔ; line AB, the radius of the circle, should move in its arc until, once again, it coincides with the same line AΔ. As it were: BΓ falls down, like a log falling, AB turns down, like a door closing (all of this metaphorical language is mine). The motions must be uniform (the log falls at the same speed throughout; the door closes with the same speed throughout). The

---

[18] As Knorr shows, this cannot be the fifth-century philosopher and must be a Hellenist geometer: see Knorr 1986: 80–6. The evidence for ascribing this to a Hippias derives from Proclus (p. 272), but the major source of evidence on the quadratrix itself is from Pappus, IV. 250.33 onwards.

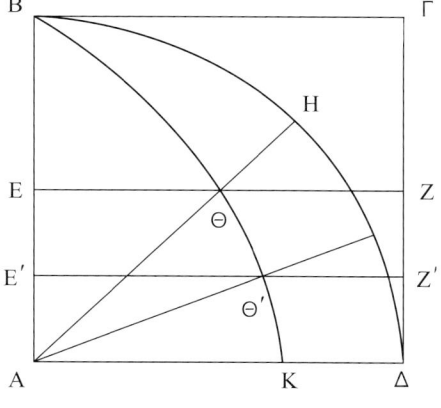

Figure 29

motions must be of equal overall speed (the log ends its falling all the way down at exactly the same moment the door ends its closing down).

At each moment during their motions, the log BΓ and the door AB coincide at some point: the point B at the beginning, and later on some such point as Θ. The points may then be conceived as tracing a curve which is called the quadratrix.

At the very last instant, true, the coinciding point gets smashed down, as it were, when the log and the door simply coincide. This adds yet another dimension of conceptual complexity to this fascinating object. Even without the problem of the end-point, the quadratrix is a perplexing object in that it is, in each moment of its life, the hybrid product of two incongruous motions: that of a straight line and that of a curve. This is not so surprising after all: as the name suggests, the curve can be used to rectify curvilinear objects. It occupies precisely this hybrid domain that so fascinated Hellenistic mathematicians, that combining the straight and the curved.[19]

The *Conchoid*, introduced by Nicomedes, is even more difficult to classify. Here a complex mechanical contraption is required even to consider the construction (fig. 30). We have a ruler KZ allowed to slide at one point on a groove, so that the point E of the ruler is always on the groove AB;

[19] Funkenstein 1986 offers a compelling analysis of the hybrid nature of the quadratrix – in Funkenstein's analysis (which was published without the benefit of Knorr's study) this is seen as a mark of the pre-Aristotelian character of Hippias' mathematics but, following Knorr, we may now see this as a deliberate deviation from Aristotelian strictures calling for the neat exclusion of motion from geometry.

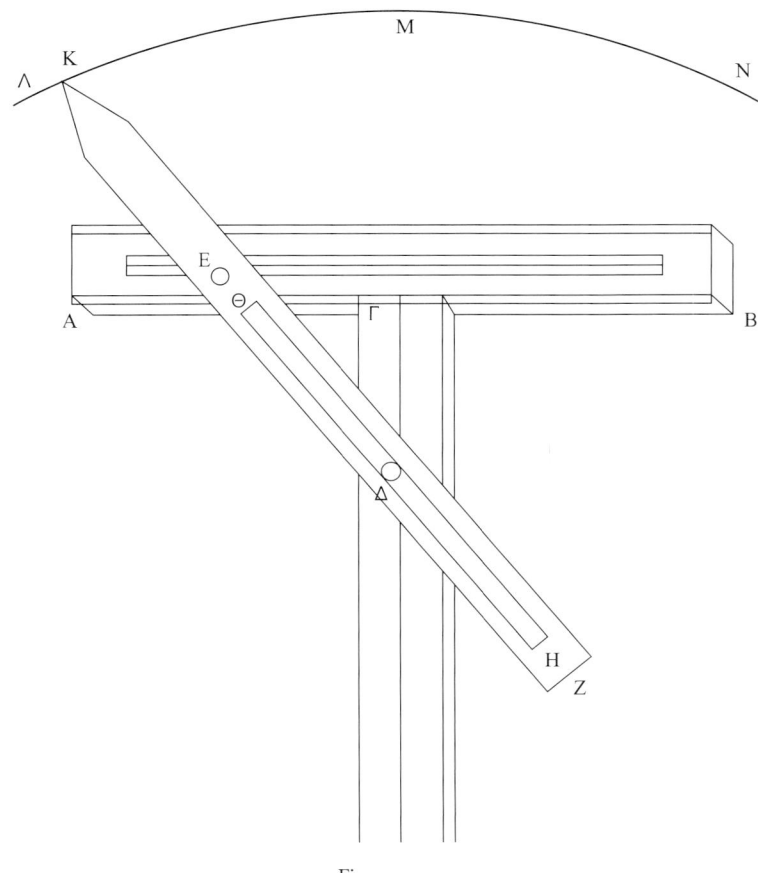

Figure 30

further, the ruler has in it a groove HΘ which is fixed to the point Δ: as it slides along the groove AB, it always must pass through the point Δ. The outcome of this operation is that the ruler KZ keeps having a certain protruding fixed length, EK, which also always, when projected, passes through the point Δ. Perhaps the best way to think about this object is as of a circle where the center, on the one hand, and the radius, on the other hand, have become discontinuous. The point Δ is a kind of center; the length EK is a kind of radius. But they have become independent (note indeed that when the point Δ is imagined resting on the groove AB so that the center and the radius are made to touch, the conchoid collapses into a circle: in modern terms, we would say that a circle is a limiting case of a conchoid).

Both quadratrix and conchoid involve not only an inherent congruity built into their defining characteristics (a straight line and a radius in the quadratrix, a center and a radius disjoint in the conchoids), but also an inherent incongruity built into their conceptual underpinnings. The conchoid essentially involves the conceptual hybrid we are already familiar with, of geometry and mechanics. The quadratrix involves another conceptual hybrid, of a new and striking nature: that between geometry and time. This would be familiar from astronomy. Indeed the two astronomical methods introduced by Apollonius – eccentrics and epicycles – are closely related to the objects described here. An eccentric is the result of a circle becoming disjoint from itself (rather like the conchoids), with its rotation defined relative to a center other than its own; the epicycle is the result of a circle hybridized with another circle. In both cases, crucially, the definition of the trajectory fundamentally involves time: the objects should not merely move in a certain way, they must do so while keeping, each, the same speed.

This is obvious for astronomical objects, perhaps: they do move after all. But the quadratrix is more intriguing, in presenting what is after all an abstract geometrical curve. And yet, a condition for the construction of the quadratrix is that the objects move in uniform speed, concluding their two motions simultaneously. Such terms as "uniform speed" and "simultaneity" do not have an obvious geometrical meaning. But if indeed (as is likely) Hippias was a relatively late Hellenistic geometer, we should then note that this striking marriage of geometry and time was not original to him. Once again, we need to go back to Archimedes – indeed, go back to the treatise I used to introduce this book. The spiral, after all (as noted on p. 5 above), is explicitly a product of motions expressed in speeds. It is the product of a point moving out from the center of a circle, progressing in uniform motion as it goes out on a radius of that circle, even as that radius rotates, again in uniform motion, around the center, both motions completed simultaneously: the crossing of the entire radius, and its rotation around the entire circle. The similarity to the quadratrix is obvious and there is little doubt that Archimedes' spiral was the direct inspiration for Hippias. And note how explicitly speeds are brought by Archimedes into the geometrical discourse: as already mentioned above when describing the narrative structure of *Spiral Lines*, the treatise begins with two propositions on speeds. I quote the second enunciation:

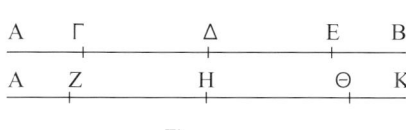

Figure 31

If, with each of two points being carried along some line – not the same – moved in uniform speed each with itself, in each of the lines two lines are taken, of which the first are traversed by the points in equal times, as well as the second; the lines taken shall have the same ratio to each other.

This intentionally enigmatic sentence can be unpacked with the diagram (fig. 31): one point is carried from Γ to E, making a stop at Δ; exactly synchronously with it, another point is carried from Z to Θ, making a stop at H at the same instant as the first did at Δ. Both move at uniform (though possibly distinct) speed. Then ΓΔ:ΔE::ZH:HΘ. This is all so puzzling because it asks us to imagine several speeds occurring together. It will not do here to think of speeds as abstract relations of abstract times and abstract spaces. The two motions must be simultaneous, so that the actual time in which events unfold must be imagined as well. At the same time, all of this has to be translated into the abstract terms of proportion.

The situation is directly comparable to Archimedes' treatment of balancing planes. Archimedes quickly establishes the law of the balance, by which objects balance when their distances are reciprocally proportional to their magnitudes. Thus the balance becomes a kind of concrete proportion. Similarly here, Archimedes develops his study of speeds to the point that the claim of "uniform, simultaneous speed" becomes equivalent to a proportion statement. From this point onwards the mathematical manipulation consists of exploiting the possibilities of considering the physical situation once as a configuration of objects in space, once again as a system of proportions. This hybrid – this duality – is at the heart of the original thought of both Archimedes' studies, in the statics of planes and in the dynamics of spirals.

Spirals are perfect hybrids, combining speeds and proportions, straight and curved motions. Archimedes was also the author of perfect mosaic objects: geometrical configurations that are literally combinations of heterogeneous constituents. What after all is the *Stomachion* if not a study in the combinatorics of a mosaic? Those fourteen, mostly non-congruent pieces, can well be taken as metaphor for the type of object studied by Hellenistic geometers (fig. 5). The object cannot be derived by any simple set of principles: it is fundamentally a set of figures thrown together haphazardly. And necessarily so: a system of mutually congruent pieces would allow far fewer combinations, far easier to detect . . . Another object marked by its many spangled variety is produced by Archimedes in another minor masterpiece, the *Cattle Problem*. There, the eight types of cattle are characterized not only by a division into male and female but also by a division into white, black, yellow – and "many-colored:" *poikilon*, again!

With the *Stomachion*, Archimedes' contribution was merely to notice the fascination of an already given object, while the *Cattle Problem* is a pure flight of fancy. Much more striking, therefore, is Archimedes' project of identifying three-dimensional mosaics – as fantastically difficult to comprehend as the *Stomachion* itself. This was Archimedes' study in semi-regular polyhedra. Here, once again, triangles, squares, hexagons, and more complex polygons are folded together to form fantastic figures. It is a distinct rule of the game that each angle – each meeting of the polygons – must involve *different* shapes, i.e. a mosaic is explicitly required. I have discussed above the semi-regular polyhedra as a phenomenon of the carnival of calculation, but no less than that, they form a geometrical carnival. And what a striking, fantastic mosaic this one is for instance – encompassing, say, thirty squares, twenty hexagons and twelve decagons in a single mosaic! This potential for visual carnival was fully exploited, finally, by another master of playful mathematics, Kepler – whose own study, based on Pappus' report, of semi-regular polyhedra (inside the *Harmonices Mundi*) is richly and variedly illustrated (the visual source for the figures on the cover of this book).

The *Stomachion* and the semi-regular polyhedra are perhaps not at the very center of the Archimedean mathematical project. So it is worth noting that at the very heart of this project lies a geometrical hybrid. I mean of course the straight and the curved. Needless to say, this is the subject matter of the *Measurement of the Circle*. Further, in both books on the *Sphere and Cylinder* Archimedes studied the relations between spheres and other objects, marked by being "less curved:" the cylinder as against the volume of the sphere, the circle as against its circumference. *Spiral Lines* and the *Quadrature of the Parabola* both reduce curvilinear planes to rectilinear ones; *Conoids and Spheroids* do the same with curvilinear solids. *Planes in Equilibrium*, as well as *Floating Bodies*, in spite of their titles, lead not so much to the study of statics and hydrostatics as such, but rather to the simplification of a parabola (in the case of *Planes in Equilibrium*) and of conoids in revolution (in the case of *Floating Bodies*). Finally, the *Method* itself offers two new results in the rectification of curvilinear solids, while revisiting many similar results from Archimedes' oeuvre. In a word:

*The hybrid object* 147

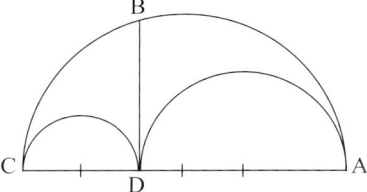

Figure 32

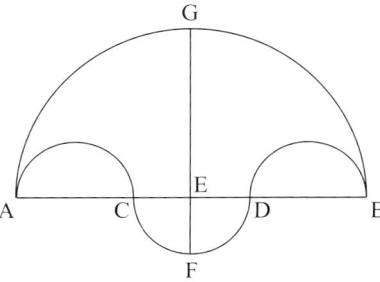

Figure 33

all of Archimedes' work can be fitted into one of two categories: either they engage primarily in a carnival of calculation (*Sand-Reckoner*, *Cattle Problem*, *Stomachion*, *Semi-regular Polyhedra*) or they are dedicated to the surprising juxtaposition of rectilinear and curvilinear objects.

To see this, let us mention the three remaining works whose Archimedean provenance is less clear, all preserved in Arabic: *Lemmas*, *Mutually Tangent Circles* and *Heptagon in a Circle*. The case of the so-called "lemmas" is very clear: Archimedes develops two new objects – as was his wont – both based on surprising curvilinear configurations. These are the *Arbelos* (fig. 32: a semi-circle minus two semi-circles) and the *Salinon* (fig. 33: a semi-circle minus two semi-circles, plus one semi-circle). Both are reduced to simpler, "less curved" objects: they are equal to a single, simple circle. This is all very reminiscent, in a miniature mode, of the major thrust of *Sphere and Cylinder* – though note here the visually appealing, mosaic-like object created by Archimedes. (I shall return to discuss the strange names themselves in the following section). Two further works are not as easy to categorize: the *Mutually Tangent Circles* and the *Heptagon in a Circle*. The first is about striking results obtained when certain lines are drawn according to the configurations obtained within tangent circles – clearly a combination of the curved and the straight, then, even if, exceptionally, no measurement of curved objects is at stake. As for the *Heptagon in a Circle*, here indeed the authorship is very difficult to detect (what we have is a treatise by Thabit bin Qurra – an able scholar and so likely to be original at least in part – ascribed by him to the authority of Archimedes). This is a sophisticated work, but its moment of surprise is based not so much on the very inscription of a heptagon in a circle (as the title implies) as on a complex construction based purely on rectilinear principles.[20] If the treatise involves more of the straight-curved combination than Euclid's own inscriptions within circles (of which more below), this is because the construction is indeed so hard to obtain. And so, the only exception to the rule that Archimedes' geometry is about the straight and the curved: a treatise titled *Heptagon in a Circle*! – an exception to prove the rule if ever there was one . . .

Of course Archimedes did not invent the circle. Indeed the little we know of the earliest Greek geometry suggests that the circle was an object of fascination from the very beginning. This was the ultimate subject matter of Hippocrates' *Quadrature of Lunules* – where bizarre objects, enclosed between arcs of different circles, are found equal to normal rectilinear areas. Aristotle's comments imply that attempts to square the circle were widespread.[21] A relation between the cone and the cylinder was noted already by Democritus before being published by Eudoxus (this we learn from Archimedes himself, in his introduction to the *Method*).[22] This result is at the heart of Euclid's *Elements* xii, i.e. one of the two advanced books on solid geometry (alongside *Elements* xiii, dedicated to regular solids). This mention of Euclid, though, reminds us immediately that much of Greek mathematics can be done without recourse to the combination of the straight and the curved. Euclid's *Elements* begin with two books where striking geometrical results are found without the circle ever being used as more than an interim instrument in the solution of problems; then book iii of the *Elements*, on the circle, hardly has room for any rectilinear figures. The first combination of the straight and the curved in Euclid's *Elements* arises in book iv, where regular polygons are inscribed and circumscribed in and about circles. Here however the circle is largely a scaffold for a book dedicated to rectilinear figures, and there is no real attention paid to any surprising combinations of the straight and the curved. Once

---

[20] See Knorr 1989b, Taisbak 1993.
[21] See especially *Physics* 185a14 ff. Simplicius' comment on this passage (*In Phys.* 53.28–69.34) is our main source of information for Hippocrates' *Quadrature of Lunules*.
[22] Heiberg 430.2–9.

again, thereafter, the curved disappears in books v and vi, dedicated to proportion as such and in plane geometry. The following three books on numbers, as well as book x on irrationals, do not lend themselves to the theme of the straight and the curved. When geometry returns to the fore in book xi, this is once again solid geometry produced with rectilinear figures alone. Book xii, as mentioned above, is the only book of the *Elements* to combine the straight and the curved in a meaningful way (in book xiii, the inscription of regular solids within a sphere is once again no more than curvilinear scaffolding for the sake of rectilinear geometry).

Among the many avenues opened up in the first two centuries or so of Greek geometry, Archimedes set himself on a single path: that of the striking juxtaposition of the straight and the curved. He made this field almost his own. We do not see his contemporaries or followers engaging in the invention of strange objects to be squared: no more spirals, conoids, arbeli, or selina. Strange objects are of course created, such as the conchoid or the quadratrix themselves, but as the very name of the quadratrix suggests, these are now tools for rectification rather than objects of rectification. Archimedes did not open the gates for an entire procession of curves – this would have to wait for the scientific revolution itself with, ultimately, its generalization of the very notion of the curve as the cornerstone of a new kind of mathematics. Familiar now with this mathematics of curves, we may even need to make an effort of imagination so as to understand how much those Archimedean objects transcended any simple definitions, how much they essentially trade on paradox and surprise: produced by a combination of the mechanical and the geometrical, or the kinematic and the geometrical, and always – by this combination – the essence of Archimedes' science – of the straight and the curved. This was, literally, a science of the hybrid.

### 3.4 A VIGNETTE: THE SCIENTIFIC NAME

I quote from Nicomachus' *Arithmetic*, our major source for the *Sieve* (*koskinos*) of Eratosthenes (D'Ooge's translation of 1.13:2):

> The production of those numbers is called by Eratosthenes the "sieve," because we take the odd numbers mingled together and indiscriminate and out of them by this method of production separate, as by a kind of instrument or sieve, the prime and incomposite by themselves, and the secondary and composite by themselves . . .

We are already familiar with the method itself, where we take a list of odd numbers written in natural order, and annotate starting from 3 every third number, starting from 5 every fifth, etc. . . . A fine example of the carnival of calculation: an open-ended process of calculation whereby the jumbled-up infinity of primes is in some sense brought under control. Indeed the metaphor explicitly brings forward the notion of order: the primes and non-primes are to start with all mixed up in the natural sequence, but the operation ends up with (up to a point) all non-primes marked as distinct from primes.

What I wish to concentrate on right now is the very presence of metaphor. Here is a new phenomenon of scientific naming: no longer a direct, literal representation of the object. Some Greek mathematician must have been the first to think of a solid composed of twelve regular pentagons – perhaps in the fourth century? – but he did not call it "the football." In the sober, literal naming typical of much early Greek scientific coinage, this was called "dodecahedron," "the twelve-faced."[23] And indeed, within the context of the precisely literal and economic Greek mathematical discourse, the presence of metaphor would be an extreme example of the presence of authorial voice. To call this operation by the name "sieve" would not arise naturally from the impersonal mathematical operation itself: it would be an authorial statement, vividly presenting to us the thought of Eratosthenes himself.

More than this: it would present to us a juxtaposition of the world of mathematical objects with that of a concrete, in this case quite mundane activity. One might call it a humble activity, even – though perhaps what may come to mind is the treatment of agriculture in the bucolic genre, where the menial and the earthly, reflected by the urbane wit of the poet, may become ironically celebrated.[24] Certainly relevant here is Eratosthenes' own poetic reference to the possible applications of the method of finding

---

[23] Such metaphor as is present in natural Greek, say, *kulindros*, "roller" – for cylinder – almost always predates scientific practice and is probably dead metaphor by the time mathematicians come to study the objects. This is very different from the process of deliberate scientific coinage, on which I concentrate in this section. It is likely that the practice has at least one pre-Hellenistic antecedent, in Eudoxus' naming a certain curve as "hippopede," i.e. "the horse-fetter" (referring to the cruel practice of tying together the legs of horses with figure-of-eight-shaped shackles): see Simplicius *in Cael.* 497.3, Proclus 127–8. Hippocrates of Chios, even earlier, has called some figures "lunules," but this perhaps should be seen not as metaphor but as the literal application of normal Greek, where a lunule-shape would be called, indeed, a "lunule."

[24] We shall briefly mention this urbane wit – perfected, of course, by Theocritus – in the following chapter. And is it an accident that the goatherd of the *Third Idyll* refers ruefully to Agroio, the κοσκινόμαντις (that is, "sieve-fortune-teller"), who found that Amaryllis cares not for him (Theocritus III.31–3)? Gow (1952 *ad loc.*) records from Philostr. *Vit. Ap.* 6.11 that fortune telling by sieve was practiced by shepherds. Is perhaps coscynomancy, rather than the sieve as a mere agricultural implement, connoted by Eratosthenes' title? For after all the method allows one to find that which, before, lay hidden (unloved by Amaryllis – or unmeasured by any number . . .)

two mean proportionals, e.g. for the measurement of "byre, or corn-pit, or the space of a deep, / hollow well."[25] This occurs in the course of Eratosthenes' epigram on his method (Powell *Coll. Alex.* 66–7), preserved inside Eutocius' catalogue of solutions to the problem of finding two mean proportionals. This method is useful for three-dimensional measurements. The prose text refers, soberly, to the use of the solution in constructing war-machines or, in general, liquid and dry measures.[26] One cannot however simply talk about "liquid and dry measures" in a poem: this would be, so to speak, too dry. Eratosthenes therefore reaches for a poetic genre available to him, that of the bucolic. We do not have the original context of Eratosthenes' *Sieve* method – was it perhaps in poem form as well? – but the sensibility seems to be similar. Into the dry arithmetical discourse is woven a metaphor suggestive not only of the concrete world but also of its literary representations. Such scientific names as "the sieve" achieve, simultaneously, several striking juxtapositions: the impersonal and the authorial; the abstract and the concrete; the literal and the metaphorical; the elevated and the humble; the scientific and the literary.

The sieve is perhaps suggestive of the bucolic. The "Lock" would be suggestive of erotic poetry and indeed had much of its life inside poetry – with the mock-erotic elevated to the level of panegyric or, perhaps, mock-panegyric. Appropriately, we also make a transition from arithmetic and calculation to the more elevated field of astronomy. And so, the most celebrated scientific name of the Hellenistic era was the *Lock of Berenice*. Our information derives from Callimachus' *Aitia* (fr. 110), and was further elaborated by Catullus, poem 66. It does derive, though, from the mathematical context we have followed so far in this book: it refers back to the work of the astronomer Conon, i.e. Archimedes' closest associate. The outlines of the story are familiar: Queen Berenice had vowed to dedicate a lock to the temple of Arsinoe, should her husband (and the dedicatee of Eratosthenes' poem), King Ptolemy III, return unharmed from his Syrian campaign. Shortly after he did in 245, the dedicated lock disappeared from the temple. Conon's brilliant contrivance had it that a loosely defined stellar constellation – between the Lion and the Virgin – was an apotheosis of the lock. We are fortunate to have (some of) Callimachus' as well as Catullus' poetic treatment, but one would very much wish to see the original text – was it prose? – by Conon. Clearly the dedication must have been shot through with irony, as after all the sobriety of descriptive astronomy is predicated upon the immutability of the fixed stars. To the striking

[25] Eutocius 96.12–13.   [26] Eutocius 90.18–19.

juxtapositions of Eratosthenes' *Sieve* one should add here the striking juxtaposition of the fixed and the changeable. As it were: compensating for the sacrilege of removing a dedication from the temple by the sacrilege of disturbing the fixity of the heavens. Callimachus' treatment would take this a step further, the story now told by the now-astral lock, mourning its removal from its beloved Berenice! – One does indeed note the theme of disjointedness we have seen already: the lock has been twice removed from Berenice's head, which I dare compare to the disjointedness of Apollonius' opposite sections or Nicomedes' center and radius in the conchoid . . . Yet there was some astronomical sense to the identification: somewhat hazy with what we now describe as the brightness of a star cluster, the area of the sky identified by Conon does present something of the glittering surface of a lock, and describing such a stellar phenomenon could be couched, among other things, as science. Once again: it is of course part of natural Greek language (as of many other languages) to name parts of the sky after mythical, often animate objects (more of this below, as we come to discuss Aratus). To have this natural language process extended into deliberate scientific coinage is however quite a different matter, and we see here a very self-conscious use of scientific naming, this time clearly as part of a courtly joke. The joke, incidentally, stuck: Ptolemy has the group as "the Lock" and Tycho has made it into a constellation, returning to mention Berenice herself as well. Hellenistic metaphor thus became part of our sky.

I have just mentioned Nicomedes' conchoid: much less famous, here is yet another example of Hellenistic mathematical metaphor, or perhaps simile (literally, the conchoid means "shell-like"). Clearly the intended simile is visual – the curve is meant to look like a shell – and one is reminded of Archimedes' "conoid" for a solid of revolution produced by parabola or hyperbola, indeed highly reminiscent of a cone, and "spheroid" for a solid of revolution produced by ellipse, where the similarity is even more obvious. But the simile of the shell is much more striking, in that it brings together the world of mathematics and that of nature – indeed, it brings together art and nature, since Nicomedes' curve is explicitly produced by a mechanical instrument. But what is so shell-like about the figure? Knorr has looked closely at this problem, his main motivation being a related problem of Greek mathematical nomenclature. Proclus tells us of the existence of another ancient curve, the cissoid, i.e. the "ivy-like."[27] What were the mathematical properties of this curve? Knorr, trying to find an answer to this question, ends up suggesting that the cissoid could have

---

[27] Proclus, *Commentary to Euclid* III, 128, 187.

been an extension of the conchoid. The last one, to recall, was produced by a ruler sliding along a straight line, producing a kind of undulating shape whose forms may vary depending on the precise parameters of "center" and "radius" of the given conchoid. Imagine now the same ruler sliding not along a straight line but along the circumference of a circle, and you have another set of undulating figures, this time enclosed. What would have been suggestive here about the ivy shape? Knorr's comments are incisive (1986: 263):

> These considerations show that for the ancients, as for us, there is no single shape which can be set out as "*the* ivy shape". . . . This in itself lends support to our identification of the "cissoids" with the circle-based conchoids; for we may distinguish at least four basic forms for the latter, many of which have a convincing resemblance to one or another of the ivy forms. There would thus be a certain poetic justice in assigning these curves this name, since the diversity of the mathematical forms so neatly matches that of their natural eponyms. One also perceives the parallel with the line-based conchoids of Nicomedes. After all, what is "*the* shell-shape"? . . . Conceivably, the mutual diversity of forms was a factor encouraging their association.

Knorr's interpretation is doubly speculative: once in his geometrical identification of the ancient cissoid, yet again in his interpretation of the name as referring to the diversity of the form speculatively identified. Even so, and even for the conchoid alone, the comments stand. The conchoid (as well as the cissoid, in Knorr's interpretation) is multiform in a deep way: with different parameters for the center and the radius, the shape may assume different topological properties. It may or may not possess a point of singularity; it may or may not contain a "loop" (fig. 34). Is it not likely that it was the very multiplicity – even open-endedness – inherent in the diversity of shell forms, which inspired its use in Nicomedes' coinage? Inventing a geometrical shape whose form is hard to characterize and is indeed essentially multiple, Nicomedes, cleverly, turned to a simile of equal ambiguity and multiplicity. The wit of the coinage consists in the double meaning of "-like" in the expression "shell-like:" at one level the likeness is merely visual (comparable to the use of "-like" in Archimedes' "cone-like" and "sphere-like"), at another the likeness is conceptual and has to do with the underlying multiplicity of form – a conceptual likeness that, in a sense, undercuts the visual one.

The above is almost too good to be true – perhaps indeed an over-interpretation. Let us note then the very use of simile in a mathematical context, this time turning to the natural world. The case is not isolated, in fact the very word "shell" appears early to have taken on a different

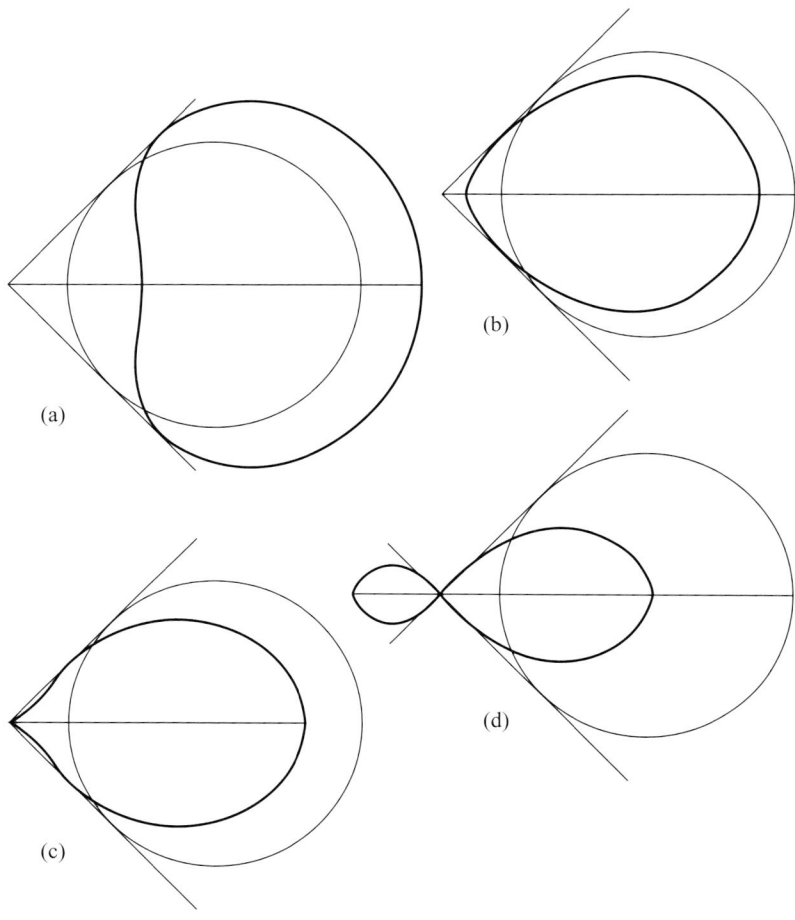

Figure 34

geometrical sense (yet another example of the diversity of the form!). This is the "cochlias," once again a shell, though this time the emphasis is clearly on the three-dimensional, repeatedly turning nature of the shell-form. The cochlias is a three-dimensional spiral form, with the motion "inside-out" of the Archimedean spiral transformed to a motion "upwards:" the point drawing the figure is located at the end of a radius that keeps rotating, even as it levitates upwards inside the cylinder (fig. 35). We are told that Apollonius has dedicated a treatise to this figure, likely in competition with

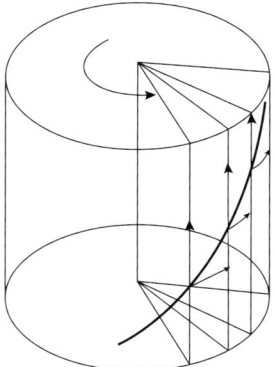

Figure 35

Archimedes' study of spirals.[28] As the figure is also the one governing the "Archimedes Screw," it may well have been an invention of Archimedes himself – though the tradition connecting the instrument to Archimedes is fairly unreliable.[29] It may be that Apollonius himself referred to the figure as "cochloid," turning it into another simile, indeed almost too similar in sound to Nicomedes' "conchoid"[30] (which of the two came first? Was the confusion intentional?). Mathematically the two are quite distinct, but the cochlias is mathematically closely related to another object: it is the product of two correlated motions, one radial, the other along a plane. This is very close indeed to the quadratrix (the product of the intersection of a radial motion and that of a line), and it is interesting to note Apollonius' metaphorical summing up of the situation: "the cochlias is the sister of the quadratrix."[31]

The "conchoid" was coined by Nicomedes, and the "cochlias" by Apollonius. While the "cissoid" is not assigned in our sources to any author, it was often assumed to derive from Diocles,[32] and is likely to come from the same generation following Archimedes. Earlier examples such as Eratosthenes' "sieve" and Conon's "lock" suggest that the practice has earlier antecedents; we do have indirect reference for Archimedes engaging in the

[28] The suggestion of (implicit?) competition is made by Knorr 1986: 295–7. The main evidence for Apollonius' study of the cochlias is *In Eucl.* 105.
[29] Dijksterhuis 1987: 21–3.
[30] As Knorr points out, it appears that the scribe of our Pappus manuscript keeps confusing the two words (Knorr 1986: 282 n. 49).
[31] Simplicius *In Cat.* 7. 192. The quadratrix itself is not named metaphorically. Instead, we see here a metonymic coinage, naming a mathematical object after one of its functions.
[32] Knorr 1986: 246.

same game of metaphorical coinage. These are the "arbelos" and "salinon" reported in the Arabic treatise of "lemmas." Both are specifically reported as "that which Archimedes calls *arbelos*" (proposition 4) or "that which Archimedes calls *salinon*" (proposition 14). The significance of "salinon," in particular, is not clear, but the Greek provenance is obvious (the terms – preserved in Arabic – are clearly of non-Semitic origin) and is most likely to be, then, by Archimedes himself. "Arbelos" is a good Greek word, meaning "leather-knife," a name quite appropriate for the shape (fig. 30). It is further reported by Pappus, though not ascribed by him to Archimedes.[33] We are back to the humble world of the "sieve," though in this case without bucolic notes to glorify it: the leather-knife connotes the lowliest of occupations. Was the "salinon," indeed – as is often assumed in modern literature – a very rare Greek word for "salt-cellar?"[34] This would fit the semantic range of the leather-knife. In fact all examples of coinage we have seen so far in this section – the sieve, the lock of hair, the shell (twice), the ivy, the leather-knife, and the salt-cellar – share this interest in the humble (sieve, shell, leather-knife, salt-cellar), the rejected and lost (lock of hair), the suspect even: the ivy, above all, was a symbol for drunkenness.[35] The scientific game of Hellenistic geometry is no place for sobriety: it is based on the jarring juxtaposition of the literal and the metaphorical, and specifically on the jarring juxtaposition of the abstract world of science with a humble stratum of human life.

Yet another dimension of metaphor and recherché coinage appears to be that of the mathematical treatise itself. Indeed often we are left without the ancient titles. But some are well documented – and are quite striking. Indeed, Archimedes' title *Stomachion* or *Stomachicon* was probably based on the name of a game established prior to his own treatise. But do note the authorial decision to name a treatise after a game called, literally, "belly-ache!" The title of Archimedes' *Psammites*, literally "the Sander" (which we refer to as *The Sand-Reckoner*) would belong to the same semantic range (if indeed authorial: there is no way of telling for sure). Once again, the title is motivated by the contents, which have to do after all with filling up the world with grains of sand. We shall in the next section return to consider the literary trope of the grains of sand, but let us note that, taken in isolation, titles such "Sander," or the "Belly-ache," suggest the same humble world of the "leather-knife" and "salt-cellar." Of a different semantic range, but no less enigmatic, is the title of what is to us Archimedes' most remarkable

---

[33] Pappus IV 208.12, 224.16. The *e silentio* is not significant: Pappus does not discuss the origins of the word or of the object.
[34] Dijksterhuis 1987: 404.   [35] Knorr 1986: 262.

treatise, the so-called *Method*. Here the modern title is quite misleading. Archimedes' own title (further corroborated by the *Suda*)[36] was *ephodikon*, the Greek word *ephodos* meaning "an approach." Archimedes' treatise was not about some method whereby results can be gained; it was about the principle that one can find a certain *approach* to a problem, even without solving it in a completely satisfactory way. The title is appropriately translated, then, "The Approacher." The modern title "The Method" is a clear invitation. The ancient title, "The Approacher" must have been intended as an enigma – as was the treatise itself. Comparable in its diffuse semantic range would be Hypsicles' *anaphorikon* – "the stander-upper," perhaps – an enigmatic, open-ended title (whose significance is only gradually resolved through the reading of this brief treatise).

We are in a position to make out something of the enigma of the titles of the *ephodikon* or the *anaphorikon*, by referring to their detailed contents. But what of Apollonius' *okutokion*? This, according to Eutocius, was the title of a study – already mentioned briefly in chapter 1 – of the boundaries on the ratio of the circumference to the diameter. (The boundaries found being finer-grained than those of Archimedes.)[37] Eutocius would hardly invent the title (which however does pleasantly anticipate Eutocius' own name . . .). Literally it means "quick delivery," though the root *oxus*, sharp, would be appropriate to the subject matter of finding fine-grained approximations. How delivery – in the obstetric sense of the Greek root *tokos* – was supposed to relate to either big numbers or the circumference of the circle, one can only guess. Was it that Apollonius' method allowed for a quick passage through the painful process of calculation? The semantic fields – of pain and of the humble – are not unlike the "bellyache" of the game studied by Archimedes and are continuous with those seen above for other Hellenistic mathematical names of either objects or treatises.

It should be said that the phenomenon may, in this case, be extended beyond mathematics itself. In general I do not pursue in this study the question of the nature of Alexandrian medicine, largely because the evidence does not allow for any direct comparisons. The main medical authors – the counterparts to Archimedes and Apollonius, such as Herophilus and Erasistratus – are known via testimony alone, nearly always in the polemic context of Galenic quotation. This provides us with practically no sense of the original texture of writing and allows us to infer,

---

[36] S.v. "Theodosius" (it appears that Theodosius wrote a commentary to the *Method*), where the title is given as *ephodion*.
[37] Eutocius 258.17.

158 *Hybrids and mosaics*

usually, no more than the dry bones of doctrine. The act of naming, however, is much more robust: later authors would often quote an earlier name and assign it to its inventor, as nomenclature after all does form an important part of medical doctrine. Indeed the bulk of Herophilus' anatomical fragments consist of quotations concerning Herophilean coinage. Sometimes these are quoted so as to unpack an implicit metaphor and in this way to discuss a piece of Herophilean doctrine, sometimes merely so as to establish an identification. The emerging structure appears as a deliberate project of medical naming in third-century Alexandria.[38] A simple, representative example is from Rufus (Von Staden 1989: 227, T129):

One of the bones is called *kneme* [tibia] . . . Herophilus, however, also calls the tibia *kerkis* [lit. "weaver's shuttle; taper rod"].

Generally speaking, some of the Herophilean names make straightforward reference to topographic relations, or to internal anatomical relations: e.g. referring to a neural structure as *parenkephalis* (latin *cerebellum*: the name survives), i.e. beyond the part where the brain proper is (T77a), or to an especially thick vein as "artery-like" (T117). Most Herophilean coinage, however, was based on quite fanciful use of metaphor and, occasionally, of metonym. Of the last, the most successful case was that of the duodenum, in the Greek *dodekadaktulon* or the "twelve-fingered" (T98) – a rather striking name for an internal organ, so called for its length as stated by Herophilus! Another somewhat bizarre metaphor is calling the testicles (and consequently the ovaries too) "twins" (T109). The majority of the names, however, follows the pattern of the *kerkis* above – a name encapsulating some humble metaphor, usually from the domain of human labor. One brain process is a "styloid" (T90), i.e. like a pen, another – still in the domain of writing! – is a "lambdoid" (T92), yet another is "pharoid" (! – T92), apparently referring to the Pharos in Alexandria. Back to writing, a cavity in the brain is the "reed-pen" (T79). (In all of this, should one detect a certain self-referential ironic reference to the "bookishness" of medical naming?) Further: a membrane is "net-like" (T121), while an eye membrane – now from the natural domain, though still quite lowly – is "cobweb-like," and yet another is "grape-like" (T88). (The eye-membranes themselves are literally "coats" (e.g. T87), so back to the world of lowly, human artifacts.) Perhaps it is worth mentioning a piece of more detailed

---

[38] While noting the limitations of ancient medical nomenclature prior to Galen – largely due to the endemic lack of consensus – Lloyd (1983: 149–67) argues that Alexandria was indeed the main site for ancient medical naming.

anatomy – not quite crystallized into nomenclature – which is highly reminiscent of the same metaphorical vein (Von Staden 1989: 218, T111b):

[The mouth of the female pudendum], in the case of women who have given birth . . . becomes more callous, similar to the head of an octopus or to the upper part of the windpipe.

Once again we see the same metaphorical domains of objects of human labor or low animals. One is reminded, indeed, of one of the most celebrated moments of ancient medicine – the anticipation of the modern conception of the heart as pump, in Erasistratus' model of the functioning of the heart which makes metaphorical use of a bellows-pump.[39] This piece of doctrine is known to us only in some very mediated forms, and it is usually taken as an example of the use of mechanistic models in Alexandrian medicine. No less, however, this can also be taken as an example of the use of lowly metaphor in describing the human body.

To conclude, let us turn to Herophilus' most successful coinage, one where he has managed, inadvertently, to attach his *own* name. The ancients sometimes refer to Herophilus calling the confluence of the great cranial venous sinuses as "lenus," or wine-press (T122–3). This metaphor connects the world of human labor and artifacts with that of the world of drinking – somewhere between Eratosthenes' "sieve" and Nicomedes' "cissoid," then. Perhaps the metaphor was so striking that later speakers felt a need to refer it to its author so as to mitigate somehow for its non-literal character: the Latin tag gradually settled on "torcular Herophili," "Herophilus' wine-press" and, through this part of the brain – through this wine-press – Herophilus earned his anatomical immortality.

The above, of course, is just a sketch of Alexandrian medical coinage. Taken together, however, with my much more exhaustive survey of Hellenistic mathematical coinage, a pattern emerges. This is a period of intensive, deliberate naming. Much of this is metaphorical in a striking way. Specifically, there is a special emphasis on metaphors based on lowly domains, so that the unexpected juxtaposition of metaphor as such is in this case enhanced by the unexpected juxtaposition of the sublime and the humble. The themes of Alexandrian naming, then, are metaphor and bathos – fitting well into our overall picture of Alexandrian science as based on jarring juxtaposition, on hybrids and mosaics.

---

[39] See von Staden 1997: 201–2 and references there, especially the ancient sources collected at n. 80. Von Staden further documents the claim that this mechanical model of Erasistratus may well refer directly to a water-pump constructed by Ctesibius.

Specifically, the phenomenon of coinage involves the activity of *metaphor*. That scientists should engage in it is typical for a cultural climate where scientists, otherwise, move towards the literary mode. To conclude this chapter, let us now look at the most fundamental genre breaking of Hellenistic mathematics – the breaking of the boundary between science and literature itself.

### 3.5 MATHEMATICS TURNS TO LITERATURE

Let us return one more time to the fragment of Eratosthenes preserved inside Eutocius' catalogue of solutions to the problem of two mean proportionals. Note that I name this catalogue in a sober, mathematical fashion: in strict geometrical terms, the problem asks that, given two lines A and D, we find two more lines B and C such that A:B::B:C::C:D. Of course, this is more often referred to as the problem of "doubling a cube." I have noted already how misleading this naming is, on p. 57 above, but the point should be emphasized now. Mathematically, doubling a cube is indeed a consequence of finding two mean proportionals: the finding of two mean proportionals contains the finding of a cubic root,[40] which would allow one, given any linear measurement of a given solid object, to find the required linear measurement of another solid object whose volume stands in a given ratio to the original solid. For example, suppose that you are given a pyramid, whose side measures thirty yards, and that you want to enlarge the volume eight times. First find the cubic root of eight – which will be two (to do this geometrically, you need to solve the problem of finding two mean proportionals). Now make a new pyramid, with the same proportions, but with its linear measurements enlarged by a factor of two, i.e. the side should now measure sixty yards. Or if you wish to double a cube, then you need to find the cubic root of two. I mention all of this so that we remind ourselves how arbitrary and limited it is to label the problem as "doubling a cube." First, the problem involves finding two values, not just the cubic root. Second, the problem is general and abstract, not applied. Third, it may be applied for any solid, not just a cube. Fourth, it may be applied for any ratio, not just that of doubling. In point of fact, this may be seen as another act of naming based on metonym – a single practical application is taken to name the entire problem. This metonymic act of naming was undertaken by Eratosthenes, who squarely

[40] It may be seen as equivalent to the finding of two powers, $x^{\frac{1}{3}}$ and $x^{\frac{2}{3}}$.

positioned this problem within a literary setting. I quote once again from the beginning of the fragment:

Eratosthenes to King Ptolemy, greetings.

They say that one of the old tragic authors introduced Minos, building a tomb to Glaucos, and, hearing that it is to be a hundred cubits long in each direction, saying:

You have mentioned a small precinct of the tomb royal;
Let it be double, and, not losing its beauty,
Quickly double each side of the tomb.

He seems, however, to have been mistaken; for, the sides doubled, the plane becomes four times, while the solid becomes eight times. And this was investigated by the geometers, too: in which way one could double the given solid, the solid keeping the same shape; and they called this problem "duplication of a cube:" for, assuming a cube, they investigated how to double it. And, after they were all puzzled by this for a long time, Hippocrates of Chios was the first to realize that, if it is found how to take two mean proportionals, in continuous proportion, between two straight lines (of whom the greater is double the smaller), then the cube shall be doubled, so that he converted the puzzle into another, no smaller puzzle.

I break the quotation to make a number of comments. First, the dramatic quotation (*TrGF adesp.* F166) is unidentified. This would be in general a very weak *e silentio* argument (so much of ancient drama is lost). Still, the double indeterminacy of "they say that one of the old tragic authors" means that – whether or not the quotation is real – the text is doubly folded within literature. Once, in that it is introduced by drama, again in that the reference to this drama is shrouded within such mythopoeic words as "they say that one of the old tragic authors . . ."[41] Eratosthenes' strategy is to refer to mathematics via myth – and to shroud it, itself, in myth.

But notice the immediate response: no sooner was mathematics mythicized – and immediately myth is mathematized. The dry, matter of fact comment that "he seems, however, to have been mistaken," with the quick technical explanation following it, is a fine example of Hellenistic use of bathos: making a very rapid transition from the elevated world of myth and drama into that of elementary calculation.

Eratosthenes reverts back into the mythicizing of mathematics with "after they were all puzzled by this for a long time," and then introduces

---

[41] For whatever its worth, Wilamowitz (1894[1971]:53–4) did rule out ascribing this passage to any known, but lost work. (We recall the "nine muses" mentioned by Apollonius' treatise on multiplying a hexameter line – p. 52 above – where the quotation looks best if we assume it was *invented*.)

Hippocrates' discovery of the equivalence between duplication of the cube and the finding of two mean proportionals. Notice a fine detail here: Hippocrates' discovery is said to have "converted the puzzle into another, no smaller puzzle." Note that the operation of converting X into another, no smaller X is the very object of the problem of doubling a cube. This kind of metaphorical self-referentiality may well be intentional, and adds a further level of playful artistry. The important consequence is that the mathematical problem at the center of this text is not allowed to stand still in a literal, abstract domain: instead, it is enmeshed in a web of literary allusions and metaphors. Let us go on reading:

After a while, they say, some Delians, undertaking to fulfill an oracle demanding that they double one of their altars, encountered the same difficulty, and they sent messengers to the geometers who were with Plato in the Academy, asking them to find that which was asked. Of those who dedicated themselves to this diligently, and investigated how to take two mean proportionals between two given lines, it is said that Archytas of Tarentum solved this with the aid of semicylinders, while Eudoxus did so with the so-called curved lines; as it happens, all of them wrote demonstratively, and it was impossible practically to do this by hand (except Menaechmus, by the *shortness* – and this with difficulty). But we have conceived of a certain easy mechanical way of taking proportionals through which, given two lines, means – not only two, but as many as one may set forth – shall be found.

At this point the text moves on to a rather sober technical description, followed by a technical mathematical proof. Once again, then, we see the mythical and the mathematical juxtaposed. We also see, once again, mathematics mythicized: the story of the Delians, the semi-mythical Plato and his academy, and finally Archytas, Eudoxus, and Menaechmus, all well known to Eratosthenes through their own writings, introduced tantalizingly with another "it is said" and vague, non-technical descriptions: semicylinders, so-called (!) curved lines, the *shortness* . . .

One further notes a certain tension in Eratosthenes' rhetoric. In the following technical account, Eratosthenes would refer to the (genuine) practical applications of the problem in the construction of war-engines, as well as in solid measurement in general. However the tendency of the mythical introduction is to undercut radically any practical motivation of the problem: it is first suggested by a tragic speech and then interest flourishes as a consequence of an oracle, the duplication in both cases motivated by purely *ad hoc* architectural requests. The text builds, at the same time, a continuity as well as a tension between myth and mathematics. Eratosthenes' solution, in particular, occupies a curious position: because one cannot help feeling that *it came too late* – the Delians shall no more build their altar . . . The belatedness effect is precisely an effect of a dissonance in the text, between mythical and literary motivation, on the one hand, and mathematical practice on the other hand.

With the mathematical exposition over, Eratosthenes reverts to ekphrasis: he describes a dedication he has set up to commemorate the invention. This involved a similar multi-modal juxtaposition: a model of the machine, a mathematical diagram, a mathematical proof and finally an epigram. The last one is quoted again to round up Eratosthenes' text, so that the brief treatise, being introduced by literature, again reverts to it at its end:

> If you plan, of a small cube, its double to fashion,
> Or – dear friend – any solid to change to another
> In nature: it's yours. You can measure, as well:
> Be it byre, or corn-pit, or the space of a deep,
> 5 Hollow well. As they run to converge, in between
> The two rulers – seize the means by their boundary-ends.
> Do not seek the impractical works of Archytas'
> Cylinders; nor the three conic-cutting Menaechmics;
> And not even that shape which is curved in the lines
> 10 That Divine Eudoxus constructed.
> By these tablets, indeed, you may easily fashion –
> With a small base to start with – even thousands of means.
> O Ptolemy, happy! Father, as youthful as son:
> You have bestowed all that is dear to the Muses
> 15 And to kings. In the future – O Zeus! – may *you* give him,
> From your hand, this, as well: a scepter.
> May it all come to pass. And may him, who looks, say:
> "Eratosthenes, of Cyrene, set up this dedication."

I have already noted above the bucolic touch of 4–5. Note now that these lead on the brief shadow of a hunting scene, in lines 5–6; lines 7–10 serve once again the mythical theme, while lines 13–16 serve as dutiful suggestion of panegyric. Finally the introductory and concluding lines 1–3, 17–18 are epigrammatic proper. Lines 11–12, alone, are suggestive of the actual mathematical detail of the treatise. The epigram, a miniature of the treatise as a whole, wraps the mathematical content within a rich mosaic of interlocking generic suggestions.

This mini-treatise is unique only in its survival. It appears that Eratosthenes was a master of the literary-mathematical mosaic. Another treatise, apparently titled *The Platonic* (another tantalizing title), must have combined the mathematical, the philosophical, and the literary. The work itself is lost, but mentions of it by Plutarch and by Theon of Smyrna suggest that here, again, Eratosthenes played a mythic version of the problem of finding two mean proportionals.⁴² (So was the repeated "it is said," in the quotations above, an arch reference to Eratosthenes' own work?) Otherwise the best extant parallel to Eratosthenes' mini-treatise, as already suggested in the previous chapter, is Archimedes' *Sand-Reckoner*. Once again, this is a very rich mosaic of a work. The rough sequence is that of quasi-philosophical introduction, followed by cosmology, then followed by astronomy proper, at first experimental and only then theoretical, which is then followed by an abstract account of the arithmetical system invented by Archimedes, leading on to the detailed carnival of calculation mentioned in the first chapter of this book, leading to a final, abrupt but well-crafted conclusion (Heiberg II. 258.1–12. I add in roman numerals):

(i) Now then, it is obvious that the multitude of the sand having a magnitude (ii) equal to the sphere of the fixed stars (iii) which is assumed by Aristarchus, (iv) is smaller than 1,000 myriads of the seventh numbers. (v) And I suppose, King Gelon, that to the multitude who are not familiar with mathematics such things may appear incredible, (vi) but will persuade, because of the proof, those who are conversant [with mathematics], and have considered the issue of the distances and the sizes of the earth and the sun and the moon and the whole cosmos; (vii) for which reason I thought it will be not inappropriate for you to consider those things.

The touch of the court is here very light: in (vii) Archimedes merely suggests – and fleetingly, at that – that King Gelon is not among the multitude of ignoramuses. But note how Archimedes brings together the elements of the mosaic: (i) the original problem, with its suggestion of poetry (to which I turn below), (ii) astronomy, (iii) Aristarchus' heliocentric theses, (iv) Archimedes' new numbers. More than this: the conclusion carefully echoes the beginning of the treatise (I mark with Arabic numerals):

(1) Some, King Gelon, think the number of the sand is infinite in its multitude ((2) I mean not only [the sand] found around Syracuse and the rest of Sicily, but that of the entire land, inhabited and not). (3) While there are others who do not suppose it < = the number of the sand> to be infinite, but still <think> that

---

⁴² The story appears twice in Plutarch – *Moralia* 386E, 579A–D – once in Theon of Smyrna, Hiller 2.3–12. Theon explicitly cites his story from Eratosthenes' *Platonicus*. Plutarch's version in 579A–D is by far the longest version and, with its dialogue setting (*The Sign of Socrates*), might perhaps suggest that Eratosthenes' original, too, might have had dialogue form – what's more suitable for "The Platonist?" – But this suggestion of a further generic component is mere speculation, which perhaps does not do justice to Plutarch's originality. For a very full discussion of the *Platonicus*, see Geus 2002: 141–94.

there exists no named number of such a size that exceeds its < = the number of the sand's> multitude.

We have already noted the fine localization of the treatise by the sly passage (2). Note now another clever combination: the (1) "some think" and (3) "others who do not suppose" at the very beginning of the treatise are responded to, with the precise Greek verbs inverted, by (v) "I suppose" and (vii) "I thought," at the very end of the treatise. Such a precise ring structure may well be intentional (Greek has many verbs of cognition, and such precise choices are therefore less likely to be accidental), but of course this cannot be proved. Just as Archimedes' touch of the panegyric is lighter than Eratosthenes', so his use of literary form is less obvious. And yet the treatise is shot through with the device of bathetic allusion to the poetic canon: this is the point of the title and the basic contrivance of the treatise, as if the subject matter is the number of *sand*. The trope is, first of all, Homeric (*Il.* 9.385: "not even if he were to give me as many gifts as sand or dust . . ."). It is used, probably independently, by Pindar (e.g. *Ol.* 2.98: "since sand escapes number . . ."), and seems to have become an established, well-recognized trope.[43] The essence of the treatise is the mock-serious treatment of poetic statements as if they were meant as technically precise – in exactly the same way as Eratosthenes builds up the image of the mythical Minos, who makes a mistake in geometry . . . It would be an error to construe this as a war of cultures, with mathematics attacking poetry: after all such an interpretation would make a fool of Archimedes, as if he does not understand the inappropriateness of applying literal standards to poetic metaphor. The critique at the end of the treatise is not of archaic poets – who used language in an expansive, careless way – but of contemporary ignoramuses who do not bother to study mathematics. Poetry is central to the *Sand-Reckoner*, but in a subtle, oblique manner. Archimedes does not criticize poetry, explicitly: he instead reacts, implicitly, against the stance of contemporaries who were ready to accept the standard authority of the poets of the past (Homer is all we need! – as in Theocritus' *Idyll* 16.20). Archimedes reveals the limitations of poetry taken too literally – thus playing with potential for bathos when set side by side with a mundane reality to which it supposedly refers. The bathos is especially clever in this case, because the very object taken – sand – can be construed as metonymically suggestive of the grandeur of the sea, metonymically represented by

[43] See e.g. Nisbet and Hubbard 1970: 321 for a series of further references, all of which appear to be quite independent of each other. The trope of the sand is so obvious that it will not do as a vehicle of intertextuality, as there is nothing to mark its appearance in the text and so alert the reader to the intertextual axis. It is not Homeric or Pindaric; it is just poetic.

its shore (which is at the origin of the poetic trope), but can also be taken as the lowliest, because smallest, object. This aspect of smallness is what comes to the fore in the *Sand-Reckoner*, as a consequence of Archimedes' treatment of the grain of sand as a measuring unit. The epic poet is chided for a trivial error; the grandeur of the sea dissolves into a minimal measure – such is the literary effect of the *Sand-Reckoner*.

One is immediately reminded of several close analogues. I start with Hipparchus. In his combinatoric study mentioned in chapter 1 above, this second-century mathematician and astronomer seems to have approached Chrysippus with an attitude precisely parallel to that Archimedes takes towards the poets. To recall: Plutarch notes that Chrysippus has argued that the number of conjunctions of ten assertibles is more than a hundred myriads, which Hipparchus has shown to be wrong in finding the precise number, 103,049. Of course the situation is not quite parallel to that of Archimedes "correcting Pindar:" Chrysippus is a *bona fide* object for critique concerning detail. And yet everything would depend on the context of Chrysippus' original comment. Let us suppose that Chrysippus did not intend any precise statement, but instead said – as is likely – that the number of conjunctions is very large, offering a suggestive hyperbole. Hipparchus would have to be construed, then, as either, pedantically, missing the gist of Chrysippus' assertion or, mock-seriously, turning a piece of suggestive prose into a claim in technical mathematics. The second option is more charitable to Hipparchus. It is likely also for the following reason: Plutarch's discussion does not suggest there was ever a Stoic reply to Hipparchus. Such a reply, however, would have been very easy to make (with a different definition of the problem, Chrysippus' claim can be made to be technically correct). Was it perhaps that no Stoic leapt forward to save the master from attack, because no such attack was perceived? If so, Hipparchus' combinatorics would be another example of a mathematician turning to a literary genre (in this case, philosophy), mock-seriously misreading it as if it contained mathematical statements – and then, mock-pedantically, proceeding to correct the errors.

The most obvious "misreading" of a literary text by a mathematician, however, is that by Apollonius: the hexameter-calculating treatise described in the second book of Pappus' *Collection*. Once again, I have had the opportunity to describe this in detail while discussing the carnival of calculation. It is now time to mention that another grotesque, carnivalesque aspect of this treatise is in its very literal act of misreading: the turning of a line of hexameter into a piece of calculation, the sound of the epic syllables removed and in its place substituted a system for calculating with the letters of the alphabet. The choice of an epic line is surely significant: for this most radical act of turning the poetic line into a literate object of disjoined characters, Apollonius has chosen the form of literature most closely associated with performance and the poetic voice. The choice of the line, once again, is striking: "Nine maidens, praise Artemis' excellent power." This is an invocation of the muses, i.e. a moment where the poet seeks his inspired voice. It is also an apparent introduction to a hymn, suggesting further an atmosphere of elevated devotion. And then: those muses are metaphorically transformed, by Apollonius' method, into the nine numerals from 1 to 9. The incongruity, the mock-pedantic tone, could not have been more exaggerated. Once again: did Apollonius himself write this perfectly appropriate line? (It is not attested elsewhere but, once again, the *e silentio* is nearly meaningless.)

With Apollonius we have a case where a single object – the line of poetry "Nine maidens, praise Artemis' excellent power" – serves both poetic and mathematical function. It is a hexameter line and, at the same time, an object for calculation. Archimedes' *Cattle Problem* goes further than this: here, the lines of poetry form, themselves, the rules for the calculation. This is comparable to Eratosthenes' epigram preserved in the mini-treatise on cube duplication. In that case, however, the epigram merely supplemented the main prose text. In the case of the *Cattle Problem* we do not know about an equivalent, prose setting of the same mathematical contents. And in fact the poetic form is deeply woven into the text. The problem describes precise equations and conditions satisfied by a set of discrete entities divided into eight subsets. The choice of animate objects would be natural, so as to make a solution with integer numbers obligatory (one cannot have "a herd with three and a half cows," for instance). This perhaps already suggests a literary setting – which Archimedes then performs in the most effective way, turning to a passage in Homer that was close to home. Odysseus' crew reaches the Island of Thrinacia, sacred to Helios. Against Odysseus' advice, his crewmembers are tempted to slaughter the cattle of Helios, on which they feast lavishly – for seven days! (*Od.* 12.) Tradition had identified Thrinacia with Sicily, so that the *Cattle Problem* is even better localized than the *Sand-Reckoner* was (recall how Archimedes turns first to King Gelon to explain to him that the sand he shall measure is not only that found along the shores of Sicily . . .). Taken as a reference to one's home island, the myth would assume a special significance: a Sicily which is sacred to the gods, a Sicily which is blessed with plenty, a Sicily which should not be interfered with. – And many were those who wished to interfere with Sicily, who wished to slaughter its cattle, during Archimedes' lifetime! Seen in such a way, the joke of the treatise – inviting one's audience to perform an impossibly huge calculation – assumes a serious meaning. Was the point perhaps that Sicily's power was indeed immeasurable?[44]

Serious or not, the effect for one's readers would have been of a striking, rich combination of the mathematical and the poetic: read superficially, the mathematician appears to misread the poetry by suggesting a literal meaning to the plenty of Helios' cattle; upon closer understanding of the mathematical structure itself, one realizes that the complexity of the calculation is such as to defy literal description. Perhaps this was the self-referential point of the joke, then: that the attempt to calculate the cattle of Helios was as doomed as that of Odysseus' crew itself.

With the *Cattle Problem*, we see a Greek mathematician turning to a well-known piece of poetry. We can go further than this: in one case, we know – and have extant – a mathematician's commentary on a work of poetry which is extant as well. This double survival is more than sheer luck: the work of poetry was among the most successful and enduring of all Hellenistic poems. I refer of course to Aratus' *Phaenomena*, and to Hipparchus' commentary to it.

I shall return to discuss Aratus in greater detail in the following chapter, and so I note briefly the main coordinates here: this is a poem from the mid-third century BC, in some sense a reflection of Hesiod's *Works and Days*, in some ways a very up-to-date work. It is composed of two parts, the first a star catalogue and the second a catalogue of weather signs (in the manner typical of early astronomical writing, the star catalogue is articulated by the *phaenomena* or, literally, appearances and co-appearances of stars, on the horizon, at various times of the year). The first part is to some extent based, for its information, upon a fourth-century prose treatise by Eudoxus, the second – upon a fourth-century prose treatise by Theophrastus.

Hipparchus, writing a century after Aratus, does not invent the concept of writing a prose commentary on Aratus. He himself notes in his introduction that several such commentaries were written, of which he considers the best to be by Attalus. Not that Hipparchus much admires Attalus. One should clear one's mind of the later concept of "commentary" as established in Late Antiquity – namely, as a work where the contents of a canonical work are explicated with due deference. Deference is far from Hipparchus' mind. Instead, he concentrates on criticizing the three authors preceding him – Eudoxus, Aratus, and Attalus – systematically looking for factual errors and gradually offering, in the process, his own outline of a star catalogue. While Hipparchus himself refers to his work

---

[44] Or is Archimedes playfully intertextually referring to a poetry that speaks directly of Sicily's political fortunes? It is a striking coincidence – pointed out to me by Fantuzzi – that Theocritus' xvi.90–1 envisages the reinvigoration of Sicily with its fields teeming with the ἀνάριθμοι χιλιάδες of cattle!

as *exegesis*, which would normally translate as "commentary," it is perhaps best rendered here by "scrutiny."

To bring a poem to scrutiny based on its factual errors – and for this sake to put it side by side with two prose treatises, by Eudoxus and by Attalus – is inherently an act of incongruous juxtaposition. This juxtaposition is quite literal: to make his point concerning Aratus' factual debt to Eudoxus, Hipparchus begins with a set of quotations from the two authors, put side by side, where the point is precisely to stress their continuity. Thus Aratus is turned into an astronomical author, in a sense on a par with Eudoxus himself. If indeed Martin is right, and Aratus' poem in fact considerably differed from its prose source in Eudoxus, this juxtaposition – this "scientification" of Aratus – is all the more incongruous.[45]

This, then, establishes a tone that can easily become mock-serious towards Aratus' poetry. Not that Hipparchus labors the point. In general, Hipparchus' tone never becomes visibly ironic, blaming Aratus for errors which are obviously allowed in poetry. For instance, Hipparchus could in principle consider the similes or the mythological comparisons in Aratus, suggesting that they were misleading for this or that reason. Instead, Hipparchus concentrates throughout on the astronomical description itself, in this maintaining a sober tone that never collapses into the sheer mock-pedantic. On the other hand, Hipparchus does not for a moment allow us to engage in a poetic suspension of disbelief: the suggestion that this or that factual error in Aratus is acceptable within some rule of poetic license is far from Hipparchus' approach. All in all, one comes out of reading Hipparchus with a sense that, according to him, there is no fundamental genre difference between the three authors criticized. This does lead to jarring consequences, in the detail of the critique. Thus, for instance, Hipparchus criticizes Attalus early on, for agreeing with Aratus (as well as with Eudoxus) on the length of the day around mainland Greece. This goes as follows.[46] First, Hipparchus asserts in his sober fashion that Aratus appears to believe the longest day in Mainland Greece is to the shortest day as five to three.

For he says concerning the Summer Tropic (our "Tropic of Cancer") that:

This then – precise as it might be – through eight parts is measured
Five of which daylong rotate and are up above earth,
Three are beneath it.

---

[45] Martin 1998: lxxvi–cii corrects, in this way, the widespread and very unreflective view as if Aratus merely "put to verse" a preexisting prose work.
[46] In what follows I sum up *In Arat.* 26.3–28.18., occasionally offering a translation (my own).

It is typical that Aratus, in context (lines 497–9) does not explicitly call the circle in question "the Summer Tropic" (though Hipparchus' identification is of course correct). The statement by Hipparchus that lines 497–9 refer to the Summer Tropic creates a hybrid text, where Aratus' elusive language coexists with precise astronomical nomenclature.

More than this: Aratus' text contained an inherent poetic and non-mathematical component, as follows. The Tropic of Cancer does not have an inherent division of parts into "visible" and "invisible." It has different segments visible, from different parts of the earth. The poem by Aratus assumes an implicit localization: it is a piece not of descriptive mathematical astronomy (from which perspective, in principle, all locales are indifferently surveyed), but of a poetic description of the sky as experienced from a certain location upon earth (which Hipparchus identifies as Mainland Greece). This is because Hipparchus assumes that Aratus did indeed follow Eudoxus, who explicitly qualified some statements by "as seen from Mainland Greece." The assumption is certainly correct, but notice that, by omitting the perspectival clause, with Aratus, or by re-inserting it, with Hipparchus, one enters and leaves a poetic domain. Eudoxus and Hipparchus impersonally survey the sky; Aratus experiences it personally, from a well-defined, single vantage point. Hipparchus' intentional misreading of that flattens the poetry of Aratus, turning it into a piece of descriptive astronomy.

So much, then, for the hybrid language and intentional misreading created by the setting of Hipparchus' scrutiny of Aratus. Let us consider the scrutiny itself. For, you see, five to three is in fact the wrong ratio. In a set of further (correct) equivalences, Hipparchus transforms Aratus' ratio of the circle into a ratio between the longest and shortest day, as well as into a latitude measurement and a measurement of the longest day. He then produces a quick calculation by which the actual latitude of Mainland Greece is $37°$, so that the longest day is 14 hours and three-fifths of an hour. On the other hand, where Aratus' calculation holds – so Hipparchus – the longest day is 15 hours and the latitude is $41°$. What Hipparchus does *not* do is to note that the ratio for the correct latitude of Mainland Greece should be (in modern notation):

14.6:9.4 or 73:46.

So that Aratus' poem should have read:

This then – precise as it might be – through one hundred and nineteen parts is measured
Seventy three of which daylong rotate and are up above earth,
Forty six are beneath it.

As I just said, Hipparchus does not draw those conclusions explicitly. By avoiding such obviously absurd statements, Hipparchus manages to maintain throughout his sober, effective polemic tone. And yet the acute reader would notice that Hipparchus, in all seriousness, criticizes Aratus for using the 5:3 ratio instead of 73:46. This Hipparchus can do, reasonably, because he goes on immediately to show the origins of the error in Eudoxus himself (a prose treatise where a precise measurement was feasible), and criticizing Attalus for not noting it himself (as he should have done). But we can immediately sense the way in which a judgment such as Aratus' could make sense, as it did even after Hipparchus' scrutiny became widely known (Aratus remained a classic, and was later to be translated into both Latin and Arabic). Given the constraints of poetry, Aratus admirably manages to combine fact – of course, as available to him – and poetic style. Hipparchus' basic device, of pretending poetic style away from Aratus' poem, endows his text with a certain artificial texture: it keeps shadow-boxing the straw figure of Aratus, the prose author. To some extent this is justified by Aratus' own claims and reception, but this fact in itself is a mark of the breaking of genre-boundaries in the Hellenistic world – as I shall return to discuss in the following chapter.

Perhaps, so as to contextualize Hipparchus' treatment of Aratus' astronomy, one may consider Eratosthenes' treatment of Homer's geography. It is especially unfortunate that Eratosthenes' *Geography* is not extant, as this treatise seems to have formed an important moment in the formation of the Hellenistic scientific attitude towards poetry.[47] As it is, we rely mostly on Strabo's critical reading of Eratosthenes (it is through such indirect testimony that we learn, for instance, of Eratosthenes' measurement of the size of the earth, mentioned in chapter 1 above). In his own geography of the first century AD, Strabo uses Eratosthenes' *Geography* (in some sense, apparently, the major work available at his time), as his main critical foil. His primary positive anchor, however – the author to whom Strabo turns for corroboration – is Homer. This would appear to be a clear example of the turning of science towards poetry, but the situation in fact differs markedly from that of the Alexandrian attitude. Strabo's basic criticism of Eratosthenes is revealing (1.2.3, Jones' translation):

[47] Notice that I concentrate on the scientific attitude towards poetry – i.e. the way in which scientific texts appropriate statements made in a poetic setting. A separate problem (and one which is much more widely discussed) is that of the philosophical attitude towards poetry, i.e., the way in which philosophers think about the role of poetry as a vehicle of truth and education. Since this question is at the heart of Platonic philosophy, the literature on it is truly enormous, but for the much more specific question of the philosophical theories concerning poetry in the Hellenistic period, a good starting point is Obbink 1995 (whose focus is Philodemus, a late author who is perhaps best understood inside the Roman, rather than the Hellenistic context).

As I was saying, Eratosthenes contends that the aim of every poet is to entertain, not to instruct. The ancients assert, on the contrary, that poetry is a kind of elementary philosophy, which, taking us in our very boyhood, introduces us to the art of life and instructs us, with pleasure to ourselves, in character, emotions, and actions. And our school [ = Stoa] goes still further and contends that the wise man alone is a poet. That is the reason why in Greece the various states educate the young, at the very beginning of their education, by means of poetry; not for the mere sake of entertainment, of course, but for the sake of moral discipline.

At this point it becomes clear that Strabo does not take Homer mock-seriously: he takes him *seriously*. This is indeed a standard Greek position from the Archaic through the Classical periods and indeed one that survives into later periods (and flourishes there) through the influence of the Athenian Stoa. In this cultural tradition, the juxtaposition of knowledge and poetry has nothing jarring about it, as poetry is understood to be a fundamentally serious activity of imparting wisdom which is, in all seriousness, considered to be, at least potentially, divinely inspired. This is the attitude with which, for instance, Plato attacks Homer in the *Republic*: for all the irony permeating Platonic writing, there is no ironic intention in the very criticism of Homer from a philosophical perspective. To the contrary, Plato makes the very serious (even to our minds) point that Homer, as a vehicle of education, suffers from important failings.

If we detect a somewhat different attitude in the Alexandrian juxtaposition of knowledge and poetry, this makes the Alexandrians stand out from this Greek cultural tradition. And we appear to see here Strabo misunderstanding Eratosthenes' unfamiliar position. For it is definitely not the case that Eratosthenes has simply consigned Homeric geography into the realm of poetic license, from that point onwards ignoring Homer's geographical claims. To the contrary: as Strabo complains, Eratosthenes had in fact a more nuanced position on Homer (VII.3.6):

Now although such difficulties as these might fairly be raised concerning what is found in the text of Homer about the Mysians and the "proud Hippemolgi" yet what Apollodorus states in the preface to the Second Book of his work *On Ships* can by no means be asserted; for he approves the declaration of Eratosthenes, that although both Homer and the other early authors knew the Greek places, they were decidedly unacquainted with those that were far away, since they had no experience either in making long journeys by land or in making voyages by sea.

This already belies a different attitude towards Homer: not to be ignored by consigning his works to poetic license, but to be refuted by considering the possible grounds of his geographical judgments. The impression formed is that Eratosthenes' attitude towards Homer was qualitatively comparable to that of Hipparchus towards Aratus. He treats him as a source, not in the sense of taking him as canonical author to be taken with deference but in the sense of taking him as critical foil. Eratosthenes treads a careful line, just as Hipparchus will do later. On the one hand, by bringing in the possibility of poetic license, he is able to maintain a sober atmosphere: he does not indulge in fanciful mock-pedantry. On the other hand, by engaging in polemic, of a sort, with Homer, he manages to create a certain continuity between his own geographic project and that of Homer. This, finally, may well be compared with the mini-treatise we do have extant from Eratosthenes, on the duplication of the cube. There, a continuity is implied between an unnamed dramatic author who has failed to comprehend correctly the problem of the duplication of the cube, which then leads through several modern treatments to Eratosthenes' own crowning achievement. The *Geography* may have ended up looking quite similar: Homer serving as foil for the main discussion, suggesting how one should *not* proceed while producing scientific geography – leading on, through various modern treatments, to Eratosthenes' own precise discoveries. The effect of juxtaposition between science and poetry would have been more light-handed in the case of the *Geography*, but would be as effective.

The fundamental claim made here is that the truth-claim of poetry – always a major force in the Greek image of the poet – was subtly transformed in the Alexandrian world. This already brings us from science to poetry itself. So as to contextualize the way in which science turns to poetry and, in general, so as to contextualize the stylistic devices of Alexandrian science, we now need to turn to Alexandrian poetry: how did it relate to science? And how could its style inform that of the scientific writings themselves?

CHAPTER 4

# *The poetic interface*

The claim of the following chapter is twofold, looking at how poetic practices are (i) *complementary* to those of the exact sciences, and (ii) *parallel* to them. Section 4.1 makes the case for (i) complementarity. It shows how Greek poets turned to scientific concepts and contents, weaving science into their poetry just as the scientists were weaving poetry into their science. Sections 4.2–4.3 make the case for (ii) parallelism. Section 4.2 takes a central example of the practices of mythography in Hellenistic poetry as a starting-point for an analysis of the familiar role of "erudition" in this poetry – now considered in light of the scientific practices discussed in this book. Section 4.3 broadens the discussion to look at the poetic parallels to the scientific practices seen throughout this book, as a whole: the narrative surprise and the mosaic text. Of course, the complementarity and parallelism are tightly connected. Section 4.4 offers a brief summary, with some tentative conclusions.

The Hellenistic world was, for generations, the least intensively studied of all ancient periods, its culture alien and uninviting for classicists inspired by Greek glory or by Roman grandeur. With changes in contemporary taste, as well as with the overall explosion of academic writing, considerable and sophisticated studies of Hellenistic civilization have appeared over the last couple of decades. Even this scholarship, however – as is not surprising – concentrates on Hellenistic literature to the exclusion of science. Thus this chapter faces a very different task from that of the previous ones. I emerge from the side lane of Hellenistic mathematics – where I was for much of the time the only vehicle in sight – to merge into the heavy traffic of mainstream Classical scholarship. What I need to achieve, for my argument to work, is to survey Hellenistic literary style as a whole so as to put it side by side with scientific style. I shall not try to be exhaustive for either primary or secondary sources. In the course of some 18,000 words, sections 4.1–4.3 sketch features of Hellenistic poetry that have mostly been noted by previous scholars. However, the recent surge of studies in the field is too recent to allow a firm sense of what the "common opinion" is. And it is, after all, in the nature of recent scholarship to engage in radical, skeptical polemic – so that no single generalization is shared by all leading scholars. Even so, I try to follow what I perceive to be the more dominant position and, in the few places where my views may deviate from what is widely accepted, I hope to make this clear, and to make my case.

Each of the three following sections has a very distinct character. Section 4.1, dealing with the use of science inside Hellenistic poetry, touches on a subject that has not been treated as such by previous scholars (though scholars have often noted various isolated references to scientific knowledge). It has therefore the character of an overview, with a relatively wide sample of cases, and it is appropriately long – about half of this chapter. Section 4.2, dealing with the carnival of erudition, touches on a familiar theme but offers a somewhat original interpretation (to a certain extent, based on the analysis of mathematics in chapter 1 above). To make my case, then, I need to offer a detailed analysis, and so this brief section is based on my own close reading of a single passage, which I take to be representative, in Callimachus. Section 4.3, finally, dealing with the wide topics of mosaic structure and narrative surprise, is the least original and so I merely recount, briefly, familiar interpretations, in a kind of rushed survey. What one needs is a *guide*, and my strategy there is to take two of them – a couple of secondary authorities, very different from each other (Hutchinson's *Hellenistic Poetry*, from 1988, as well as Fantuzzi and Hunter's *Tradition and Innovation in Hellenistic Poetry*, from 2004), and to follow their interpretations in order.

## 4.1 LITERATURE TURNS TO SCIENCE

Eratosthenes' *Geography* is not extant and so our understanding of his adjustment of heroic epic to scientific knowledge must be mediated by the kind of indirect guesswork put forward at the end of the last chapter. I suggested there that Eratosthenes ultimately took the sober view according to which Homer's geography should be brought under poetic license, and yet he did not forego the pleasure of discussing in some detail Homer's precise as well as imprecise statements, thereby creating a rich texture of ironic turning from science into poetry. Clearly, at any rate, Eratosthenes signals a certain literary option: within a heroic epic, factual knowledge might be intentionally blurred via the soft lens of poetic license, so as to create a distinctively poetic atmosphere. Significantly, this is not the route taken by the extant Hellenistic epic. Moving away from Eratosthenes to obtain another view of the same field, we may look, not from science towards poetry but from poetry towards science. This time no guesswork is called for, as Apollonius Rhodius' heroic epic, the *Argonautica*, is extant. It also goes without saying that the poem is primarily a response to Homer, and that it recalls Homer's fundamental spatial structure of voyage and return. No shortage of opportunity for geography, then, whose remarkable structure is among Apollonius' central literary devices.[1] There is, throughout, a clearly established vein of the purely scientific, with precise information delivered in a tone suggestive of the genre of prose geography (retouched metrically so as to form a kind of didactic passage within the heroic epic). This then verges on other passages, whose resonance is not so much with scientific geography as with paradoxography – a genre distinct from the kind of geography Eratosthenes, say, would produce, but often put forward side by side with geography proper in such works as, say, Herodotus' *History* (which seems to be a major generic reference point for the Apollonian geographical passages). Both geography and paradoxography are ambiguously positioned in the Apollonian text, in that they evoke a world which the reader may well take to be not merely mythical but also contemporary. However, paradoxography can easily verge into more obviously mythical descriptions, where Apollonius evokes not the stable realities of contemporary places and nations but rather a realm explicitly ruled by poetic license – the connection between this realm and the real geography is however made reliable, and finds a lot of "occasions," in the frequent practice of aetiological interpretation of geographical places. Thus Apollonius' use of geography, once again, proceeds via a certain modulation so that the jarring incongruity of poetry and science is subtly played out. Apollonius manages throughout to keep the reader uncertain as to the intended boundaries of suspension of disbelief. Lines 1.936–52 – to take an example nearly at random – may illustrate this type of transition (Seaton's translation):

There is a lofty island inside the Propontis, a short distance from the Phrygian mainland with its rich cornfields, loping to the sea, where an isthmus in front of the mainland is flooded by the waves, so low does it lie. And the Isthmus

---

[1] This is widely recognized in the literature; see Meyer 2001 and references there. One can also find in Apollonius a certain interest in astronomical data, evident especially in some of his similes (Bogue 1977: 70–92), which however typically do not go beyond quite elementary knowledge. The interest in medical science is far more striking, with for instance some very precise, and very recent psychophysiology summoned so as to account for Medea's anguish (III.761–5, see Solmsen 1961. I thank G.E.R. Lloyd for this reference), and I mention more of this further below. Geography, however, remains the science closest to the very subject matter of the *Argonautica* and the one to influence it the most.

has double shores, and they lie beyond the river Aesepus, and the inhabitants round about call the island the Mount of Bears. [So far: purely topographical information – notice for instance how the "bears" are not going to play any narrative role in what follows. The precision is, in narrative terms, redundant, and there is nothing especially colorful about the facts mentioned: thus one has the sense of facts for facts' sake. Note also the strong anchoring of the text in the present of the poem's narrator – "there *is*," "the inhabitants *call*."] And insolent and fierce men dwell there, Earthborn, a great marvel to the neighbours to behold; for each one has six mighty hands to lift up, two from his sturdy shoulders, and four below, fitting close to his terrible sides. [An apparent turn into paradoxography – note the word "marvel," *thauma*, nearly a paradoxographical technical term. This prepares the ground for a transition into the poetic past.] And about the isthmus and the plain the Doliones had their dwelling, and over them Cyzicus son of Aeneus was king, whom Aenete the daughter of goodly Eusorus bore. But these men the earthborn monsters, fearful though they were, in nowise harried, owing to the protection of Poseidon; for from him had the Doliones first sprung.

Now that we have reached into the past tense of individual heroes, the gods reappear as well and it is clear that we have moved into a strictly poetic mode. But note the seamless transition effected here from secular geography to sacred myth, from present to past. This, one should note, is all related to a fundamental choice made by Apollonius, to pick a myth – and then to further localize it – so that its locations are well within the civilized world of the third century, making sure in this way that the present and its facts cannot be avoided. This was a choice: he could after all have produced a poem on Aethiopia or on Thule – or indeed he could have ventured into geographically safer places such as Hades or the Island of the Blessed. Apollonius has constructed his problem in such terms so as to prevent, from the outset, the possibility of a solution based purely on poetic license.

Let us take just one further example of the same type of transition. Phineus the seer is to prophesy the future of the voyage. This is a long speech – lines II.311–407, 420–5. In what must be a mildly comic effect, the bulk of his prophecy is no more than what the heroes could have picked up by, say, buying up a copy of some kind of equivalent of Herodotus. I quote to provide a sense of this down to earth, factual tone (ll. 360–8):

Now there is a headland opposite Helice the Bear. Steep on all sides, and they call it Carambis, about whose crests the blasts of the north wind are sundered. So high in the air does it rise turned towards the sea. And when ye have rounded it broad Aegialus stretches before you; and at the end of broad Aegialus, at a jutting point of coast, the waters of the river Halys pour forth with a terrible roar; and after it Iris flowing near, but smaller in stream, rolls into the sea with white eddies.

Such descriptive passages are intertwined with moments of oracular advice, exhorting the voyagers to act in precise ways so as to succeed in their journey. This however is not quite of a divine order: the advice, for instance, that at a particularly frightful passage they first send a dove forwards, is indeed couched in pathetic language, but is perhaps to be read as a piece of nautical advice. On the whole, the theme of Phineus' speech is set by Zeus's reluctance to share his secrets (311–16). The readers' expectations – as well as those of the heroes – are for divine revelation, but they are deliberately frustrated as Apollonius produces the bathetic effect of the Baedeker prophet. At this moment of inspired speech – i.e. the very moment where poetry is traditionally assumed to possess its unique truth value – scientific-style, geographic information is provided.

Such examples might be multiplied at will, as Apollonius' epic is so closely woven around geography and ethnography.[2] I will not offer here any specific interpretations of Apollonius' poetics – a contested field which calls for more discussion than is appropriate in this book. I merely sum up noting that – complementary to what I conjecture for Eratosthenes' own geographical perspective on myth – Apollonius' myth keeps referring to scientific geography, modulating his text between the divine and the secular, evoking, ever so gently, something of the tone of mock-seriousness.

With the *Argonautica*, we clearly consider one of the major moments of Alexandrian culture: here, after all, is the Hellenistic attempt to master the dominant cultural form of heroic epic. Less obvious to us is the significance of Callimachus' poem on the *Lock of Berenice*, already discussed above in the context of scientific coinage. The hyperbolic absurdity of the poem as well as its anchoring in ephemeral courtly events, both suggest to modern sensibilities the likelihood of a mere passing exercise. And yet Callimachus himself chose to revise and reinsert the poem as some sort of culmination of his main work, the *Aitia*, and some of the most receptive readers of Hellenistic poetry – the Roman readers of the Late Republic – appear to have found in it a major source of inspiration.[3] Indeed much of our knowledge of the poem is derived from a close Latin paraphrase by Catullus (poem 66) – a rendition produced by a poet and read by an audience to whom Ptolemaic court affairs meant nothing. Gutzwiller (1992) has convincingly shown the effectiveness of the poem in blending together various inflections of the feminine gendered voice, all present through the voice of the lock (absurdly, the narrator of the poem). To this one

---

[2] For several more examples see Zanker 1987: 116–18 (which however, once again, does not aim to be exhaustive), as well as Meyer 2001 mentioned above.
[3] See Puelma 1983.

should certainly add the effective blending together of the poetic and the scientific. Now, to say that Callimachus' invocation of astronomy is mock-serious is to state the obvious. Indeed his starting-point is a piece of astronomy that must have been, itself, mock-serious. To recall: Queen Berenice's lock, dedicated to the gods, has disappeared from the temple and Conon has identified it as a new constellation in the sky. Callimachus' poem celebrates, or rather mourns, this catasterism, as the lock laments her double separation from her beloved queen (note that in the poetic version, the lock is most definitely a maiden).

It takes a little while for us to realize that the lock is the narrator of the poem. The mosaic, surprising effect of the poem is attained at its very beginning: the yet to be defined speaker begins with a magnificent evocation of the sky, calling forth its grandeur as both physical and scientific subject:

Πάντα τὸν ἐν γραμμαῖσιν ἰδὼν ὅρον ᾗ τε φέρονται

"Having surveyed the entire sky in geometrical configuration, and whereby [stars?] are moved" (who did the surveying? We are not told and may well expect a mythical person; that this is the geometer Conon would come as a moment of shocked surprise, bringing together, once again, the heroic and the scientific).

Note that my translation brings out the geometrical sense of *en grammaisin*: in the Greek exact sciences, for an activity to be based on *grammai* has the technical sense of its being conducted "geometrically" or more precisely "based on diagrammatic representation."[4] With Conon being primarily a geometer (the best among his peers, to judge by Archimedes' constant references to him in his introductions),[5] this term is likely to have this technical sense. Thus Callimachus begins by evoking the stars as geometrical objects, as well as by evoking their magnitude: the very first word, *panta*, sets a tone of awed hyperbole that Catullus picked up in his Latin first word, *omnia*. Otherwise Catullus removed – as is not surprising from a Latin pen – the precise geometrical reference, keeping however a very clear sense of the scientific context:[6]

1        He, who surveyed all the fires of the universe,
         Who calculated the risings and settings of stars,

---

[4] See Netz 1999: 35–8. For further discussion of the technical terminology in Callimachus' poem, see Pfeiffer 1949, 1953 *ad loc.* (who however sees in *grammai* an *astronomical* technical term; probably one should read the text as over-determined in this respect).
[5] Heiberg I 4.14 (*SC* I), 168.5 (*SC* II), II 2.2–21 (*SL*), 262.3–10 (*QP*).
[6] Lines 2–6 are available only from Catullus' paraphrase.

>       How the brightness of the burning sun is darkened,
>       How the heavenly bodies disappear at well defined times,
> 5     How sweet Love, sending away Trivia (= Hecate, = Moon) furtively
>         to the Latmian rocks
>       Seduces her from her aerial rotation,[7]
> 7     Me, too, Conon saw in the air.

Notice first of all the ironic duality of science and of poetry, that involving the transition from lines 1–4 (where the stars are approached scientifically) and lines 5–6 (where the stars are approached poetically) – with the fine witty touch of the astronomer as the scientist capable of predicting where ladies depart for their amorous trysts! (This indeed fits well the feminine themes of this poem.) The scientific setting itself is one we are familiar with: the astronomer lays claim to the hyperbolic task of attempting to capture the unbounded, in this case the totality of the heavens. The juxtaposition of this huge task with the minuteness of the lock is typical not only of Hellenistic poetry but of Hellenistic science as well. The introduction to the poem seems to make an ironic comment on the *impossibility* of surveying the entire heavens (can you measure up the heavens one lock of hair at a time?). This duality of huge tasks, and their deflation by reduction into minute measuring units, is one we have seen repeatedly in chapter 1 above. We now see how this duality fits into the Hellenistic poetic program as well. The jarring juxtaposition of the minor and the major, the lock and the heavens, was intentionally absurd but it did not preclude – for either poets or scientists – the serious treatment of the major cultural object itself. Through the comedy of the lock, one also senses certain serious concerns: scholars from Gutzwiller onwards have successfully shown how the poem broaches such subjects as that of femininity in a masculine world, of the transition from girlhood to womanhood, of the role of the monarch – as well as the grandeur and sheer beauty of the sky. The minute and ironic perspective of the lock is the place of standing from which the Alexandrian poet moves an Earth. And equally, the scientists, even while stressing the impossible precision required for tasks such as measuring cosmic values, produce such values with the greatest precision possible. The minute, as a key for greatness, is a cultural theme for both Alexandrian science and poetry.

The fundamental literary duality of the lock – that of the mythical and the literal – is tied to another duality, that of its political setting.

---

[7] Lines 5–6 invoke a mythical aetiology for, probably, lunar eclipses (the moon goddess keeping her secret trysts with Endymion, at the Latmian rocks).

The Ptolemaic kings did present themselves as in some sense members of a mythical order, while at the same time protagonists of the political, contemporary scene. This went hand in hand with another duality, felt throughout Alexandrian life: the monarchs presented themselves twice over, once as Egyptians and once again as Greeks – a duality made central by Susan Stephens in her interpretation of Hellenistic poetics.[8] Did the political duality account in some sense for the literary one? Whatever our interpretation of that, we may certainly say that, in Alexandria, both poets and the court displayed a similar semiotic principle of *duality*: here is a culture where ambiguity was not shunned but was rather actively engaged with as a medium of meaning.

Hence a special role for the skies: these after all serve, at the same time, as depository for mythical references, and as literal, scientific objects. Callimachus is by no means alone in exploiting this duality. Eratosthenes has produced what must have been a long poem on the same topic of catasterism, the *Hermes* (now known almost wholly from later astronomical testimonies that mined the poem for its facts). Apparently the basic contrivance was to follow Hermes from youth to catasterism. The construction of Hermes' lyre gives rise to a description of the harmony of the spheres. And at some point – in the mosaic structure we are now familiar with – this catasterism would evolve into an astronomical description produced from the vantage point of the heavenly Hermes. At the literary level, then, this poem would perhaps at first suggest a hymn, only then to reveal itself as didactic epic[9] (more in keeping with its dimensions – apparently some 1,600 lines!).

Astronomy and geography are intertwined in this poem (as always with Eratosthenes: here is the author who measured the earth by astronomical principles). Hermes, from his position on high, seems to survey the regions of the earth, much like a modern-day astronaut. One should note that the relationship between astronomy and geography was indeed tight in antiquity: the fundamental principle of Greek scientific geography was the role of different latitudes in defining different regions of the earth, and it seems that Hermes' gaze upon the earth was structured by such latitudes. Even so, the description is very literary in character, playing the astral gaze for all of its visual potential: the polar zones darker than enamel, the torrid zone red as fire (fr. 16) etc., all of this quite out of place in a genuine

---

[8] Stephens (2004). Her argument is, in fact, that many perceived tensions in Hellenistic poetry begin to make sense as soon as we see them as the juxtaposition of Hellenic and Egyptian themes.
[9] At the very least, this would have appeared to be at first a poem *about* Hermes – gradually revealed to use the figure of Hermes as a vantage point, literally, for astronomical observation.

piece of descriptive geography. Traditional myth transformed into a kind of imaginary space travel – indeed, a special pity that this work is lost – perhaps an early precursor of science fiction . . . (Kepler's *Somnium* comes to mind).[10]

Eratosthenes' *Hermes* survives only in fragments; Aratus' *Phaenomena* not only is fully extant but was among the most widely read of all Hellenistic works; for its extraordinary influence on Roman culture, see Gee 2000.[11] Thus it serves as the most obvious example for the cultural centrality of this duality of the stars, as both myth and science. We have already encountered Aratus and considered him from the perspective of science looking at poetry, with Hipparchus' commentary on the poem. But the poem might equally be considered from the perspective of poetry looking at science.[12] Indeed, the astronomical part of Aratus' work would have to look towards Eudoxus' own *Phaenomena*[13] (the work is bipartite, with its second part based on Theophrastus' treatise on weather-signs; more on this below). Now, it should be said that, among available astronomical models, Aratus chose a relatively simple source. We have extant, for instance, Autolycus' fourth-century treatise on *Risings and Settings* of stars (a subject closely related to the field of *Phaenomena*, whose ultimate theme was the appearances, i.e. risings of stars according to the time of year). This is a strictly geometrical study, where the risings and settings of stars are considered as an optical-astronomical problem: depending on the position of

---

[10] This poem may well have inspired a previous *somnium* – Scipio's (Geus 2002: 128), as well as the satirical variant of Lucian's *Icaromenippus* (whose paragraph 6 is a direct parody of the mathematical attempt to encompass the cosmos). See, in general, Geus 2002: 110–28 for discussion of the *Hermes* as well as further references.

[11] The *Phaenomena* was Aratus' greatest achievement, celebrated in antiquity and, alone of his works, extant today. The scholia mention other works by him that may well represent a wider project of scientific-minded poetry: a *Description of Bones*, *Medicinal Properties*, a *Scythicon* (possibly an epic work with Scyths as its topic but more likely an ethnography?), a *Division of the Canon* (i.e. on mathematical music?). We know next to nothing on all such works and indeed cannot be sure that they were in verse. Did he perhaps write science in both prose and poetry? Likely not: and as for the anecdote repeated by the scholia, as if Aratus was a doctor while Nicander was an astronomer, hence their errors – this clearly is a joke of no biographical value. (Martin 1974: 9.17–21, 11.9–15 for other works; Martin 1974: 8.25–9.1, 11.14–12.3, 20.10–15 for the anecdote.)

[12] Besides looking at science, this poem may – or may not – be looking at philosophy. A scholarly debate rages as to the possible anchoring of the poem in Stoic cosmology – a debate whose very possibility suggests, to my mind, that no such dogmatic affiliation was intended by the author of the poem. (See Kidd 1997: 10–12, Gee 2000, chapter 3, Fakas 2001: 18–39.) Be that as it may, I leave aside here Aratus' possible indebtedness to the Stoics, to concentrate on his certain indebtedness to Eudoxus.

[13] Martin 1998 qualifies this judgment and suggests that perhaps the reference is not so much to the prose work as to its system of constellations as encapsulated in the globe produced by Eudoxus; but surely even such a globe would have to be "read" via the prose work, and on the whole, Hipparchus' careful textual comparison – however biased it must have been – appears to have some substance in it.

the observer, and the relative position of the stars and the sun, different stars are visible at different times of the year. Autolycus discusses this in the abstract terms of spherical geometry, without mentioning particular stars. Earlier than Autolycus, Eudoxus himself was author not only of the *Phaenomena* used by Aratus, but also of the planetary system discussed by Aristotle. This was perhaps the first Greek attempt to characterize the planetary motions by a geometrical model, in this case one involving a nested system of rotating spheres. This treatise (perhaps titled *On Speeds*, referring to the velocities of spherical rotations) is not extant. We do have extant treatises of "Sphaerics," from the beginning and end of the Hellenistic era, the first by Euclid, perhaps, (and so early third century?) and the second by Theodosius of Bithynia (late second century), both belonging to the same tradition of abstract spherical geometry. Aratus could in principle have produced a poem – very different from the actual *Phaenomena* – with abstract spherical geometry couched in the diction and meter of didactic epic. He deliberately chose not to.[14] This clearly would be very alien to his approach and, in seeing why, we may perhaps better understand his poetics.[15]

At one level, the main consideration is Aratus' wish to display a cultural continuity with the past: a poetic version of Autolycus (or of Eudoxus' *Speeds*) would have no poetic precursor, whereas a poetic version of Eudoxus' *Phaenomena* harks back to the major model of epic didactic, that of Hesiod (whose *Works and Days* contains substantial descriptive astronomical passages). This is established at the beginning of the poem: with a proem addressed to Zeus[16] and then, immediately afterwards, the

---

[14] As Hunter (1995: 6–7) points out, it is noteworthy that Aratus chose to foreground his avoidance of the theme of the *planets* – ll. 454–61 very emphatically assert that the poet *would not* write about this all-important feature of the sky. Why is that? Hunter suggests that perhaps this is because the planets lack *kosmos* – but would they, to a reader of Eudoxus? Rather, the outcome of this emphatic avoidance is to underline Aratus' choice to narrate in poetry the *Phaenomena* – as against *On Speeds*.

[15] Couat, writing in France in 1882, discusses the same point. His mistake is telling and worth noticing. He tries to mitigate what he perceives as the "mediocrity" of Aratus' poem by pointing to a supposed transitional character of the science of his times, "the grandiose and simple-minded conception of its earliest days no longer exists" (i.e. we have already moved beyond early metaphysical speculation); "it has not yet the confident and courageous bearing of adult science" (i.e. it is not yet modern science). A footnote expands on this theme: "To put in verse the great work of Laplace, such would be approximately the task of a poet who sought to-day to do something equivalent to what Aratus has done. But while it was possible to translate Eudoxus, who would venture to translate Laplace?" (Couat, tr. Loeb 1930: 472). The telling point is that Aratus did have available to him a model directly comparable to Laplace – namely, Eudoxus' *On Speeds*; and he made a *deliberate* choice to work from precisely the kind of prose source that occupies the middle ground between myth and science – the star catalogue.

[16] This proem, as one would expect, meaningfully differs from Hesiod's in conjuring an image of a rational, perhaps not anthropomorphic Zeus. This is the main basis for the Stoic allegiance on

major poetic set-piece of the poem – where Aratus momentarily foregoes astronomical description for the sake of myth – which is clearly meant to evoke Hesiod. This passage combines the Hesiodic themes of justice spurned, and the world's ages, into yet another tale of catasterism, this time of Justice exiling herself to the sky in the form of Virgo (ll. 96–136).

Note indeed that we seem to return again and again to the theme of catasterism – which is closely related to the fascination with dualities of high and low which must have motivated the Hellenistic interest in poetic astronomy to start with. This duality is reflected, in this particular case, as that of prose and poetry. And here is another reason to reproduce the *Phaenomena*, not the *Speeds*, in poetic form. It is not just that Aratus has re-poetized a piece of prose (which would have been the case had he chosen the *Speeds* as model). He has re-poetized simultaneously prose *and* poetry. The real achievement of Aratus was not just to make Eudoxus poetical, but rather to mix Eudoxus with Hesiod: the act involved is not just that of genre transformation, from the prose of Eudoxus to a poetic form, but rather that of genre hybridization, entwining together two great models.[17] For the modern reader, Aratus' work might at first glance appear rather arbitrary in its subject matter, but for the knowledgeable Hellenistic reader it would appear that Aratus has set himself a monumental task: combining the greatest work of epic didactic, with the achievements of the greatest scientist who has ever lived.

The task would be complicated by the fact that the sources were so easily available. Aratus' more sophisticated audience – arguably, the one intended – must have had access to Eudoxus' text. Hipparchus' reading was not at all against the grain: the most natural thing to do – for one capable of that – was to read Aratus in light of one's knowledge of Eudoxus. This must be stressed, as it involves the main duality of the text. Even while scanning Aratus' hexameter, the audience would pick up another layer of text, a kind of continuous shadow of prose to accompany the poetry. We should be grateful for Hipparchus' setting of the two texts side by side, as we may for instance read lines 184–5 to this prose accompaniment:

> From her tail-tip [cynosure] to both his [Cepheus] feet
> Stretches a measure equal to that from foot to foot.

Aratus' part, but possibly all that is intended is a lively sense of anachronism, setting Hesiod's god against that of a more contemporary Zeus; later on in the poem a more anthropomorphic, "Hesiodic" Zeus is displayed – which would not be allowed by any card-carrying Stoic.

[17] For, it should be said, Eudoxus was to the scientific readers of the third century as much a towering presence as Hesiod was to the readers of poetry. Archimedes, we recall, constantly refers to Eudoxus as the model against whom he wishes, himself, to be measured (see Intro. n. 6 above).

This, Hipparchus notes, is based on Eudoxus' statement that "[the feet of Cepheus] make an equilateral triangle [with] the tail of cynosure" (Hipp. 14.13–16 – quoted by Hipparchus, critically, as according to him the statement is not technically correct: the "base" between the two feet is shorter than the other sides of this triangle). The audience – even without referring at all to Eudoxus' text – would immediately recognize that Aratus' periphrastic expression must stand for a precise geometrical statement. More than this: the audience would recognize that there is another lexicon available for just the purposes required by Aratus' description, that of the exact sciences. And the audience would finally recognize that this lexicon is not allowed into Aratus' text because of the formal consequences of the generic choice to employ epic didactic. The result is perhaps some subtle self-irony, with the text suggesting its *limitations* as a piece of science, by suggesting the incongruity of Hesiod and Eudoxus; or perhaps the audience would focus on the positive achievement of providing the Eudoxean information in spite of the Hesiodic genre, that is focusing on the positive achievement of generic hybridization. Either way, the shadow accompaniment of scientific prose and the constant sense that the poetry is periphrastic to it, would heighten the fundamental sense of duality.

Duality is the key to the work in some other, even more direct ways. It is primarily a bipartite text: while the astronomy is the more visible, first part, it occupies no more than about two-thirds of the poem (732 lines of 1154), the second part being devoted to weather signs. Here once again the source is venerable, if not quite as monumental as Eudoxus – the eminent author Theophrastus. The sense of bifurcation is deep, as the two topics are distinct in many ways. The weather signs part does not evoke the grandeur of the mythical heavens, nor does the constant shadow prose accompaniment become as marked. (Theophrastus' treatise would be written in a lexicon much looser than that of Eudoxus' treatise, so that the gap between Aratus and Theophrastus would have to be much smaller than that separating him from Eudoxus.) This bifurcation is at bottom the duality we are already familiar with, between the high and the low: the high of the sky with the low of the weather and even (I would suggest) the high of Eudoxus' systematic science with the low of Theophrastus' more haphazard collection. Once again, Aratus worked in some ways to highlight this sense of bifurcation: for instance, the invocation to Zeus at the start of the poem contains elements that can, in retrospect, seem to suggest the topic of weather signs, but it ends with the poet asking Zeus to help him, simply, "to tell the stars" (*asteras eipein*, l. 17). By failing to suggest in the introduction that the poem should go beyond a star catalogue to include a section on weather signs, he prepared for a moment of surprise as the reader reached the transition into the second part. On the other hand, the transition itself is fairly smoothly handled: the star catalogue is partly arranged on the principle of first appearances of stars, essentially a way of making the skies into calendrical signs. Then again, the weather signs pick up with a survey of signs related to appearances in the sky (such as the phases of the moon). Most important, Aratus sets up the poem, from its very beginning, in the most general terms of Signs. Zeus is the one who (l. 10)

Αὐτὸς γὰρ τά γε σήματ' ἐν οὐρανῷ ἐστήριξεν

Himself set up the signs in heaven.

And Aratus would repeatedly refer, in the course of the star catalogue, to the stars as "signs." A random example (l. 233):

Ἔστι δέ τοι καὶ ἔτ' ἄλλο τετυγμένον ἐγγύθι σῆμα

There is yet another sign fashioned nearby [referring to another constellation]

This insistence on the word "sign" must be understood as another case of the shadow prose accompaniment; for the sophisticated reader would have to pick up the word *semeion* as the prose shadow to accompany poetic *sema* – and as the central object of epistemological discussion. Hellenistic philosophy of science was organized around the problem of "inference from signs," a problem couched in explicit binary terms: under what conditions can one object be considered as sign for another, i.e. to constitute grounds for inferring the existence of the other?[18] In the elevated poetic setting of the star catalogue, the unscientific reader might read off Aratus' *sema* as, say, "mark" (an established epic sense), i.e. the star is a *sema* in that it is *visible*, so that it serves as a reference point. But for the scientific reader – already familiar with the philosophical sense – the section of weather signs would be decisive, favoring the reading of *sema* in the prose sense of *semeion*, i.e. of the star as a sign of *something else*. Which something else is that? This is generally left unsaid, but the poem provides us with many examples of stars serving as signs for other things such as calendrical and (in the second part) weather events; possibly, Aratus could have had astrological signs in mind as well. So, instead of the star catalogue as a static survey, detailing a depository of nightly marks, the first part of the poem comes to be

---

[18] Allen 2001, esp. chapter 3 on the Stoics (whose definition of a sign is "an antecedent in a sound conditional revelatory of the consequent," Sextus Empiricus *M.* 8.277 – note the inherent dual structure).

understood as an introduction to a dynamic system. The stars stand in an open-ended set of semiotic relations to a variety of other, mostly unnamed phenomena. To learn the stars, so Aratus suggests, is to learn a language – literally, a system of signs – which may then be employed in a host of other ways. The poem does not really just "tell the stars;" it rather teaches us how to "tell *with* the stars." In other words, the star catalogue casts not one shadow, but two. One is formal: a prose shadow, that of the Eudoxean text sensed by the reader through the medium of Aratus' poetry. The other is substantial: a semiotic shadow, that of the stars as vehicles of meaning, sensed by the reader through the medium of Aratus' static description. We may even begin to appreciate here something of the achievement of the poem. It repeatedly enacts the principle of binary composition, mostly tied to the fundamental bivalence of the stars, as both poetic and scientific object.

Aratus' *Phaenomena* most centrally plays on the duality of high and low, in this case literally – the duality of stars and earth. The very subject matter of catasterism is an enactment of this theme, and we return time and again to its cultural fascination. This, after all, was the time that poets were for the first time made, literally, *stars* – in the group of the Pleiad. As is well known, many sources (though all in the commentary and Byzantine traditions) refer to a group of poets, especially a group of tragic poets, as the Pleiades.[19] The numbers in the list fluctuate, as debates over inclusion gave rise to textual confusion: there ought to have been seven. Of course, to produce a list of seven is not an original move for a Hellenistic author – the ancients had Seven Sages[20] as well as Seven Wonders,[21] all rather like the contemporary American "Best Ten . . ." (though once again, similarly contested, lists of seven sages or wonders would also swell to include more than seven). What is striking, and apparently original, is that, for Hellenistic poets, this seven-hood came to be represented by the metaphor of an astronomical constellation.[22] Was this a *Hellenistic* invention? As Fraser points out (see n. 19), the *terminus ante quem* is no earlier than Strabo (who does refer in 675 to Dionysiades as "counted among the Pleiad"), but the fact that so many of the authors mentioned flourished in the reign of Ptolemy

---

[19] The evidence is summed up by Fraser 1972: 871 n.6.
[20] See Martin 1993 – who believes, against Fehling 1985 – that such lists of sages were very early, possibly archaic; they certainly were pre-Hellenistic.
[21] Clayton and Price 1988.
[22] As pointed out by Martin 1993: 121, Vedic literature has its own version of Seven Sages who are widely correlated, among other things with the stars – but rather than assuming some deep Indo-Arian roots, one should see here a parallel process motivated in each case by its own separate context. For, after all, no one in Greece prior to the third century thought of *a constellation of poets*.

Philadelphus suggests that the list may have been made canonical then or soon after: the Pleiad, in short, could well have been contemporary with Berenice's lock and the product of the same cultural pattern.[23]

Another enactment of this theme would be the science of astrology (especially in its judiciary form, providing individual horoscopes). Here after all is a science whose essence is the tying together of high and low: eternal stars and transient lives. Astrology, one can say, is catasterism turned upside down. A word is called for, as astrology should be seen as yet another form in which mainstream Hellenistic culture turned to look at science. Now, it is well known that Greek astrology came into being in the third century BC, as a somewhat transformed version of earlier Babylonian astronomy. (This antecedent differs from the Greek model in that Babylonian astronomy was mostly concerned with state affairs, though there are Babylonian sources for the individual horoscope as well.) The standard account is a simple contact and diffusion story: the Greeks come to occupy Babylonia, and the Hellenistic world allows for the unhindered travel of experts; hence Babylonian astrology leaves its ancestral home at Mesopotamia to begin its world-wide journey.[24] This is obviously an important part of the truth, but one needs also to provide an account for why Greeks at this time and place would be receptive for this particular cultural form (we do not see Greeks taking to circumcision, say, as an outcome of Hellenistic expansion). There are certain suggestions in the secondary literature, say, having to do with the roles of "fate" and "fortune" as cultural themes in the Hellenistic world.[25] This may well be true as well. To this, however, one should add that astrology, with its essential bipolar structure of high and low, was *structurally* ready for assimilation into Alexandrian civilization – which served as foundation for its later

---

[23] One could think of poets as stars – or one could think of them as *flowers*. So did Meleager as the Hellenistic era was coming to its close, towards the end of the second century BC. Meleager summed up the achievements of the Hellenistic epigram by creating the metaphor of the "wreath" (whence our "anthology") – a collection of earlier poets, each represented by *a flower species*. The analogy between Meleager's project and the notion of the Pleiad runs deep: in both cases, a group of poets is mapped onto a scientific taxonomic system, whether in astronomy or in botany; and in both cases, the group is composed of poets we would recognize as "Hellenistic." How did Hellenistic poets come to sense their identity as a literary movement? By perceiving themselves in the terms of a scientific system. (The curious thing, of course, is that the metaphor of "poetry as flowers" has for us become so saturated that we already fail to see the *botanical* import of Meleager's metaphor.)

[24] See Jones 1999 for the best documented account of the contact and the diffusion – apparently the consequence of Babylonian knowledge traveling to Egypt in the Hellenistic world, there to be produced gradually in Greek. As Rochberg points out (2004: 242–4) the spread of Babylonian astrology should be seen within the context of a much wider influence of Babylonian divination practices that seem to have won very wide acceptance throughout much of the Old World.

[25] So, venerably, Tarn 1959: 340–7. Of course, such interpretations of a Zeitgeist have gone out of fashion with our own, more sober, spirit of the time.

spread. What we repeatedly see is that the Hellenistic fascination with the stars is related to a fascination with bipolarity as such.

The same bipolarity is evident in the other major work of didactic epic surviving from antiquity – where the subject matter is not at all the elevated theme of the stars. The "high" derives from the epic form, the "low" – in this case, from the subject matter itself. In the second century BC, Nicander wrote a number of epic didactic works: a couple, lost, on land-tilling and honey-making (an influence, probably, on Virgil's later *Georgics*), that is "low" themes of a certain kind.[26] The two extant poems are, so to speak, lower: the *Theriaca* (on poisonous creatures) and the *Alexipharmaca* (on antidotes to poisons). Thus the subject matter taken by Nicander is not merely low but also grotesque and morbid. Nicander, among other things, versifies a specific prose work – just as Aratus did – in this case a study of poisonous animals by Apollodorus. The last-mentioned author was a third-century Alexandrian medical author, so that in Nicander we see Hellenistic poetry turning to Alexandrian science itself for inspiration (unlike Aratus, who versified the pre-Hellenistic Eudoxus and Theophrastus). This, however, may well represent no more than the accidental availability of models. At any rate, the distance between prose source and poetic treatment must have been crucial to Nicander's poetry: the language is not merely that of hexameter, but is also particularly rich and poetic, making use of Homeric *hapax legomena*, neologisms, as well as of complex syntactic and semantic arrangements.[27] The audience is invited to imagine a doctor – or a safety-conscious lay reader – scanning Homeric scholarship so as to be sure about the precise treatment of a serpent's bite . . . In other words, Nicander does not aim at the sobriety of Aratus' style. The absurdity of setting this particular material in poetic form is, instead, celebrated. Let us read for instance *Theriaca* 128–36 (adapting Gow and Schofield):

Beware you of meeting at crossroads the dusky
Male viper as he has escaped from her bite, and is maddened
By the blow of the smoky hued female, at the season when lustfully
She fastens upon him and tears him with foul fangs, and cuts off her lover's head;
But then as they come to be born, the young vipers
Avenge their sire's destruction, by gnawing their way
Through their mother's thin side – being born, they are motherless.

[26] On Nicander in general see Jacques 2002. Another lost work is "on things changing to each other," an inspiration for the later *Metamorphoses* by Ovid – and a theme obviously linked to the Alexandrian structural interest in mosaic and hybrid structures.
[27] See e.g. Jacques 2002: xciv–cvi.

For alone of all snakes, she, the female viper, is burdened with pregnancy:
Oviparous snakes of the forest warm their brood enclosed in a membrane.

The undeniable fascination of such lines has little to do with the conscientious study of medicine or zoology. And still, the source of the poetry in the prose of zoological and paradoxographical works is obvious to the readers (the word "oviparous" – in hexameter!). The prose sources provide an anchoring of meaning, so that, as much as the poem will go over the top, one's sense of an underlying reality would be preserved. This is not just Nicander inventing stories of snakes: snakes really are – or at least, really are purported to be – as paradoxical as that. Overall, the poem enacts, though on a different scale, the modulation seen in Apollonius Rhodius' use of geography. Just as Apollonius allowed poetic space and geographical space to blur together, so Nicander allows zoological monsters and poetic monsters to cross together (for once, the biological metaphor is apt) – the sharp opposition between the two serving a particularly shrill poetic effect.

The titles of Nicander's works are interesting in themselves. *Theriaca*, in particular, may be suggestive of prose in a precise sense: the ending *-ca*, i.e. an adjective formed from a noun, meaning roughly "having to do with . . ." may have been calculated to bring to mind the ancient *technē* genre. This may be compared with a spectacular find from the Hellenistic era – a papyrus, first published in 2001, containing some 600 lines. This papyrus forms perhaps the bulk of a book of poetry, usually agreed now to contain a collection of epigrams by Posidippus: one of the foremost epigrammatists of the third century BC. The papyrus roll itself is from the end of the century, and, aside from being now our major source for Posidippus himself, it also forms our best indication of what a third-century book of poetry could have looked like. Now, the poetic medium chosen by Posidippus, the epigram, is very far from the technical. Formally it is based on brevity of expression which precludes long descriptive passages. In terms of its content, the epigram derives from the tomb inscription, and its generic identity always keeps a trace of this origin: typically it has a localized, personal voice (even if a contrived one), speaking to a particular object, often associated with a deceased person.

All the more remarkable, then, that Posidippus' collection of epigrams is organized into sections which are mostly (eight of the extant ten) headed by *-ca* titles: so that we have epigrams purportedly on *lithica* ('things having to do with stones'), *oionoscopica* ('things having to do with the reading of omens'), or *hippica* ('things having to do with horses') – all suggestive of *technai*. Were those titles by Posidippus himself? The clever, ironic interplay between title and epigrams suggests an authorial control (perhaps later than that of the epigrammatist, but bespeaking, for sure, of Hellenistic sensibilities).[28] What is most interesting for my purposes here is the deliberate play with the possibilities of jarring juxtaposition of scientific expectation and poetic fulfillment. The title *Lithica*, "On things having to do with stones" would invite the reader to expect a string of scientific and paradoxographical statements, perhaps a kind of versification of a Peripatetic treatise such as Aristotle's *Meteorology* IV or Theophrastus' *On Stones*. In truth the epigrams do answer the title in a quite straightforward way – these are all epigrams about precious stones and especially about jewels made with such stones. But are these written primarily within the generic bounds of ancient epigram or of ancient mineralogy? I quote two of the epigrams:

14 (K. Gutzweiler):

> The horse Pegasos has been well-carved
> On sky-blue chalcedony by a craftsman using both hand and mind.
> For Bellerophon fell into the Aleian plain of the Cilicians,
> But the steed flew up into the dark air.
> For this reason he molded the creature riderless,
> Still trembling under the reins, on this airy stone.

17 (E. Kosmetatou and B. Acosta-Hughes):

> Reflect how this stone that the Mysian Olympus
> Unearthed is marvellous in two ways:
> One side deftly attracts the opposing iron
> Just like a magnet, the other side repels it,
> Which is both counteractive and a wonder: how one
> And the same stone emulates the course of two.

Epigram 14 belongs to the genre of *ekphrasis*, i.e. it describes a piece of art and – as is often the case with ancient *ekphrasis* – it takes the opportunity to expand on the mythical subject depicted in that art. This would of course be completely out of place in a treatise on minerals. The evocation of a particular object as the crystallization (literally!) of a scene, fits well the generic bounds of the ancient epigram. Epigram 17, on the other hand, derives directly from the mineralogical tradition, and even its paradoxography is of a kind that the most sober-minded scientific text would allow. I quote it of course as a very obvious example of the aesthetic we have been pursuing throughout this book: here is a culture that marvels

---

[28] See Lavigne and Romano 2004 for the deliberate interplay of text and title (concentrating on the *oionoscopica* sequence.)

at how "one and the same . . . emulates the course of two" which may well be said of Posidippus' collection, emulating both the epigram and the *technē*.

Some of the titles would be more transparent: *Andriantopoiika*, "Things related to statues," invites the reader to expect "normal" ekphrastic epigrams, an expectation largely fulfilled. *Hippica* is a more cunning title: suggestive of the actual genre of prose manuals of horse-training, it is instead a sequence of epigrams on victors in horse races. Perhaps *Nauagica*, too, could invite one to expect some sea-faring advice (it is in fact lamentations for shipwrecks). Aside from the *Lithica* itself, two sections actually do bring in some science: the *Oionoscopica* (whose subject matter would be perceived by its audience as scientific) as well as the *Iamatika*, "recoveries of health." The first of the *Iamatika* poems is especially complex:

95 (P. Bing):

> Like this bronze which, drawing shallow breath up over
> Its bones, scarcely gathers life into its eyes,
> Such were the ones he used to save from disease, that man who discovered
> How to treat the dreadful bite of the Libyan asp,
> Medeios, son of Lampon, from Olynthos, to whom his father
> Gave all the panacea of Asclepius' sons.
> To you, O Pythian Apollo, in token of his craft
> He dedicated this shriveled frame, the remnant of a man.

The poem is strangely ambiguous between an epitaph and a dedication – though both would mark it formally as epigram. Within the generic bounds of the epigram, however, the poem makes a precise medical statement: the physician in question discovered a treatment for the bite of a specified animal. This medical theme, however, is not treated at all neutrally, "scientifically." The bite itself is suggestive in its horror (the same horror which Nicander would later use to such effect), and the complex simile of lines 1–2 establishes a marked pathetic tone which is then made almost grotesque in the concluding lines. In short, this brief epigram plays on the same duality of medicine which we have seen in Nicander – a subject matter which is simultaneously scientific *and* emotionally charged.

In general, medicine would be easily available for poetic treatment. Just as heroic epic is essentially the poetry of voyage, opening up the possibilities of geography, many mythical themes bring up the subjects of wound and pain, opening up the possibilities of medicine. This intersection of science and poetry is the one to have been most often noticed by the secondary literature, and I shall confine myself here to two examples, one from each of the two major Hellenistic poets, Apollonius and Callimachus.

To take first the *Argonautica*: the hero Mopsus meets the very same Libyan asp whose bite we have just seen mentioned as cured (poor, pre-scientific Mopsus! – and who of the two, Posidippus and Apollonius, is intertextual with whom?) I quote extensively IV.1518–31 (Seaton's translation):

Now Mopsus stepped on the end of its [the asp's] spine, setting thereon the sole of his left foot; and it writhed around in pain and bit and tore the flesh between the skin and the muscles. And Medea and her handmaids fled in terror; but Canthus bravely felt the bleeding wound; for no excessive pain harassed him. Poor wretch! Already a numbness that loosed his limbs was stealing beneath his skin, and a thick mist was spreading over his eyes. Straightway his heavy limbs sank helplessly to the ground and he grew cold; and his comrades and the hero, Aeson's son, gathered round, marveling at the close-coming doom. Nor yet though dead even for a little space. For at once the poison began to rot his flesh within, and the hair decayed and fell from the skin.

The passage brings together the human pathos of the comrades' reactions, the grotesque terror of paradoxographical, exaggerated description, and finally what is likely to be scientific observation. Zanker points out the close parallel in Nicander's *Theriaca* 186–9, which suggests both are drawing on similar medical sources.[29] Of course, Nicander would certainly also draw on Apollonius: the key fact for us is how literary and scientific intertextuality could definitely co-exist.

Most has studied in detail another case of combined literary and medical intertextuality, in Callimachus' *Hymn to Delos*. The context is as follows. Leto's wanderings are over, she finally reaches the spot, Delos, where she will give birth. The wanderings, indeed, allow for some geography so that in lines 206–8 Leto (Mair's translation) "sat by the stream of Inopus, which the earth sends forth in deepest flood at the season when the Nile comes down in full torrent from the Aethiopian steep" – a recondite piece of paradoxical geography (the Delian stream of Inopus was supposed to be subterraneously connected to the Nile), to set the stage for the truly recondite piece of medical advice to follow (ll. 209–10):

And she loosed her girdle and leaned back her shoulders against the trunk of a palm-tree, oppressed by grievous distress.

---

[29] Zanker 1987: 125.

Most observed that Callimachus had in fact revised the mythical tradition (that had Leto lying on the ground in her pain). Leto's upright, supported pose, must certainly be a reflection of Herophilus' obstetric advice. In other words, the goddess is allowed to follow the most up-to-date (and consciously innovative) medical advice – and yet to suffer the agony of delivery in its full pathetic form, highlighting the suffering of the goddess and perhaps also ironically undercutting the power of the science.[30]

With these last examples, our sampling of poetic uses of science in Alexandria has covered the range of fields from mathematics to medicine. An author such as Callimachus, it appears, was equally familiar with both Conon's astronomy as well as with Herophilus' obstetrics. Before we conclude, it would be fascinating to see some reflections not only of the science, but also of the scientists themselves: does the scientist emerge as a cultural figure worthy of poetic celebration? The answer is complicated: Alexandrian poetry firmly aligns itself within the narrative range it inherits from its literary past. Even its contemporaries are draped with the clothes of Homeric figures – so that when Callimachus attacks his critics, they are called not by name but are, famously, made to be "Telchines" – mythical, impish smiths known to Archaic poetry. The elegant way to bring in the present was through the lens of the past. And so we can find the same Callimachus remaking the past to make it appear much more scientific, in this way perhaps bringing in the scientists of the present. Thus Callimachus' first iambus – traditionally a form used for invective but, in typical genre-breaking, employed by Callimachus for a historical tale praising the virtue of peace among scholars.[31] Hipponax, the sixth-century master of iambic invective, arises from the dead and admonishes contemporary scholars to behave well to one another, recalling the seven sages for their *exemplum*: when offered a cup as prize to the greatest of the sages, each insisted on the other being worthy of the prize until Thales (who emerges from the tale as first among equals) finally dedicated it to Apollo. Here is how Thales' wisdom is described (lines 52–62, adapted from Trypanis' translation):

For Thales was the winner: he was clever in other things, and was also said to have measured the little stars of the Wain, by which the Phoenicians sail their ships. And the Arcadian [who handed the prize, lit. "pre-lunar," a standard epithet for Arcadians, applied here as a pun] by happy chance found the old man in the shrine of Didymean Apollo, scratching the earth with a staff, drawing the figure which the Phrygian Euphorbos [Homeric hero, said by Pythagoras to be his earlier

---

[30] Most 1981.
[31] On Callimachus' iambs in general see Acosta-Hughes 2002; for the first iamb in particular see also Konstan 1998.

reincarnation – a device which allows Callimachus to bring in the anachronistic Pythagoras] discovered, he who first among men both drew triangles, even scalene, and extended a circle [about them], and taught men to abstain from living things . . .

The verb which I translate by "extended" (a circle) is fragmentary: we have επ . . ., for which I follow Pfeiffer's very likely επαγε: the verb should be analogous to the verb ἔγραψε used for the triangles (drew), which is a technical geometrical term – a constraint that leaves few options. These are not the only technical terms in this passage, where Thales is found γράφοντα τὸ σχῆμα "geometrically drawing and proving concerning the figure," and triangles are σκαληνά, a good technical word. It is curious – and likely intentional – that the verbs are mixed. In mathematical Greek, circles are drawn, straight lines extended; I take it that either Hipponax or Thales are considered to have not yet mastered the technical language of Callimachus' age. Assuming the technical side is as meticulously planned as that, one would wish to find an interpretation for the figure which an ur-Pythagoras was the first to devise and which Thales contemplated. The "even scalene" triangles must be the right-angled triangle, which was associated with Pythagoras – via the so-called "Pythagoras' theorem" – perhaps as early as the fourth century.[32] Now, no standard proof of Pythagoras' theorem calls for a circle. However, the drawing of a circle around a right-angled triangle – the poem makes best sense if we have the two objects conjoined – immediately determines the identity of a very important problem. This is the problem of finding a mean proportional between two given lines, A and C. The solution: let them stand side by side and treat the resulting line as a diameter of a circle; then the resulting perpendicular B forms the desired mean proportional (fig. 36, Euclid's *Elements* II.14). If this is indeed the problem we should imagine here, then we see Thales contemplating the antecedent of the major geometrical problem of Callimachus' own time. For the problem of finding a single mean proportional is the antecedent to the problem of finding *two* mean proportionals – the so-called "duplication of the cube" (a name which may arise with Eratosthenes and so would not be known to Callimachus). In this poem of anachronism, where Hipponax rises from the dead to serve (perhaps) as Callimachus' mouthpiece, and where Pythagoras is represented by his previous ghost, should we imagine Thales himself as standing in, among other things, for the mathematicians of Callimachus' time? This is speculative, of course (though, I consider it

---

[32] The reason for assuming that is that by the third century BC, the tradition seems to be fixed. Eudemus would certainly ascribe this theorem to *someone* (Zhmud 2002 argues convincingly that Eudemus' history was organized by "first discoverers" of famous results), and so it is difficult to see how a tradition would arise against his ascription. I return to the evidence, immediately below.

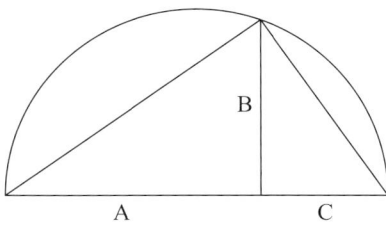

Figure 36

very likely given the mention of both triangles and circles): it was essential to Callimachus' poetics to make references to contemporary science vague and allusive and so, with a subject as technical as geometry, they would have to become very difficult for us to pick up with any certainty.

Of course Thales and Pythagoras invite poetic treatment more than, say, Euclid would. Here is the evidence for Pythagoras' theorem – tantalizing, and yet suggestive of the treatment of science in Hellenistic poetry. Plutarch (1094B), Athenaeus (418f) and Diogenes Laertius (VIII.12)[33] all quote the same distich (with no more than scribal variations):

> Ἡνίκα Πυθαγόρας τὸ περικλεὲς εὕρετο γράμμα
> κεῖν' ἐφ' ὅτῳ κλεινὴν ἤγαγε βουθυσίαν
>
> When Pythagoras discovered that famous proof,
> For which he gloriously drew[34] a glorious oxen sacrifice

– quite clearly the fragment of an epigram. Athenaeus ascribes it to Apollodorus "the arithmetician;" Diogenes, to Apollodorus "the calculator." A number of authors – starting from Vitruvius (IX. praef. 7)[35] – connect this episode with the specific discovery of "Pythagoras' theorem" (obviously the original epigram, even in its complete form, would only allude to the mathematical contents themselves). While the earliest quotation of the poem itself is by Plutarch, there is no reason to believe it is as late as the first century AD and it is perhaps more likely that the author of the source of Vitruvius' anecdote was already familiar with the epigram, in which case this would likely form a piece of Hellenistic poetry. Where

---

[33] Diogenes repeats a prose paraphrase of the same story in 1.24.
[34] Once again, the verb *agein* which – just possibly – may be read as a geometrical pun.
[35] Other authors who connect the anecdote to the discovery of Pythagoras' theorem include Diogenes Laertius, Plutarch, and Porphyry; for the full list see Pease 1958: 1207–8 n. *ad* III.88. The important observation for us is that likely the Greek authors do not rely on Vitruvius, which suggests a common Greek origin for the anecdote already in the Hellenistic world.

should we position it then? It was written by an "arithmetician" or probably, more precisely, a "calculator" (a kind of *lectio difficilor*: this is the less obvious epithet). Perhaps then a Hellenistic mathematician, an author of a treatise in calculation – who also dabbled in poetry. Or perhaps a poet who was famous for his treatment of mathematics and numbers? It might be significant that we cannot tell for sure. At any rate, note the poetic touch of jarring juxtaposition: abstract geometry with concrete sacrifice; in particular (surely, the point of the epigram), the jarring juxtaposition of Pythagoras, antiquity's most famous vegetarian, and the sacrifice of oxen (Cicero, pedantically, notes that the anecdote is for this reason unlikely to be true[36]).

The mention of Apollodorus, the obscure calculator-poet, brings to mind another scientist-poet, this time a physician. The evidence is only slightly better for this author – Nicias of Miletus. He is addressed quite frequently in the extant works of Theocritus – four times[37] – as the doctor-poet who best knows the cures for love. The irony of such lines is that they transform the "love as illness" metaphor into a literal statement, perhaps (if we transform "love" into "medicine") suggesting an obscene reading of the poetic trope, perhaps (if we transform "medicine" into "love") suggesting a comic figure of the love-lorn doctor. This irony is of a kind essential to Theocritus, whose poetry keeps subverting the poetic tropes of love without ever completely abandoning their pathetic power. And so, the dual skill of Nicias made him, for Theocritus, into an especially useful semiotic device. Nicias, the person who juxtaposes within himself the poet and the doctor could serve as sign for this juxtaposition of the metaphorical and the concrete, the amorous and the pharmaceutical, which Theocritus so much valued. It is unfortunate that so little is known of Nicias' own poetry – a mere handful of epigrams that survive, apparently, via Meleager's *Anthology*.[38] Those epigrams do not bring up a particular medical theme (they do, however, tend to focus on love from what one may call a bucolic angle, suggestive of the poet who corresponded with Theocritus) – this of course may represent no more than the accidents of survival. The remaining piece of evidence on this poet derives from Meleager himself who, in describing the "wreath" put together in his so-called *Anthology*, refers to Nicias as "verdant bergamot-mint" – which, as Lai points out, refers to a

---

[36] *Nat. D.* III.88.
[37] Addressed at the first lines of *Id.* XI, XIII, and the main figure in both *Id.* XXVIII.7 and the main figure of epigram VIII.
[38] *Anth. Pal.* VI.122,127, 270; VII 200; IX 315, 564; *Anth. Plan.* 188, 189. A further fragment, addressed to Theocritus, survives from the scholia to the latter (*Suppl. Hell.* 566).

plant famous for its pharmaceutical uses, sacred to Aphrodite, whose name even connotes the female sexual organs – in short, raising the same complex of ideas for which Theocritus has found his poet-doctor friend such a useful addressee.[39] Perhaps Meleager had in mind Nicias as a Theocritean figure but, more likely, the original body of work by Nicias, itself, was based on this ironic treatment of love and love's remedies.

And so we find, in Hellenistic poetry, references to a entire range of scientific phenomena; we find references to such heroic figures of science as Thales and Pythagoras; we even find some poet-scientists, whether the famous polymath Eratosthenes or the obscure calculator Apollodorus, the obscure doctor Nicias. Can we finally find some reference to the major scientists of the Hellenistic era? Any poetic celebration of our heroes from the previous chapters? Not quite, which is, of course, a pity: for among those poets lived a giant of mythical magnitude; perhaps, of all Greeks the one to have achieved the most. In extant literature, it remained for a Roman poet to celebrate Archimedes, and even then, indirectly:

> You – the measurer of sea and earth as well as
> The numberless sand – Archytas, are now confined
> By such small dust near the Matine shore . . .

Thus begins the well-known Ode 1.28 by Horace, an epigram in its manner: for the first twenty lines, it appears to be an inscription on Archytas' tomb, and then it is found in the final lines 21–36 that Archytas is addressed not by an inscribing poet but by another corpse, that of a sailor (washed up near Archytas' tomb?), asking to be buried . . . (apparently, he has only the dead Archytas to ask favors from: a desolate scene.)[40] The transposition of the "measuring numberless sand" from Archimedes to Archytas has long perplexed editors; Nisbet and Hubbard suggest finally, with a shrug, that "a poet would have no respect for facts in a matter of this kind," but one notes that the audience would probably recognize the shadow of Archimedes (who not only measured sand, but also was the author of *On Floating Bodies* – the major "measure of the sea" of antiquity). Perhaps Horace wished to transpose the standard depiction of geometrical genius to his native Apulia (where Archytas, conceivably, was buried), perhaps he needed to avoid the more specific historical and pictorial associations of

---

[39] Lai 1995.
[40] Could the desolate tomb specifically call to mind the description – presumably well known to Horace' readers – of the desolate Archimedean tomb rediscovered by Cicero (see next footnote)? On the Archimedes tomb trope as a whole, see Jaeger 2008, chapter 2.

the actual Archimedean tomb.[41] But what we must assume, either way, is that Horace's audience, in turn, must have assumed that Horace knew his scientific facts – and also must have allowed him to invert the facts so as to refer, vaguely and therefore elegantly, to the achievements of the past. By now, both Archytas and Archimedes are as historical and mythical as Thales and Pythagoras were for Callimachus. I like to believe that, in its exaggerated play of mosaic structure and surprise – the two parts so violently disjointed, the re-definition of the first twenty lines so shockingly unprepared for – Horace was also acknowledging the greatest Hellenistic master of surprising, fragmented and yet tightly arranged narrative, Archimedes. Which brings us from the question of complementarity – how poetry looks at science just as science looks at poetry – to the question of parallelism: which were the stylistic features of Hellenistic poetry, and how can they serve to explain those of Hellenistic mathematics?

## 4.2 THE TEXTURE OF ERUDITION

Among the epithets commonly applied to Hellenistic poetry are "erudite" or "scholarly," sometimes indeed (less so in recent decades) "pedantic." Indeed some of the Hellenistic poets were scholars, a term which in the Hellenistic context refers to the systematic study of the papyrus collections at Alexandria, concentrating mostly on literary works. What makes us classify this study as "scholarly" – rather than as the pastime of literary connoisseurs – is the systematic attempt to catalogue, analyze, and textually criticize the literary heritage.[42] Display of the erudition accumulated in this way could take several forms, which we may divide according to their engagement with (i) sign or with (ii) the signified. (i) In their reading and especially their textual critical study, Hellenistic scholars would explicitly articulate the verbal variety used by different authors and its appropriateness to its various themes. This awareness could then inform the poetry itself, in the poet's choice to use this or that word, especially with rare words or with words applied in rare meanings (perhaps with certain intertextual implications in mind: I use this word the way X did). For more on this Hellenistic practice, see e.g. Cusset (1999, part 1, concentrating on Homeric

---

[41] The tomb was visited, of course, by Cicero (*Tusc.* v. 23). Its association with the siege of Syracuse would bring in an entire nexus of associations having to do with the subjugation of Greeks by Romans, not the theme of Horace's poem. Finally, we should mention that while Horace' scientific portrait of Archytas is all wrong, his association with Pythagoras (relevant later on in the poem) was historically correct, and might have been more important for Horace.
[42] For the nature of Hellenistic scholarship, see Pfeiffer 1968.

*hapax legomena*). In what follows, I concentrate on (ii), the signified. The domain of archaic poetry is myth: the beliefs and rituals of Greeks across the Mediterranean. Hellenistic poetry retells this myth, providing it with rich geographical and ethnographical detail. In the rest of this section I take a single well-known example – the second part of Callimachus' *Hymn III*, or the *Hymn to Artemis* – and use it to describe the resulting texture of a scholarly text in a kind of carnival of erudition.[43]

The *Hymn to Artemis* is yet another Hellenistic bipartite work (with an elaborate transition between the two parts).[44] Both parts take off from the archaic model of the so-called Homeric hymns, departing from them in different ways. A Homeric hymn often (though not always) has for its subject some kind of biography of the deity, perhaps concentrating on certain episodes; it also provides along the way some information about the worship of the deity. The first part of Callimachus' *Hymn to Artemis* offers a close-up look at the biography, concentrating largely on one strange episode: the baby Artemis seeks permission from her father Zeus to remain forever a virgin! This is described in detail, playing out the contrast between the childishness of the goddess and her adult request. The episode is then allowed to progress somewhat: Zeus assigns Artemis a retinue of nymphs and they all go to Hephaestus' cave to collect the goddess' weaponry, with a lively encounter between the nymphs and the Cyclopes at the cave. Artemis then proceeds to test her new bow, and the hymn bursts into a genuine celebration of the goddess' prowess, with the poet addressing her in sincere, moving terms. All this leads on to her entrance, newly armored, to Olympus, to be seated next to Apollo. This sequence takes 170 lines,

---

[43] For discussions of this section of the hymn, see Plantinga 2004 and references there. Plantinga notes that previous authors have dismissed this section as mere "parade of learning," and her strategy is to show that it is more than that, displaying interesting thematic concerns. This I do not deny, but for my purposes I need to discuss a very different problem, namely: just what is it about this text – in formal, or cognitive terms – that makes it *appear* as a "parade of learning?" An answer to this question will serve to unpack a certain underlying structure which we may then use for our comparison of poetic and scientific styles.

[44] How are we to understand the relation between the two parts? Most modern readers feel that the tension between the two can hardly be resolved. Bing and Uhrmeister (1994) argue for the "unity" of the hymn, and indeed certain themes can be shown to hold through the hymn as a whole (their program of displaying this unity holds best, though, insofar as they deal with the first part of the hymn and show it as an organic unity devoted to the goddess' growth towards civilization; the argument that deep unities are to be observed between the second and first part comes down to some relatively weak connections – e.g. both parts refer to the themes of "hunt" and "outdoors" [p. 32], hardly striking for a poem about Artemis, or that the mention of many temples serves to locate Artemis within civilization [p. 33]). All in all, it is obvious that every work of art displays both dimensions of unity and diversity, that different styles, artists, and works strike a different balance between these two dimensions, and that in this particular hymn diversity is much more pronounced than unity – as it tends to be in Callimachus' work as a whole and in Hellenistic literature.

of which about half are dedicated to Artemis' original dialogue with Zeus, and half – to the following narrative sequence. The poem may well appear to end here, but then Callimachus goes on to say that he should not have his cattle plow the fields while the nymphs dance around Artemis (how he is to judge when that happens, is not clear). Here is how the dance is localized (171–4 Mair's translation):

> Near the spring of Egyptian Inopus[45] or Pitane – for Pitane too is thine – or in Limnae[46] or where, goddess, thou camest from Scythia to dwell, in Alae Araphenides, renouncing the rites of the Tauri.[47]

Retelling yet again, in simple prose form, Mair's prose translation, what Callimachus appears to be saying is that there are four locations he can think of for the dance of the nymphs surrounding the goddess:
(a) Delos
(b) Pitane
(c) Limnae
(d) Alae Araphenides

Each location is specified via the refracting lens of scholarship: (a) the reference to Delos is mediated via a piece of geographical lore, (b) that to Pitane – the simplest – evokes a comment where the poet, speaking as the expert scholar, notes that the location is indeed fitting (this is fundamentally a piece of geography: what Callimachus is implying is that Pitane has a major shrine to Artemis). (c) The reference to Limnae is perhaps intentionally obscure, while (d) that to Alae Araphenides is especially curious, with the poet refracting the location – an Attic deme – via a location where the goddess does *not* dance: a negative location which, however, allows the poet to bring in a piece of ethnographic lore. More than this: the temple at Alae Araphenides had specific connotations with the Black Sea, making the reference depend, for its full meaning, on the poet's scholarship.[48] Among other things, the description of a location as negatively defined by another where the goddess is *not* has a certain delightful absurdity, no doubt intended by the author.[49]

---

[45] Inopus is a stream at Delos; Callimachus obliquely refers to a geographical doctrine according to which the river is connected with the Nile.
[46] The reference of this Limnae is not well determined: ancient commentators thought an Attic deme was intended, while modern scholars often prefer a Laconian location (Bornmann 1968 n. *ad* 172).
[47] This is an oblique reference to an ethnographic tradition according to which the Tauri at Scythia worshipped Artemis with human sacrifice.
[48] Bornmann 1968: n. *ad* 173–4.
[49] One cannot resist quoting a modern parallel to this priamel construction: who is the most beautiful woman in our town, asks Georges Brassens? "C'est pas la femme de Bertrand / Pas la femme de Gontrand / Pas la femme de Pamphile / C'est pas la femme de Firmin / Pas la femme de

Note that there are *four* elements in this list. This is precisely one element above the rhetorically effective listing of three. This is in line with the overall strategy of this list, to numb its reader so as to gain, simultaneously, a sense of the wide geographical reach of the goddess – as well as the wide erudition of her poet. Certainly the reader does not come out of this description with a sense that all of the shrines have been identified, or even those who are most important. The sense, to the contrary, is that such a listing could in principle go on for much longer. And indeed, the poem did not end. Lines 170–82 were a mere transition to the second part of the poem, as we move now from the lively narrative of the first part (represented in the transition by the dancing nymphs) to the detail of erudition (foreshadowed by the quadripartite localization of the nymphs). It turns out that the first 182 lines of the hymn have still left many unanswered questions (183–5):

Which now of islands, what hill finds most favour with thee? What haven? What city? Which of the nymphs dost thou love above the rest, and what heroines hast thou taken for thy companions?

To be precise, these are six questions, phrased with the *pleiston*, "most" adverb, promising a single reply to each. The "or . . . or . . . or . . ." structure of the preceding lines cannot be repeated, and if the replies are to be delivered with as much dispatch as the questions, the end of the hymn should not be far away. Indeed the reply starts on a promising note of brevity (187–8):

Of Islands Doliche hath found favour with thee, of cities Perge, of hills Taygeton, the havens of Euripus.

While rapid, the replies need not be obvious (the mention of Doliche, in particular, may be a quaint display of specialized knowledge concerning the spread of Artemis' temples). But all of this is within the simple facts of cultural geography: which parts of the Greek world are most closely associated with Artemis? The two following questions are mythological in character and so leave much more room for play. Thus begin lines 189–91:

And beyond others thou lovest the nymph of Gortyn, Britomartis, slayer of stags, the godly archer; for love of whom was Minos of old distraught . . .

Germain / Ni celle de Benjamin / C'est pas la femme d'Honoré / Ni celle de Désiré / Ni celle de Théophile / Encore moins la femme de Nestor / Non, c'est la femme d'Hector." – Note the carnival of philandering erudition constructed by this priamel.

At which point Callimachus is set loose. We are told the story of Britomaris escaping from Minos, finally falling off a cliff to be saved by fishermen's nets (!), *hothen* – "whence" – always a significant word with Callimachus (lines 197–200):

Whence in after days the Cydonians call the nymph the Lady of the Nets (Dictyna) and the hill whence the nymph leaped they call the hill of nets (Dictaeon), and there they set up altars and do sacrifice.

In other words, we are allowed to cross momentarily into the favorite Callimachean theme of an *aition*, most typically the mythical story said to underlie a piece of worship – i.e. a combination of literary knowledge with Greek ethnography. (This combination is the subject matter of Callimachus' major work, the *Aitia*). But wait: we were not told yet how the worship of Dictyna is carried out! (lines 200–2):

And the garland on that day is pine or mastich, but the hands touch not the myrtle. For when she was in flight, a myrtle branch became entangled in the maiden's robes; wherefore she was greatly angered against the myrtle.

I wish to linger for a moment on this avoided myrtle. We should note that, in order to bring in this fact concerning the ritual, Callimachus has to go back to the narrative – apparently already concluded – concerning the flight of Britomaris. This undercutting of narrative closure is decisive, because now it becomes clear that there are other possible details one could in principle tell about the flight. At the same time, we cannot reconceptualize the story on the basis of the alternative narrative principle – as if Callimachus was in fact telling the story of the flight of Britomaris from the perspective of the ritual, accounting detail by detail for its various features until all are given their proper aetiology. For it is clear that we were given, as yet, only a very minimal sense of how the ritual proceeds. Structurally, we see Callimachus telling more details than the bare necessity for sustaining a narrative, and at the same time telling them in a disorderly manner which foregrounds the absence of narrative closure. Thus the outcome of reading the episode of Britomaris is that we are overwhelmed not only with the wealth of information presented by Callimachus, but also by the sense that there is so much more information to cover, so many stories to tell and so many details to fill in.

This digression, then, is fatal: closure has been ruled out and the implied promise of the *pleiston* adverb has been forgotten. As we move from nymphs to heroines, we are no longer looking for a single reply (and are no longer sure even which question we answer). Next is mentioned Cyrene – as nymph, probably? Or as heroine? Then further mythical female figures are mentioned, probably intended as possible replies for the "heroine" question, Procris, Anticleia, and Atalanta, each with a certain scholarly refraction (Procris named obliquely by reference to her husband, on Anticleia we are told that "they say" she was loved by Artemis – which foregrounds Callimachus' scholarly activity of looking for sources – and Atalanta is provided with a mythical narrative comparable to that of Britomaris). In short, while the four questions on islands, cities, hills and havens took two lines to answer, the two questions on nymphs and heroines took the thirty-seven lines 188–224, by which end we no longer have any expectations of closure at all: why not go on telling of more nymphs and heroines? Instead, Callimachus proceeds to tell us about more shrines and cities, i.e. undercutting even the brief replies he did give. The following lines provide a list of shrines, one mentioned briefly (at Miletus, lines 226–7), one alluded to in extreme brevity (a vocative in line 228: Χησιὰς Ἰμβρασίη πρωτόθρονε, "Lady of Chesion and of Imbrasus, throned in the highest," suggestive of a shrine to Artemis at Samos (where the Chesion cape as well as the Imbrasus stream are located – another piece of Callimachean geography),[50] ore a mere *ad hoc* mythical dedication (lines 228–32: Agamemnon's dedication of the rudder of his ship), then two in Arcadia are allowed a more expansive mythical treatment (lines 233–6). So far five shrines in lines 225–36, presented without any clear ordering principle and certainly numerous enough to blur any sense of structure – whereupon Callimachus can proceed to what is perhaps the most notable structure associated with Artemis, the temple at Ephesus. Lines 237–58 tell the mythical story of its foundation by Amazons, leading on to the historical narrative of the failure at Ephesus' gates of a seventh-century campaign led by Lygdamis, a Cimmerian ("milkers of mares," Callimachus notes in line 252 – an epithet simultaneously Homeric and ethnographic). This is not yet the ending of the hymn: Artemis' defense of Ephesus establishes yet another theme, that of the goddess' terrible, unyielding nature. A couple of vocatives introduce the elaboration of this theme (and allow Callimachus to sneak in two further pieces of cultural geography, l. 259): "O lady of Munychia [i.e. there is a temple to Artemis at the harbor of Athens . . .], watcher of harbours, hail, lady of the Pherae [. . . and another, at Thessaly]." Then line 260 incants:

μή τις ἀτιμήσῃ τὴν Ἄρτεμιν

Let none disrespect Artemis.

---

[50] Bornmann 1968: n. *ad* 228.

For – the text continues down to line 267 – οὐδέ (then a line and a half), μηδέ (then one line), for οὐδέ (then one line), μηδέ (then half a line), for οὐδέ (then half a line), οὐδέ (then a line), μηδέ (then half a line), for οὐδέ (then a line and a half): An extravagant, condensed catalogue with four admonitions and five mythical examples to support them (thus, for instance, none should shun the yearly dance [ll. 266–7]): "for not tearless to Hippo [queen of the Amazons] was her refusal to dance around the altar." At which point Callimachus departs on this simple note (l. 268):

> Hail, Great Queen, and graciously greet my song.

Part of the point of line 268 is, in context, to request the goddess to treat the poet better than she did Hippo, but the abruptness of the departure is much more marked than its appeal. After all, the poet's address to the goddess at the middle of the poem (lines 136–41) was more heartfelt, maybe even more appropriate as an ending. Line 268 does not so much provide closure, as provide the marker for where closure could, in principle, be inserted – and is instead avoided. The final catalogue of lines 260–7 functions not merely as yet another instantiation of the open-ended catalogue. It is the third catalogue of its kind (the first was nymphs and heroines, the second was temples). The texture of each of these catalogues is so dense that even three of them are much more than can be synoptically inspected: by the end of lines 267, the reader can no longer recall which items precisely Callimachus has listed. Thus there is one further, open-ended meta-catalogue: the catalogue of types of items that can be catalogued for the goddess. In this case these are: (i) beloved nymphs and heroines, (ii) temples, (iii) consequences of disobedience. Clearly no principle governs this list and it is not only that countless more items may be added to each individual list; the list of lists can be indefinitely extended as well. Borges' often-quoted Chinese Encyclopedia does come to mind. And so, lines 183–268 begin on the note of trying to sum up the most important mythographic detail concerning Artemis, and end up suggesting the impossibility of any such summary.

The above forms an analysis of just one text of Hellenistic scholarly poetry. It is not a minor example, as the *Hymn to Artemis* 183–268 is one of the more extended scholarly passages in the hymns of Callimachus. It is remarkable in its scholarly focus and somewhat extreme in its structure – though not in its intended effect. In a fundamental study of Callimachus' hymns, Harder (1992), notes that the presence of the "mimetic" – the localization of the speaker of the hymns in space and time – serves to emphasize a limited, "perspectival" character of the knowledge claimed by the poet. He speaks not from the perspective of genuine omniscience but rather from the markedly artificial perspective of the scholar-poet. This is a fundamental ironic play with the claims of the poet to divine truth. And it is therefore interesting to note that Hymn III.183–268, where the ironic, asymptotic character of the carnival of erudition is at its most marked, is also the place where the "mimetic" character of Callimachus' hymns is the least obvious (reduced, in fact, to the direct questions addressed to the goddess in lines 183–5.) When not marking, ironically, his human limitations via marking himself as a mere mortal, Callimachus marks his text directly – through an ironic, carnivalesque structure.

The best place to investigate this in detail would have been Callimachus' *Aitia*. I chose to concentrate on the *Hymn to Artemis* merely because it is extant in full and so can sustain such formal analysis with better claim for certainty. But clearly very similar formal principles seem to underlie the *Aitia* as a whole. Fantuzzi and Hunter are worth quoting (2004: 58, focusing on fr. 43 but making an argument for the *Aitia* as a whole): " . . . the whole project of 'completeness' is exposed for what it is . . . : catalogue style in fact advertises, rather than conceals, silences. The poet may indeed find any gap in his knowledge intolerable, but the undertaking is as doomed as the wish to make decisions between competing *aitia*." (2004: 63, again concentrating on fr. 75 to make a general point): "These verses . . . display a brilliant control of poetic voice, exploiting the claims to omniscience by a poet who sets himself up to narrate 'origins', but is defeated by the multiple ramifications of the material he chooses." The *Aitia* was a work setting out to tell everything about everything; it was the appropriate vehicle for a literature that seems to have valued the deliberate frustration of closure. In this way, the carnival of erudition is by no means a marginal phenomenon of Hellenistic poetry: it is right at its heart.

What are the consequences of all of this for my intended parallel between mathematics and poetry? One can point at many stylistic parallels between the text discussed above and the Greek mathematical texts discussed in the first three chapters. The repeated false ending of the *Hymn to Artemis*, for instance – the way in which it repeatedly resumes even as the reader expects a closure – gives rise to narrative surprise of the kind discussed in chapter 2. The basic bipartite structure of the hymn, as well as the articulated, many-times disjunctive structure of the second part, are clear examples of mosaic composition directly comparable to many structures seen in chapter 3. Such considerations will be further pursued in the coming sections of this chapter. My interest here is of course mainly with the parallel to chapter 1. The carnival of erudition, evident in so many literary Hellenistic works, is an important context for the understanding of the carnival of calculation discussed in the first chapter. I even dare to suggest that, by bringing in the carnival of calculation, some further light may be thrown on the carnival of erudition itself.

The Bakhtinian notion of the carnival is as difficult to apply to Hellenistic erudition as it is to its mathematics. While sex and excrement are easy to find in Greek myth, their presence in Hellenistic poetry would be unmarked, simply because such functions are integral to myth already in its archaic, canonical formulation. In Greek literature, the lower bodily functions do not ironically undercut the sublime but rather enhance it by bringing out the pathetic presence of the human inside the divine order itself. (This, incidentally, is why Rabelais can simultaneously enact a late medieval carnival while at the same time pretending to be a classicizing humanist.) And yet, one can look for functional, structural ways in which the Hellenistic flights of erudition are sensed as a contrast to the serious sublimity of canonical poetry. The sense of irony towards the sublime is achieved not by an up-down inversion of bodily functions (as is done by Rabelais) but by a more subtle process of undercutting: at the very moment of addressing the divine order, the Hellenistic author suggests the futility of such an address and focuses the reader's attention away from divinity, towards the decidedly human, mundane practice of book learning.

There are two interrelated ways by which the futility of discussing the divine order is suggested by the carnival of erudition. The first has to do with the unit of measurement. Callimachus sets out to express Artemis' grandeur, but this is immediately translated into the details of myth and ritual, both taken in their minute and, most important, *non-transparent* detail (why *this* detail? why *now*?): a close-up on the baby Artemis pulling the hairs of Zeus's chest; the purported origins of the name of a hill in Crete. This bathos yields the effect not only of comedy, but also of profound self-irony. The poem builds a contrast between its goals and its means, as the divine goal is measured against the mundane, humble means of expressing it. So this is one way of subverting the sublime: through the *minute*.[51]

---

[51] The accumulation of detail does not have to end up in the minute canceling itself out: details can also *add up*. To do so, however, they must become explicitly structured. Thus Theocritus' panegyric of Ptolemy, which explicitly evokes this *very* topos of the multiplicity of praise (Theocritus XVII.11–12): "How shall I first pick up? Since the telling can proceed by myriad ways, of how the gods favored the best of kings." This question however is immediately, curtly answered in line 13 (ἐκ πατέρων, "from his forefathers") – no ironic answer here. The panegyric proceeds in clearly defined units of text, never attempting to surprise and to throw the reader back: from the forefathers (conceived widely to include his native island Cos) we proceed to current possessions, which finally form the basis for his *euergeia*. From beginning to end the poem marks the notion of the well

As a consequence of the limited means themselves, but especially through the use of complex structures that thwart the achievement of closure the poems are not merely minute but are also *asymptotic*. The implicit suggestion is that such poems could go on indefinitely and never exhaust their subject. In this way, the very project of singing the divine is being questioned. Setting out to capture the divinity of Artemis, Callimachus also suggests, implicitly, the impossibility of such a task.[52] To further augment this effect, the poems indulge in an opaque, difficult to parse texture of obscure details, very rich with proper names that are often only vaguely known to the reader from elsewhere. This explosion of obscure proper names replicates, in miniature as it were, the same structures of the minute and the asymptotic. I quote from lines 226–8:

Sojourner in Miletus; for thee did Neleus make his guide when he put off with his ships from the land of Cecrops. Lady of Chesion and of Imbrasus, throned in the highest . . .

There are fourteen words in the Greek, of which five are proper names. I intentionally avoid footnotes with explanations of the names: the Greek reader would have picked up many of them quickly (not so much the two last place names in Samos, though), but the very effort of mentally picking them up and finding their associations to the text would be a hindrance to any natural, "flowing" reading: the hymn thus deconstructs itself into minute details that do not add up to a sum of their parts.

---

ordered ("We begin from Zeus, Muses, and end with him," line 1 – a promise fulfilled with the word "Zeus" at the final line 137): it is after all a praise of *hierarchy*. The one non-transparent moment is, appropriately, numerical. How many cities in Egypt? lines 82–4: τρεῖς ἑκατοντάδες τρεῖς δ' ἄρα χιλιάδες τρισσαῖς ἐπὶ μυριάδεσσι, δοιαὶ δὲ τριάδες, μετὰ δέ σφίσιν ἐννεάδες τρεῖς, i.e. 3*100+3*1000+3*10000+3*2+3*9, which by my count is 33,333. The vacillation up and down the numerical scale, together with the lovely breaking of 33 into 3*2+3*9 is calculated to achieve a sense of the immeasurable with, perhaps, a whiff of humor. All in all, this panegyric shows that, when they wanted to, the Hellenistic poets knew how to make themselves clear. The opacity of the *Hymn to Artemis* is clearly intentional – and highly effective in its irony. (I thank Marco Fantuzzi for suggesting this comparison to me.)

[52] Once again, one cannot resist a modern parallel, in this case a very close one, from Nabokov's *Pale Fire*: "Now I shall speak of evil as none has / Spoken before. I loathe such things as jazz; / The white-hosed moron torturing a black / Bull, rayed with red; abstractist bric-a-brac; / Primitivist folk-masks; progressive schools; / Music in supermarkets; swimming pools; / Brutes, bores, class-conscious Philistines, Freud, Marx, / Fake thinkers, puffed-up poets, frauds and sharks." The loathings are genuine (and genuinely Nabokov's) and some of them of deep significance; but the chaotic structure, as well as the immediate bathetic descent from "evil" to "jazz," construct this self-irony: the impossibility of the attempt to capture the sublime (an impossibility which is the main theme of that poem, *Pale Fire*). This is achieved precisely through the combination of the minute and the asymptotic (the latter achieved via the prevention of closure). The difference between Callimachus and Nabokov is – surprisingly – that Callimachus is much more subtle, Nabokov much more blunt in using this technique.

This combination of the minute and the asymptotic is, of course, already directly comparable to the mathematical carnival of calculation – where the mathematician sets himself a seemingly impossible task such as measuring the ratio of the circumference to the diameter, or counting all prime numbers, or finding the size of the cosmos, and ends up, in one sense, encompassing such a task while, in another sense, he further underlines the task's impossibility. This effect is obtained through the implicit emphasis on the means of calculation, which are based on indefinitely small units of measurement that in principle cannot be made powerful enough for the task at hand so that it can only be obtained in an asymptotic way: however big the n-gon may be, a 24-gon, a 48-gon or a 96-gon, the minuteness of the sides can no more than approximate the precise, infinite circularity of the circle; however precise one's astronomical observations are, their underlying imprecision as well as the approximative nature of trigonometric calculation will undermine any astronomical calculation; primes cannot be exhausted, they can merely be found one by one. To further augment this asymptotic effect, the mathematicians also employ an opaque, difficult to parse texture of writing, often based on the numbing repetition of number words, a texture that further deepens the distance between the reader and the task obtained.

   This comparison serves to remind us of the common cultural themes animating both poetry and mathematics. I have already noted in chapter 1 above how size – taken to the extremes of the big and the small – seems to have been a culturally charged sign in Hellenistic Alexandria. The contrast of big and small, the way by which the latter cannot achieve the former except as an asymptotic, ironic exercise: we can see how this would be a powerful symbol to both poets and mathematicians active in a culture of courtly grandeur. At any rate, regardless of how we situate this symbolism in historical terms, we should concentrate on the structural similarity of the two enterprises. Let us sum up the structure. An author sets out to capture objects that are, within their cultural setting, considered to be sublime. He employs: (i) for themes, an emphasis on the minute, (ii) for the telling of those themes, an implicitly asymptotic (= lacking in closure, difficult to parse) presentation. The result is an ironic undercutting of the very enterprise, giving rise to a certain irony towards the sublime itself. Since the sublime remains present as the background to the work, the work ends up subverting the sublime (and not just ignoring it), constructing a carnivalesque effect. The work performs the paradox of a certain holiday away from sublimity while still being directly engaged with it. The sublimity may be that of precise truth, in the mathematical case, or of divine reality, in the case of poetry but, once again, the structural result is the same.

One needed to argue in minute detail for the parallelism between a mathematical carnival of calculation, and the poetic carnival of erudition: this parallel has to do with a complex structural effect. The two next parallels I wish to draw – with surprise and with mosaic, hybrid structures – are much more obvious, and I now change gear to a completely different mode, going rapidly through some fairly non-controversial claims. Let me start however by suggesting the outlines of a controversy whose edges, in what follows, I must skirt.

### 4.3 MOSAICS AND SURPRISES: INTRODUCING A SURVEY

Writers of the classical period were citizens of a city which they preferred to all others . . . Poets of the Alexandrian school abandon, at an early age and without hope of return, the place in which they were born . . . [their] poetry is no longer the mouthpiece of the people's thought; it is merely the echo of an entirely personal imagination . . . Alexandrianism is the victory of what in our day has been called "art for art's sake." . . . it was through the Alexandrians that love became and has since remained the main theme of imaginative literature . . . they understood the gain that accrues to poetry from an accurate delineation of the most humble reality . . . they attempted to introduce science into poetry . . . the rigid frame in which tradition has enclosed each kind of poetry was enlarged or shattered . . . [yet] it was reserved for other ages to make their ideas productive and with their aid to create masterpieces. In the decline of a civilization which already has to its credit centuries of great literature, it is not without effort that we can find that freshness and sincerity of impressions that constitute poetry. For new-comers it is hard not to wish to improve upon their predecessors, and not to seek for new and rare forms . . . [poets] choose whatever is unusual or morbid . . . Such was the special plight of the Alexandrian poets, placed as they were on the confines of two worlds, the ancient and the modern, the last born of the one and the forerunners of the other. Our own plight is almost the same, nor can we read the Alexandrians without a glance into our own hearts.

So Couat in 1882, in the peroration to his great study of Alexandrian poetry, *Alexandrian Poetry under the First Three Ptolemies*.[53] In its main tendency, this passage sums up brilliantly a position to which, today, most scholars of Hellenistic poetry would violently object. This main tendency has to do with the question of poetry and citizenship – which, for scholars of Couat's generation, would come to be expressed through the Hegelian diction of civilization passing through its ages of youth and decline. Thus,

[53] Loeb tr., Couat 1930: 542–7.

the youthful civilization of the citizen-poet came to be contrasted with the decayed one of the poet-for-poetry's sake. "Poetry for poetry's sake" – what an absurd notion, in truth, when so much of Hellenistic poetry so clearly speaks for the concerns of royals and their empires! No, this aspect of Couat we must avoid, nor is any such implication intended by my reference, in the title, to the "ludic" – as if the science, or the civilization that gave birth to it, were engaged in the playful *as against* the serious. As if the ludic should be seen as a kind of holiday taken from the central issues of either science or poetry.[54]

It is almost as if the goal of scholars of Hellenistic civilization working today is precisely that: to salvage the persuasive core of judgments such as Couat's, while avoiding the pitfall of a Hegelian interpretation of "decadence." The generation of scholars from Couat (1882) down to Kroll (1924, with its famous metaphor of the "hybridization of genres") has set down a certain path for studying the style of Hellenistic poetry, which was more recently abandoned as interpretation while, mostly tacitly, taken over as description. The historical account is all different; the key formal properties are similarly identified. Belatedness is crucial to Fantuzzi and Hunter, writing in 2004, just as it was to Couat himself – only now it is understood as an active engagement with a past of "models" chosen by a poet, instead of Couat's burden to which poets were passively subjected. And the central metaphor of duality – of lying in between two worlds – is remarkably vigorous in so many various studies of Hellenistic civilization, in Selden's "Alibis" from 1998 as well as Stephens' *Seeing Double* from 2004. The latter study, in particular, may be seen as the direct opposite of Couat's. Stephens produces an interpretation of Hellenistic literature which is fully political. The poets, far from producing "art for art's sake," engage instead with the central political problem of their civilization: the construction of a new political identity in colonized Egypt. And yet the theme of this new identity is the duality, the in-between status of two worlds, the Hellenic and the Egyptian.

Certain formal intuitions seem to hold even as our contextual sense of Hellenistic civilization becomes more sophisticated and historically responsible. The presence of past genres and the intentional effort of subverting them; the fascination with dualities and ambiguities – these seem to be real

---

[54] Compare Fantuzzi and Hunter 2004: 17: "The concept of 'contamination of literary genres' has often, and rightly, been identified as one of the distinctive characteristics . . . Much less correctly, however, such 'contamination' has at times been associated with . . . a ludic and subversive sophistication which was wholly preoccupied with books and only too ready to sacrifice the traditional literary system."

212                    *The poetic interface*

features of Hellenistic literature to which one can find wide agreement, from Couat down to Fantuzzi, Hunter, Selden, and Stephens. I shall now concentrate on such formal intuitions that are widely shared in the scholarship. I shall follow them, taking – true to the Hellenistic aesthetic – not one, but *two* guides. In between the two, an image of Hellenistic poetry is to be gained. One guide is *Hellenistic Poetry*, a survey by Hutchinson from 1988. With little claim for originality, this book can be taken to represent the entire tradition from Couat onwards (even if shunning, at Hutchinson's historical stage, Couat's Hegelianism). The other is *Tradition and Innovation in Hellenistic Poetry*, a major piece of original research by Fantuzzi and Hunter. This can be taken to represent the more sophisticated scholarship of recent years that aims to go beyond the more easy generalizations of past scholars. Hutchinson's book is the explicit "survey," and therefore my plan is to follow him as he surveys the various authors, turning then to Fantuzzi and Hunter to get, as it were, the more critical view.[55] We begin, therefore with Hutchinson – and with Callimachus.

### 4.4 MOSAICS AND SURPRISES: A SURVEY

Hutchinson begins with the notion of Callimachus the "pedant," where he immediately points out that Callimachus' device is, typically, to construct (in my terms) a mosaic, surprising composition where the pedantic stands in contrast to other elements. Often Callimachus constructs narratives of real human emotion, to have them disrupted by statements of learning or by comparable meta-textual devices. Take fr. 75 of the *Aitia* (already mentioned above in connection with the carnival of erudition). Following upon the touching mythical love story of Acontius of Ceos, Callimachus adds (ll. 58–60, adapting Whitman):

and this love of yours we heard from Xenomedes of old, who once set down all the island in a mythological history.

This leads on to a kind of abstract of the book by Xenomedes: the erotic and the bibliographic follow upon each other without interruption. We notice the rich comic effect, as well as the tight connection between mosaic composition and surprise. As Hutchinson sums up: "the difference is made salient through vigorous contrasts and extravagant surprises." The same can

---

[55] Adding on to the Hellenistic theme of duality, Fantuzzi and Hunter are two co-authors – who further disavow the current fiction of co-authorship, signaling instead that the different parts of their book are, each, the responsibility of only one author. I ignore this complication to refer throughout to a single multiple author, "Fantuzzi and Hunter 2004."

be said for the hymns: as we have seen already with the *Hymn to Artemis*, the structure of a hymn is sometimes that of a mythical story, framed by, e.g., the singing voice of the poet. In the *Hymn to Artemis*, the framing is distinctly scholarly. In hymn v, it is a description of a ritual (where the voice of the poet addresses the participants even as the ritual is being described). Myth and ritual may form a seamless whole, but Callimachus instead creates a tension: the participants in the ritual await Athena's arrival and, with it being delayed, Callimachus has to fill in the time with a story. Hymn iv, to Delos, has a more complex structure, not so much a mosaic as a hybrid: the single narrative line of the hymn is predicated upon the wild incongruity of its subject matter, Leto searching for a place to accept her childbirth – with Greek localities anthropomorphized to absurdity. This then leads to the framing-composition of the *Aitia* themselves. Here the author (at least in the first two books) seems to be referring time and again back to the muses, to instruct him on details of scholarship that he cannot solve himself – to use an analogy later than Hutchinson's, the Muses at Helicon appear as some kind of search engine to help the poet where his library fails . . . Once again we see the complex hybridization of the sublime and the pedantic.

We now turn, following Hutchinson, to the *Iambi* (of which we have mentioned above the first, with its reference to Thales and, implicitly, to Pythagoras). The theme stressed by Hutchinson is that of contrast between tones: the one expected from the generic bounds of the iambus (a tone of scurrilous invective), the other urbane and measured. Often the two are set in direct opposition to each other, in a debate within a single iambus; in the programmatic iambus 1, Hipponax – the master of the archaic genre in its full scurrility – is portrayed to rise from the dead to preach good manners.

Callimachus comes close to treat an epic theme, on an epic scale, in his *Hecale* – a poem the size of some two or three Homeric books. Its theme immediately gives away the basic device: Theseus, on his way to fight the Marathonian bull, takes shelter with the poor old peasant-woman Hecale. On his way back, he discovers that she is dead, and founds an Athenian deme and cult in her name (among other things, this poem is another Callimachean *aition*). The contrast is obvious: between the grand and the humble. Much guesswork is required to make sense of the fragments we have, and so we could sin here in circularly reconstructing Callimachus' poetic persona (reconstructing the poem from the fragments on the basis of our assumptions concerning Callimachus, and then using the poem to sustain those very assumptions). And yet one can quote Hutchinson's summary: "We can at least see the divergence, and perceive something of how the elevation of Theseus' heroism stands against the lowly element in Hecale's pathos, and goes to make up the tonal structure of the poem."

Following a brief discussion of Callimachus' epigrams (where once again Hutchinson stresses the theme of abrupt transition, now in the miniature span of an epigram), he moves on to some programmatic elements in Callimachus. The evidence is well known (and subject to fierce debate, notably in Cameron 1995). It is also very directly helpful for our immediate purposes. In the final iambus, Callimachus imagines a critic who objects to his many-stranded productivity as a whole as well as to the genre mixture within the *Iambi* themselves. (A Byzantine summary of the *Iambi* refers to their *polyeidia*, "many-formedness," which was taken as the title of the recent major study of that work, Acosta-Hughes 2002.[56]) In the well-known prologue to the *Aitia*, against the Telchines, Callimachus' main point is of course difficult to reconstruct with certainty, but clearly it does involve the scale of elaboration of individual themes. In some sense, Callimachus claimed to avoid the lengthy. The *Aitia* is a long work, but it consisted of many transitions between highly individualized, small units. Thus the two extended ars-poetic pronouncements, from the end of the *Iambi* and from the beginning of the *Aitia*, both cohere around a single theme: Callimachus' preference for a poetry with many strands to it, many transitions. This may well set the scene for Hellenistic poetry as a whole.

Fantuzzi and Hunter return to a similar theme, emphasizing the poet's relation to his past poetic authorities and its implication for his poetic persona. Their interpretation of the Telchines serves to sum this up (75–6): "When the Telchines tell Callimachus 'to grow up', what they mean is that he should adopt a poetics sanctioned by time and archaic practice . . . together with the moral seriousness that attends it. Callimachus rejects both the poetics and the *gravitas* in his extraordinary wish to start all over again." Allusion as a central theme of Callimachean poetics, in other words, is there to serve the contrast between Callimachus and his tradition. Fantuzzi and Hunter's analysis of a brief passage in *Hecale* may be taken to spell this out (254–5): (vv. 22–3) "But they did not sleep for long. Quickly came the frosty dawn-hour . . . (στιβήεις ἄγχαυρος)."

If v. 22 varies easily recognizable Homeric patterns, the following verse is radically innovative. For the Homeric formula "Dawn with her beautiful throne" (six times in Homer) Callimachus substitutes στιβήεις ἄγχαυρος, 'frosty hour close to dawn'; στιβήεις 'frosty' is a neologism . . . As for ἄγχαυρος, this is not only

---

[56] See Acosta-Hughes 2002: 9.

very rare (Cypriot, according to Hesychius α 922 Latte) but also grammatically ambiguous . . . [Callimachus] juxtaposes the very Homeric v. 22 to the marked linguistic innovation (in enjambement) of v. 23, a striking shift which is matched by the sudden intrusion of a typically Hellenistic description of the time of day, drawn from the daily life of humble people, which places *en abîme* the dominant taste of the Hecale as a whole.

The relationship to one's model assumes a special meaning in the case of the *Hymns*. The Hellenistic authors need not have thought of Homer as essentially oral, but they were definitely aware of the cultic significance of a hymn. To the extent that they produced a non-ritual, purely textual hymn, they therefore had to produce a text radically alien to its intertext in the *Homeric Hymns*. This is a major theme of Fantuzzi and Hunter's (2004) interpretation of Callimachus' hymns:

As for the long hymns to Artemis and Delos, these poems construct an audience crucially interested in sacred spaces, rites, and their history as practised by others – often very remote 'others' . . . sometimes the effect can be disorienting, as the text pays little attention to the boundaries and categories with which we are familiar; we may feel, as in the *Hymn to Artemis*, overwhelmed by a body of disparate ritual experiences . . . [moving to the *Hymn to Delos*] In this mixture of third-person description of cult and an empathetic involvement in it by the poet, Callimachus found the seeds of some of his most striking experiments with poetic voice.

The point is that Callimachus' hymns work by variously disturbing the way in which a hymn is supposed to be anchored in the here-and-there of cultic experience: whether by the heaping together of various here-and-theres, as in the *Hymn to Artemis*, or in the mixing of the here-and-there of the empathetic involvement with ritual, together with its distant, "scholarly" description, as in the *Hymn to Delos*.

As we have already seen in their treatment of *Hecale*, Fantuzzi and Hunter emphasize Callimachus' verbal texture. In it, they see his poetics (43–4):

[H]is whole style reveals, and demands of his readers, an extraordinarily easy familiarity with the Greek literary heritage and with the various levels of literary and non-literary Greek. Callimachus' choice of words, and the order in which he places them, is constantly surprising; it is this, more than anything else, which distinguishes his poetry from that of all other surviving Greek poets. Words of high literary parentage or of the greatest rarity occur alongside others drawn from the contemporary world of mundane activities . . .

So much for this, our first and most important stop in the tour of Hellenistic poetry. Callimachus – the major poet of the third century – was a poet marked by his sharp verbal and thematic contrasts, by his striving to achieve the surprising effect, and by his conscious engagement with, and subversion of, his literary models.

We may now turn to Apollonius of Rhodes. Once again, we approach a subject vigorously debated – that of the relationship between Callimachus and Apollonius[57] – but we still follow a consensus view as we follow Hutchinson's identification of an essential continuity between the two poets. The Argonauts' song in praise of Apollo is a useful example (2. 701 ff.): an epiphany of the god, rendered with full emotional force, is set alongside a scholarly discussion of the origins of a certain ritual-cry. This juxtaposition of the divine and the scholarly – bathetic, ironic, and somehow not disruptive of the emotional power of the poem as a whole, is of course one we have seen already in Callimachus himself. Indeed, the theme of *aitia* is central to Apollonius (Hutchinson counts forty *aitia* in the three books 1, 2 and 4), and they may have a similar function to that we have seen in Callimachus' *Hymn to Artemis*: a certain ironic distancing between the poet and the divine order he confronts. Certainly they serve to frame individual episodes (Apollonian *aitia* frequently serve to provide closure to a narrative episode), making the work as a whole somewhat more "episodic" in character. A further effect is specifically that of mixture: the notion of the *aition* involves a chronological duality, of the mythical past (which provides the *aition*) and the historical present (for which the *aition* is provided). This duality is especially marked within the mythically defined genre of epic poetry – where the intrusion of the present is very vividly felt. (We have seen this duality, in effect, in considering the use of geography in Apollonius, where the same topography serves as arena for both mythical event and contemporary geography, and this duality, of a past felt as present and yet alien, is the main theme of Fantuzzi and Hunter's own reading of Apollonius.)

The *Argonautica* has often, in modern times, been criticized for its lack of unity. Hutchinson emphasizes that this critique must be beside the point for Apollonius' original conception. The poem does display a clear overarching narrative structure (the Argonauts, after all, do sail and return), as well as a set of unifying emotional tones. Within this framework, though, Apollonius' intention was also to create a complex pattern, whose unity would not be too obvious. I quote some comments (pp. 105–6):

The poem deliberately plays on the reader's conception of its unity as it develops. On a first reading Books 1–2 seem far from possessing a tight or radical unity;

---

[57] See Köhnken 2001 and references there.

attempts to eliminate this impression are misguided. The author highlights the discontinuity of his narrative ... Book 3 as we read it appears to join the whole poem into a simple kind of unity through contrast: love, cunning, women, now have superiority over courage and men ... We seem to find unity through pointed reversal and forceful opposition ... The fourth book takes both sides of the antithesis between male and female, valour and guile, and so forth, and causes them to undergo a whole variety of mutations, grim, playful, and fantastic, in a disruptive series of episodes.

I have already mentioned the poem's relation to its past as the main theme of Fantuzzi and Hunter's reading of the *Argonautica* – understood in a rich sense: the historical Apollonius reacting to Homer, the implied author's position *vis-à-vis* the past recounted by him and even the heroes' relation to what is, to them, the deeper past of deeper mythological realms. The emphasis is on the complex nature of this relation towards the past: it is that of originality with continuity. The stylistic analysis may serve as central example; Apollonius' very use of epic formulae is distinctly Hellenistic (266–7):

Apollonius uses repetition with great care ... and it is variety, not faithfulness, which is sought. ... The Golden Fleece occurs fifteen times in the *Argonautica*, and it is not easy to imagine that poetic language offered many different ways to say "fleece"; moreover, "golden" was only χρύσε(ι)ον. Apollonius succeeds, however, in achieving a level of internal formulaic expression that avoids repetition as far as possible, by making use not only of a careful alternation between κῶας "fleece" and δέρος "skin" (the former eight times, the latter seven times) and between χρύσειον (eleven times) and χρύσεον four times), but also of hyperbaton: κῶας and δέρος are regularly separated from their adjective.

(One is indeed reminded of the complex patterns by which Archimedes varies the repetition of conclusions, see p. 124 above). The same observation is generalized from the verbal to the narrative level as well (123): "Apollonius largely avoids repetition of the most familiar Homeric kind, that of 'formulaic' language and of scene-type; variation, rather than sameness, is the principal determinant". The poem as a whole stretches across a wide literary domain, from the quotidian to the strictly fantastic, and Fantuzzi and Hunter develop the emphasis on variation in the context of book 4 (124):

Repetition ... always foregrounds similarity and difference ... The fantastical landscapes of book 4 in fact extend the horizons of epic in both time and space: the difference but clearly pointed relationship between the allusive obscurity of Argos's speech and the dry and detailed ethnography of the prophet Phineus [which we have considered in section 4.1 above] is a paradigm case of difference within epic sameness.[58]

Plurality indeed appears to be a major theme of the *Argonautica* (95):

> The most important single difference between the inner design of the Homeric poems and that of the *Argonautica* is that no character is as central to the latter as Achilles and Odysseus are to the poems in which they appear ... the plurality of Argonauts imposes its own shape upon the generic pattern.

This however is not a point Fantuzzi and Hunter wish to push too hard and they immediately point out that the cyclic poems may have resembled the *Argonautica* better. On the whole, their position on Apollonius' poetics is that this represents (92): "not a matter of a radical break with the past through the creation of a new poetics, but rather of a rearrangement of emphasis giving new meaning to particular elements within a pre-existing repertoire." The case of the formulaic expression is indeed the central example: Apollonius directly borrows the Homeric epithet, but rearranges its function, in this case to obtain the exact opposite effect from that of Homer himself – from constancy, to variation.

So far in this book, we have discussed Theocritus less than we did Callimachus and Apollonius. His themes of love, nature and myth do not easily call up the exact sciences (he does of course have his share of medicine and botany, and we have mentioned in particular on pp. 197–8 above his relation with the poet-doctor Nicias). And yet his poetics is very tightly related to the stylistic features discussed in this book. Indeed, it is curious that, arguably, the two most consistent exponents of the "ludic" – that is, in my view, Archimedes and Theocritus – should both hail from Syracuse.[59] But we should perhaps avoid such speculation, to follow Theocritus' style.

Hutchinson notes the following function of the evocation of nature's beauty in Theocritus (p. 146):

---

[58] *Variatio* is so well known as an Apollonian technique that Fantuzzi and Hunter do not describe it in much greater detail. I refer the reader further to Nishimura-Jensen 1998, "The poetics of Aethelides: silence and Poikilia in Apollonius' *Argonautica*." This article (with references to the literature on the topic, much of it from early in the twentieth century) concentrates on the place for *verbatim* repetition *par excellence* – the transmission of messages by heralds – and on the Apollonian technique of infusing this repetition with *variatio*.

[59] More to the point: both Archimedes and Theocritus wrote in Doric – a decision which would have different meanings, however, in poetry and in prose. What precisely Theocritus' dialect was, or what its significance was among the various possibilities of more or less artificial and archaizing modes available to poems of his time, is not at all clear (see e.g. Abbenes 1996, Fantuzzi and Hunter 2004: 371–7). What the same choice meant for Archimedes is even more obscure, for the simple reason that there is nothing to compare to: *no other Doric prose* is preserved from this period. It might have been simply the most natural vehicle for him to use; or it might have been a deliberate act of patriotic obscurity: we do not know.

The use of scenery . . . must be seen as part of a wider characteristic . . . typically one of jarring or piquant juxtaposition. The tranquil and melodious description of the spring in 22 is abruptly succeeded by a description of the man who was sitting there, a hideous and alarming figure: the first thing we learn of his appearance is that he was 'a terrifying sight, his ears crushed by harsh boxing' (45).

He then sums up Theocritus' poetics as follows (p. 148): "It delights to place the beautiful and the passionate in opposition to the grotesque, the unattractive, and the low." For this Hutchinson provides the fantastic example of Priapus' song to the love-sick Daphnis (1.82–91): first assuring Daphnis in lyrically intense phrases that his beloved is seeking him through every brook and grove; then comparing him to a goat-herd who watches his goats mate and cries at envy because he is not a he-goat himself (!); finally cashing out the analogy in terms that are once again lyrical and touching – as he sees the maidens, he is sad not to dance with them.

The well-known poem 15 performs such contrasts on the large scale of the poem as a whole. Here is another Hellenistic bipartite work, whose core is a song to Adonis sung in his festival, while its framing (more than twice the core) follows two loquacious philistines as they make their way to the festival and back. The contrast in this case is almost too obvious: an exquisitely elevated song is set against a delightful parody of coarseness. In general, it appears that the theme of duality was very much present in Theocritus' own mind.

Duality is related to Theocritus' standard device of represented dialogue (remember how he had *two* women going to the festival in poem 15). Bipartite structure is often formally marked by Theocritus, in the arrangement (by no means unique to poem 15 discussed above) of a poem enclosing a song. In various ways, Theocritus makes sure the two components – framing poem and framed song – will be as formally distinct as possible (e.g. by the use of refrain in the song, or by writing it in couplet structure). In other words, the Theocritean poem is typically an explicit mosaic structure. As Hutchinson sums up this formal effect (p. 173): "So firm a stratification of the poem makes it possible to exploit the levels in a fashion both elaborate and striking." Poems 11 and 6 offer an obvious case. Both deal in different ways with the same subject, whose appeal to Theocritus would be obvious – the ancient version of "Beauty and the Beast," which has the Cyclops Polyphemus pining in unrequited love towards the nymph Galatea (a theme of polar opposites if ever there was one). In poem 11 the singer is the Cyclops; his song is framed by Theocritus himself, speaking in urbane, measured irony to his friend, the poet-doctor Nicias. In poem 6 the songs are sung by herdsmen, once again, who compete in song (in a rather amicable agon), each offering his own striking version of the same story. We see Theocritus enacting duality at several levels: two poems dealing with the same theme; each based on the dualities poem/song, frame/framed; one based on a dual competition; the theme itself based on the polarity of opposites Polyphemus/Galatea.

Fantuzzi and Hunter begin their study of Theocritus emphatically (p. 133): "Within the panorama of Hellenistic literature, Theocritus of Syracuse reflects, as much or more than any other author of his period, the taste for *polyeideia* 'writing in many literary genres'." This is a simple statement about the variety of Theocritus' production but is then extended to the study of individual genres pursued by Theocritus, in particular the bucolic whose generic nature forms the main theme of Fantuzzi and Hunter (p. 134): "[W]hat most sets the bucolic poems of Theocritus apart is the detail and consistency of the new world for 'high' poetry in hexameters which he creates." Much of the discussion is then dedicated to the marked "realistic" vein of the bucolic setting which in Theocritus – unlike his imitators – does not become merely idealized but instead evokes a consistent, and constantly compelling, image of an actual countryside. The central outcome of this is to underline the tension between the elevated nature of the sign – hexameter – and the humble nature of the signified – the countryside (p. 138):[60] "This is not to say . . . that when Theocritus elaborated the possibility of hexameter bucolic mime . . . he realized that he was 'inventing' a 'new' literary genre; nevertheless, he was bound to be aware that few, if any, precedents existed for his combination of rustic contents and epic metre . . ." This discussion of genre may be summed up as follows (p. 140): "If Theocritus did not specialize in any particular genre, his poetry as a whole in some ways challenged the traditional system of genres."

Beyond Theocritus' challenge to the system of genres as a whole, stand his original contributions within the terms of accepted genre. Idyll 24 follows an appropriate heroic theme (Heracles the infant struggling with the snakes) and so it reshapes the hexameter in a manner less radical than that of the bucolic idylls and more comparable to that of Apollonius. The effects of reworking of the past are however as marked (pp. 205–6): "Idyll 24 offers an excellent opportunity to observe a Hellenistic poet's creative exploitation of the literary heritage . . . Theocritus' reworking [of his Pindaric source] . . . 'contaminates' Nemean 1 both with material of his own and details drawn from Paean 20." So much for what I may call mosaic-structure ("contamination" in Fantuzzi and Hunter's terms), but

---

[60] "Sign" and "signified" are my terms; they are not in Fantuzzi and Hunter's style.

in some other ways the treatment of Heracles is not all that different from that of the bucolic poems (p. 257):

Theocritus both blurs the superhuman elements of this tale of extraordinary, precocious heroism and exaggerates the all too human reactions of the characters; as far as possible, this heroic tale becomes a story of everyday domestic reality. Theocritus' allusions to archaic epic reinforce this narrative strategy, for these are used to suggest, with subtle irony, the differences between the archaic heroic world and the less heroic attitudes and situations of Theocritus' characters . . .

This thematic point is then reinforced by a stylistic analysis, e.g. (p. 264): "Echoes of archaic epic texts litter the narrative of the serpents' attack, establishing a series of high analogies or, more commonly, ironic differences between Homeric heroes and the protagonists of Theocritus."

To sum up somewhat crudely: we have seen the role of surprise in Callimachus, of variation in Apollonius, and of sharp contrasts and generic experimentation in Theocritus. From the three major Hellenistic poets, we may now return to follow Hutchinson with a quicker survey of four figures: Aratus, Herodas, Lycophron, and Asclepiades, adding in Posidippus (whose re-discovery, too late for Hutchinson, forms the basis of a long discussion in Fantuzzi and Hunter).

Of course we have already looked closely at Aratus, a prime example of the mixing of science and poetry in Alexandria. We have also pointed out the various dualities inherent in his *Phaenomena*, to which Hutchinson, of course, pays attention as well (p. 215): "One of the work's most salient features is its conjunction of two different areas of subject-matter, taken from two different sources" (referring to the combination of star catalogue and weather signs). As Hutchinson points out, this duality also translates into an opposition of high and low. Inside the star catalogue, he stresses a duality inherent in the poetic treatment of the stars as both visual and metaphorical. The poet keeps referring to the splendor of the object seen in the sky, while at the same time singing the praises of the objects mythically represented by the stars. Yet another duality is the one inherent in the technical treatment: there is a trace of the pedantic in Aratus, which Hutchinson describes well for the Milky Way (p. 219):

In 469ff. a lavish subordinate clause is accumulated, in which the glory of the Milky Way and the rapt amazement of the spectator are richly expressed. If ever the addressee has marveled at this sight – γάλα μὲν καλέουσιν 'they call it milk'. The dry clause obtrudes abruptly as if the glory of the heavens were subordinate to this essential information.

As Hutchinson sums up for the astronomical section of the poem: "We have an impression of elevation continually made distant, playful, fantastic, or tremendously fanciful." As for the second part, having to do with weather signs, Hutchinson focuses mainly on its "low," ironic aspect, where frogs are (946 ff.) a "most unhappy race, a blessing for water-snakes, the fathers of the tadpoles." This, as he points out, serves as a vehicle for maximal variety: while the mythical stars keep interacting with each other in the first part of the poem, the second part goes one humble fact at a time, each standing apart from its predecessors. Once again, we see a varied mosaic structure. As with Apollonius' variation, all of this is so well known that Fantuzzi and Hunter prefer not to dwell too much on those aspects of Aratus, concentrating instead on the way in which his text subtly modulates Hesiod's model. Their main point is that all of the above does not remove from the "seriousness" of the poetry as didactic (233–4): "[W]ithin the tonal range of ancient 'factual' poetry, stylistic *poikilia*, wit, variability of voice, irony and so forth are often alleged to show that the poet is not 'serious' about his material . . . [but] such phenomena are ordinary features of the poetic mode and poetry, no less than science, has its own conventions." – A very important point which is strengthened by my observation that contemporary science often was as poikilic, witty, variable and ironic, while of course maintaining its seriousness about its material. If Fantuzzi and Hunter say less on Aratus' style, we may note that they consider Hutchinson's own survey of it as its best appreciation (p. 242 n. 189), adding their own brief comments (pp. 242–3):

Aratus' night sky is never dull. Within the overall fixedness of eternal patterns there is constant motion . . . Paradox indeed is central to Aratus' construction of the nightly drama of the heavens . . . this is a world in which rivers rise out of the sea, rather than flow down into it, and the "endlessly pursued" hare survives to go down "with all its limbs intact". There are, on the other hand, strange dismemberments: "as for the figure on his knees, since he always rises upside down, the other parts then emerge from the horizon, the legs, the belt, all the breast, and the shoulder with the right hand; but the head with the other hand comes up at the rising of the bow and the Archer" (Aratus, *Phainomena* 669–73, trans. Kidd).

Herodas' poems are very different in character from anything we have seen so far: while the combination of the high and the low seems to be central to much Hellenistic poetry, there is hardly any trace of the "high" in Herodas. We recall the two ladies going to the festival in Theocritus' poem 15. There, the framed song presents an elevated level of poetry to set against the vulgarity of the philistines. Herodas' vulgarity is unrelieved, his themes violence and sex, his protagonists – slaves and their obnoxious mistresses. Formally, Herodas adopts dramatic conventions so that the poet does not usually speak in his voice and instead has his protagonists speak for themselves, once again eschewing the possibility of setting different kinds of voices against each other. The dramas, however, are all based on expectations raised and surprisingly thwarted: the pimp who complains of a client's treatment of one of his prostitutes, suddenly turning to the client to offer the prostitute for sufficient pay (poem 2); the lady at the cobbler's shop, about to ask, delicately, for the merchandise that actually interests her (a dildo) thwarted twice; first it appears the cobbler is about to ask a sexual favor from her in return for the merchandise; then the sudden entrance of another customer seems to cut the whole transaction short (poem 7). All of this is indeed very far from Aratus' turning of Eudoxus' astronomy into poetry, and yet the inversion of established norms of high and low, as well as the focus on surprise as a narrative principle, are all continuous with the aesthetic of surprise seen elsewhere in Hellenistic poetry. As Hutchinson sums up (p. 257): "the vividness and concreteness of imagined drama [also] served Herodas in the creation of foils, disparities, and contrasts which could help mark out particularly important low material in the poems." Fantuzzi and Hunter (2004) do not discuss Herodas further and perhaps neither should we.[61]

Hutchinson – generally a very patient reader – has less patience for Lycophron[62] (p. 257): "only the most scholarly of my readers are likely to persevere . . . with so obscure a poem as the *Alexandra*." This is indeed a strange work: we are witnesses to a scene with a slave recounting (to his silent master Priam) the prophecies he has just heard uttered by Cassandra as Troy fell. The main, bizarre device – worthy of modernist theater – is to have this prophecy continue for 1,474 lines, the length of a play. The bizarre is the main theme of the poem, recounting its grotesque events in awkward, obscure periphrastic expressions. We may follow Hutchinson and quote from the very beginning of Cassandra's narrative (ll. 35–7):

---

[61] We may of course quote Hunter from elsewhere. Hunter 1993: 31: "The mimiambi of Herodas reveal familiar hallmarks of the poetry of the third century: characters drawn from socially humble backgrounds; a literary re-casting of sub-literary 'genres' . . ." 39: ". . . this knowing game of 'revealing' and 'not revealing' would carry particular force in a written literature which always asks us to 'see' what we cannot actually see. Here the mimiambi may be thought not only to be poised between 'reading' and 'performance' but also in fact to acknowledge and exploit the problem of their own 'performance status'."
[62] Whether indeed he is the author of the *Cassandra* (Fantuzzi and Hunter 2004: 437–9) is of little importance for our purposes; the work clearly is Hellenistic.

Still alive, he was a carver of liver; he was made to seethe by the smoke of that cauldron, on that hearth without a fire, and through the heat the hair dropped out like water from his head on to the ground.

The scene described is of a myth already disturbing in itself: Heracles killing a sea-monster by entering it and cutting its innards from the inside. The inconvenience of this heroic deed is made absurdly graphic – here, for sure, myth is being *undercut*. It is relevant that Heracles is mentioned because of his sack of Troy: Cassandra is not circumspect about her hatreds, so that she ends up subverting Greek mythology as a whole by making her various heroes subject, above all, to the emotion of hatred. Hutchinson sees the theme of the poem (in his analysis of the Odysseus scene, ll. 648–819) in (pp. 263–4) "a characteristic mixture: harsh passion from the speaker, agile distortion from the poet." That is, the techniques of ironic distancing we have often seen in Hellenistic poetry are here juxtaposed with a narrative of raw anguish and hatred, creating a sense of extraordinary tension. Fantuzzi and Hunter follow West in seeing a possible intertext in the widespread apocalyptic literature of the Near East, noting the consequences of this intertextuality (2000: 440):

We will have here another example of the raising to high literary status of a largely 'sub-literary' form, . . . It is not merely in the area of form that the *Alexandra* explores inherited dichotomies; poetic voice is central to this project. The uninvolved epic narrator is set off against Cassandra's pathetic involvement . . . The metre of the poem, a very strict and repetitive iambic trimeter which all but avoids resolution, associates the Alexandra with the tragedy of the "Pleiad," but the lavish scope and verbal style of the prophecies clearly draws inspiration from the lyric tradition.

Fantuzzi and Hunter relate all of this ultimately to their basic conception of Hellenistic drama as a genre of fragmentation for which they argue, based on Ezekiel's *Exagoge* – a Hellenistic drama by a Hellenized Jew (436) that: "[T]raditional dramatic structure could rapidly disintegrate . . . the tendency to anthologize, the performance, often by solo artists, of famous monologues from plays, the decline in the importance of the chorus – led to the privileging of the individual scene over the whole drama." Hellenistic drama, as far as we can tell, was made of sharp contrasts within an episodic, that is mosaic structure.

From the extreme expansion of Lycophron, we move into the extreme concision of epigram – a genre which Hutchinson chose to illustrate with Asclepiades. Indeed this poet is much more directly delightful, as in poem

2 (my translation – in this case it would give a false impression if we substitute a prose paraphrase):

> You treasure maidenhood. And what's so great about it? When you go
>     To Hades, girl, a lover you will find there not.
> Among the living, Venus' pleasures are – while in Acheron
>     Bones and Ashes, maid, we lie.

Hutchinson uses this quatrain to stress its effect (reminiscent, incidentally, of Khayyam) of contrasting death in the strong sense of decayed flesh, to that of the living body and its pleasures. The harshness of "bones and ashes" is the original aspect of this poem, the one that would register most directly with its original readers.

Now consider poem 5:

> By the eyes Didyme grasped me – oh my! – and I –
>     I melt, like wax by fire, watching beauty.
> What if she be dark? So coals are, and yet when
>     We heat them – they shine out, like roses.

Hutchinson notes the many layered contrast and surprise in the transition from the first couplet to the second: from conventional beauty to darkness (not generally praised by ancient lovers); from conventional, indeed clichéd metaphor (the wax) to one original and harsh (the burning coals); from waxing lyrical (excuse the pun!) to sophistic argumentation.

It will be appropriate to sum up briefly this master of brevity: in Asclepiades we see the principles of juxtaposition of opposites, and of sharp turns and surprises, made sharper by the strong closures of epigram. This reminds us just how widespread such principles are in Hellenistic poetry – not at all limited to this or that genre, so that one can find sharp contrasts both in the ponderosities of a Lycophron as in the small confections of an Asclepiades. Indeed, will it not be of the essence of the culture, to embrace the two extremes of size – to embrace, that is, *opposites*? Be that as it may: in our study in binarity, we now move on from Hutchinson's Asclepiades to Fantuzzi and Hunter's Posidippus. Their concern is far from formal – indeed, they consider Posidippus in the context of Hellenistic encomia, concentrating on the several epigrams that directly concern the Ptolemaic house. Their emphasis therefore is on the "seriously" political, yet their interest is not only in the precise political stance taken by Posidippus but also in the nature of the poetic problem confronting him. This may be summed up – in my terms – as two sets of oppositions. First, traditional Greek encomia, focusing on athletic and military valor, had to be extended to encompass female monarchs – representing the special role of the sister-wife in Ptolemaic royal ideology (Fantuzzi and Hunter 2004: 377–7). Second, the encomiastic stance had to have a dual focus – mainland Greece (to which Posidippus' propaganda may be directed) and Alexandria (to which the encomia are dedicated: Fantuzzi and Hunter 2004: 389–93) In both ways, Posidippus needs to extend the established tropes of praise to encompass this new and paradoxical type of material.

Yet, to sum up, it should be said that purely stylistic questions are not the center of Fantuzzi and Hunter's attention, for Posidippus as for their general project. The following quotation on Apollonius is very typical (p. 100): "It is . . . clear that the cosmic resonances of the *Argonautica* are far less pervasive than those of the *Aeneid*, or even of Homer . . . *and a Hellenistic aesthetic of tonal poikilia is not the sole reason for this*" (my italics). This "not only" is at the heart of the explanatory strategy adopted by Fantuzzi and Hunter, which is to acknowledge the presence of a "Hellenistic style" – largely speaking, of the kind I would call "ludic" – and yet to situate this poetry within a wider and different perspective. So the introduction (vii):

The catalyst for such views [the Hellenists as proto-"modernists"] came, often enough, from the emphasis in Wilhelm Kroll's seminal studies on "Kreuzung der Gattungen" and effects of surprise in Hellenistic and Roman poetry. The phenomena to which Kroll pointed are real enough, and are given deserved prominence in this book, but his insights – and particularly his most famous catch-phrase – have too often been used as a substitute for serious analysis and hard thinking about the complexity of the Hellenistic engagement with the past.

The "not only" of Fantuzzi and Hunter is not only the statement that, even after one has studied style, one should also study further elements. It is a stronger claim: that a mere catalogue of stylistic devices provides a misleading sense of the nature of the poetry. Coming out of Hutchinson's survey, we may well still share Couat's sense of an art for art's sake, one that revels in the sense of a radical break from the past. Fantuzzi and Hunter identify similar stylistic devices, but they anchor them in a certain practice of intertextuality so that, overall, they make the case for a Hellenistic aesthetic where the two terms of their title – tradition as well as innovation – are equally important. All of this is worth repeating here, as after all Fantuzzi and Hunter can be taken to represent the dominant research program today in Hellenistic literature, where the stylistic observations made by past generations of scholars are re-interpreted in more historically nuanced ways. My own strategy – of re-extracting the formal core out of such historically nuanced studies – is somewhat unfair, then, but, at the end of the day, it is best simply to explode once and for all the supposed opposition between the formal and the historical. After all, works of art – or of science – do possess both. If I put aside the questions of history to concentrate on the form this is primarily because it is much more difficult (as I will return to explain below) to argue for the *historical* continuity between poetry and science in the Hellenistic world. To anticipate: just how, for example, would we map "tradition" and "innovation" from poetry on to science? Let us first of all concentrate, then, on the formal continuity – which is not hard to come by. This section, after all, has been an exercise in the obvious, reiterating well-known facts – that Hellenistic poetry was characterized by surprise, variation, and experimentation with genre. Let this brief statement suffice.

## 4.4 SCIENCE AND POETRY IN ALEXANDRIA

We have seen, therefore, an extended stylistic parallelism between science and poetry: in both, one can find a certain carnivalesque play of detail, with its ironic self-undercutting; mosaic composition; narrative surprise; indeed a certain tendency to experiment with one's very generic boundaries. In a sense, the extended nature of the parallelism – the fact that it pertains to several stylistic aspects – should not surprise us. For after all, it is only natural that a style based on mosaic composition should also engage in narrative surprises (if you wish to make the individual components of your text stand out in isolation, it is good strategy to make narrative transitions appear rough and unexpected). The crossing of genre-boundaries is a natural consequence of a fascination with surprise and mosaic composition – or vice versa, that is, if your system of genres is subject to experiments, you should mark this to your readers by the employment of rough transitions between textual elements. Then again, the meta-textual awareness inherent in the breaking of genres goes hand in hand with an ironic self-undercutting and, given the preference for mosaic composition, goes well with sustained attention to individual detail. In short, styles are not produced by some kind of blind combinatorics of stylistic features. The stylistic features must hang together so that, finally, there are only so many "stable states," so to speak, of style. Other things being equal, then, we may expect different but contemporary forms of cultural expression to converge around similar styles.

Of course, other things may well be unequal. In our own culture, for instance, science and poetry generally speaking display very divergent styles. Perhaps it is possible to identify, in both, a certain preference for the hermetic: both science and poetry, especially in the West, value today the sense of cultural activity as belonging to a professionalized elite (whose enjoyment – of either art or science – is never the direct sensual delight valued by many previous generations, and is instead highly mediated and based on the exercise of one's professional skills).[63] But this is precisely the point: the cultural tendency to professionalize delight means, among other things, that different cultural spheres may develop different canons of aesthetic pleasure. Thus, for instance, contemporary poetry is all about fragmented experience while contemporary mathematics is all about large-scale isomorphisms. Why should this not be the case? The people who read and write mathematics lead a life totally separate from that of the people who read and write poetry.

This of course was not the case in Alexandria. Eratosthenes, at least, was both poet and scientist, and we have seen plenty of evidence for mutual awareness between the two fields. This was definitely an elitist culture, but one where skills were not considered inherently limited to isolated activities: to the contrary, it appears that the transfer of skills from one field to another was valued as such. It is thus, once again, only predictable that we should see the styles of science and poetry converge. But indeed more than this can be said: a theme we have returned to again and again was that of the mosaic: the construction of a single work out of diverse elements. The way in which Eratosthenes crosses over from science to poetry (as in the mini-treatise on the duplication of the cube) or from poetry to science (as in the *Hermes*), is not an accident of an individual who happens to be diversely talented: this is the direct expression of mixture as a cultural principle.

We may even suggest as follows. In the course of his analysis of the relation between scientific and technological research in the early twentieth century, Galison uses the metaphor of "critical opalescence" – the stage of phase transition where matter can settle on either liquid or gas, and so clusters of molecules keep forming and reforming now as this, now as that – a bubbling medium of indeterminacy. Thus the same author whether Poincaré or Einstein, can go back and forth between scientific and technological research, now producing this, now that, now using insights from one in the service of the other. The crucial thing is that we should not envisage one realm as informing the other; rather, at this time and place, we should stop thinking of them as separate realms. Of course, it is not

---

[63] For the origins of this cultural tendency for verbal art, see Bourdieu 1993, an argument that may well be repeated for other forms of art as well as of science – though in science, of course, the sociological forces driving professionalization are more straightforward.

my intention here to endorse or to criticize Galison's interpretation of the early twentieth century. But it is obvious by now that I envisage Hellenistic culture as undergoing just such a moment of critical opalescence where, by the very nature of the way in which generic boundaries are constantly explored and inverted, cultural life is expected to cross domains; the very nature of the "cultural domain" becomes somewhat inappropriate. The molecules settle somewhat differently in the *Duplication of the Cube*, and in the *Hermes*, making us call the first "science" and the second "poetry," but both truly belong to the same scientific-poetic program of multigeneric experimentation.

Finally, this essential opening up and inverting of generic domains gives rise, in the Hellenistic world, to an almost perverse interest in otherwise minor genres. In particular, the very recherché genre of advanced mathematics assumes an almost central position. The outcome is an unprecedented – and, until modern times, never repeated – period of mathematical activity. Its culmination is in the work of a master story-teller, Archimedes.

# *Conclusions and qualifications*

The overall structure of the argument is simple. First, we have covered, in the first three chapters of this book, a substantial body of evidence pointing to a certain style of Hellenistic mathematics. Its three major constituents are: (1) mosaic composition, (2) narrative surprise, (3) generic experimentation (a more specialized phenomenon is that of the carnival of calculation). Second, we have briefly noted, in chapter 4, how such stylistic features may also be typical of the major literary works of the same period (with the carnival of calculation paralleled by the carnival of erudition). The minimal claim of the book, then – the one backed up by evidence – is of a certain homology of style between the exact sciences and poetry in the Hellenistic world. In the conclusion to the preceding chapter I have already pointed beyond, to much more tentative claims. It is tempting to postulate a historical force underlying the homology. More than this: if indeed we suggest that a certain historical process led to a Hellenistic interest in generic experimentation, then it becomes very tempting to suggest that the rise of the exact sciences as a major cultural phenomenon should be seen as part and parcel of this practice of experiment in genre, where a hitherto minor genre suddenly gains in prominence.

All of this, however, is highly tentative, largely because our evidence can support such historical interpretations only with difficulty. In this section I acknowledge and address the limitations imposed by our evidence. This qualifies the argument of this book so that we can better see what conclusions can, finally, be made.

We may consider the following three questions in order. The first is whether there is indeed a historical force underlying the two stylistic practices, in science and in poetry, or whether instead the two should be seen as analogous, perhaps, and yet as historically distinct. A positive answer to this first question gives rise to another set of questions. Should such an account be seen in terms of some underlying principle common to both poetry and science – so that both form independent expressions of a single theme of

Hellenistic history – or should it instead be seen in terms of literary style influencing scientific style? (The third logical option – that of science as an influence on literature – is sufficiently unlikely in its cultural context to be ruled out.) Finally, should this account be understood primarily in terms of outside historical forces or in the terms of the history of style?

The questions have a cascading order: not only in that questions two and three depend upon question one but also in that an account in terms of literature as an influence on science already determines a stylistic account (for, after all, literary practices could not have informed scientific practices – unless they did so through the example of their style; literature does not wield any other force). And so we can say there is a fundamental question – whether there is a causal story to be told about science and literature in the Hellenistic world – and then a more detailed question, which of the following four forms such a story should take:

1 Outside historical forces shape, independently, both science and literature.
2 Outside historical forces shape literature, whose style then influences that of science.
3 The parallel development of style acts simultaneously on both science and literature.
4 The stylistic development of literature gives rise to a certain Hellenistic style which, in turn, impacts upon Hellenistic science.

I believe a story should be told, and, less confidently, I believe it is unlikely to be provided in the terms of (1) above. Which of (2)–(4) is to be preferred is a question I cannot answer (as it touches mostly on the history of literature) and one which I am not sure can be answered at all.

And yet one should admit: even the basic question, of whether a causal story is to be told at all, is hard to answer. It might perhaps appear excessively skeptical to deny the very historical connection between the styles of science and poetry in Alexandria. After all, the stylistic homology is plain to see, the cultural setting is closely related, and contacts between the two fields are well documented, as already abundantly seen by now. Indeed, at the end of the day, I do consider such skepticism excessive. But it is not groundless, and it is appropriate to acknowledge the grounds for such doubt.

The fundamental difficulty is that we cannot, in truth, differentiate the styles of either poetry or science from those of preceding periods. To tell a causal story with greater certainty, we would need to document the rise of a new style, present in both science and poetry, through the first half of the third century BC. Otherwise the coincidence of two styles at the same time could be seen as the mere overlap of two phenomena whose origins lie elsewhere. In reality we cannot document this new departure. The coincidence of science and poetry is very much the coincidence of survival.

The situation is especially dire with the exact sciences. Nearly nothing survives that is dated securely to before the Hellenistic era. Two fragments stand out, a quadrature of lunules by Hippocrates of Chios, from around 450–430 BC,[1] and a complex three-dimensional solution to the problem of finding two mean proportionals, by Archytas, from the first half of the fourth century.[2] Both present considerable philological difficulties in extracting the original style of writing.[3] Further testimonies to early Greek mathematics (in particular, within Plato's works, or occasionally in the scholia to Euclid's *Elements*) provide us with even less information about the original style of writing. We can then move later in time. Substantial chunks of mathematics are extant in the Aristotelian corpus – always inserted for a philosophical purpose and set within the stylistic constraints of Peripatetic prose. Under the name of Autolycus we have two small astronomical treatises, likely to date from the second half of the fourth century BC.[4] It is customary to date Euclid to the very beginning of the Ptolemaic period, a plausible date, with very little evidential support.[5] With this ends our evidence for "early" Greek mathematics: following upon Aristarchus' surviving treatise, the next substantial figure is already that of Archimedes himself.

Among the early authors mentioned above, one should perhaps make a distinction between Hippocrates and Archytas, on the one hand (which we may label "early Greek mathematics"), and Autolycus, Euclid, and the fragments extant in the Peripatetic corpus, on the other hand (which

---

[1] For the (standard) date and the crucial argument that this is among the earliest pieces of Greek mathematics, see Netz 2004, containing also a text.
[2] See Huffman 2005: 342–401 for text and extensive discussion.
[3] This difficulty is the main theme of Netz 2004. See Huffman 2005: 347–8 for a summary of the *status quaestionis* regarding Archytas.
[4] This, on the force of a statement of Diogenes Laertius (IV.29) – which one has no special reason to doubt – that Autolycus was Arcesilaus' teacher.
[5] Doubts on the standard dating of Euclid were first voiced by Schneider 1979. The main piece of evidence is as follows. Proclus *In Eucl.* 68 states that Euclid lived under the first Ptolemy, explicitly making this an inference on his part, based, moreover, on the dubious grounds that Archimedes refers to Euclid (this likely refers to a comment in our received text of *Sphere and Cylinder* I.2 which, as explained in Netz 2004: 44 is most likely a gloss). On the other hand, let me note briefly that The Archimedes Palimpsest contains a new reading of a text following upon proposition 16, referring once again to Euclid. If this is indeed admitted to the text of Archimedes – which is by no means clear – then Proclus' statement may stand). Be that as it may, the coincidence between Euclid's *Elements* and the toolbox of previous results used by Hellenistic mathematicians (Saito 1997, Netz 1999, section 5.4) appears to me unlikely to be completely fortuitous, so that a relatively early date for Euclid is, all in all, the likeliest hypothesis.

we may label "pre-Archimedean Greek mathematics"). Each presents a separate problem of differentiation. It is difficult to differentiate early Greek mathematics from Hellenistic mathematics as regards its style. It is difficult to differentiate "pre-Archimedean" Greek mathematics from Hellenistic mathematics as regards its date.

Hippocrates and Archytas present us with surprising configurations of objects and narration, combining, in the case of Hippocrates, calculation with geometry and, in the case of Archytas, offering some of the most delightful spatial puzzles of all of Greek mathematics.[6] I would have no difficulty at all in joining those two mathematical gems to my survey of Hellenistic mathematical style. While the Peripatetic fragments, as well as Autolycus and Euclid, present us with a style which is decidedly more sedate and pedagogic, we cannot tell whether this is not a mere accident of the nature of the works surviving (all three groups of text form some kind of "elementary" function), and, most worrying, it is difficult – as stated above – to show that Euclid really predates all other Hellenistic mathematics.

The lack of comparanda further complicates our ability to offer causal accounts. It would be useful if we could compare the growth of mathematical style with that of medical style and then tie the two lines of developments to the historical setting of mathematics and medicine. As it happens, the survival of medical works neatly complements that of mathematical works: as the mathematical works begin to be available in abundance, the medical works peter out. We have, in medicine, effectively nothing extant from the Hellenistic age. Herophilus, the Archimedes of medicine, is an author known through testimony – largely that of Galen. On the other hand, early Greek medicine, mostly from the fifth century (though apparently some of it from the fourth century) is very extensively documented in the so-called Hippocratic corpus, which indeed may serve as the basis for stylistic study.[7]

The comparable difficulty with differentiating Hellenistic literature is familiar, a litany repeated in all introductions to the subject. Non-dramatic poetry is not represented well in our evidence for the fifth and fourth centuries BC so that we end up comparing Callimachus with Hesiod,

---

[6] Plutarch's mention of Hipparchus' numbers – a key example of the Hellenistic carnival of calculation – goes on to mention Xenocrates, who, says Plutarch (733A, Heinze fr. 11) gave the number of syllables as 100,000,200,000! This number is not as well accounted for as Hipparchus' numbers are now, and could possibly represent some extravagant feat of calculation in a fourth-century author. Though, on the other hand, the number in this case is remarkably "neat." From what we know of Xenocrates' version of Platonism – with its number ontology verging on the numerological (see e.g. Thiel 2006) – one may think that such a number may emerge from a rather non-technical context comparable, say, to Plato's nuptial number.
[7] A study which has been pursued, most notably in van der Eijk 1997.

Apollonius with Homer – much, perhaps, as Callimachus and Apollonius would have liked us to do. Sober historical judgment would call, instead, for comparison with Callimachus' and Apollonius' more immediate, but no longer extant predecessors. What does survive in any abundance from the fourth century – Plato's prose as well as Menander's drama – already fits well many characteristics of Hellenistic literature. We may note the subtle mixture of the comic with other dramatic forms in Menander,[8] as well as Plato's generic experimentation, not to mention Plato's use of irony.[9]

In short, it may be that there is nothing specifically Hellenistic about the styles of both Hellenistic literature and Hellenistic mathematics. One could just as well compare the ludic in Archytas' finding of two means with the ludic in Plato's *Timaeus* – pointing out even the likely historical contacts between those two authors. Nothing specific to the third century. Alexandria, as always, arrives too late. Not that this would matter that much: a Hellenistic style that starts off at the fourth century would be just as good, for our purposes, as one that starts with the third (and this is now a standard response to the possible blurring of the border between the fourth and third centuries: see e.g. Kassel 1987). The problem, for the specific project of this book, is obvious: if we wish to set against each other a pre-Hellenistic mathematical style with a Hellenistic mathematical style – say, the more pedagogic strain of Euclid as against the more ludic strain of Archimedes – then, if Archimedes is seen as a reaction to Callimachus, who does Euclid react to? A normal assumption would be that Euclid reacts to the main philosophical developments in fourth-century Athens,[10] that is to an intellectual environment dominated by Plato who, from a stylistic point of view, may foreshadow Alexandria most closely.

In other words, the main observation appears to be that if Archimedes could have reacted to a *literary* style, Euclid did not. Which is precisely my position: the main new development of Alexandrian science is, I suggest, a cultural alignment where the scientific merges with the literary.

As for early Greek mathematics, this indeed should be contextualized historically – in its own terms. The one obvious thing about our evidence for Hippocrates and Archytas is that those authors should be seen against the background of the philosophy and medicine of their time – that is, compared to "Sophists" or to "Hippocratics," authors for whom the flourish of rhetorical argument is the dominant stylistic requirement. It makes simple historical sense to compare Hippocrates of Chios with, say,

---

[8] See e.g. Zagagi 1995. [9] See e.g. Nightingale 1996.
[10] Regardless of his possible specific philosophical affiliations, often discussed, inconclusively, by past scholars (see e.g. Mueller 1991 for a balanced position).

Gorgias; by the same token, Archimedes should be compared with, say, Theocritus. Even if different historical periods may give rise to somewhat comparable texts, this is no reason for us to avoid placing texts in their appropriate historical context.

While I cannot speak with the same authority for Greek literature, I do after all follow in the trend of most scholarship in Hellenistic literature in identifying a specifically Hellenistic vein of literature, whose major achievement and all later inspiration lie in the work of Callimachus in the second quarter of the third century BC.[11] While of course one should not imagine such watersheds as clear breaks from the past, this should not diminish the importance of perceiving Hellenistic poetry as a specific historical reality, to be understood, once again, on its own historical terms. In short: both Callimachus and Archimedes, in their respective field, seem to constitute a point of departure, and so, at the end of the day, it makes perfect sense to treat the two near-contemporaries inside a single historical account. Perhaps the point should be put, very generally, as follows. At the background of the stylistic issues broached by this book are some trans-historical tensions. Literature brings together diversity and unity: the tension between diversity and unity is thus a constant of literary history. Mathematics brings together certainty and surprise: the tension between certainty and surprise is thus a constant of mathematical history. Some literary cultures emphasize diversity, others emphasize unity. Some mathematical cultures emphasize certainty, some emphasize surprise. While the tension is trans-historical, and the need to resolve it in some form or another is indeed a basic constant of any cultural history, it is also resolved, always, within some specific, *historical* context.

What shape this account should take is, as suggested above, much more difficult to argue. For one thing, the difficulties of differentiation carry over here as well: any explanatory account should be corroborated by comparisons, e.g. by showing that fourth-century literature had a different character from its third-century counterpart because, say, the political structures underlying it were different – but how to argue this when so little is known of fourth-century literature? But much worse than this: we know so little of the actual social realities of the third-century practitioners.

---

[11] Was this awareness shared by the ancients themselves? Fantuzzi and Hunter (2004: 444–9) tend to a qualified "yes" while stressing the difficulty of the question. Perhaps the best evidence is that of survival itself: it was for a reason, after all, that papyrus makers and then (to a lesser extent) parchment makers chose to perpetuate the generation of Callimachus; the same papyrus and parchment makers also ignored, much more consistently, the generations immediately preceding them. This represents at least a tacit acknowledgment of a literary watershed set at the beginning of the third century.

I shall soon come to discuss the chronologies of science and of poetry – and almost all of the evidence would have to be pulled out from internal evidence from the works themselves. We do have some precious scraps of evidence – literally, scraps of papyrus, most notably *P.Oxy.* 1241, with a fragmentary list of Alexandrian librarians from which we learn that both Apollonius of Rhodes as well as Eratosthenes served as librarians at Alexandria. But what social reality did such a post represent? Effectively no reliable evidence survives for such specific questions.[12] Sure enough, authors may write encomia to monarchs. But what does that mean of their position *vis-à-vis* the court? The lack of external evidence makes all such interpretations speculative. Scholars from Kroll in 1924 down to Stephens in 2004, arguing, respectively, for the poetics of refined alienation following the collapse of Classical civic tradition, or for the poetics of biethnic court culture, always rely on a combination of some general historical understanding of Hellenistic civilization, on the one hand, and the poems themselves, on the other hand – in the absence of the crucial connecting evidence showing how the poems were socially anchored in their historical setting. So much for the case of literature – where, at least, we have some extant encomia. The scientists do not write encomia, and their social position is almost entirely a matter for speculation. Reading the works of Archimedes, we can deduce a lot about spheres and parabolas and, at a further remove, we can learn something about style of presentation. But there is very little to go by in terms of Syracusan sociology.

Of course, it is not just that we are hampered by the lack of evidence: decisions between explanatory approaches are always inherently subjective. The account most appealing to contemporary historical taste would probably take the form I defined above as "outside historical forces shape, independently, both science and literature." This is because the tendency in contemporary scholarship is to ground culture in outside, extra-historical forces, largely speaking "political." The most obvious format such an account could take would be to ground Hellenistic culture, in its various manifestations, within Hellenistic court culture; another related route would involve the history of literacy, with a more "bookish" culture in Alexandria, one all too aware of its belatedness in literary history. Indeed, such have been the most common explanatory strategies in Hellenistic literary history since Kroll (1924), indeed since Couat (1882) and before.

---

[12] Fraser 1972: 320–35 is still the authoritative summary of our evidence – in which pride of place goes to Tzetzes and the *Suda*, i.e. authors writing from within the late civilization of Constantinople.

Both the court and the book, however, do not translate easily from poetry to mathematics. Eratosthenes does dedicate a small mathematical treatise to Ptolemy Euergetes, as Archimedes dedicates the *Sand-Reckoner* to King Gelon. Yet these are, in some sense, minor works, not to be compared with the main works of Archimedes – addressed to the relatively obscure Dositheus – or of Apollonius – addressed to the truly obscure Eudemus. In both cases a colleague is addressed from another city (Archimedes writes from Syracuse to Alexandria, Apollonius – from Alexandria to Pergamon). Hellenistic mathematics was not court mathematics: it was the science of an international, self-conscious elite. As for bookishness, the Greek pursuit of mathematics was, from its very inception, a reflective, literate activity (fundamentally based on the *lettered* diagram).[13] Furthermore, the past would hardly weigh as heavily on science as it did on poetry. Archimedes did not compete against a distant, unattainable Homer; he competed against the fully historical Eudoxus, scarcely a century old – and he must have known that he, Archimedes, was the better. For all the stylistic homologies between science and poetry, let us not lose sight of a crucial divergence: the reflective subtlety of Hellenistic mathematics has nothing to do with allusion to past works. For such reasons, then, the very stylistic analogy between mathematics and poetry would serve, if anything, to undermine a purely socio-political interpretation of the Hellenistic style: the socio-political setting of mathematics was very different from that of poetry.

This however should not be pressed too hard. Perhaps it is difficult to provide a single socio-political account for both poetry and mathematics, but this would be a problem for the socio-political account for poetry only if we insisted on a single, independent line of cause and effect impacting on both cultural fields. But this perhaps we should better avoid. My own tendency – my own subjective preference – would be for an account where the stylistic properties of Greek mathematics are understood as a consequence, primarily, of the stylistic properties of Greek poetry. However weak this *post hoc ergo propter hoc* might be, the fact remains that Archimedes' work is somewhat later than that of Callimachus. So far in this book my chronology tended to be vague, "the third century" serving as my favorite chronological term. Indeed, usually, not much more can be said, on either poetry or on science. But people do not typically occupy the neat compartments of Common Era centuries, and some kind of measure of chronological reality should be helpful in considering our historical account. In true Hellenistic

---

[13] See Netz 1999, chapters 1–2, for the nature of the Greek diagram – and chapter 4 for a non-oralist interpretation of the formulaic language of Greek mathematics.

238  *Conclusions and qualifications*

narrative style, then, I turn now – right towards the end of this book – to the underlying chronology.

As it happens, the key to the chronologies of both science and poetry in the Hellenistic world is, as usual, in astronomy – though in a strange way. I refer to Conon's naming of the *Lock of Berenice*, an event dated not by its astronomical properties (nothing special did take place in the sky, after all – which is part of the irony of the act of naming). This is dated however securely enough, by the external circumstances of Ptolemaic campaigns, to the year 245 BC. In an elegant manner, this single event then bifurcates, to function as the major chronological terminus for both poetry and science, *ad hoc* for poetry and *post hoc* for science.

In poetry, the key observation is that Callimachus weaves the *Lock of Berenice* into the closure of the *Aitia*, right towards the end of book IV. It is a standard position of Callimachean studies that books III–IV form a late addition to a much earlier, two-book work – though this has little hard evidence. However that may be, Callimachus' *Deification of Arsinoe*, referring as it does to a proximate event – the death of Arsinoe – that took place in 270, provides us with at least twenty-five years of activity and confirms the image of Callimachus' *Lock of Berenice* as the product of old age. Callimachus appears to be active mainly in the second quarter of the third century.[14]

In science, the key observation is that Archimedes refers, in the introductions to some of his major works, to the death of Conon.[15] We further know of Archimedes' death in the fall of Syracuse in 212, so that Archimedes' major period of activity must have been at around 240–215 BC.[16]

Those three dates, then, frame the chronological discussion: the death of Arsinoe in 270; the disappearance of Berenice's lock in 245; the death of Archimedes in 212. Neatly spaced roughly a generation apart, these dates serve to underline the one fact of consequence to our argument: the major figure of Hellenistic poetry was active one generation prior to the major figure of Hellenistic science. As it happens, these figures are not only the most important in their respective fields: they also happen to

---

[14] See Fraser 1972: 719–20, as well as 1004 n.1 there. Cameron 1995, ch. VII offers an argument for transposing the prologue to the *Aitia* from c. 245 to c. 270, which however is strictly based on transposing Callimachus' age at the time from c. 70 to c. 45: a birth c. 315 and death not much later than 245 seems to be a cornerstone of Hellenistic studies, not to be tampered with even by a skeptic such as Cameron.

[15] These references are in the introductions to *Sphere and Cylinder* I, II, *Spiral Lines* and *Quadrature of Parabola*.

[16] See Knorr 1978b, Vitrac 1992 for an attempt at a more fine-grained Archimedean chronology – one which however is not necessary for our attempt at a coarse-grained comparison between science and poetry.

be the most securely dated, other authors often defined, chronologically, in relation to them. The major difference in the chronologies is that the literary one looks both backwards and forwards from its Callimachean acme, whereas its scientific counterpart tends much more to look forward from its Archimedean acme. An inscription from 263/262 mentions Posidippus already as (likely) an acclaimed poet:[17] this could make him, as often stated, somewhat older than Callimachus, an identification now supported by the encomiastic range of the newly discovered epigrams.[18] Apollonius of Rhodes was chief librarian preceding Eratosthenes (i.e. preceding Archimedes' contemporary).[19] We have from Theocritus' encomia of both Ptolemy Philadelphus (Idyll 17) and Hiero (Idyll 16), specifying enough detail to allow us to say for certain that he was active between 276 and 270 BC. Aratus is sometimes taken to be endorsing a Callimachean aesthetic by inserting the acrostic *leptē*, "fine," into the *Phaenomena* (lines 783–7: see Jacques 1960), though other arrangements of allusion and influence are possible as well.[20] All that is clear is that the bulk of what we know as Hellenistic literature was known or produced by people alive at around 270 to 245 BC – Callimachus' own period of activity.

Now let us turn to mathematics. Apollonius of Perga is certain to have been active early in the second century BC, making him considerably younger than Archimedes.[21] Many Hellenistic mathematicians are known to us through their relation – often polemical – to authors such as Archimedes himself. Eratosthenes is the addressee of Archimedes' *Method*. Dionysodorus and Diocles both offer a solution to a problem they perceive to have remained unsolved by Archimedes.[22] Nicomedes boasts a solution better than one by Eratosthenes,[23] Diocles – a solution better than one by Dositheus[24] (both Eratosthenes and Archimedes are, of course, contemporaries of Archimedes). Hypsicles reacts to what he sees as a defective treatment by Apollonius.[25] Hipparchus' relatively late date in the second century is secured by his astronomical observations. Of course, some of the authors discussed in this book were earlier than Archimedes: so, I still believe, Euclid, and so surely was Aristarchus (to whom Archimedes refers in his *Sand-Reckoner* – and who is known to have been attacked

[17] *IG* ix i².17: 24–25.   [18] Thompson 2005.   [19] *P. Oxy.* 1241 ii 5ff.
[20] Such questions of allusion and reference are peculiarly problematic. So Köhnken, on the relationship between the three main Hellenistic poets (2001: 73): "Research on early Hellenistic chronology is in a bewildering state ... scholars are far from agreeing on who alludes to whom." This is typical of the lack of genuine, external evidence on any of the cultural figures of the Hellenistic world.
[21] Toomer 1970.   [22] Netz 2004, sections 1.4–1.5 respectively.
[23] We have discussed this polemic on p. 99 above.   [24] Toomer 1976: 34.
[25] We have discussed this polemic on p. 93 above.

by Cleanthes).²⁶ But it remains clear that the bulk of the mathematical writings displaying the stylistic features described in this book were written from around the middle of the third century to the middle of the second century BC.

It remains possible – and plausible – to argue that the cultural forces active at around 270 BC were not all that different from those active at around 230 BC. The same courts, the same libraries. And yet, it also becomes possible – and plausible – to suggest that the Hellenistic exact sciences took their shape in a culture informed, among other things, by the rearrangement of literary taste achieved by the generation of Callimachus. It is a simple and straightforward assumption that authors, writing in the Greek Mediterranean between the mid-third and the mid-second centuries, could have had their aesthetic sensibilities shaped by their readings of Callimachus, Theocritus, or Apollonius of Rhodes.

Readers might perhaps feel cheated by such an account. Do I say that Greek mathematicians wrote the way they did, because they "happened to enjoy writing this way?" This indeed may appear as if, instead of offering an explanation, I was avoiding one. In a sense, this is fair criticism, to the extent that I do shift much of the burden of explanation from science to literature. I explain Archimedes by reference to Callimachus whose style, in turn, I do not try to explain here – as such an explanation is beyond the scope of my expertise or of this book. But the point on which I do wish to insist is that the account suggested here does not mean as little as "authors writing in a manner they happen to like." Rather, the account should be read as arguing that authors write in a way which *they cannot help* liking. It is this, non-contingent nature of pleasure, which makes it an important historical principle. For, after all, people cannot simply choose what they like or do not like, no more than they can choose which language to speak and how to take in food. People learn how to take pleasure, in exactly the same tacit way in which they learn all other aspects of their culture. To say that Hellenistic mathematics was characterized by a certain style – which I label "ludic" – because this was the type of verbal experience its readers were trained in, is therefore a meaningful historical statement, explaining why, in some sense, Hellenistic mathematics could not have been otherwise. This then is the simplest argument possible, stated right at the outset of this book: people do the things they enjoy doing. I wish my reader to admit no more than this.

---

²⁶ Plutarch's *On the Face of the Moon* 922F–923A.

*Conclusions and qualifications*

Be that as it may: I wish to conclude on a cautious note. Hellenistic mathematics displayed a style closely resembling that of its immediate literary heritage. This was probably not the result of some coincidence: through whichever causal route, the styles of science probably did respond to those of poetry. And so, to this extent, this mathematics was the creature of its own age.

In this book I have tried to push forward our understanding of what is involved in mathematics being of this or that age. One of the ways, I claim, in which this ought to be understood, is in the terms of shifting aesthetic sensibilities. Mathematicians seek a certain kind of beauty. Perhaps mathematical beauty is a constant – as far as the contents of mathematics are concerned – and yet the *forms* this beauty takes are certainly cultural. And while the history of mathematics surely is many stranded, one of its most important strands is formed by such cultural forms of mathematical beauty. In this book I have begun tracing this strand, in the main achievement of Hellenistic mathematics, centered around the figure of Archimedes.

# Bibliography

Abbenes, Jelle G. J. 1996. "The doric of Theocritus. A literary language," in M. Annette Harder, Remco F. Regtuit, and Gerry C. Wakker (eds.), *Theocritus*. Groningen (Hellenistica Groningana 2), 1–19.
Acerbi, F. 2003a. "Drowning by multiples. Remarks on the fifth book of Euclid's *elements*, with special emphasis on Prop. 8," *Archive for History of Exact Sciences* 57: 175–242.
   2003b. "On the shoulders of Hipparchus: a reappraisal of Ancient Greek combinatorics," *Archive for the History of Exact Sciences* 57: 465–502.
Acosta-Hughes, Benjamin. 2002. *Polyeideia. The Iambi of Callimachus and the Archaic Iambic Tradition*. Berkeley and Los Angeles (Hellenistic Culture and Society 35).
Aigner, M. and Ziegler, G. M. 1998. *Proofs from the Book*. New York.
Allen, J. 2001. *Inference from Signs: Ancient Debates about the Nature of Evidence*. Oxford.
Amthor, A. 1880. "Das Problema Bovinum des Archimedes," *Zeitschrift für Mathematik und Physik* 25: 153–71.
Argentieri, Lorenzo. 2003. *Gli epigrammi degli Antipatri*. Bari (Le Rane Studi 35).
Barker, A. 1989. *Greek Musical Writings II*. Cambridge.
Barnes, J. 1997. "Roman Aristotle," in J. Barnes and M. Griffin (eds.), *Philosophia Togata II: Plato and Aristotle at Rome*. Oxford, 1–69.
Benveniste, E. 1932. "A propos de κολοσσός," *Revue de Philologie* 58: 118–35.
Bing, P. and Uhrmeister, V. 1994. "The unity of Callimachus' *Hymn to Artemis*," *Journal of Hellenic Studies* 114: 19–34.
Bogue, P. 1977. "Astronomy in the *Argonautica* of Apollonius Rhodius," Ph.D. thesis, University of Illinois.
Bornmann, F. 1968. *Callimachi Hymnus in Dianam*. Florence.
Bos, H. J. M. 2001. *Redefining Geometrical Exactness: Descartes' Transformation of the Early Modern Concept of Construction*. New York.
Bourdieu, P. 1993. *The Field of Cultural Production*. Cambridge.
Bowen, A. C. 2001. "La scienza del cielo nel periodo pretolemaico," in S. Petruccioli (ed.), *Storia della scienza: 1. La scienza greco-romana*. Rome, 806–39.
Bruins, E. M. (ed.) 1964. *Codex Constantinopolitanus palatii veteris no. 1*. Leiden.
Burnyeat, M. F. 2000. "Plato on why mathematics is good for the soul," *Proceedings of the British Academy* 103: 1–81.

Cameron, A. 1990. "Isidore of Miletus and Hypatia: on the editing of mathematical texts," *GRBS* 31: 103–27.
  1995. *Callimachus and his Critics*. Princeton.
Chandrasekhar, S. 1987. *Truth and Beauty: Aesthetics and Motivations in Science*. Chicago.
Chemla, K. 1994. "Similarities between Chinese and Arabic mathematical writings 1 : root extraction," *Arabic Science of Philosophy* 4 (2): 207–66.
  2003. "Generality above abstraction: the general expressed in terms of the paradigmatic in mathematics in Ancient China," *Science in Context* 16: 413–58.
Clagett, M. 1984. *Archimedes in the Middle Ages*. Philadelphia.
Clayton, P. A. and Price, M. J. 1988. *The Seven Wonders of the Ancient World*. London.
Cleary, J. J. 1995. *Aristotle and Mathematics: Aporetic Method in Cosmology and Metaphysics*. Leiden.
Couat, A. 1930 (tr., J. Loeb, originally published in French 1882) *Alexandrian Poetry under the First Three Ptolemies*. London.
Cullen, C. 2004. *The Suàn Shù Shū. "Writings on Reckoning": a Translation of a Chinese Mathematical Collection of the Second Century BC, with Explanatory Commentary*. Cambridge.
Cuomo, S. 2001. *Ancient Mathematics*. London.
Cusset, C. 1999. *La Muse dans la Bibliothèque: Réécriture et intertextualité dans la poésie alexandrine*. Paris.
De Falco, V., Krause, M., and Neugebauer, O. 1966. *Die Aufgangszeiten der Gestirne*. Göttingen.
Decorps Foulquier, M. 2000. *Recherches sur les Coniques d'Apollonius de Pergé et leur commentateurs grecs. Histoire de la transmission des Livres I–IV*. Paris.
Dijksterhuis, E. J. 1987. *Archimedes*. Princeton.
Djebbar, A., Rommevaux, S., and Vitrac, B. 2001. "Remarques sur l'histoire du texte des *Eléments* d'Euclide," *Archive for History of Exact Sciences* 55: 221–95.
D'Ooge, M. L. 1926. *Nicomachus of Gerasa: Introduction to Arithmetic*. New York.
Duhem, P. 1908. "ΣΩZEIN TA ΦAINOMENA," *Annales de Philosophie Chrétienne* 6: 113–39, 277–302, 352–77, 482–514, 561–92.
van der Eijk, P. J. 1997. "Towards a rhetoric of ancient scientific discourse: some formal characteristics of Greek medical and philosophical text (Hippocratic Corpus, Aristotle)," in E. J. Bakker (ed.), *Grammar as Interpretation. Greek Literature in its Linguistic Contexts* (Mnemosyne Supplement No. 171). Leiden, 77–129.
Fakas, C. 2001. *Der hellenistische Hesiod. Arats Phainomena und die Tradition der antiken Lehrepik*. Serta Graeca: Beiträge zur Erforschung griechischer Texte, Band 11. Wiesbaden.
Fantuzzi, M. and Hunter, R. 2004. *Tradition and Innovation in Hellenistic Poetry*. Cambridge.

Fehling, D. 1985. *Die sieben Weisen und die frühgriechische Chronologie: Eine traditionsgeschichtliche Studie*. Bern.
Fowler, D. H. F. 1999. *The Mathematics of Plato's Academy*. Oxford.
Fraser, P. 1949. *Callimachus: Fragmenta*. Oxford.
  1953. *Callimachus: Hymni et Epigrammata*. Oxford.
  1972. *Ptolemaic Alexandria*. 3 vols. Oxford.
Fried, M. and Unguru, S. 2001. *Apollonius of Perga's Conica: Text, Context, Subtext*. Boston.
Funkenstein, A. 1986. *Theology and the Scientific Imagination from the Middle Ages to the Seventeenth Century*. Princeton.
Gardies, J. L. 1991. "La proposition 14 du livre v dans l'écomomie des Éléments d'Euclide," *Revue d'histoire des Sciences* 44: 457–67.
Gee, E. 2000. *Ovid, Aratus and Augustus: Astronomy in Ovid's Fasti*. Cambridge.
Geus, K. 2002. *Eratosthenes von Kyrene*. Studien zur hellenistischen Kultur- und Wissenschaftsgeschichte. Münchener Beiträge zur Papyrusforschung und antiken Rechtsgeschichte, 92. Munich.
Glucker, J. 1978. *Antiochus and the Late Academy*. Göttingen.
Gow, A. S. F. 1952. *Theocritus. Edited with a Translation and Commentary*. Cambridge.
Grasshoff, G. 1990. *The History of Ptolemy's Star Catalogue*. New York.
Green, P. 1990. *Alexander to Actium: The Hellenistic Age*. London.
Gregory, A. 2000. *Plato's Philosophy of Science*. London.
Gutzwiller, K. 1992. "Callimachus' 'Lock of Berenice': Fantasy, romance, and propaganda," *American Journal of Philology* 113: 361–85.
Habsieger, L., Kazarian, M. and Lando, S. 1998. "On the second number of Plutarch," *American Mathematical Monthly* 105: 446.
Harder, M. A. 1992. "Insubstantial voices: some observations on the Hymns of Callimachus," *Classical Quarterly* 42: 384–94.
Heath, T. L. 1921. *A History of Greek Mathematics*. 2 vols. Oxford.
Heiberg, J. L. 1891. *Apollonius: Opera. Vol. I*. Leipzig.
  1893. *Apollonius: Opera. Vol. II*. Leipzig.
  1910. *Archimedes, Opera Omnia, Vol. I*. Leipzig.
  1913. *Archimedes, Opera Omnia, Vol. II*. Leipzig.
  1915. *Archimedes, Opera Omnia, Vol. III*. Leipzig.
Helden, A. van 1985. *Measuring the Universe: Cosmic Dimensions from Aristarchus to Halley*. Chicago.
Henderson, J. A. 1991. *On the Distances Between Sun, Moon and Earth*. Leiden.
Hoepfner, W. 2003. *Der Koloss von Rhodos und die Bauten des Helios. Neue Forschungen zu einem der Sieben Weltwunder*. Sonderband der Antiken Welt, Zaberns Bildbände zur Archäologie. Mainz am Rhein.
Hoyrup, J. 1997. "Hero, Ps.-Hero and Near Eastern practical geometry. An investigation of *Metrica*, *Geometrica*, and other treatises," in Klaus Döring, Bernhard Herzhoff, and Georg Wöhrle (eds.), *Antike Naturwissenschaft und ihre Rezeption*, 7. Trier, 67–93.

Huffman, C. 1993. *Philolaus of Croton: Pythagorean and Presocratic*. Cambridge.
   2001. "The Philolaic method: the Pythagoreanism behind the *Philebus*," in A. Preus (ed.), *Essays in Ancient Greek Philosophy VI*. Albany, NY, 67–85.
   2005. *Archytas of Tarentum*. Cambridge.
Hunter, R. 1993. "The presentation of Herodas' *Mimiamboi*," *Antichthon* 27: 31–44.
   1995. "Written in the stars: poetry and philosophy in the 'Phaenomena' of Aratus," *Arachnion* 2 (http://www.cisi.unito.it/arachne/num2/hunter.html).
Hutchinson, G. D. 1988. *Hellenistic Poetry*. Oxford.
Immhausen, A. 2003. "Egyptian mathematical texts and their contexts," *Science in Context* 16: 367–89.
Jacques, J. M. 1960. "Sur un acrostiche d'Aratos (Phen. 783–787)," *Revue des Études Anciennes* 62: 48–61.
   2002. *Nicandre: Oeuvres*. Paris.
Jaeger, M. 2008. *Archimedes and the Roman Imagination*. Ann Arbor.
Jones, A. 1999. *Astronomical Papyri from Oxyrynchus*. Memoirs of the American Philosophical Society vol. 233, Philadelphia.
   2002. "Eratosthenes, Hipparchus, and the obliquity of the ecliptic," *Journal for the History of Astronomy* 33: 15–19.
Kassel, R. 1987. *Die Abgrenzung des Hellenismus in der griechischen Literaturgeschichte*. Berlin.
Kidd, D. A. K. 1997. *Aratus' Phaenomena*. Cambridge.
Kidd, I. G. and Edelstein, L. 1988. *Posidonius*. Cambridge.
Knorr, W. 1978a. "Archimedes and the pre-Euclidean proportion theory," *Archives Internationales d'Histoire des Sciences* 28: 183–244.
   1978b. "Archimedes and the 'Elements': proposal for a revised chronological ordering of the Archimedean corpus," *Archive for History of Exact Sciences* 19: 211–90.
   1978c. "Archimedes and the spirals: the heuristic background," *Historia Mathematica* 5: 43–75.
   1985. "Archimedes and the pseudo-Euclidean 'Catoptrics': early stages in the ancient geometric theory of mirrors," *Archives Internationales d'histoire des Sciences* 35: 28–105.
   1986. *The Ancient Tradition of Geometrical Problems*. Boston.
   1989a. *Textual Studies in Ancient and Medieval Geometry*. Boston.
   1989b. "On Archimedes' construction of the regular heptagon," *Centaurus* 32: 257–71.
   1996. "The wrong text of Euclid: on Heiberg's text and its alternatives," *Centaurus* 38: 208–76.
Köhnken, A. 2001. "Hellenistic chronology: Theocritus, Callimachus and Apollonius Rhodius," in Papanghelis and Rengakos (2001): 73–92.
Konstan, D. 1994. "Foreword to the reader," in J. C. Clay, P. Mitsis, and A. Schiesaro (eds.), *Mega Nepios: il ruolo del destinatario nell' epos didascalico*. Special issue of *Materiali e discussioni per l'analisi dei testi classici* 31: 11–22.

1998. "The dynamics of imitation: Callimachus' first Iamb," in M. A. Harder, R. R. Regtvit, and G. C. Wakker (eds.), *Genre in Hellenistic Poetry*. Groningen, 133–43.
Kosmetatou, E. and Papalexandrou, N. 2003. "Size matters. Poseidippos and the Colossi," *Zeitschrift für Papyrologie und Epigraphik* 143: 53–8.
Kroll, W. 1924. *Studien zum verständnis der römischen Literatur*. Leipzig.
Lai, A. 1995. "Il χλοέροον σίσυμβρον di Nicia, Medico-Poeta Milesio," *Quaderni Urbinati di Cultura Classica* 51: 125–31.
Landels, J. G. 1978. *Engineering in the Ancient World*. Berkeley, CA.
Lavigne, D. E. and Romano, A. J. 2004. "Reading the Signs: the arrangement of the new Posidippus roll (*P. Mil. Vogl.* VIII 309, IV. 7–VI.8)," *Zeitschrift für Papyrologie und Epigraphik* 146: 13–24.
Lloyd, G. E. R. 1978. "Saving the appearances," *Classical Quarterly* 28: 202–22.
  1983. *Science, Folklore and Ideology: Studies in the Life Sciences in Ancient Greece*. Cambridge.
Lorch, P. 1989. "The Arabic transmission of Archimedes' *Sphere and Cylinder* and Eutocius' *Commentary*," *Zeitschrift für Geschichte der Arabische-Islamischen Wissenschaften* 5: 94–114.
Mach, E. 1912. *Die Mechanik in ihrer Entwicklung historisch-kritisch dargestellt*. Leipzig.
Magnani, S. 2002. *Il Viaggio di Pitea sull' Oceano*. Bologna.
Mair, A. W. 1921. *Callimachus: Hymns and Epigrams (et al.)*. Cambridge, MA.
Martin, J. 1974. *Scholia in Aratum Vetera*. Leipzig.
  1998. *Aratus: Phénomènes*. Paris.
Martin, R. 1993. "The Seven Sages as performers of wisdom," in C. Dougherty and L. Kurke (eds.), *Cultural Poetics of Archaic Greece: Cult, Performance, Politics*. Cambridge, MA, 108–28.
McAllister, J. W. 1996. *Beauty and Revolution in Science*. Ithaca.
McCartney, E. S. 1960. "Vivid ways of indicating uncountable numbers," *Classical Philology* 2: 79–89.
Meyer, D. 2001. "Apollonius as a Hellenistic geographer," in Papanghelis and Rengakos (2001): 217–35.
Minonzio, F. 2000. "Lo 'Stomachion' di Archimede," *Lettere Matematica* 35: 41–7, 36: 36–42, 37: 38–45.
Most, G. W. 1981. "Callimachus and Herophilus," *Hermes* 109: 188–96.
Mueller, I. 1981. *Philosophy of Mathematics and Deductive Structure in Euclid's Elements*. Cambridge, MA.
  1991. "On the notion of a mathematical starting-point in Plato, Aristotle, and Euclid," in A. Bowen (ed.), *Science and Philosophy in Classical Greece*. New York, 59–97.
Nagy, G. 1996. *Poetry as Performance: Homer and Beyond*. Cambridge.
Netz, R. 1997. "Classical mathematics in the Classical Mediterranean," *Mediterranean Historical Review* 12: 1–24.
  1998a. "Proclus' division of the mathematical proposition into parts: how and why was it formulated?" *Classical Quarterly* 49: 282–303.

1998b. "The first Jewish scientist?" *Scripta Classica Israelica* 17: 27–33.
1999. *The Shaping of Deduction in Greek Mathematics: a Study in Cognitive History.* Cambridge.
2003. "It's not that they couldn't," *Revue d'Histoire des Mathématiques* 8: 263–89.
2004. *The Transformation of Mathematics in the Early Mediterranean: from Problems to Equations.* Cambridge.
2005. "The aesthetics of mathematics: a study," *Proceedings of the Conference on Mathematics as Rational Acitivity.* Roskilde University, 252–93.
forthcoming. "The texture of Archimedes' writings: through Heiberg's veil," in Karine Chemla *et al.* (eds.), *Proof in History.* Cambridge.
Netz, R., Saito, K. and Tchernetska, N. 2001–2. "A new reading of Archimedes' use of indivisibles: preliminary evidence from the Archimedes Palimpsest," *SCIAMVS (Sources and Commentaries in Exact Sciences)* 2: 9–29, 3: 109–25.
Nightingale, A. 1996. *Genres in Dialogue: Plato and the Construct of Philosophy.* Cambridge.
Nisbet, R. G. M. and Hubbard, M. 1970. *A Commentary on Horace's Odes.* Oxford.
Nishimura-Jensen, J. M. 1998. "The poetics of Aethalides. Silence and 'poikilia' in Apollonius' Argonautica," *Classical Quarterly* 48: 456–69.
Obbink, D. (ed.) 1995. *Philodemus and Poetry: Poetic Theory and Practice in Lucretius, Philodemus, and Horace.* Oxford.
Otterlo, W. A. A. van 1944. "Untersuchungen über Begriff, Anwendung und Enstehung der griechischen Ringkomposition," *Mededelingen der Nederlandse Akademie van Wetenschappen, Afdeling Letterkunde* 7: 1–46.
Packard, D. W. 1974. "Sound patterns in Homer," *Transactions of the American Philological Association* 104: 239–60.
Papanghelis, T. D. and Rengakos, A. (eds.) 2001. *A Companion to Apollonius Rhodius.* Leiden.
Pease, A. S. 1958. *Cicero / De Natura Deorum.* Harvard.
Pfeiffer, R. 1968. *History of Classical Scholarship From the Beginnings to the End of the Hellenistic Age.* Oxford.
Plantinga, M. 2004. "A parade of learning: Callimachus' *Hymn to Artemis* (lines 170–268)," in M. A. Harder, R. F. Regtuit, and G. C. Wakker (eds.), *Hellenistica Groningana, Callimachus II.* Leuven, 257–78.
Prager, D. F. 1974. *Philo of Byzantium: Pneumatica.* Wiesbaden.
Puelma, M. 1983. "Gli Aitia di Callimaco come modello dell'elegia romana d'amore," *Atene e Roma.* 28: 113–32.
Rashed, R. 2000. *Les Catoptriciens Grecs: Les Mirroirs Ardents.* Paris.
Reynolds, L. D. and Wilson, N. G. 1974. *Scribes and Scholars.* Oxford.
Rice, E. E. 1983. *The Grand Procession of Ptolemy Philadelphus.* Oxford.
Rochberg, F. 2004. *The Heavenly Writing.* Cambridge.
Saito, K. 1997. "Index of propositions used in book 7 of Pappus' Collection," *Jinbun Kenkyu: The Journal of Humanities* (Faculty of Letters, Chiba University) 26: 155–88.

Schiesaro, A., Clay, J. C. and Mitsis, P. (eds.) 1994. *Mega Nepios: il ruolo del destinatario nell' epos didascalico.* Special issue of *Materiali e discussioni per l'analisi dei testi classici* 31.

Schneider, I. 1979. *Archimedes: Ingenieur, Naturwissenschaftler und Mathematiker.* Darmstadt.

Seaton, R. C. 1912. *Apollonius Rhodius: Argonautica.* Cambridge, MA.

Sedley, D. N. 1997. "Plato's *Auctoritas* and the rebirth of the commentary tradition," in J. Barnes and M. Griffin (eds.), *Philosophia Togata II: Plato and Aristotle at Rome.* Oxford, 110–29.

Selden, D. L. 1998. "Alibis," *Classical Antiquity* 17: 289–411.

Sidoli, N. 2005. Review of R. Netz, *The Works of Archimedes: Translation and Commentary,* Vol. 1 (Cambridge: 2004), *Aestimatio* 1: 148–62.

Siu, M. K. and Volkov A. K. 1999. "Official curriculum in traditional Chinese mathematics: how did candidates pass the examinations?" *Historia Scientiarum* 9: 85–99.

Solmsen, F. 1961. "Greek philosophy and the discovery of nerves," *Museum Helveticum,* 18: 150–97.

Sorabji, R. 1972. "Aristotle, mathematics, and colour," *Classical Quarterly* 22: 293–308.

Spada, S. 2002. "La 'Syrakosia' di Ierone, fra gigantismo e misura," Συγγραφη, *Materiali e Appunti per lo Studio della Storia e della Letteratura Antica* 4: 135–51.

Staden, H. von. 1989. *Herophilus: the Art of Medicine in Early Alexandria.* Cambridge.

  1997. "Teleology and mechanism: Aristotelian biology and early Hellenistic medicine," in Wolfgang Kullmann. and Sabine Föllinger (eds.), *Aristotelische Biologie: Intentionen, Methoden, Ergebnisse.* Stuttgart, 183–208.

Stanley, R. P. 1997. "Hipparchus, Plutarch, Schröder and Hough," *The American Mathematical Monthly* 104: 344–50.

Stephens, S. A. 2004. *Seeing Double: Intercultural Poetics in Ptolemaic Alexandria.* Berkeley.

Stirewalt, M. L., Jr. 1991. "The form and function of the Greek letter-essay," in K. P. Donfried (ed.), *The Romans Debate.* Peabody, MA, 147–71.

Suppes, P. 1976. "Archimedes's anticipation of conjoint measurement," *Role and Importance of Logic and Methodology of Science in the Study of the History of Science.* Colloquium presented at the XIII International Congress of the History of Science, Moscow.

Suter, H. 1899. "Der Loculus Archimedius oder Das Syntemachion des Archimedes. Zum ersten mal nach zwei arabishchen Manuskripte der Koeniglichen Bibliothek in Berlin Herausgegeben und Uebersetzt," *Abhandlungen zur Geschichte der Mathematik* 9: 491–9 (reprinted in F. Sezgin. ed.) *Islamic Mathematics and Astronomy, vol. 62, Archimedes in the Arabic Tradition, Texts and Studies,* Frankfurt am Main, Institut für Geschichte der Arabisch-Islamischen Wissenschaften 1998, 1–9).

Swerdlow, N. 1969. "Hipparchus on the distance of the sun," *Centaurus* 14: 287–305.
Taisbak, C. M. 1982. *Colored Quadrangles. A Guide to the Tenth Book of Euclid's Elements.* Opuscula Graecolatina, 24. Copenhagen.
  1984. "Eleven eighty-thirds: Ptolemy's reference to Eratosthenes in 'Almagest' 1.12," *Centaurus* 27: 165–7.
  1993. "Analysis of the so-called 'lemma of Archimedes' for constructing a regular heptagon," *Centaurus* 36: 191–9.
  2003. *Euclid's Data: The Importance of Being Given.* Copenhagen.
Taliaferro, R. C. 1997. *Apollonius of Perga: Conics Books I–III* (Diagrams W. H. Donahue, Introduction H. Flaumenhaft, Editor D. Densmore). Santa Fe.
Tarn, W. W. 1959. *Hellenistic Civilization.* London.
Thesleff, H. 1961. *An Introduction to the Pythagorean Writings of the Hellenistic Period.* Acta Academiae Aboensis, Humaniora 24.3. Åbo.
  1965. *Pythagorean Texts of the Hellenistic Period.* Acta Academiae Aboensis, Humaniora 30.1. Åbo.
Thiel, D. 2006. *Die Philosophie des Xenokrates im Kontext der Alten Akademie.* Munich.
Thompson, D. J. 2005. "Posidippus, poet of the Ptolemies," in K. J. Gutzwiller (ed.), *The New Posidipppus. A Hellenistic Poetry Book.* Oxford, 269–82.
Toomer, G. J. 1970. "Apollonius of Perga," in C. C. Gillespie *et al.* (eds.), *Dictionary of Scientific Biography*, vol. 1. New York, 179–93.
  1976. *Diocles on Burning Mirrors.* New York.
  1985. "Galen on the astronomers and astrologers," *Archive for History of Exact Sciences* 32: 193–206.
  1990. *Conics: Books V to VII / Apollonius: The Arabic Tradition.* New York.
Trypanis, C. A. 1958. *Callimachus: Aetia, Iambi, Lyric Poems, Minor Epic and Elegiac Poems, Fragments of Epigrams, Fragments of Uncertain Location.* Cambridge, MA.
Tybjerg, K. 2003. "Doing philosophy with machines: Hero of Alexandria's rhetoric of mechanics in relation to the contemporary philosophy," Ph.D. thesis, University of Cambridge.
Vitrac, B. 1992. "A propos de la chronologie des oeuvres d'Archimède," in J. Y. Guillaumin (ed.), *Mathématiques dans l'Antiquité.* Saint-Étienne, 59–93.
  2004. "A propos des démonstrations alternatives et autres substitutions de preuves dans les *Éléments* d'Euclide," in *Archive for History of Exact Sciences* 59: 1–44.
West, S. R. 2000. "Lycophron's Alexandra. '*Hindsight as Foresight Makes No Sense?*'" in Mary Depew and Dirk Obbink (eds.), *Matrices of Genre. Authors, Canons, and Society.* Harvard, 153–66.
Wilamowitz-Moellendorff, U. von. 1894. *Ein Weihgeschenk des Eratosthenes.* Repr. in *Kleine Scriften II* (1971), Berlin.
Young, G. de. 2005. "Diagrams in the Arabic Euclidean tradition: a preliminary assessment," *Historia Mathematica* 32: 129–79.

Zagagi, N. 1995. *The Comedy of Menander: Convention, Variation, and Originality*. Indiana.

Zanker, G. 1987. *Realism in Alexandrian Poetry: a Literature and its Audience*. London.

Zetzel, J. E. G. 1993. "Religion, rhetoric and editorial technique: reconstructing the classics," in G. Bornstein and R. G. Williams (eds.), *Palimpsest: Editorial Theory in the Humanities*. Ann Arbor, 99–120.

Zeuthen, H. G. 1886. *Die Lehre von den Kegelschinitten im Altertum*. Copenhagen.

Zhmud', L. 2002. "Eudemus' history of mathematics," in István Bodnár and William W. Fortenbaugh (eds.), *Eudemus of Rhodes. Rutgers University Studies in Classical Humanities, XI*. New Brunswick, 263–306.

# Index

Abbenes, J.G.J. 218 n.59
Acerbi, F. 19–20, 43 n.29, 123
Acosta-Hughes, B. 194 n.31, 214
Alexander the Great 56
Alexandria 54–6, 59–60, 93, 99, 107, 158, 181, 199, 209–10, 228, 234, 237
*Alexipharmaca*, see Nicander
algebraical symbols 48
alphabetic numerals 51–2
alternative proofs 96, 125–30
analysis 75, 108
anthyphairesis 42
Antipater of Sidon 60 n.42
Apollodorus (calculator) 196–8
Apollodorus (physician) 189
Apollonius of Perga 29, 61, 77, 93–4, 99–100, 107, 110, 113, 120, 127–8, 139, 141, 152, 154–5, 157, 166–7, 237, 239
    *Conics* 8 n.9, 61, 64–5, 91, 112
        Book I 91, 99–100, 102, 104, 105 n.33, 109–10, 117–20
        Book II 91
        Book III 88–91, 100, 108
        Book IV 91, 109
        Book VI 91, 109
        Book VII 71–4, 91, 108
    *Cutting off of a Ratio* 108–9
    *Hexameter Line* 49–54, 56, 58, 61, 110, 112, 166–7
    *Okutokion* 157
Apollonius of Rhodes 176–8, 190, 193, 216–18, 220–2, 226, 234, 236, 239–40
Arabic mathematics 64–5, 71, 75, 78–9, 82, 88, 108, 112, 156
Aratus 33, 110, 152, 168–71, 182–7, 189, 221–3, 239
Arbelus 147, 156
Arcesilaus 232 n.4
Archimedes, works by
    *Balancing Planes*, see *Planes in Equilibrium*
    *Cattle Problem* 33–4, 56, 58, 136, 146–7, 167–8

    *Conoids and Spheroids* 81, 122, 136, 138, 146
    *Floating Bodies* 135, 146
    *Heptgon in a Circle* 147–8
    *Lemmas* 147, 156
    *Measurement of Circle* 21–8, 29, 32, 45, 58, 63, 146
    *Method* 5 n.6, 75–80, 103–4, 120–2, 126, 128–9, 131, 146, 148, 157, 239
    *Mutually Tangent Circles* 147
    *Planes in Equilibrium* 40–1, 48, 77, 80–1, 103, 123–5, 135, 137–8, 145–6
    *Quadrature of the Parabola* 126, 128–31, 146, 238 n.15
    *Sand-Reckoner* 30–3, 56–8, 105–6, 136, 147, 156, 164, 166–7, 237, 240
    *Semi-Regular Solids* 44–5, 146–7
    *Sphere and Cylinder I* 3, 5 n.6, 66–70, 77, 80–2, 100–4, 113, 128, 136, 146, 238 n.15
    *Sphere and Cylinder II* 3, 67, 106, 123, 126, 136, 146, 238 n.15
    *Spiral Lines* 1–15, 19, 40, 45, 75 n.9, 80–1, 126–7, 136, 138, 144–6, 154–5, 238 n.15
    *Stomachion* xiii 17–20, 22, 35–6, 58, 66, 136, 145–7, 156–7
Archimedes' axiom 4, 129
Archimedes' screw 155
Archytas 8 n.9, 162–3, 198–9, 232–4
*Argonautica*, see Apollonius of Rhodes
Aristaeus 94–6
Aristarchus 28–31, 42, 45, 55, 58, 107, 110, 164, 232, 239
    *Sizes and Distances of Sun and Moon* 28–9, 37–40, 56, 112
Aristotle 5 n.6, 8 n.9, 23, 133–4, 148, 191, 232–3
    *Physics* 5
arithmetic 8 n.9, 30
Asclepiades 221, 224–5
astrology 186, 188
astronomy 5, 28–9, 32–3, 35, 54, 85 n.21, 92 n.26, 112, 127–8, 133, 136, 144, 151–2, 164, 169–71, 176 n.1, 179–87, 221–2, 238–9

251

Athenaeus 196
Athens 234
Attalus (astronomer) 168–9, 171, 173
Attic dialect 5 n.6
Autolycus 54, 107, 182–3, 232–3
axiomatics 13, 80

Bakhtin, M.M. 17, 59, 61–2, 207
Barker, A. 24 n. 12
Basilides of Tyre 93
Bing, P. 200 n.44
Bogue, P. 176 n.1
Borges, J.L. 205
Bornman, F. 201 nn.47–8
botany 188 n.23, 218
Bourdieu, P. 228 n.63
Bowen A.C. 127 n.10
Brassens, G. 201 n.49
*Bucolic Genre* 151, 156
*Burning Mirrors*, see Diocles
Burnyeat, M.F. 23 n.10

Callimachus 33 n.19, 59–60, 151–2, 175, 178–81, 193–6, 198, 200–8, 212–16, 221, 233–5, 237–8, 240
 *Aitia* 151, 178, 194, 206, 212–13, 216, 238
 *Epigrams* 214
 *Hecale* 213–15
 *Hymn, 3 (Artemis)* 200–8, 213, 215–16
 *Hymn, 4 (Delos)* 193–4, 213, 215
 *Hymn, 5* (Bath of Pallas) 213
 *Iambi* 194–5, 213–14
Cameron, A. 60 n.41, 65, 214, 238 n.14
catesterism 179, 181, 184, 187–8 see also Lock of Berenice
Callixenus of Rhodes 59 n.40
*Cattle Problem*, see Archimedes
Catullus 151, 178–9
center of gravity 40
Chemla, K. 42 n.26, 46
Chinese mathematics 46, 48
Chrysippus 34–5, 166
Cicero 66, 182 n.10, 197, 199 n.41
cissoid 152–3, 155, 159
Cleanthes 240
Cleary, J.J. 134 n.13
Cleomedes 54–5
cochlias 154
cochloid, 155, see conchoid
*Codex Constantinopolitanus* (Hero) 47 n. 32
Colossus 60
combinatorics 19–20, 34, 145, 166
conchoid 142–4, 152–3, 155

cone 12, 139, 148
conic sections 76, 83, 88–9, 100, 118, 129–30, 133, 135, 139–40 *see also* ellipse, hyperbola, opposite sections, parabola
conoid 3, 135, 152
*Conoids and Spheroids, see* Archimedes
Conon 67, 101, 129, 151, 155, 179, 194, 238
Couat, A. 183 n.15, 210–12, 226, 236
Ctesibius 86 n.23, 159 n.39
Cullen, C. 46 n.31
Cuomo, S. xiii, 112 n.39
Cusset, C. 199
Cutler, B. 20
cylinder 120–2, 131, 148, 150

Decorps-Foulquier, M. 65
definitions 8 n.9, 98, 100–1
Democritus 148
Diaconis, P. 20
diagrams 7, 38–9, 41, 43, 45, 47–51, 53, 74, 84, 86, 97, 101–3, 124, 137, 237
didactic epic 104
Dijksterhuis, E.J. 41, 63, 80 n.15, 155 n.29
Diocles 75, 82–8, 91, 107, 132–3, 155, 239
 *Burning Mirrors* 79, 82–7, 95, 99, 108
Diogenes Laertius 196, 232 n.4
Dionysodorus 239
Diophantus 46, 48, 113
Djebbar, A. 65
Doric dialect 63, 218 n.59
Dositheus 2–3, 67, 101, 103, 106, 129, 237
Duhem, P. 128 n.11

ecliptic 35
Egyptian Mathematics 45–6, 48
Eijk, P.J. van der 233 n.7
Einstein, A. 118
ekphrasis 106, 163, 191–2
*Elements, see* Euclid
ellipse 71–4, 117–18
enunciation (as stylistic element in proofs) 84
Epicurus 105
epistolary form 104–5
Erasistratus 157, 159
Eratosthenes 30, 35, 54–7, 85 n.21, 103, 105, 111, 132, 150–1, 155, 159–65, 167, 171–3, 175–6, 178, 181–2, 195, 198, 228, 236–7, 239
 cube duplication, *see* two mean proportionals
 geography 171–3, 175–6
 *Hermes* 181–2, 228–9
 *Platonicus* 57, 163
 *Sieve* 30, 58, 149–52, 155–6, 159
 *Two Mean Proportionals* 108, 132, 160–4, 228–9

erotic poetry 151
Euclid 12, 48, 61, 64, 78, 82, 94, 100, 102, 110,
    115–17, 120, 139, 196, 232–4, 239
  *Catoptrics* 134–5
  *Data* 108, 123
  *Elements* 21, 43, 65, 74, 81, 98, 107, 109, 113,
    115, 118, 123–4, 125 n.8
  Book I 47, 98, 102–3
  Book II 195
  Book IV 148
  Book V 149
  Book VI 149
  Book IX 30
  Book X 50, 61 n.45, 78, 93, 108, 149
  Book XI 149
  Book XII 148–9
  Book XIII 61 n.45, 82, 91, 93, 95, 108–9, 112,
    115–17, 148–9
  "Book XIV," see Hypsicles
  *Optics* 134
  *Spherics* 183
Eudemus (correspondent of Apollonius of Perga)
    99–100, 237
Eudemus (historian of science) 195 n.32
Eudoxus 5 n.6, 56 n.38, 67, 148, 162–3, 168–71,
    182–5, 189, 223, 237
Eutocius 8 n.9, 29, 42, 57, 75 nn.9–10, 99, 106,
    111, 113, 123, 151, 157, 160
Ezekial (dramatist) 224

Fakas, C. 182 n.12
Fantuzzi, M. 168 n.44, 175, 206, 208 n.51, 211–12,
    214–26, 235 n.11
formulaic language 38, 97, 123–4
Fowler, D.H.F. 42
Fraser, P. 187, 236 n.12, 238 n.14
Fried, M. 120 n.6, 140 n.17
Funkenstein, A. 142 n.19

Galen 112, 157, 158 n.38, 233
Galison, P. 228–9
Gardies, J.L. 43 n.29
Gee, E. 182
Gelon 106, 164, 167, 237
Geminus 111
geography 171, 177–8, 181, 192–3,
    216
Glucker, J. 110 n.36
Goldstein, B. 127 n.10
Goldstein, R. 102 n.30
Goodman, N. 141
Gorgias 235
Grasshof, G. 33 n.21, 42 n.27
Green, P. 59–60
Gutzwiller, K. 178, 180

Harder, M.A. 205
Heath, T.L. 79
Heiberg, J.L. 17, 19, 63–4, 75 n.9, 79, 101,
    103
Helden, A. Van. 29 n.15
Henderson, J.A. 56. n.38
Hero 48, 64–5, 86 n.23, 111
  *Metrica* 47, 63
Herodas 221–2
Herodotus 176–7
Herophilus 157–9, 194, 233
Hesiod 105 n.32, 168, 183–5, 233
Hesychius 215
Hipparchus 19–20, 29, 33–5, 56. n.38, 58, 110, 112,
    166, 168–71, 173, 182, 185, 233 n.6, 239
Hippias (author of quadratrix) 141, 144
Hippocrates of Chios 148, 150 n.23, 161–2, 232–4
  *Quadrature of Lunules* 148
Hippocratic Corpus 233–4
Hipponax 194–5, 213
hippopede 150 n.23
Homer 52 n.34, 165, 167, 171–3, 176, 200, 213–15,
    218, 221, 226, 234
Horace 198–9
Hoyrup, J. 65
Hubbard, M. 165 n.43, 198
Huffman, C.A. 23 n.10, 232 nn.2–3
Hunter, R. 175, 183 n.14, 206, 211–12, 214–26, 235
    n.11
Hutchinson, G.D. 175, 212–14, 216–26
Hypatia 113
hyperbola 89, 140–1
Hypsicles 92–100, 102, 107, 110, 157, 239
  *Anaphoricon* 92 n.26, 157
  "*Elements XIV*" 92–7, 108, 112

Immhausen, A. 46
indivisibles 131
inequalities 25–7, 32, 39, 42, 71, 119
intertextuality 92–5, 102
introductions (as literary genre) 2–4, 9, 67, 78,
    83, 88, 91–107

Jacques, J.M. 239
Jaeger, M. 66 n.2, 198 n.40
Jones, A. 188 n.24

Kassel, R. 234
Kepler, J. 146, 182
Kidd, I.G. 55 n.37, 182 n.12
Knorr, W.R. 1–2, 21, 23, 43 n.29, 63–5, 126, 127
    n.9, 134 n.14, 141 n.18, 142 n.19, 148 n.20,
    152–3, 155 n.29, 238 n.16
Köhnken, A. 239 n.20
Koine dialect 5 n.6, 63

Konstan, D. 104–5, 194 n.31
Kroll, W. 136 n.16, 211, 226, 236

Lai, A. 197, 198 n.39
Landels, J.G. 135 n.15
Laplace, P.S. 183 n.15
Lavigne, D. 191 n.28
Lloyd, G.E.R. 128, 158 n.38
*Lock of Berenice* 151–2, 155, 178–80, 188, 238 *see also* Callimachus, *Aitia*
Lucian 182 n.10
Lycophron 221, 223–5

Martin, J. 169, 182 nn.11, 13
Martin, R. 187 nn.20, 22
*Measurement of Circle, see* Archimedes
mechanics 86–7, 104, 129–33, 142–4, 159, 162–3
medicine 157–9, 192–4, 197, 218, 233
Meleager 188 n.23, 197–8
Menaechmus 162–3
Menander 234
Mendell, H. 63
Menelaus 112 n.38
*Method, see* Archimedes
Meyer, D. 176 n.1
Mitchel, J. 52 n.34
*Moscow Mathematical Papyrus* 45–6, 48
Most, G. 193
Mueller, I. 30 n.17
music 8 n.9, 23–4, 34, 133
Mykonos 102 n.30

Nabokov, V. 208 n.52
Nagy, G. 64
*Nature Magazine* 102 n.30
Naucratis 99–100
Nicander 182 n.11, 189, 192
  *Alexipharmaca* 189
  *Theriaca* 189–90, 193
Nicias of Miletus 197–8, 218–19
Nicomachus 30, 112, 149
  *Arithmetic* 149
Nicomedes 99, 142–3, 153, 155, 159
Nightingale, A. 234 n.9
*Nine Chapters, The* 46, 48
Nisbet, R.G.M. 165 n.43, 198
Nishimura-Jensen J.M. 218 n.58

Obbink, D. 171 n.47
opposite sections 89, 140–1, 152
optics 8 n.9, 83–4, 133–4
Orpheus 52 n.34
d'Orville, 301 Ms. (Euclid) 47
Otterlo W.A.A. van 124 n.7
Ovid 189 n.26

Packard, D.W. 52 n.34
*Palimpsest, the Archimedes* 17, 232 n.5
panegyric 151
Pappus 44, 49–54, 108, 113, 141 n.18, 146, 155 n.29, 156
  *Collection* 43 n.29, 112 n.38, 126–7, 166–7
parabola 49, 75–8, 84, 103, 122, 129–31
paraboloid 85, 87, 132
paradoxography 190–1, 193
pedagogy 13, 108–9, 111–15, 123, 234
perfect numbers 30 n.17
Pergamon 99, 237
Pfeiffer, R. 179 n.4, 195, 199 n.41
*Phaenomena, see* Aratus
Pharos 60, 158
Philo of Byzantium 86 n.23
Philo of Gadara 29
Philodemus 171 n.47
Philolaus 23
physics 4–5, 8, 12–13, 15
Pindar 32, 165–6
*Planes in Equilibrium, see* Archimedes
Plantinga M. 200 n.43
Plato 8 n.9, 23, 35, 62, 102 n.30, 133, 162, 171 n.47, 172, 232, 234
Pleiades 187–8, 224
Pliny the Elder 33
Plutarch 19, 163, 164 n.42, 166, 196, 233 n.6, 240 n.26
*poikilia* 17, 19, 136, 146, 226
Poincaré, H. 228
*polyeidia* 214, 220
Porphyry 196 n.35
Posidippus 60 n.43, 190–2, 225–6, 239
Posidonius 54–8, 110
prime numbers 30, 150
Proclus 113, 141 n.18, 150 n.23, 152, 155 n.28, 232 n.5
Protarchus 93
pseudepigraphy 64
Pseudo-Apollodorus 172
Pseudo-Justinus Martyr 52 n.34
Ptolemaic monarchy 55, 57, 106, 151, 161, 163, 181, 187, 225–6, 232, 237–9
Ptolemy (scientist) 29, 42, 112–13, 127, 152
  *Almagest* 33, 35 42 n.27, 112
Puelma, M. 178 n.3
Pythagoras 195–9, 213
Pythagoreanism 23
Pytheas 56

Q.E.D. 123–4
*Quadratrix* 141–2, 144, 155

Rabelais 207
regular solids 82, 92, 94, 115–16, 149
Reynolds L.D. 64
Rhodes 54–6
ring composition 124, 165
Rochberg, F. 188 n.24
Romano, A. 191 n.28
Rufus 158

Saito, K. 43, 232 n.5
Salinon 147, 156
*Sand-Reckoner*, *see* Archimedes
Schneider, I. 232 n.5
Sedley, D. 5 n.6
Selden, D.L. 211–12
Sesiano, J. 64, 83 n.17
Sicily 167–8
Sidoli, N. 67
Simplicius 148 n.21, 150 n.23
Siu, M.K. 48 n.33
Solmsen, F. 176 n.1
Sophistic movement 234
sphere 49, 66–70, 86–7, 104, 132
spherics 183, *see also* Euclid, Theodosius
*Sphere and Cylinder*, *see* Archimedes
spheroid 152
*Spiral Lines*, *see* Archimedes
Staden, H. von 158–9
Stephens, S. 181, 211–12, 236
stereometry 8 n.9
Stirewalt M.L. Jr. 105
Stoics 19, 172, 182 n.12, 183 n.16, 186 n.18
*Stomachion*, *see* Archimedes
Strabo 171–2, 187
*Suàn Shù Shū* 46 n.31
*Suda* 157, 236 n.12
Suppes, P. 80 n.15
surveys 108–9, 111
Syene 55
Syracuse 106, 164, 199 n.41, 218, 237
*Syracusia* 60 n.44

Taisbak, C.M. 93, 108, 148 n.20
Taliaferro, R.C. 89
Tarn, W.W. 188 n.25

Thabit bin Qurra 148
Thales 194–6, 198–9, 213
Theocritus 150 n.24, 165, 168 n.44, 197–8, 207 n.51, 218–22, 235, 239–40
Theodosius 109, 157 n.36
  *Spherics* 109, 112 n.38, 183
Theon of Alexandria 113
Theon of Smyrna 29 n.16 163, 164 n.42
Theophrastus 168, 185, 189, 191
*Theriaca*, *see* Nicander
Thesleff, H. 64
Thiel, D. 233 n.6
toolbox of results 43, 74, 75 n.9
Toomer, G.J. 72, 83–4, 86 nn.22–3, 112 n.40, 239 n.21
two mean proportionals 132–3, *see also under* Eratosthenes
Tybjerg, K. 86 n.23
Tycho Brahe 151
Tzetzes 236 n.12

Uhrmeister, V. 200 n.44
Unguru, S. 120 n.6, 140 n.17

Vat. Gr. 218 Ms. (Pappus) 50, 155 n.29
Virgil 189
Vitrac, B. 125 n.8, 238 n.16
Vitruvius 196
Volkov, A.K. 48 n.33

West, S.R. 224
Willamowitz-Moellendorff, U. von 161 n.41
Wilson, N.G. 64

Xenocrates 233 n.6
Xenomedes 212

Young, G. de 47 n. 32

Zagagi, N. 234 n.8
Zanker, G. 178 n.2, 193
Zetzel J.E.G. 64
Zeuthen, H.G. 120 n.6
Zeuxippus 106
Zhmud, L. 195 n.32
zoology 190